A People Among Peoples

A PUBLICATION OF THE CENTER FOR THE STUDY OF

THE HISTORY OF LIBERTY IN AMERICA

HARVARD UNIVERSITY

A PEOPLE AMONG PEOPLES

Quaker Benevolence
in Eighteenth-Century America

Sydney V. James

HARVARD UNIVERSITY PRESS

Cambridge, Massachusetts

1963

Distributed in Great Britain by Oxford University Press, London

Publication of this book has been aided
by a grant from the Ford Foundation.

Library of Congress Catalog Card Number 62–20248

Printed in the United States of America

To my mother and the memory of my father

Introduction

AMONG the salient characteristics of the history of liberty in the United States was the development of modes of voluntary action. Americans were thoroughly familiar with power and devoted a good deal of attention to the procedures for its proper use through the state, as well as to prevention of its abuse. But not everything that they wished to do in society had to be done through the coercive instruments of the government. In the eighteenth century they brought into being alternative means of action, immensely significant for the future. The communities that then took form supplied a basis for the pluralistic organizations of the century that followed.

In this evolution, the Society of Friends and its members played a critical role. Their religious commitments compelled them to abjure violence and to refrain from using the instruments of the state. Yet the same beliefs also compelled them to take an active concern for the affairs of the world. In England they had already learned to live as dissenters, as a permanent minority among others who thought differently from them. But in the New World they learned to be a people among peoples. In Pennsylvania they quickly discovered that they would not permanently be a majority and that as control slipped out of their hands they would have to work out modes of action that did not depend upon the instrumentalities of the state.

Professor James's thoughtful study reveals the subtle interplay of forces that enabled them to do so. The early concern of the first American Quakers to assure the survival of their own community gradually broadened to take in the entire society about them. Benevolence, initially a concept that described relations among Friends, was transformed into one that described obligations toward Negroes, Indians, and other dependent persons. By the time the American Revolution created a serious challenge to the Quaker conscience, a pattern for organized, voluntary co-operative action was established.

The Society of Friends thus assured its own survival as a group within the whole society. But it did more than that. It was to live on not as an isolated enclave, but as a people among peoples, engaged in constant, fruitful interaction with others. The Quakers thus established precedents of immense importance for cooperative social action. They also showed how an ethnic group could retain its identity and yet exist in intimate contact with — enriching and enriched by — others. To the understanding of the process by which they did so this meticulously worked-out study brings together a wealth of material that illuminates the main trends of American social and intellectual history.

OSCAR HANDLIN

Preface

Taking my departure from an interest in humanitarianism as it appeared in the American colonies, several years ago I set out to discover what Quakers had done in the years when Englishmen and Americans of other faiths were investing disinterested benevolence with new importance. If Low Church or comprehensionist Anglicans, Massachusetts Congregationalists, and German pietists turned to associations for practical piety by the beginning of the eighteenth century, and the Great Awakening left the ideal of social service as one of its few durable after-effects, where did the renowned Quaker philanthropy fit into the picture? The Friends, it seemed likely, had not shared the background of these others who exalted projects born of good will to all mankind.

My first surprise came from the discovery that Quakers had scored a most uneven record in philanthropy. Even though they steadily held beliefs which later were used to justify large-scale ventures, long stretches of the colonial years yielded no evidence of any special action on their part. Rather, mutual aid in the religious community turned out to be their only charitable behavior, a polar opposite to what we now think of as Friends' humanitarianism. Though Quaker historians and historians of Quakerism have minimized the distinction and occasionally obliterated it, a serious inquiry into humanitarianism must begin with a reasonably precise concept of the phenomenon.

I therefore examined the Quaker religious fellowship to discover how its strong emphasis on in-group charity had changed to make room for attitudes more akin to the ideals of benevolence arising in other quarters. I confined my attention more and more to the views and actions of organized Quakerism. The problem lay in explaining how the sect acquired either a devotion to humanitarianism or at least the reputation of having it.

Bent on analyzing what "the Quakers" thought or did, I soon had to face the possibility that such a category would crumble at my touch. Perhaps the sectarian opinion was a will-o'-the-wisp. Modern Quakers are far from unanimous in support of the pacifism for which they are famed; many of them tolerantly accept as their forebears men whose views or behavior earned their expulsion by Quaker Meetings in the past. Evidence quickly accumulated to show that eighteenth-century Friends could not maintain complete uniformity in the ranks even by vigorous disciplinary measures. Was not Quakerism the religion of the Inner Light? Worst of all, the widespread ignorance of their faith by colonial Friends, and the narrowness of the circle of active participants in the Meetings, indicated that the Quakers displayed roughly the same variation in commitment to their church as was found in other communions. The Meetings imposed fairly precise standards of fidelity to the faith, and the standards were in the hands of the active participants. To a large degree the ignorant and lukewarm were only passive endorsers of the official views and programs of their church.

My search then proceeded to the question of how the church's leadership acted and why it turned toward humanitarianism to an extent which made that quality characteristic of Quakers even outside ecclesiastical business. Benevolence, for the Friends, was, after all, an attitude toward outsiders; it could not be of great moment in the early years when outsiders were expected to become insiders or be forgotten. Humanitarianism implied acceptance of some working relationship, more or less permanent, between the Quaker sect and the human race from which it was recruited. But other general plans were possible for such a relationship, and specific projects in philanthropy other than those adopted by the Quakers could have been chosen. Satisfactory explanations of what had happened, I became convinced, were to be found in the special conditions of colonial America and the political ordeals of the Quakers between 1755 and 1783.

The eighteenth-century record, viewed in one light, told the story of the failure of the Quakers to remain a major American religion. However, unless percentages of total population were the only indices of success, the Quakers had not failed the test of significance. Their idealism — the pacifism, humanitarianism, and public spirit which emerged from their eighteenth-century trials — remained an example of what Americans can achieve, and to some degree pervaded the estimates of what the nation best exemplifies. The crucial question therefore remained: Why did the Quakers respond to their experience in the eighteenth century in a way that brought them out as active members of the civil community rather than to immure them in sectarian isolation? Why did they become Americans and not domiciled aliens? The answer is to be found in the fact that in America — above all, in Pennsylvania — they had the opportunity to be Quakers and leading citizens simultaneously. Even after Pennsylvania had ceased to be a Quaker commonwealth, and the American Revolution had stirred up suspicion against pacifists, the barriers separating the Society of Friends from the community at large were so low that the Quakers themselves tried to raise them to hold their church together. But it proved at least as attractive to devise ways to make participation in the affairs of the community compatible with membership among Friends.

Acknowledgments

LIKE most scholars, along my way I ran up debts of a sort that cannot be repaid. Here I can post notice of my gratitude, if nothing more. Numerous people — friends and Friends — have helped me with advice, the facilities of libraries and hospitality. The committee in charge of the Department of Records of Philadelphia Yearly Meeting (302 Arch Street, Philadelphia) kindly gave me the freedom of its collections in 1954 and later years. Eleanor Melson, and more recently Mary Ogilvie, showed me the way into these materials. I also want to thank Eleanor Brenn, another anchor of Friends' Arch Street Center, for her special assistance. Howard H. Brinton, as Custodian of the Department of Records of the now reunited Philadelphia Yearly Meeting of the Religious Society of Friends, has given permission to quote manuscripts under his jurisdiction. The Historical Society of Pennsylvania has granted permission to quote manuscripts in its collection. In more general ways, Richard Wood and his family, Phyllis and Morton Keller, and Wallace E. Davies have made my journeys to Philadelphia enjoyable.

In Providence, Robert Cool pled my case before the Vault Committee of New England Yearly Meeting of Friends and secured permission for me to use the archives under its care. Mrs. William Paxton, Librarian of the Moses Brown School, graciously gave me her time to put the documents in my hands. At the Quaker Collection of the Haverford College Library, Friends Historical Library at Swarthmore College, and the Rhode Island Historical Society the several staffs and librarians have put their facilities at my disposal.

The editors of the *Bulletin of Friends Historical Association* and *The William and Mary Quarterly* have kindly given permission to use material which has appeared in articles that I wrote for those periodicals.

Frederick B. Tolles of Swarthmore College has discussed my

ACKNOWLEDGMENTS

work with me, to my great benefit, on several occasions, though by means of his books I have received even more guidance from him. Perry Miller, Samuel Eliot Morison, Bernard Bailyn, David Riesman, and Donald Fleming of Harvard University have similarly given both precept and example which I hope I have used well. My greatest debt, however, is to Oscar Handlin, under whose sponsorship I wrote a preliminary version of this book as a Ph.D. thesis. His accessibility and willingness to give me as much of his time as I might claim made him the graduate student's ideal. More recently, his steady encouragement (in addition to the more tangible benefits conferred in his capacity as Director of the Center for the Study of the History of Liberty in America) has helped me bring to presentable form whatever value lies in this book.

My wife, Jean M. James, deserves a special paragraph. She has done her highly competent best from the start of this project to make domestic life a help rather than a hindrance to scholarship. More recently she has applied her sharp eye for detail to the entire manuscript.

SYDNEY V. JAMES

Providence, Rhode Island
June 1962

Contents

A PEOPLE AMONG PEOPLES

I

The Quaker Religious Fellowship
in the American Colonies

Quakers in the twentieth century enjoy a reputation for humanitarianism. Some of them fear that the general public regards their Religious Society not as a church in which God's will is done and men's souls are saved, but as a philanthropic agency. In spite of the danger of such misunderstanding, many Friends, quite justly, think humanitarianism is a quality of their fellowship which proves its worth. There are Quakers, in fact, who take it so for granted as an attribute of their sect that they assume it must always have been there.

A record could be drawn up filling the three centuries and more of organized Quakerism with incidents of philanthropy on the part of individual members. Yet, as a religious community Friends have not always accepted humanitarian concerns. The Society did not undertake projects to do good for outsiders until near the end of the eighteenth century, and did so at that time in circumstances which made it evident that their motives were not unalloyed humanitarianism. Moreover, though Quakers then spoke of benevolence to all mankind, they reached outside their own ranks, at first, only as far as those to whom they felt a special obligation in addition to common humanity. Once the basic shift in policy had been made, however, the initial boundaries blurred and lost their powers to confine.

To discover how this change in policy occurred it is necessary to trace the internal affairs of the religious fellowship and the impact on it of external ideas and events. The structure of the church and of its operations crystallized during the first half of the eighteenth century. "Charity," the guiding concept which embraced the practice of mutual aid among Quakers and their behavior towards outsiders, even then proved incapable of guiding its practitioners in all their dealings with non-Friends. However, the long ordeal of the French and Indian War and the Revolution provided the occasion for Quakers to find a new relationship between their church and the surrounding society. The period of almost three decades between the beginning of border raids on Pennsylvania and the return of peace was a time of recurrent outbursts of religious zeal among Friends. A pattern of piety then emerged in Pennsylvania and spread to New England, New York, and the South which carried a new approach to religion throughout American Quakerdom.

Two lines of development, seemingly antithetical, then came to characterize the history of the Society of Friends in all parts of America: the intensification of asceticism, sectarian exclusivity, and corporate solidarity, on the one hand, and a desire to use the church to improve the world around it, on the other. These modifications, evolving simultaneously, combined to allow Quakers in the late eighteenth century to make a creative response to the ordeal of war and civil unrest.

In addition, the Quaker response to the ideas circulating in America at the time of the Revolution bore fruit in a resolution of the conflict over what charity required of a conscientious Friend in respect to Negro slaves. Later, the specific demands of patriots in the Revolution gave Quakers throughout America the occasion to bring unity to their own ranks and to embark on new projects for the benefit of outsiders. But not until peace had returned were the Friends able to proceed freely with endeavors to reform their religious Society in the light of their new conception of it and to undertake a large program of humanitarian projects to demonstrate their value to a civil community where other religions were vastly more popular. If the new adjustment of the Quakers to the rest of their compatriots was destined to be no more permanent than the one made under the name of charity, at least for the post-Revolutionary generation there had been established not only a role for the Society of Friends but a common ground in ideas shared by those in it and those outside, a jointly held property which guaranteed that the Quakers would not go the way of the Mennonites into obscurantist isolation. From the late eighteenth century the humanitarianism of Friends became a lasting feature of their church's operations and their outlook toward the world.

The organizational and theological features of the Quaker fellowship, in the larger outlines, remained the same from near the beginning of the sect to the middle of the nineteenth century. While not slighting the developments which took place in this period, therefore, it will be possible to treat a great deal of the routine of the church as constant. True, in the late seventeenth century many details remained unfixed which a century later would become highly formal. But for the most part the change only gave precision and regularity to practices which had been started in England during the Restoration.[1]

The great importance that Friends of the eighteenth century gave to their ecclesiastical Society and its regulations may seem to have been illogical on the part of a people who believed in direct and frequent inspiration as the foundation for all religious life. Indeed, the contradiction implicit in the strict control of each believer by his fellow members of the church and commitment to the doctrine of the Inner Light, provided one of the never-failing dynamic forces in the Quaker church. But to colonial Friends there was no contradiction; the opposing concepts were held together by a theology reinforced by sectarian traditions.

Quakers accepted the two traditional branches of the theological description of the church: the totality of souls united with God, or invisible church; and the organized religious fellowship on earth, or visible church. Robert Barclay stated the matter clearly in his *Apology for the True Christian Divinity*, first published in Latin in 1676, the book which Friends promulgated as the comprehensive, official exposition of their views until well after the eighteenth century. According to Barclay, there was "one catholic church" composed of all who were "called and gathered truly by God, both such as are yet in this inferior world, and such as having already laid down the earthly tabernacle, are passed into their heavenly mansions." The "members" of the true church were scattered "among heathen, Turks, Jews, and all the several sorts of Christians," of both sexes. Their understandings were "blinded in some things," notably "the superstitions and formality of the several sects in which they" were "engrossed," but they remained "upright in their hearts before the Lord." They strove "to be delivered from iniquity" and loved "to follow righteousness." Their significant religious activity was secret, occurring in the "touches of . . . holy light in their souls" which enlivened and quickened them and united them to God as "true members of this catholic church." The union of souls into the invisible fellowship gave glory to God and expressed his love to the world.[2]

While this definition of the true church enabled the theologian to assess its worth in the moral universe, a description of the visible church yielded more useful details. Quakers, like many other Protestants, believed they had restored the Christian fellowship to the purity of the Apostolic age. The Lord had released them "from the impressions and teachings of men, to inspire them with degrees of the same universal love, by which the dispensation of the gospel was ushered in." The church on earth was a number of particular churches, each consisting of "a certain number of persons gathered by God's Spirit." As the Lord had given the Children of Israel fleeing from Pharaoh "Lawes; and statuts, to keep & doe & appoynted" Elders and Overseers "to see y^t theye keept ye Lords waye; . . . & Likewise in ye primative times" to the first Christians, so too in the seventeenth century the "Blessed power" of Jesus Christ again raised up "ffaithfull men & women" to assemble pure meetings of "the Lords peculier People." Once gathered and united in the love of God, the "Holy Lawgiver" directed them "to meet together for the worship of God in spirit" and "also for the exercise of a tender care over each other in regard to faith and practice," and through these religious exercises "to bear a joint testimony for the truth against error." As a result of this communion and of the suffering imposed on them for their faith by the world around them, they became "as one family and household in certain respects." Membership in the actual congregation, like that in the invisible church, resulted from an "inward work of holiness," and a forsaking of iniquity.[3]

Once established, the church had to maintain itself, with divine aid. Although "God hath given to many of his saints and children, and is ready to give unto all a full and certain assurance that they are his, and that no power shall be able to pluck them out of his hand," they could always turn from justification and grace. They would be given every encouragement to do so: there was "nothing more certain, than that the great Enemy of Man's Soul" sought daily to "catch those, who have in some measure escaped his Snares." The pastors, Overseers and teachers, under appointment of the Spirit of God, helped guard other Quakers from the wiles of the fiend. "What serves the ministry for but to perfect the saints?" They "lead people out of sin into righteousness." Overseers watched over the conduct of fellow members to warn them privately of any drift toward the downward path, and overlooked no chance to preserve "peace, love, unity, concord, and soundness . . . in the church of Christ." So, beyond the basic truth of being a people gathered from the mass by the Spirit of the Lord to his greater glory, the visible church was a community of people for preaching the gospel and helping one another to persevere in righteousness and to achieve perfection.[4]

To accomplish these ends the religious fellowship on earth was further elaborated and coordinated by the institution of several sets of officials and "meetings." The familiar idea of a Quaker meeting is that of the session for worship. The traditional picture is substantially correct for the eighteenth century. A number of people wearing unornamented clothes of an old-fashioned cut gathered in a plainly furnished room, most of the men sitting on one side, women on the other, both facing the front benches on which sat the dignitaries of the meeting. From time to time someone broke the silent waiting with a prayer or with exhortations to virtuous living. If the congregation included a person who had so frequently felt called upon to deliver divine messages as to be formally "recognized" as a minister, he might deliver a sermon, presented without books or notes, expounding a scriptural text and applying it to doctrine and conduct. During all communications of divine Light the men removed the hats which they wore tenaciously in the presence of all earthly power. One of the dignitaries ended the meeting by shaking hands with a Friend next to him. At this signal the rest of the congregation did likewise and relapsed into ordinary conversation.

Meetings for worship were open to the public and were held every First day (as Friends called Sunday, to adhere to Biblical precedent and avoid pagan distortions of Christian life) and once during the week. They were held either at a private home or a meetinghouse, the times and places being determined by the Monthly Meeting for business, which ordinarily included several groups of Friends who worshiped together. In New England, especially, there were annual gatherings for worship to which people from outside the regular congregation flocked in large numbers. But every Meeting for Discipline or business devoted some time to worship, too.[5]

Less familiar but more important historically were the business Meetings which supervised the activities engaged in in the name of "charity" and later undertook humanitarian projects. These Meetings, too, were under the direct government of the Holy Spirit; segregation of business from worship meant no disparagement of its spiritual character. The "Glorious Light" of Christ in Friends' hearts "from Tim to Tim mad manifest" to them many "things Reprouable Inconsisting wth Truth & Plainness." The church — in the ancient metaphor, the mystical body of Christ — had different members who, when acting according to the divine intent, found themselves sorted into the various offices of the body where they were gifted to serve. The multiplicity of kinds of meetings merely carried the differentiation of function in the body one step further.[6]

Some willingness existed to grant the business of the fellowship a secular foundation. William Penn argued that since all civil societies agreed that their existence and reputation required a wide range of regulation of their members, and since there was a scriptural command exhorting Christians "to be ready to every good word and work," Friends did not need to make all business "an *act* of *faith,* or other *exercise* of *conscience.*" He proposed to exempt such branches of "charity" as giving aid to the "poor, aged, sick, and orphans," recording vital statistics, controlling marriages, reconciling differences between members, and any efforts "to pre-

6

vent, rebuke, and restore disorderly walkers." In short, he would have released most of the work of the Meetings for Discipline from the necessity of specific inspirational authority. His views did not prevail, in theory. In practice, however, many kinds of business, such as investment of money and fixing times of meetings, were consigned to mundane calculation without anyone's making a formal decision that it should be so. Ultimately, the emphasis in Quaker theorizing about church government fell on divine authority for the general types of business, rather than on the inspiration for each act.[7]

Men's Meetings for Discipline (or business) formed a pyramid of four main strata, with a nearly complete duplication in Women's Meetings. The smallest assembly was the Preparative Meeting, which met weekly in most places. It consisted of a group of Friends living close to each other, sometimes the same group as one in an ordinary meeting for worship. During the eighteenth century Preparative Meetings usually kept no records. They had Overseers (named at a Monthly Meeting) to keep watch over the rest of the members and present cases to the next higher Meeting when they could not deal with them alone. Preparatory Meetings also presented to the Monthly Meeting such items of business as the establishment of a new place of worship. By the late eighteenth century the campaign to establish schools in sufficient array to accommodate all Friends' children had reached the point where the Preparative Meetings were diligently undertaking to set them up, notably in New Jersey.[8]

Just above the Preparative Meeting was the basic unit in the Quaker organization, the Monthly Meeting. To it pertained the significant function of defining membership. In any such body the members constituted a group of some bulk, spread over a territory of the smallest possible size. A few instances were to be found, however, of a tiny community of Friends being placed in a Monthly Meeting which invariably met at an astonishing distance, when it was thought that the stability and resources of a larger group were needed to preserve them in good practice.[9]

The Monthly Meeting appointed trustees to hold titles to meeting-houses and other property. It kept graveyards, supervised marriages,

7

provided aid for those in "low circumstances," and reproved improper conduct on the part of its members. It received and issued epistles and the several kinds of communication from one Meeting to another known as "certificates."

There were several kinds of certification: Monthly Meetings issued certificates of removal to members who planned to live in the territory of some other Meeting, attesting the members' acceptability in church fellowship. If Friends felt some reservation to full endorsement, they either explained their attitude in the document or refused to issue it to the member until he had removed the cause of their dissatisfaction.[10]

Meetings gave three kinds of temporary certificates. A member going to marry a woman in the territory of another Meeting needed a document from his own expressing satisfaction with his conduct in general and specifically declaring his "clearness" for marriage — that he was free of marital or romantic entanglement with other women. Boys sent away to school or apprenticeship required a paper recommending them to the care of the Meeting in whose territory they would be. Friends traveling in the ministry took certificates from their Meeting for Discipline, and often from their Meeting for Ministers and Elders as well, testifying to their spiritual gifts and the concurrence of the home Meetings in their "concern" to travel.

Business Meetings considered proposals to modify the regulations of the Society, whether in organizational practice or refinement of individual conduct. If approved at a Monthly Meeting, such proposals were taken (often put as questions) to the immediately superior Quarterly Meeting, and, if successful there, to the Yearly Meeting, which might refer them to London Yearly Meeting to start general consultation among the whole Quaker world. Or the Yearly Meeting in America could refer them back to its subordinate Meetings for deliberation and report, a process that might be carried on for years without much recorded outcome.

The most important functions of the Monthly Meeting were those of preserving good conduct among the members and aiding the brethren in need. To accomplish these tasks, Meetings developed highly formalized devices of mutual surveillance and mutual aid.

The process of surveillance was initiated and carried on most constantly in the Preparative Meeting. Upon detecting fault in another, a Quaker was supposed to speak to him and warn him of his error or the likelihood of falling into it. The two might wait on God together or discuss the standards of conduct which Friends approved. If a man made no progress with a stumbling brother, he could call on the aid of others in the Meeting who were known for their experience and skill with the wayward. Before 1700 this practice gave rise in some places to the appointment by the Monthly Meeting of Overseers for each Preparative Meeting, a system which spread after the turn of the century. The Overseers had the duty to give help, advice, and spiritual "labor" in such cases. They were also to seek out the erring and to initiate "dealings" if no one else did.

Once a "disorderly walker" had been reproved, his case might take several courses. If the Overseers reformed a drunkard before he had become notorious, the business could be left off the record. If they found repentance in the heart of a well-known sinner, they would take his paper of self-condemnation to the Monthly Meeting, where it might be rejected as insufficient or accepted to be read with appropriate publicity — perhaps at a First day meeting for worship. But if private and discreet labor failed, the Overseers asked the aid of the Monthly Meeting, which might then form a temporary committee on the case. Then the offender had either to repair as much of the damage he had done as was in his power and sign a paper condemning his behavior, or be expelled ("disowned") from the Meeting. A testimony of disownment (or "denial"), like a paper of self-condemnation, was read on an occasion that would bring it to the knowledge of as many as possible. The objective in publicizing these documents was to remove the blame for the offense from Quakerism.[11]

As an aid in preventing misconduct, a list of "queries" was read to Monthly Meetings, covering the main points of the sect's code of behavior. In 1755 Philadelphia Yearly Meeting decided that each Monthly Meeting Clerk should write down the responses and transmit them to his Quarterly Meeting, where a summary would be made for its territory and sent to the Yearly Meeting, which would make a grand total of the "state of Society." This practice, always against some opposition, spread to other Yearly Meetings' jurisdiction. In epistles the higher Meetings could then guide the attention of lower ones to common kinds of misbehavior or important dangers. In this way the mutual surveillance in Monthly Meetings was given direction and prevented from falling into decay or becoming a local eccentricity.[12]

Mutual aid, the other central part of Monthly Meeting business will be examined in detail in later chapters. It influenced the basic organization of the Meeting, however, simply by requiring that funds be steadily available. Monthly Meetings kept a "stock," money collected primarily in the name of "charity," which included aid to the poor and most of the rest of the church business. In many places collections were taken up at Meeting; in others the Meeting's Treasurer solicited regular subscriptions to augment the stock. The Treasurer had custody of the money and sometimes invested it, with the aid of prudent Friends. Investment was especially important if the Meeting received large donations for the poor or for a school. Other common expenditures were for the building and maintenance of meetinghouses.

Though the accepted Quaker theory of church government was not developed to justify the practice, Meetings often did not conduct their business entirely in general session; instead, they assigned the preparation of most items to temporary committees — to investigate for certificates, inspect for clearness for marriage, and audit accounts. When appropriate, the committees brought back drafts of documents, such as "denials," but always submitted their recommendations to the whole Meeting. Committees also performed services for the members between sessions of the Meeting; they found places for apprentices who needed the care of Friends, or arbitrated disputes over property.[13]

Every Meeting of whatever sort had a Clerk, whose duties were crucial, though hard to define. Christ was the Head of the Church and dictator of its affairs, but since he communicated his will to the group through individuals and the sense of the Meeting, a Clerk was necessarily the highest human official to record the divine pleasure.[14] The Clerk started and stopped the sessions, but his role in recording decisions gave him his greatest importance. He assessed the views of those present and formulated "minutes" of what he believed was the extent of unanimity. The members assented or remained silent to wordings which he produced unless they felt right in objecting. In most matters before a Monthly Meeting the Clerk's duties were perfunctory. He recognized items of business and recorded appointments of committees. But in an intangible way his influence was great.

Although all adult male Friends were members of a Monthly Meeting and were urged to attend its sittings, a handful did most of the work. The predominance of an inner group of regulars was even more striking in the Quarterly Meetings. These embraced several Monthly Meetings, from each of which a few members were named to "the service of the Quarterly Meeting." All others were free to attend, but few did; and in any case the appointed representatives were considered to bear the opinion of their Monthly Meeting. In America, Quarterly Meetings were established to conform with English usage, in which they had jurisdiction over a shire, but there proved to be no subdivision of the colonies which had an equivalent importance. In parts of New England Friends did not bother to set up Quarterly Meetings to cover the whole territory until the early eighteenth century, and even then these did not coincide with such seemingly important divisions as the boundaries between the different colonies.[15]

Not until the 1750's, when the Society of Friends set on foot major undertakings against slave-holding and for moral regeneration, and began the practice of writing detailed answers to queries, did the Quarterly Meetings became useful. They could send committees of "weighty" Friends to aid Monthly Meetings. In some places the Quarterly Meetings also undertook to found and run schools, a project normally assigned to Preparative or Monthly Meetings.

Quarterly Meetings chose representatives who comprised the official core of their Yearly Meetings, of which there were six in colonial America. Yearly Meetings deliberated on such important matters as declarations of principle. They formulated norms of conduct for Friends through queries, minutes of advice, or a series of flat statements called a "Discipline" (at first, an accretion of advices given to the Overseers for their guidance). They prescribed any additional duty to the members and resolved ambiguities in existing standards. After consideration of the state of the church they gave timely "Advices" (often merely recommendations to call attention to specific previous minutes), which they sent as an epistle to the lower Meetings.

The Yearly Meeting had its own stock, which it raised by requisition on the subordinate Meetings and placed in the custody of a Treasurer or Treasurers. The money was used for the welfare of the fellowship, sometimes to pay for petitions for laws desired by Friends, at other times to finance the printing of broadsides, pamphlets, or books explaining the Quaker position. Even when it was not asked for financial backing, a Yearly Meeting reserved the right to veto the release or alter the text of any publication touching upon religious or even political matters that could affect the reputation of the faith; it did this to prevent members from misrepresenting the views of their church or taking internal disagreements into the public arena. In Philadelphia, the Monthly Meeting took care of this business through a committee of Overseers of the Press for several years before 1709, when the Yearly Meeting established its own committee.[16]

Lobbying and supervision of publications were two aspects of the Yearly Meeting's broader task of speaking to the world at large in the name of Friends. For American Quakers there were two limits on this function of the Yearly Meeting: one, the responsibility taken by the Meetings for Sufferings which came into existence in the colonies only in 1756 and later; the other, the role of London Yearly Meeting. Apart from the historic primacy of the English Quaker community, the British Meetings were communications centers, for the American Yearly Meetings corresponded with London but not always with each other. Major decisions on belief and practice were often deferred by one American Meeting until it put them before London, which would inquire into the views of Quakers everywhere, render a verdict, and transmit it to all Yearly Meetings in its annual Epistle. Even after 1783, London and its long-established Meeting for Sufferings held first rank as public spokesmen.

The procedures of the Yearly Meeting changed slowly during the eighteenth century in a direction similar to those followed in the lower Meetings. At first the preparation of items of business had been put in the care of temporary committees, which returned to the whole group with drafts or plans. As the years went by, however, a standard order of business developed, and reliance increased on standing committees. The Overseers of the Press were an early permanent committee. Later, Meetings for Sufferings had something of this character. By the end of the eighteenth century there were others, some of which had the duty to oversee subsidiary institutions of the Meeting, notably Indian missions and boarding schools. By that time committee reports accounted for so large a part of the recorded business of an annual session as to suggest that the Yearly Meeting served mainly to inform the members about the affairs of their Society and elicit their enthusiasm.

In addition to the regular pyramid, some exceptional Meetings were held in a few places. What later became Baltimore Yearly Meeting met twice a year for many years, once on each side of Chesapeake Bay. In Pennsylvania, Fishing Creek Half-year Meeting was a kind of Quarterly Meeting without much to do and embracing Monthly Meetings too far apart for the members to gather frequently. A few special Meetings took responsibility for the poor. One of them met at each sitting of the Yearly Meeting in Maryland for many years after its establishment in 1678. Another was called several times by Philadelphia Monthly Meeting, which in 1699 also experimented with a gathering to take care of the Meeting's school, publications, "matters of difference, acco&tt &Cᵃ," but gave it up after a short time. Later, when the Monthly Meeting at Philadelphia divided into three, it found it impossible to divide some of the assets, as was normally done in such cases, and therefore obtained the permission of the Quarterly Meeting to establish a committee of the three Monthly Meetings in the city, to supervise the Almshouse, inspect the schools, care for the poor, manage endowed funds, and various other branches of business.[17]

Parallel to all the Men's Meetings there existed a pyramid of Women's Meetings. Their members, too, preserved each other in virtuous conduct and investigated for certificates and for clearness for marriage. They helped in the care of the poor, saw that the meetinghouses were cleaned, and performed other duties appropriate to their sex. But there were limits to what the Women's Meetings might do. They often had to rely on money from the Men's stock to supplement their own. In many places they could not have the last word on certificates and denials of their own members. The attitude of the men of South Kingstown, Rhode Island, who indignantly protested that this policy degraded the women's meetings where it prevailed and set up a "Preheminence" of the males "where Truth admits of none," was unusual in the middle of the eighteenth century. Even those who came out four-square for equality of the sexes in the eyes of God found that there were many times when the men had to act for women members, and few when women performed duties for the men.[18]

Another set of Meetings of record, those of Ministers and Elders, later called Select Meetings, grew in importance during the eighteenth century. Ultimately they existed in weekly, monthly, quarterly, and yearly forms, hierarchically arranged. In various places, however, Select Meetings were either not wanted or not practical because of the small number of potential members. Only those specially designated went to these meetings. Early in the century monthly and quarterly Meetings of Ministers were set up, often convening in the morning before regular business Meetings. Soon, Monthly Meetings for business began to appoint Elders to join the gatherings of ministers. The Elders, according to a minute adopted at a Yearly Meeting in Philadelphia, 1723, were to cultivate the ministry. The old hands were to guide the young, encourage them in study of Scripture, remind them to "keep to true patience, and submission to the will of God"; not to parade learning or "strive to extend their declarations further than they find the life and power of God to bear them up," but "abide in the simplicity of the Gospel." As they learned to do this, with the help of Elders and other ministers, they would "witness a gradual growth" of purity in their ministry and "be content to wait for it in the will of God." [19]

The Select Meetings had a tendency to cultivate elitism as well as the ministry, however. In Philadelphia Yearly Meeting they obtained the right to propose new members in 1747, and eight years later interpreted a special set of queries to give them complete disciplinary jurisdiction over their members. Monthly Meetings protested this infringement of their own powers, but not until 1792 did the Yearly Meeting rule in their favor. During their ascendancy, the Select Meetings occasionally delivered forceful statements of how all Friends ought to behave.[20]

If the Ministers and Elders threatened to disrupt the basic structure of the Quaker fellowship by establishing a spiritual elite, the Meetings for Sufferings (now called Representative Meetings or Permanent Boards) created a greater peril, an oligarchy. These bodies were set up by the Yearly Meetings, beginning with Philadelphia in 1756. Designed to meet emergency conditions in the French and Indian War and the Revolution, they consisted of members appointed by the Quarterly and Yearly Meetings, and met as often as business required, but normally at least once a month. At first they were concerned with the relief, legal aid, and public reputations of those Friends who fell afoul of military exactions or Indian warfare. They also corresponded with each other, and sometimes with Yearly Meetings elsewhere on behalf of their own. In 1771 Philadelphia Yearly Meeting gave to the Meeting for Sufferings some of its functions, such as control of the press, an arrangement that allowed swift action in time of crisis. After the Revolution the Meeting for Sufferings provided legal protection to re-enslaved Negroes, served as the voice of the church to the various governments, and — conspicuously in New England — moved toward the role of interim committee between sittings of the Yearly Meeting.[21]

The Meetings for Sufferings had access to ample funds. The one at Philadelphia was born with £1000 in its hands and was promised more as it might be needed. During the Revolution these Meetings commanded even greater resources, which they could transfer from one Yearly Meeting to another. Because they were intended to be powerful, they had to be controlled. Until 1768, apprehensions of creating a monster were so strong among Delaware Valley Friends that they made their Meeting for Sufferings dependent on annual renewal of its powers. Their Quarterly Meetings retained the right to name representatives to it even though it might be quite impractical for them to attend its deliberations. It was also made clear that the new organ could decide no question of faith or discipline.[22]

The danger of losing control of the church to some ungovernable coterie of members came not from careless delegation of powers; it was not to be curbed by formal restrictions. Actually, the religious community had long before come under a sort of oligarchy which conducted the business Meetings and staffed the new institutions, the Select Meetings and the Meetings for Sufferings. The active leaders of the church — ministers, Overseers, the perennial committee members — constituted a large, imprecise ruling element, but one with a fairly good record for using its power in the interests of the Society. Perpetuating this feeling of responsibility and the qualities of the fellowship that had brought it into being were the most effective means to preserve the church from domination by selfservers.

In an even broader sense the operation of the great structure of Meetings depended less on nice definitions of power than on the spirit in which the leadership conducted them. As long as the sense of the Meeting was truly sought, the authority of any gathering in the church rested on the concord among the members rather than on parliamentary maneuvers, or even majorities. Yet to achieve a harmony of understandings among people who cultivated the individual conscience as zealously as the Quakers required a great deal of guidance of consciences and special skills on the part of the leadership.

The elaborate organization of the church itself produced a uniformity of attitudes among Friends. Solidarity was, indeed, deliberately aimed at. With Christ the head, how could wrangling be tolerated in the body? With the divine will constantly revealed in countless Meetings, each had to heed developments in all the rest to be sure of the validity of its own decisions. As a result, precipitate action rarely occurred, and local peculiarities were ironed out. The Select Meetings preserved orthodoxy in the ministry. But a decline in the general vigor of ministry probably did more to stabilize the tone of the Society in the eighteenth century; soon the Elders became as important as the Ministers, and in the Meetings for Discipline the predominance of the business-minded regular participants was even heavier.

These leaders lacked the advantages of esoteric wisdom, the magic of oratory, or a stirring new Gospel to control their brethren. Though they acted cautiously, as a rule, some of them crusaded for new concepts of right; a few grew too vehement in their methods and were disowned. When they managed to remain in the fellowship, they did so by taking care not to damage the "unity of Friends." Notable Quakers maintained more exacting standards of conduct than their Society set for the general membership, drawing the admiration of those who did not wish to imitate them.

It was the task of the ruling element to hold together not only the exemplary purists in the fellowship, but the ordinary members as well. The leadership never ran out of recommendations for bringing the members' behavior up to the perfectionist standards long established by Friends, but in performing the duty of helping the straggling saints to persevere, they had to tolerate many chronic ills in the body — frivolity of the youth, neglect of the education of slaves, and absenteeism from First day meetings. Ardent preachers of purity were needed to keep the ideals alive. It was the task of the leadership, then, to act as brokers between the fervor of the few and the tepidity of the many.

This state of affairs in the church had special importance to the entry of humanitarian concerns into the affairs of the Meetings. Such innovations had to be introduced without destroying the church and driving out those members most in need of the inspiration of the loftier ideals. Advocates of change had to wait until conditions outside the Society favored their cause, and until a widespread presumption in their favor destroyed the moral grounds for opposition. Only then would the Meeting move to their side. The active participants in Meetings had to retain the confidence of all, regardless of personal inclination. What sometimes appeared to be spiritual dullness was often merely the cautious adherence to the sense of the Meeting on the part of a ruling element which lacked such attributes of sacerdotal authority as the power to remit sins, withhold sacraments, or even claim a superior spiritual rank. The decisive moments were often those when the leadership put the faithfulness of the spiritual laggards to the test.

One divisive force with which the Quaker ruling element did not have to cope was theological controversy. As a sect, Friends exhibited a low level of intellectual activity in the eighteenth century. There were individual Quakers of great mental ability and cultivation. Many doctors and lawyers on both sides of the Atlantic, and gentlemen such as the Norrises and Logans of Philadelphia, or Moses Brown of Rhode Island, were well educated. Some had been trained at universities. But they did not use their minds to explore divinity. Some notable ministers had little schooling and never made up the deficiency with study. With few exceptions, no new theological works of stature went on Quaker shelves during the eighteenth century. Instead, Friends reprinted the seventeenth-century authors, some of whom had been bred in controversial reasoning in the days before their conversions — Robert Barclay, William Penn, and Isaac Penington, for example. New "Friends' books" tended to be short tracts which often consisted of passages from the earlier writers, journals of terrestrial and spiritual experience, histories, or occasional pieces, such as John Woolman's and Anthony Benezet's, on slavery and Indians, or Moses West's on marriage.[23]

No need was felt for new treatises on theology. All Truth was consistent, and Barclay, for example, had inquired quite far enough into his subject — perhaps even too far, if the strictures on the learned world in the *Apology* were applied to the work itself: God had given man "a spiritual divine light, to rule him in things spiritual, and the light of reason to rule him in things natural," but the best results could be obtained by combining the two. For the ministry, however, God could make up the lack of learning "in the most rustic and ignorant," and "one that comes to be a true minister," who has learned logic and philosophy, would be safer if he could "forget and lose" his training, "for it is the root and ground of all contention and debate, and the way to make a thing a great deal darker than clearer." Without the interference of invalid human reasoning, "the truth proceeding from an honest heart, and spoken forth from the virtue and Spirit of God" enjoyed a "natural logic, by which

rational men . . . deduce a certain conclusion out of true propositions, which scarce any man of reason wants." [24]

The proof of spiritual soundness, whether in ministry or in the
government of the church, was in the effect. If ministry promoted
sanctification and did not stray from accepted tenets, if Meetings
for Discipline preserved "comely order" and unity, analysis of the
phenomena was superfluous. The theory of the ministry emphasized the immediacy of the message. John Griffith's *Journal* revealed a minister's conviction that he had been "serviceable" when
he was enabled to speak of private faults at a Meeting where he
had no acquaintance with the members. Correspondingly, there
was no purpose in writing down sermons. The spiritual resources,
rightly tapped, could have no limit, and divine wisdom would supply the needs of specific times and places beyond the ability of
human ingenuity. To the restless intellect unable to descry the divine logic there was always the consolation that revelation had not
stopped, so consistency might eventually appear, harmonizing what
the mind had previously grasped only in seemingly irreconcilable
parts.[25]

If highly wrought human reasoning yielded place in Quakerdom
to a communal sentiment, or sense of the Meeting, the leaders of
the church still had to contend with sharply conflicting ideas, traditions, and articles of faith. These contradictory elements have sometimes been analyzed in Troeltsch's terms, attributes of the polar op-
posites, "church" and "sect," with the history of Quakerism one
of oscillation between the two. Certainly, in early Pennsylvania,
Friends emphasized those qualities of their fellowship that made it
resemble a "church" seeking to embrace all men and dominate the
world, and finding it necessary to compromise with earthly realities.
More commonly, elsewhere, they behaved like a "sect," withdrawing from the world to cultivate purity among the select few in the
face of any external opposition. Yet Friends never adhered strictly
to either of the two varieties of religious community and at any
given time embraced in brotherhood men who exhibited traits appropriate to each. Sectarian discipline was always prized, though
never ruthlessly enforced. During their most churchly period, Pennsylvania Quakers would not deliberate in Meeting to give ideological

direction to the Holy Experiment; on the contrary, they defined the business of their religious Society more narrowly than at any time before or after. All the peculiarities of Friends' behavior, such as keeping on hats before judges and using the old singular second person pronouns, could be freely practiced for the sake of individual purity or public example. Furthermore, Quakers inherited from the seventeenth century the remnants of an attitude quite outside the categories of "church" and "sect." The first Publishers of Quaker "Truth" had thought of the re-establishment of the true church on earth as the Second Coming, the founding of the kingdom of God which would embrace all mankind and, far from compromising with the corrupt world, would renovate and purify it in every particular after weathering the final tempests of opposition.[26]

The reformist zeal which lingered after the chiliastic vision had faded, and the attitudes toward religion embodied in Troeltsch's concepts of church and sect, were ways of defining a group purpose. The distinctive tenet of Friends, however, was the belief in the Inner Light, potentially one leading to the utmost individualism and the destruction of religious fellowship, as it did when John Perrot and a few followers refused to meet for worship except on inner prompting from the spirit. The spirit failed them, and they quickly disappeared as a sect.[27] To maintain a society devoted to the Inner Light required all the support to group coherence offered by the ideals of "church" and "sect." Friends, to remain in brotherhood, had to bear a joint testimony to the truth of the Inner Light by giving the world an example of a pure community governed by Christ's spirit.

As it happened, the various group purposes frequently found their agents in different individuals. Zealous apostles arose who felt drawn to preach to outsiders, and Quaker courtiers appeared, like William Penn and Dr. John Fothergill, who ingratiated themselves with the high and mighty. But contemporary with them were men like George Whitehead and William Edmundson, who devoted themselves to the purity and order of the sect, and John Woolman, who exemplified the sectarian ideals of meekness, purity, and intense religious experience. The presence of men with such different talents posed a formidable, never-ending problem of utilizing them in the fellowship; no one of them could prescribe the outlook of all his fellows.

The problem, viewed from another angle, was one of upholding reliance simultaneously on individual and corporate experience of the "motion of the Spirit." The existence of the sect depended on both, but individual "openings" had to be orthodox. Select Meetings could usually ensure doctrinal soundness; the Bible and the pragmatic results of preaching could supply further checks. But bland correctness could not preserve spiritual life.

To some extent, Quakers required eccentricity and tendencies to heterodoxy. At least, spiritual good health entailed some straining at the leash of accepted ideas, because the continued outpouring of novel messages gave evidence of divine revelation as well as did group approval of the reiteration of long-accepted ones. Since Friends on principle regarded their understanding of Truth as incomplete, many new ideas which were in the air outside the fellowship probably drifted in readily when not prevented by a conflict between individual religious leaders and the body. Yet conflicts raised opposition to several important proposals to expand the social duties of the church — for example, by the establishment of missions to Indians.

In such cases, the need for a corporate purpose could easily work on the side of the novelty. If the practical "fruits of the spirit" in sanctification of conduct proved the worth of Quakerism and its ministers to individuals, greater accomplishments by the fellowship, whether merely as an example of a purified community or more actively as an agency to do good, might demonstrate the value and validity of the church as a whole. Opposition to some new proposal could be carried on in the name of some virtuous older generation which had not needed it, as well as on the grounds of absence of an inward corroboration for it on the part of the church in general. But veneration of the ancestors, while strong among Quakers, could never completely dissolve the explosive element of belief that revelation was still unfinished. When the possibility of a new duty for Friends was raised, the leadership in the Meetings had the delicate task of keeping both the advocates and the opposition in the fellowship from destroying it, until some accommodation of

2 1

standing practice could be made which would satisfy all of the members.

While political conditions left the Quaker church free, its inner strains and its very nature kept it changing steadily. But when people of the world began to attack the Meeting for the standards of behavior it required of its members, and ultimately as an undesirable conspiracy, Friends had to defend their church on a wider front than usual. Shifting conditions in the world spoiled the adjustment Quakers had made. In the period of the American Revolution, though at first the church tried to hold itself aloof from the struggle and compel its members to do likewise in their private capacities, it had to abandon this simple policy lest it alienate many of its members and provoke an irresistible attack on the Quaker organization from the Revolutionary governments. To make the church acceptable to Friend and non-Friend, it had to be given a firm connection with the whole society. Quakers sounded anew the call to forsake the world and form a perfect community, but at the same time, paradoxically, had to find a special role in the world for themselves which would be consistent with their principles and appreciated by outsiders.

When the leaders of the church had worked out a program which met these specifications, the conflicting aspects of Quakerism tended to be embodied in different individuals, as before, making patterns of inner tension in the church even more complex. On the whole, Friends increased institutional control over each other, surcharging the tensions with more exacting confinement of individual inspiration. Simultaneously, the church took up the institutional development of humanitarian concerns, making social service through its organization a duty of the members. These changes, of course, no more brought stasis than had earlier ones: they led to further changes in the nineteenth century and to several severe breaks in the unity of the body; but these events are beyond the scope of the analysis to be offered here.

The Rise and Progress of "Charity"
Among the People Called Quakers

Before they raised the standard of benevolence to all mankind, Quakers upheld an ideal of conduct to each other and their fellow men which they often called charity. This term applied to a fairly well-wrought concept, understood by colonial Friends and shaped from materials provided in the yeasty days of the First Publishers of Truth. Charity — including both the specific duties and their grounds in theology or piety — kept little of the outgoing vigor of early Quakerism. Rather, it cultivated the sectarian solidarity which persecution had early encouraged on both sides of the Atlantic. As upheld by Friends' Meetings, charity entailed only general and rarely enforced requirements of good behavior to outsiders. It meant mainly the members' mutual aid and surveillance.

In the Middle Ages the Church had the responsibility for providing Catholic Europe with various social services. In its jurisdiction nearly all the inhabitants automatically assumed allegiance to it; it had no competition, although local rivalries and bickering went on incessantly within it — between rival monastic houses, for example, or between bishops and their cathedral chapters. Pious laymen endowed religious houses for special purposes, such as caring for the sick or providing refuge for travelers. The vast majority of the beneficiaries of charity, however, received it in the agricultural villages where they lived. In the ideal parish the poor were supported out of the funds collected as tithes. Even though the right to collect a tithe had often lapsed or fallen into secular hands, the parishes kept the duty of caring for their needy, and performed it as best they could. From time to time conscientious prelates tried to get parish revenues rededicated to their canonical uses. Monasteries fostered agricultural improvements and stored grain to tide their districts over famine years. Outside the framework of the Church only a few institutions, such as guilds in the towns, joined in the work of maintaining or educating the poor.[1]

In sixteenth-century England the feebleness of the old institutions and the creation of a separate national church, together with changes in economic behavior, new social aspirations, and the efforts of the monarchy to gain control over all forms of public authority, compelled redistribution of the institutional responsibilities for social welfare. An upsurge of social conscience, especially in the urban middle class, provided the necessary will. The state took a share of the responsibility, which it entrusted to local authorities. While making the parish one of its agents, thereby preserving the old system to that extent, the monarchy also dissolved many monastic establishments, after which other ways had to be devised to perform some of their old services. Lay donors rushed to found new institutions, most conspicuously to cope with growing urban poverty and to prevent it from increasing. Still, the readjustment of basic institutions of the realm between 1540 and 1640 was not total; Englishmen continued to have one king and one faith.[2]

More far-reaching, though less dramatic, alterations came later with the division of the Christian fellowship in the kingdom. Few Englishmen accepted happily the fact that they no longer agreed on how the Church of England should be organized. Puritans for years insisted just as strongly as other Anglicans that the law should permit one true church only. Even after many of the successors to Puritanism had formed dissenting communions and had gone over to toleration and nonestablishment, the traditional ideal of political and religious unity retained a strong appeal. Quakers, too, felt the attraction of this ideal. Penn, in the act of pleading for religious freedom, thought it wise to endorse uniformity. "I am for a national church," he insisted, "so it be by *consent*, and not by constraint." However, since religious unity might be preserved only in love and conviction, in proper response to the spirit within, fidelity to religion required toleration of disunity of churches.[3]

24

As a practical consequence of the multiplication of sects and the voluntary basis of church fellowship, dissenters from the established church brought on themselves perplexing problems in charity. For what part of the social services of the formerly universal church were they responsible? They had little desire to shuffle the burden off on civil authorities. Was a minority sect, in its own estimation the true visible church, obliged to feed the hungry or care for the sick among the multitudes whose hearts were hardened against God? As long as the Church of England carried on some of the old services or left them in the hands of corporations which became autonomous, such as colleges or hospitals, it was possible for men of all persuasions to postpone drawing the new lines between secular and ecclesiastical business. Many new philanthropic institutions had no connection with a church community, though Puritan merchants put up much of the money for them.[4] Yet the current ran strongly in the direction of governmental responsibility for social welfare, whether on the level of the nation or the city. So long as church and state were linked, non-participants in the one had to face the need for doing without the services of the other to some extent. They had to draw their own line between the civil and the religious, write their own definition of their obligations to and reliance on the state. Cutting the connection with the government down to a minimal level, in turn, sooner or later put the responsibility for their own social services on the shoulders of dissenters.

Early Quakers, filled with missionary zeal, avoided a full confrontation with this problem. Since all men could respond to the sure guide within and by denying self-will enable themselves to obey the divine, they were all eligible for spiritual brotherhood. By doing non-believers the supreme good, by drawing them to Truth, the early Friends knew that they would arrive at a state of affairs where no problems about charity to people of other persuasions would exist. Just as they subscribed to the old ideal of religious unity, these Quakers also behaved in accord with time-honored precepts by distributing money or bread to the poor in the world around them. They saw their own immediate needs, though, and organized to aid each other systematically. They wanted to create a perfect circle and enlarge it.[5]

By the late seventeenth century, Quaker missionary attitudes took on a nonreligious aspect also. While George Fox, Thomas Lawson, and others had appealed to the government for greater attention to the Christian duty of caring for the poor, even prior to the Restoration, the years of persecution which followed stimulated Friends to preach to their nation social duties that went beyond those which had long been recognized. The defense of their religious Society proved the occasion for speaking as the tribunes of prisoners and the poor, for demonstrating good will and good citizenship.[6]

To combat the united church and state which proclaimed that dissent from the one meant treason to the other, Quakers had also to clarify their ideals of the relations between the two. Especially did they need a definition of the civil authority which would make loyalty compatible with religious diversity. Penn's arguments for toleration kept returning to the ancient axiom that government existed for the temporal good of the citizens. To preserve those under it, the government had duties which men of all sects endorsed: to relieve the "oppressed" and uphold the interests of the fatherless, as well as to repress wickedness. The behavior of the body politic, then, would not be thwarted by a variety of churches. In fact, the state had a positive obligation to avoid religious persecution which impoverished the people and thus raised taxes for the support of the poor! Let the diverse congregations improve individual conduct, Penn argued, and the task of government would be lightened, and the general welfare advanced. If civil society had a unity independent of the religious fellowships in it, and some of its right ends were attainable by helping the weak and needy, then the virtuous of whatever persuasion had reason to strive for the good of all. Penn hoped that the promotion of *"practical* religion" would put a stop to doctrinal bickering, persecution, and sloth, and lead to social unity.[7]

While Penn directed his ingenuity primarily to the political problem, the mind of John Bellers dwelt on projects for the public welfare. He wanted Quakers to use their Society to preach social service to the nation. The years of persecution before 1687 had made charity within the Society a matter of first importance and of such magnitude as to forestall concern for outsiders. Bellers told them that when Friends enjoyed toleration, God expected them to work "an Improvement to his Honour, upon every Talent he hath given You," and that they should create a good example among themselves of a method to abolish poverty. He advocated "Colleges of Industry," workhouses carefully regulated to make the inmates productive and improve themselves in skills and piety. He devoted great effort to making a case for the economics of the system, in order to show not only that the poor could support themselves but could at the same time yield profit to the rich investors and strength to the nation. His nimble mind produced further plans — for a world government, the improvement of medicine, penal reforms which included abolition of capital punishment, permanent national prosperity, better elections, education, and rehabilitation of criminals.[8]

But Bellers' enthusiasm was by no means contagious. While other Friends were becoming preoccupied with the affairs of their religious Society, he went on hoping to persuade them to join him in advocating or demonstrating the practicality of his projects for the benefit of all mankind. By 1718 he had to appeal to the Quarterly Meeting of London and Middlesex to stir up the old spirit. How could they convert the heathen in foreign lands without systematic social services? How could they ward off the damage done by "the prophane and vitious Lives of our present *Sea-Men*" without creating a sound operating base in England? Worse still, others were doing better! Friends must make a start by filling their charitable institutions with outsiders whose moral and economic beings could be purified.[9]

That Bellers' influence on Quakerdom was remarkably small was shown by the only attempt to carry out his ideas: a "College of Industry" set up according to his specifications by London Friends in 1701. It seemed entirely plausible that his program to end poverty was getting a trial in the best possible place; Bellers had based his plan on a domestic flax-spinning business run by Quakers in the same city earlier to aid their own poor without expense to the Meeting's stock. Nevertheless, the "College of Industry" failed to function as a pilot plant in a chain of such establishments to work the temporal and moral salvation of England; instead of managing it as a model community and profitable enterprise, the men in charge began to transform it into a refuge for aging Friends. Soon they sent poor boys and pensioners, too, and finally converted the institution into a Quaker school! Bellers had added to the original model only the educational activity. Although he and Penn had urged Christians to rally to their common beliefs and "practical Christianity," Quakers were among the least willing to do so. (Penn, be it noted, had also cautioned them: "be careful not to mingle with the crowd, lest *their* spirit enter *us*, instead of *our* spirit entering *them*.") [10]

The clue to Friends' growing devotion to a self-contained sectarian life and their rejection of plans for world conversion by social service can be found in a comparison with other religious circles. In the seventeenth century, several sorts of Europeans and Americans began to stress the obligation of Christians to do good to their fellows. In New England, Cotton Mather called on them to form societies to reform morals, stamp out vice, and relieve the poor. He wanted to revitalize piety and reunite the fractious Congregationalists on several new planes of voluntary association to replace the old ties enforced through the magistracy. He learned of the method from English Nonconformists and German pietists. In the Established Church of England a comparable development took place. Such prelates as Archbishop Tillotson preached unity of Christians under the fundamental tenets they shared, and collaboration in benevolent projects to keep their minds off their disputes. This plan did not bear fruit at once. At the beginning of the eighteenth century Anglicans sought to hold together only the factions in their own Church by promoting the Society for the Propagation of the Gospel and the Society for the Promotion of Christian Knowledge. These organizations, furthermore, gave a new flicker of life to an old form of church-state unity; their activities were intended to strengthen the Empire. As the century wore on, though, redoubled emphasis on the benevolence of God, the good order of his creation, and the duty of man to imitate and be grateful for the divine intent, inspired Anglicans to acts of "practical Christianity" of a less political nature — such as founding hospitals or catechizing young slaves.[11]

By contrast with Congregationalists and Anglicans, Friends had no need of benevolent societies to distract them from bickering or to make up for a lost partnership with the state. The last dispute over fundamental Quakerism had been the Wilkinson-Story controversy over church government in the 1670's, and several years before Mather wrote his *Essays to do Good* or the founding of the Society for the Propagation of Christian Knowledge or the establishment of the orphanage at Halle, Quakers had weathered the storm blown up by George Keith, which led to their last major schism until the Hicksite separation. The expulsion ("disownment") of Keith by Philadelphia and London Friends had a curious quality. He was disowned more for his inharmonious spirit than for his views. Many of the proposals he had made too vehemently were later adopted.[12]

The ouster of Keith, in spite of all the acrimony it stirred up in Pennsylvania and London, created only small, short-lived schismatic groups and left no enduring antagonistic factions within the Society. Keith himself, without intending to do so, helped restore internal harmony by leading an attack from outside. By 1700 the excommunicate had found his way to the Church of England and two years later set out on a missionary tour for the Society for the Propagation of the Gospel to inspire Protestants to unity in opposition to Quakerism. When the potential allies failed to gather for a concerted attack, he carried on the battle simply as champion of the Church of England against the Society of Friends. Though he converted few of the enemy he managed to restore the Quakers' sense of being a beleaguered garrison holding out against a vastly more numerous foe, and thus dashed their hopes for full freedom to promote their beliefs and compete in the contrivance of social benefits.[13]

Keith's campaign reinforced the unifying effect which English Friends received from two other kinds of hardship imposed on them from outside — difficulties which left them in unaccustomed isolation from other advocates of religious liberty. Toleration as established in 1689 had given to Dissenters the right to worship freely in public and to take Oaths of Allegiance which ignored the Established Church. But Quakers had wanted more than a revised form of oath to the king; they asked an alternative to all oaths, especially in courts of law. When, as it happened, Friends fell to arguing over the exact wording which their consciences would let them use in an affirmation, they baffled their supporters outside the Society, few of whom could sympathize with such refinement of scruples. In addition, Friends continued to suffer distraints of property that was sold to satisfy tithes which conscience forbade them to pay. English Quakers, however, knew that their troubles with oaths and tithes after 1689 were minor matters compared with the persecutions under Charles II. The main points of religious toleration had been won; Friends could hope to persuade their government to grant legal exemptions from the remaining requirements contrary to their consciences. In pressing their suit for the parliamentary acts which they wanted, Quaker leaders pointed to their brethren's peacefulness, innocuousness, and detachment from national affairs.[14]

The pleas of the leaders were well founded. Since the departure of Story and Wilkinson in 1678, there had been a loss of missionary vitality in the Society as well as a strengthening of its organization which the two men had tried to resist. The church government had been developed primarily to defend itself, and special organs had been created, notably London Meeting for Sufferings, to secure relief from persecution and civil disability. By the end of the seventeenth century Friends had not only been relegated to the position of a minor sect; they had accepted it. Instead of heeding the call of Bellers to advance as reformers into the English social structure, they strove to be cautious and detached from public affairs, to hold what religious liberty they had and persuade the government to give them more. In 1689, London Yearly Meeting advised Friends to "Walk wisely and circumspectly towards all men, . . . giving no offence nor occasions to those in outward government, nor way to any controversies, heats or distractions of this world." In this frame of mind they turned to the leadership of

George Whitehead, a man who was dedicated to sectarian orthodoxy and gave the positive obverse to this advice: Friends should
love one another and cultivate "charity." [15]

A number of circumstances combined to make the developments
in England acceptable to Friends in America. The relationship of
American to English Quakerdom was close at all times. In the
seventeenth century, most American Friends were English emigrants. Their spiritual guide was the London Yearly Meeting, and
it largely remained so for their descendants until late in the following century. In colonies where they were persecuted (notably
Massachusetts and Virginia) the main problem was the same as in
England: survival and legal relief. In North Carolina, Friends enjoyed a brief prominence, but this period came to an end with the
arrival of men and money from the Society for the Propagation of
the Gospel in Foreign Parts and the growth of other nonconform-
ing denominations. In fact, Quakers quickly became an embattled
minority as efforts to establish the Anglican church and to restore
the requirement of taking an oath to hold office gained strong
support. [16]

In the Quaker colonies along the Delaware, the religious organization readily took the role of a non-established sect, though at
first for novel reasons. The colonial ventures themselves had virtue
in Quaker eyes both as demonstrations of good societies and havens
from persecution. Enjoying control of the government as well as
religious freedom, Friends as a matter of principle chose not to give
their church any of the attributes of a state church, and limited the
business of the Meeting to internal affairs while they sought
through other channels to create a perfect society and evangelize
the nonbeliever. This basic decision about the proper sphere of the
Meeting, though ignored occasionally in early Pennsylvania, was
rigorously applied in the first quarter of the eighteenth century
as outsiders came to outnumber Quakers in the province. Though
Friends continued to be active in public affairs of all sorts, prudence
and principle alike required that they precisely restrict the functions of the Meeting to internal matters and prevent it from undertaking any action which would provoke the united hostility of non-

Quaker Pennsylvanians or, at their instigation, interference with religious liberty in the colony by the imperial authorities in London.[17]

When the spirit of Bellers failed to suffuse and orient it, the Society of Friends was left supporting the longer-established practices of mutual aid and surveillance as the chief obligations of individuals to each other. Though hope of converting and reforming the world had enlivened Quakers on both sides of the Atlantic, the beliefs and recommendations for conduct which they called charity came to limit the functions of their religious Society. The limitation prevailed in the Delaware Valley roughly from 1700 to 1756; elsewhere in the colonies it began earlier and lasted longer — to the Revolution, or even a few years later.

Charity was a sectarian version of the church's traditional duties of social service — and more. Its central features were the mutual aid and encouragement to avoid sin which Friends gave each other. In fact, charitable practices included most of the activities of the Monthly Meeting, and nearly any contact between Friends when conducted virtuously. Even launching a business without adequate training and credit was a case of failure to do "unto all Men, as we would they should do unto us." But Robert Proud, writing just before the American Revolution, mentioned features of charity which show surprising ramifications of the concept and complicate the task of explaining it. Together with such easily justified duties as the use of arbitrators rather than suits at law, he put the love of enemies (and seeking their welfare), the care of Friends' poor by the Meeting while members also paid taxes for support of the "public poor," education of all children to be self-supporting, civic spirit, the promotion and support of benevolent institutions, and even pacifism.[18]

Basically, Friends regarded charity as an expression of "the love of God, which first made us love one another." Love, Penn explained, was the "natural" binding material of the universe and gave both religion and secular government their true effectiveness. The role of the Quaker Meeting, however, was not to be deduced from such broad principles alone.[19]

Early in the eighteenth century, Philadelphia Yearly Meeting recommended to its members a "Fervent & Inward charity one towards another, & to all Men." This endorsement was hardly debatable: there had been "those Commendations given unto Charity by the Apostle in his Day," and the example of early Christians whose type of religious fellowship Friends believed they were restoring. In Penn's day there was a remnant of an ancient Christian attitude: that the poor were the image of God and as such were to be loved as God was loved. A Quarterly Meeting at Philadelphia began a collection for the needy, "that we may continue to have a true feeling sence of such among us, as are the Lords true poor, who may cry to the Lord for relief"; none should justly "complain in our streets, but that our Bowels may be open to them for their Relief." By 1721 practical expressions of charity were praised as "friends antient Care and practice." [20]

Yet the authority of the past was not enough; explanation seemed necessary, and the Meeting supplied it by calling upon "Experience." Without charity not only did "Zeal towards God" fail, but "Men speak Evil of Dignities, Detract & Lessen the Name of their Neighbours, & Evilly Intreat in Secret the Reputations of those that think them no Harm." But "where Charity is, there is Love to God, & Love to Man," and since it "preserves Unity, & as it were Teaches all Duty," it inspired "Acts, and Expressions of Love & Goodwill to all." The Meeting in 1719 clarified the concept in abstract terms as "Social affection, and communicative good," calling it "the foundation of the people of God, And as they abide in it," the authority of their Meetings. The peculiar aspect of this occasion to define charity was that the words were included in the preamble to the Discipline to be enforced. [21]

Maintaining virtuous conduct among the members of the Meeting was part of the practice of charity, and, like aid to needy Friends, was explained by one of the Quakers' definitions of their religious fellowship. They thought of the church as Christ's "Family of Love," and tried to behave as members of one family ought to behave toward each other, "taking due Care one of another for their Preservation from all Uncleanness, Disorder, Snares and Entanglements that are in the World." The brotherhood in Christ, however, did not impose an over-riding equality on the partakers, but gave divine sanction to other relationships, made it virtuous for *"Husbands to love their Wives, and Wives to love and reverence their Husbands; Children to honour their Parents, and Servants their Masters."* Spiritual kinship even created the moral need for *"Widows to be chaste; also young Men and Maids to be soberminded, and not to marry with Unbelievers; and all to labour, for he that will not work, must not eat; and rich Men to be rich in good Works."* [22]

Quakers also used the concept of family solidarity among the believers to justify mutual aid. The Meeting assumed the duties of a poor, disabled, or missing father or husband when flesh-and-blood kin could not take his place. It cared for widows, fatherless children, the sick and lame, kept watch over the treatment of apprentices placed with its help, and supported the aged.

Friends went so far as to use the human family as a subassembly of the church. They believed that the "divine principle of Grace" was sufficient to "preserve children" in "Obedience to that divine Command, of Honouring of Parents." In New England, standing officers of Monthly Meetings visited their brethren family by family to help strengthen these vital units. Elsewhere, Meetings sponsored programs of visits whenever Friends could be found who felt adequate spiritual power and a "concern" to do the work.[23]

The Meeting made the heads of households responsible for the spiritual training and welfare of the other members. They were expected to encourage and invite their dependents by a "pious Example . . . to love retirement; & to seek in stillness for the Counsels of Wisdom that they may become happily acquainted with the voice of the true Sheapherd." This function of the parent gave much of the explanation for Friends' condemnation of those who married outsiders, a step which was sure "to introduce great Confusion, by destroying the proper and joint Authority of the heads of Families, and abating of Love between themselves." There were even cases when a man and wife both in membership were disowned for quarreling and separating.[24]

Throughout the seventeenth and eighteenth centuries, moreover, the family or household included more than just parents and children. In addition to other dependent relatives, it embraced bound servants and slaves. The Meeting insisted that such persons ought to be treated exactly as actual kin. In practice Negroes were not taken fully into the family, though apprentices probably were, especially if they were young Friends. An obvious corollary to the standards set for treatment of apprentices was that parents ought to bind their children only to fellow members. Meetings insisted on this article of virtue only to encounter sporadic misbehavior, probably occasioned by the desire of parents to break out of the economic restrictions which obedience would have imposed; at any given time, a community of Quakers could offer only a limited assortment of openings for apprentices.[25]

When conducting their church government Friends always strove to safeguard the reputation of Truth (that is, Quakerism) by maintaining "the comely Order of the Gospel." They believed that the restoration of the "ancient Beauty" of functional relationships between the believers with their various "gifts" attracted converts and produced an institution with an excellence lovely in itself and glorious to God. The distinctive beauty of Christian fellowship was perfection of individual conduct. The discipline of the Meeting preserved "Christ's liberty," that is, perfect freedom from sin and human will. If each one persevered as he ought to in his worldly employment, spent money on nothing "vain" or corrupting, stayed within bounds of prudence, what need had he of charity beyond watchfulness of the Overseers? Christ's vineyard was not to be kept in order by preserving people in sin; nor was his Truth to be promulgated if its professors were allowed to behave scandalously without reproach. The Meeting, therefore, had to be sure that a Friend's need of aid did not arise from behavior below standard, or that such aid would improve him.[26]

Various events could reduce Quakers to want and dependency in spite of blameless "conversation." Orphans and poor widows obviously could not be held responsible for their hardships when there was no suspicion of murder. Even those orphans with an inheritance needed to have legal aid or supervision of their training for both secular and religious life. Victims of fire, flood, and sickness bore no blame for these disasters; nor did victims of religious persecutions. Those brought to distress by military campaigns or capture had to qualify for aid by maintaining Friends' peace testimony. Business failure could logically be a legitimate occasion for the Meeting's aid in the form of temporary relief or measures calculated to restore the unfortunate man's earning power, provided he had carried on his affairs in accord with Friends' standing recommendations. Even the dependents of an alleged counterfeiter, "in want of immediate Relief & Assistance" received "the necessary care." They were, after all, innocent victims of radically corrupt human nature.[27]

Though Quakers spared no pains to prevent their religious community from suffering "any Reproach by the Vicious or Uncomely Practices" of any members, they did not serve this goal by swift expulsion of the wayward. Brotherhood in the love of Christ required them to defend each other from the "Mischievous Attempts of Satan the Adversary." Their beliefs about sanctification and the worth of aids to divine grace led them to expand charity in several directions beyond simple encouragement to virtue.[28]

The emphasis on the Inner Light in Friends' doctrines has left inconspicuous their commitment to the view that every man was "originally disordered, and actually depraved." The seed of grace which they believed present in everyone, was a divine principle distinct from the animal nature of Adam's posterity. Through it each man received God's guidance sufficient to enable him to lead a holy life, unless he silenced it by persistently refusing to accept its direction.[29] Even after diligently trying to obey the divine promptings a Quaker's natural depravity influenced his conduct all too often. Some Meetings tried in their testimonies of disownment to explain relapses into corrupt ways, or called on repentant sinners to do so in papers of self-condemnation.

In these documents eighteenth-century Friends used two approaches to the subject of disorderly behavior and distress. In the practical conduct of the Meeting, emphasis was often put on immediate causes. In testimonies of disownment, such causes of reprehensible behavior were given as "loose and Unprofitable Company, and . . . frequently drinking strong Liquors to Excess," disregard of "the Duty due to . . . Parents, and the Unity of Friends, contrary to the Rules of Discipline Establish'd for the maintenance of Good Order among Us," and "Neglect of Meetings for Divine Worship." Sometimes the link between cause and effect was explained more fully by the use of common sense. Excessive drinking introduced "discord, strife & many other evils," or deprived a woman "of the use of her understanding, And caused her to Speak, and Act in an Imprudent and unseemly manner." Though misbehavior could be traced to such understandable human circumstances, it had to be condemned. Friends could elude the snares of such evil ways. Commonly, the fact that they did not was set down discreetly to "unwatchfulness" or "carelessness," which assigned responsibility to the sinner, but might also hint at insufficient vigilance by the religious fellowship.[30]

But a basic explanation for failure was also given, sometimes in conjunction with these immediate causes. One man "Transgressed the wholesome Rules Of Friends" by marrying a girl within the forbidden degrees of consanguinity "through inatention to that Light and Wisdom which by Divine Goodness has [been] placed in every Intilgent mind"; an unfortunate woman "so far disregarded the dictates of the divine Principle of Grace in her own Mind as to have a Bastard Child." If she had been properly attentive, "the Principle of Truth . . . would have preserved her from Evil." Less often, the finger of blame pointed to an ultimate cause, "the Snares of the Tempter" or seduction "by the Enemy of Mankind." Satan seized every chance to introduce disorder into the community of Friends, as he had successfully done into the early Christian church. He tempted individuals to "Indulge themselves" in an infinitude of ways and thereby turned them from the love of God and unity in Christ.[31]

Emphasis on the Inner Light as the built-in defense of each man gave Quaker explanations of sin the corollary injunction: cultivate the personal religious experience, subdue the human will. Emphasis on bad company, drink, or the devil gave a different one: fight worldly temptations, cling to the pure religious fellowship. The former made a self-reliant Christian, the latter a successful sectarian or ascetic, able to persevere in virtue amid a worldly community. Either emphasis could be given, since Friends believed that they had the capacity individually to cultivate "that good seed universally sown in every heart, by the great and good Husbandman," or collectively to shore up the defenses of the band of saints against the mass of reprobates bombarding them with temptations to the vain delights their own natures yearned after.[32]

Charity put the individual's inner cultivation into the context of the church's collective struggle with the world. Conduct evil enough to warrant disownment was forgiven in members when new evidence of regeneration came forth. The soul felt an orderly process of rebirth. An acute awareness, then horror of sin and the helplessness of the natural man, welled up, to be relieved by a glimmering of God's law. The soul expanded in knowledge and freed itself from bondage to sin. Ministry and dealings helped to bring on such a renovation, which could happen in anyone. Where signs of it existed, the care of the Meeting continued. Timely administration of aid also could help by removing material "hindrance to . . . inward growth." The tie of mutual love between members was not broken when one erred; the rest had the obligation to help him back in ways which they did not use with outsiders. They continued to assume that he was in their league against the snares freely accumulated by the world. This united stand of the embattled saints, though itself an aspect of charity, could be interpreted as offering a benefit to mankind when the world was regarded less as the enemy and more as the audience to be edified by the comely order of the Gospel in action.[33]

Another important feature of charity among Friends logically followed from their doctrine of grace: that they should help each other to be in a receptive condition for the process of regeneration. Though the effect of the process in no way depended on human will, a successful outcome was known to be assisted by deliberate religious exercises and by favorable circumstances in earthly life. Obviously, illumined by pure love Quakers should do their best to give each other the benefit of such exercises and circumstances. These considerations gave one of the reasons for Friends' educational charity and some of its special character. They gave a purpose to the distribution of denominational literature to Meeting libraries or directly into the possession of a member too poor to buy it.[34] They also reinforced desires to make giving aid to the needy an act calculated to produce long-range benefit.

Quakers believed that wealth should further God's purposes. The moral ideal of stewardship did not imply giving all they had to the poor. The "persuit of worldly Riches, . . . within due Bounds for the comfortable subsistence of our Selves and Families, . . . is not only Lawful but commendable." But they urged each other to "stand loose in" their "affections to the world," and realize that "we were not created barely to serve ourselves"; that "if there be any good use for . . . [riches], it is to relieve others in distress," since men are "but stewards of the plentiful providences of God, and consequently accountable for" their stewardship. Though they saw virtue in the charitable act apart from the benefit which it conferred on the poor man, as wise stewards they tried to control the economic consequences of gifts. When rich Friends gave money for charity, they often specified that it could be used either for relief of the needy or for putting out the children of the poor to learn a trade. A responsible use of money would prevent future poverty as well as alleviate the hardships of the present. Refined moral fervor, of course, did not always accompany wealth, but Friends were usually at hand to remind the rich brother of his obligations.[35]

Thus Friends in their own circle carried out the medieval expectations that the church would attend to a large number of the temporal as well as spiritual needs of its members. Even though Quakers confined the more positive and detailed manifestations of charity to the members of the Meeting — they took care of their own poor and fatherless only — as they pointed out, by assuming this limited responsibility they contributed to the public welfare.[36] In this way Friends' mutual aid could be justified as expressing charity to the public at large.

As expounded in the Philadelphia Yearly Meeting Minute of 1706, charity could logically extend more directly to those outside the Society. Endorsement of such extension was *pro forma* to some degree; Meetings neither enforced nor specified it. Certainly Friends did not call on each other to do unto outsiders through the religious Society what they did for each other. The Meetings did not think it right to take under their care poor orphans who were not the children of Friends, but referred them to public authority. Yet in some extraordinary cases of need, members contributed through the Meeting to the relief of outsiders.[37]

In the late seventeenth century, Quaker writers had preached greater duties. Penn had urged that Christians "relieve the necessitous, see the sick, visit the imprisoned, administer to their infirmities, and indispositions, endeavour peace amongst neighbours," and that women help others of their sex who lacked domestic servants. Thomas Budd, in 1685, urged the rich with idle funds to invest in transporting the jobless to the banks of the Delaware, "in order to bring them out of that Slavery and Poverty they groan under." [38]

In the early days of the Quaker colonies, a few gestures were made by Meetings to regulate members' business with outsiders in the interest of general moral purity. Friends were told, for example, not to keep wares in their shops to sell to others which they thought it wicked to buy for their own use. A Friend discovered with a stock of "Jew's harps" received a visit from a committee of his Monthly Meeting to tell him to sell no more and to get back those already sold, refunding the price. But after the beginning of the eighteenth century the Society neglected such details, to say nothing of the broader recommendations of Penn and Budd. Meetings required of individuals only the negative duty of not damaging or deceiving outsiders.[39]

In the main, Friends expressed love well enough to those outside their Society by affording an example of love to one another. In their Yearly Meeting at Philadelphia, 1786, they wrote to their "fellow Labourers in the Vineyard of Jesus our Lord" across the ocean, calling on all Quakers to persevere in "the Upright Performance of our respective Duties as individual Members of his mystical Body when separate," and in their religious Society, "as united Branches of his heavenly Household, to promote the Glory of his holy Name among ourselves." By preserving each other in good discipline, they could ensure that "an Increase of Brightness & Strength" would "be known to ourselves, and visible to enquiring Beholders." [40]

There were other ways in which good conduct might have effect beyond its value as example. Friends' pacifism also constituted a branch of charity. Fighting was "contrary to the peaceable Principle" they had "always profess'd"; their religious ideal breathed "Love to all our Fellow Creatures" and led them to cultivate the useful instead of the destructive arts.[41]

In some cases Quakers considered participation in civic affairs a branch of charity. In this field, even more than the others, the Meeting left good works to individual initiative. When a plan for an Academy of Philadelphia, for example, got under way, the Meeting officially ignored it, but some Friends backed it, willing to cooperate with men of other faiths. They withdrew support in this case when others converted the institution to sectarian and party advantage. Philadelphia Quakers in their private capacities promoted the public Alms House and engaged in relief of paupers.[42]

More often, though, the concept of charity had such a strong element of corporate solidarity that Friends faced their neighbors as "a People." Since other denominations had a similar attitude and degree of self-sufficiency in the colonies where most Quakers lived, this posture helped the Friends to live harmoniously in their civil communities. Yet the Quakers had built up corporate solidarity partly as protection from the "World." As early as 1726, the Yearly Meeting urged the members to look back on the settling of Pennsylvania and try to be as worthy as their forebears. The tumultuous, profane crowd of the world's people posed a special threat. Since Quakers controlled the government, outsiders could not "persecute them as in times past," but strove "to give them disturbance and trouble of another sort" in their immoralities and deceits, "using many artful ways to draw others to fall in with them."[43]

Friends had to resist with virtue, as they refused to seek revenge or hurt their enemies. They could take Penn's advice to English Friends in 1678, that they be ready for contact with outsiders, but determined that "they must come to *us*, we must not go to them." Morality required sympathetic help for the "infirmities" of the others: Friends "must make their case as [their] . . . own, and travail alike in spirit for them as for [themselves]." [44]

But they could go further, illumined by charity. In Pennsylvania, especially, Quakers kept feeling the responsibility to produce a general reformation. In their capacity as a People they could bring benevolent pressure to bear on other appropriate social entities for the good of all. When the Monthly Meeting in Philadelphia weightily considered the prevalence of swearing and drunkenness, it decided to present a memorial to the Mayor, Aldermen, and Commonalty of the City expressing their concern and that of "all other the Sober and well minded Inhabitants." They asked that the government take action to do everybody good by suppressing vicious ways. Save for considering such a petition, they "as a Religious Society ever carefully avoided admitting Matters immediately relating to Civil Government into our Deliberations." They thought it right, however, to discuss and act on a request for aid to victims of a fire in Charleston, which the Proprietor and Governor of Pennsylvania had received from the Governor of South Carolina and transmitted to the "several Religious Societys." They had even taken a plan for a common burial ground to other societies, saying, "We as a people shall be willing to allow our share towards the charge thereof, if they think well of it." [45]

As a People among Peoples, a sect among sects, Friends found a place in their social milieu as one of several similar groups of citizens each of which could initiate or be called on for certain kinds of social action. The Quakers relieved their own poor and expected other religious divisions of society to do the same. They left to civil society certain functions thought to be appropriate to it in a governmental sphere, notably those relating to "interest" or embracing the affairs of all religious subdivisions. They expressed their religious obligation to outsiders by corporate leadership in virtue and by individual help to persons for whom no "People" felt a responsibility. In this way, Friends participated in the colonial American solution to the problems in social action raised by the breaking up of the monastic foundations and the national church. The solution of Quaker charity preserved the voluntary element which

Penn had insisted on from the start in church affairs. It managed the duties of mutual aid and surveillance. Its success was most limited in dealing with the duties of the individual to outsiders; these it handled partly by making them functions of the Meeting (notably in preaching moral and decorous behavior), partly leaving them to individual discretion, partly letting them go.

Mutual Aid in the Monthly Meeting

THE concept of charity invested some very practical matters
with deep religious significance. It did not, however, determine
how the problems of individuals should be handled. Tradition,
realities of experience, and pre-Quaker sectarian precedent guided
Friends as they worked out their system of religious fellowship.

American practices had English origins. Emigrating Quakers
carried familiar organizational methods across the Atlantic and used
them in new Monthly Meetings. Even before many of them had
settled in the New World, traveling ministers and epistles from
England had urged the colonial brethren to conduct business after
the fashion developed at home. In New England a few distinctive
local practices persisted until the Revolution, but in most respects,
by the end of the seventeenth century, Quakers everywhere were
able to keep a high degree of uniformity in the operations of their
fellowship.[1]

It proved possible to frame "advices" which applied to all
Friends. Even though such basic institutions as the family and apprenticeship kept changing in America away from the European
forms, the divergence did not proceed so far as to render the common terminology obsolete or the moral objectives of the "advices"
irrelevant. Standards developed in England to deal with apprenticeship, servitude, shopkeeping, manufacturing, overseas trade, debt or
inheritances, were transferred to America. The judgment of con-
crete events, however, required common sense and attention to the
particulars in any case. Local circumstances, such as the large size
of the Quaker population of London, the elimination of Quakers
from farming in England, and the existence of Indians and Negroes

in the colonies, rather than disagreement in original views of what charity required, made the charitable acts of the English and American Meetings differ during the eighteenth century.[2]

Quakers did a more thorough job of mutual aid than other English sects. The Friends' system was developed by the end of the seventeenth century, although refined thereafter. From the Seeker communities which provided many early converts to Quakerism, and from the techniques of English private philanthropy, the Friends took ingredients that they put together in a distinctive fashion. Seventeenth-century Friends combined devices for encouraging the poor to become self-supporting with measures to make the religious fellowship self-sufficient. They created officials of the Meeting to carry out the work in normal cases. In addition to generally accepted secular goals of philanthropy in England at that time — such as promoting the stability of families, by making them self-supporting and disciplined, and providing a helping hand for any type of temporary distress — Quakers put unusual stress on their own objectives.[3]

This commitment to self-sufficiency as a church had religious justification, but it also gave a practical reply to those who demanded that Friends be well-adjusted members of the body politic, accept military duties, and support the established cult. If Quakers could not in good conscience meet all the normal obligations to society, they could balance the score by relinquishing some of the benefits. The refusal of their compatriots to accept this bargain and their efforts to extirpate Quakerism created an urgent necessity for mutual aid.

In the early years of colonial Quakerdom, persecution created the same demands for relief as in England. Friends enjoyed legal toleration in Lord Baltimore's colony and in Rhode Island, and in New Netherland and Carolina after 1663, but their sectarian "testimonies" kept them at odds with provincial governments for years. In Maryland, as in England, for instance, they waited long for permission to use the affirmation in court and lost the privilege to hold public office for a few years after 1691 when oaths were insisted upon. In America the burdens of taxation for religious establishments were similar to those in the home country. In Connecticut and Massachusetts, "priests' rates" to pay clergymen were levied on Friends sporadically until the middle of the eighteenth century, and in Maryland, Virginia, and the Carolinas until the Revolution. The victims' Meetings recorded their "sufferings" diligently and sometimes gave material help, as when Newport paid the jail expenses of some Massachusetts brethren imprisoned at Bristol for not paying ecclesiastical assessments. Meetings also tried to aid those who suffered in other ways from maintaining the distinctive Quaker testimonies. Military requirements — training with the militia, or serving in war — existed everywhere outside the Quaker colonies on the Delaware. The refusal of Friends to pay fines for noncompliance, or to hire substitutes, brought sheriffs to their doors to seize property to auction off for the forfeit and costs. Meetings gave aid when the exactions led to economic distress and, when laws allowed the exemption of conscientious pacifists, gave documentary proof of membership to men of fighting age.[4]

From their earliest days Monthly Meetings called on members to "take Notice of the Poore to Ease one another." But the Quaker colonies at first faced the special problems of charity in pioneer settlements. Immigrants died, leaving widows and orphans stranded in the near-wilderness. Families became separated. Newcomers lacked practical knowledge about what to do. Provisions ran short, and people arrived sick. Burlington Monthly Meeting in 1678, Philadelphia in 1682, and Newark, Delaware, in 1686, took up collections "to administer present supplies" to those who "may through sickness, weakness, or death of Relations be reduced to want or distress." The Meetings appointed men to collect the money, and others to visit the poor and sick and minister to their needs.[5]

The urgency of the situation soon compelled Philadelphia Friends to improve their policies and institutional methods. In February, 1684, upon considering the great necessities of "dutch" Friends at Germantown, the Monthly Meeting called a special session "to consider what to do in relation to poor friends." When the Philadelphians met they decided that it was their duty to provide aid for poor Friends only; "such as walk disorderly may not receive [care] . . . when the faithful and honest hearted want due help." Friends agreed that they should cheerfully contribute for the relief of outsiders "as the magistrates see meet." The Meeting designated men to collect and administer a fund for the relief of Friends' poor to which each member would monthly contribute a sum appropriate to his means. These Overseers of the Poor were to "provide work for them according to their Capacity, and if they have children to acquaint the meeting thereof, that they may be placed out." But in spite of this provision, Philadelphia continued for several years to be especially burdened with the poor of the province, including a large number of widows.[6]

Burlington Friends, putting their faith in prevention, in 1682 "took itt into Consideration of what Service it might be to Visset Such friends y^t are newly Come Over & are Yet unsettled to Advise" them and find out "what their Intent is Either to take up Land or follow Some Other Imploy & to ye Utmost Endeavour to assist them in their Intentions." Philadelphia resolved to do likewise only on the exhortation of the dying Frances Taylor, and both Men's and Women's Meetings appointed members to the service. Subsequently, only the more affecting cases of immigrants in distress went before the Meeting. For instance, Philadelphia gave over thirty pounds to Samuel Massey who, on his way from Ireland, was "taken by the french and lost all, and Indebted for his and families passage from Antigua." Aid to the newly arrived became a minor matter after 1719, though one incident did take place on the eve of the Revolution.[7]

Even after such diligence to supply an ounce of prevention, Friends had to spend pounds for cure. Meetings which had a continuing heavy burden of poor relief soon developed a routine administration to deal with it. Instead of naming special committees for each case they let the Overseers of the Poor take the whole job, from discovering needy members to helping them. The Overseers presented their account to the Meeting periodically; then a committee inspected the records and, when it was satisfied, the Meeting directed the Treasurer to reimburse the Overseers. This system had the added advantage of preserving the anonymity of the beneficiaries. (Philadelphia Monthly Meeting still has bundles of case records which are kept sealed from all eyes.) Paying for this charity was fairly well arranged through regular contributions and spontaneous donations at business Meetings. Subscribers could be dunned when they neglected their obligations; only when war played havoc with prices and currency did the system come to grief.[8]

In such unsettled times even the smaller Meetings were driven to appoint Overseers of the Poor. During the Revolution, for instance, refugees from Newport created a burden on neighboring Meetings in Rhode Island which required the service of these regular officers. Until then, poverty among the members had either been rare enough to be handled by *ad hoc* committees or so endemic as to require constant assistance from whole Quarterly, or even Yearly, Meetings. Country Friends, furthermore, had no use for an elaborate system to raise money. The collection at Monthly Meeting created a stock which provided for ordinary expenses, and in emergencies the members answered special appeals for the price of board of a poor widow, as they did for the Yearly Meeting stock or repairs to a meetinghouse.[9]

As a rule the Friends in charge of the needy tried to supply immediate wants. They gave gifts in money or kind. On learning that William Parlet, for example, was "very poor" and lacked clothing, Falls Monthly Meeting directed "Joseph Kirkbride, Samuel Dark and Peter Worrall to get a good pair of leather breeches and a good warm coat and waistcoat, one pair of Stockings and shoes for the said Parlet." Chesterfield Monthly Meeting sent a Friend in similar circumstances some cloth, buttons, and thread, and let him do his best with them. Elsewhere they used the panacea, cash: Philadelphia sent the aged Thomas Makin twenty shillings in 1725. When winter set in, the poor needed wood. A prudent Meeting set a committee to work to purchase fuel in September when the price was still low. On other occasions, Men's Meetings paid for food, bedding, a house, "Chirurgical" operations by Drs. Thomas Bond and William Cowper, medicine, and, when these measures failed, a coffin. Women's Meetings deliberated on aid to the needy in even more minute detail.[10]

Some Quakers continued as the Meeting's charge for years. A certain Friend John, for instance, required aid from Philadelphia intermittently from 1706 to 1722. Others received their board at the Meeting's expense. The city Friends early thought it wise to find places for aged brethren "in the country," and after 1768 made it a regular practice to save money.[11]

Meetings also looked out for the spiritual needs of their poor. Just before the Revolution, Philadelphia Yearly Meeting made a special effort to put the Bible and more specifically Friendly religious books in the hands of members unable to afford them. Philadelphia Monthly Meeting had long had a library built upon the collection of books left to it by Thomas Chalkey, and bought some additional volumes especially to circulate among the needy. An epistle from the London Meeting for Sufferings, however, sparked interest in this concern among Friends in Bucks County. When the Revolutionary War had actually begun, Philadelphia Yearly Meeting began to print and distribute Friends' books to make it easier for Quakers to defend their religious profession. The project was revived after the peace, and the Pennsylvanians encouraged similar undertakings in other parts of the Quaker world.[12]

Loans formed a regular feature of the Meeting's charity, ordinarily without interest and often on inadequate security. They helped a man or woman set up in a trade or shop. John Needham, for example, asked Philadelphia Monthly Meeting for "Ten pounds to be paid again in twelve Months he having present occasion to lay it out in a Stocking Weavers loom, whereby he is in hopes to be better able to Support his Family." He returned the money "with a gratefull acknowledgement of Friends Kindness in the Loan." It was just as common, however, for the Meeting to lend money to poor persons who had some property, rather than give them aid. The Meeting let Adam Lewis borrow money on his house rather than sell it. When his heirs who had not supported him claimed the property the dispute was settled by an agreement to put the value of the estate at the disposal of his grandchildren as they needed it.[13]

Friends' Almshouse, a unique institution, provided a home in Philadelphia for those who, through age or infirmity, were unable to earn a living. It owed its start to the generosity of John Martin, a tailor who died in 1702 and left his estate "for the use of poor friends" as the Monthly Meeting might see fit. Three trustees took ownership of the property, consisting of a house in town and 500 acres in Chester County. The house, sometimes called the "Hospital" in early years, sheltered poor Friends from 1704 until 1729. When the Meeting petitioned Penn for a charter for its school in 1705, it asked unsuccessfully for similar recognition of the Hospital. By 1726 Martin's house had deteriorated to such an extent that the Meeting decided to replace it with "six small Tenements on part of the Lot," leaving the rest of the land "to Let at a ground rent toward the support of poor friends that may be placed in the Tenements proposed to be Erected." Building began in 1729, and a campaign for funds soon elicited donations and several large bequests. By 1746 eight more units had been added.[14]

These new structures, often called the Almshouses, gave a roof to poor Friends, especially women, too old to work. Of two dozen persons admitted between 1744 and 1773, only a quarter were men. It is hardly surprising, then, that while the Men's Meeting deliberated over the construction and upkeep of the buildings, the Women's gave more attention to the inmates. Both Meetings appointed overseers to carry out their decisions, but the women also acted more directly. Every month they sent money "to Friends in the Alms House" — about two pounds per month during the 1750's, more in later years. In 1758 the men imposed regulations to reduce the expense and make inmates "more helpful to each in Case of Sickness or otherwise." The chief innovation put two persons in each unit, doubling the total which could be housed — a desirable end in itself in the difficult year of Indian depredation.[15]

Women's Meetings had a role in many branches of charity, though mainly to their own members. In Philadelphia the Women's Meeting continued to give close attention to the poor long after the men had put such business into the hands of special officers. Their accounts record many small sums given to the needy — "for Cloathing & Nursing Ann Roberts," for example, or "to Eliz. Martin for Linnen for the Child placed with her by Friends." When two children entrusted to the Philadelphia men Friends proved to be girls, they were turned over to the women. The Women's Meeting supplied temporary domestic help for sisters who for a time were unable to take care of their families, and sometimes helped arrange board for poor widows or care of young children.[16]

Ordinarily the women were quite as cautious as their menfolk, but there were times when impulse won over prudence. The accounts of Philadelphia women Friends offer such items as: "Sent as a token of Friends Love to Wᵐ Stockdel," "Given a poor Friend at this Meetᵍ," "To some Persons in great want," "Paid for a Gown for M D," or "Borrowed out of the Yearly Meeting Stock for the Assistance of a Young Woman that is likely to be Suddenly Marryed — £5." [17]

In several respects the Women's Meetings were not in a position to act independently. Their financial resources were not great, and they often had to apply to the men for funds to refill their coffers. (No doubt the Quaker wives found it more effective to act in concert than individually when they wanted money from their husbands.) Even the Burlington women, who had invested funds of their own, spent more for poor relief than came in from interest or the monthly collection. In Newport the women virtually abandoned the attempt to supply their needs by contributions and instead, secured permission from the Men's Meeting to get money from its Treasurer whenever their own supply ran out. Such arrangements did not make the women dependent on the men. On the contrary, it put the care of the poor more fully in female hands. The women in Newport appointed the Overseers of the Poor and conducted the routine aspects of relief. Since the men had not undertaken the usual amount of this work, it was only fitting that they supply the cash, especially as they enjoyed an ample stock, much of which came in as rent on a large tract of land.[18]

Some charitable services were considered out of the female province. The Men's Meeting had to stand in for the man of the family. When a woman lost her husband or became separated from him, she received small gifts from Friends of her own sex, but needed the advice of the men if she was able to earn her living, or their support if she was not. The men sought out relatives of unfortunate women and put pressure on them to give aid as a part of family duty. When no other course was available, however, the Men's

Meeting arranged for the most lucrative disposal of the property and then paid for the board of husbandless women, often in a Friend's family. They also assisted widows to execute the wills of their late husbands and to enjoy their rights to the estates during probate. When a man had been imprisoned, the Meeting helped his family while his support was denied them, and eased his stay in jail if he had been committed for acts upholding Quaker principles.[19]

The family whose provider had failed in business presented a special case. Occasionally a Meeting kept a man out of prison. It expected a bankrupt to offer all he had to his creditors, and urged them to be lenient. It appointed a committee to help arrange an equitable division of the assets. Far from disowning the bankrupt, the Meeting might help restore his financial standing, sometimes by promoting a subscription of money "to help him and his family with something to begin again towards their relief . . . on condition the Creditors do Release him," which those who "were friends ought to do." Or Friends might make a loan to enable a man to satisfy creditors. The Meeting could even help by using its superior facilities of communication to locate distant creditors. Sometimes it gave timely advice in an effort to stave off insolvency.[20]

When a Friend lost all he had by accident, the Meeting was very generous. Indian incursions and capture by the French were occasions for aid. But the most frequent cause of total loss was fire. Quakers gave each other as much as might be needed after such misfortune, whether a few pounds "for a present supply" or a subscription on a large scale to replace a house or barn.[21]

One of the most important varieties of aid was in binding out fatherless children. The service not only had the virtue of practicality but the sanction of George Fox as well, and Meetings sometimes insisted upon it over the objections of the supposed beneficiaries. To put a child in a household where he would receive his keep, in exchange for doing some chores, was to take a burden off his mother. The Meeting might even pay for his care in the foster home and for tuition to a schoolmaster. When old enough and equipped with the rudiments of the three R's, a child could be apprenticed to learn a trade in the normal fashion. This not only lessened the current expense to the Meeting, but also insured against charges in times to come, since it was likely that an untrained poor boy would "be chargable in future to friends by reason of his incapacity to get his own Livelihood unless some Measures be taken to enable him by learning to do it." The Meeting's assistance in apprenticing children was, in its view, the most proper kind of care, whether a father was dead or merely poor.[22]

In performing its duty the Meeting faced the same difficulties as natural parents. Children had to be put out among Friends; so a member had to be found who could offer a suitable trade. Making the arrangement cost five pounds or more, including a fee and necessary clothing for the child. And the young person might not take to the career laid out for him. Philadelphia Monthly Meeting met a wide assortment of these problems in the case of "Seymour Hood an Orphan Child descended from Friends." The Meeting sent him to Friends School until he attained the "proper age to be putt out apprentice." Since he was lame, "a Sutable Master" could not "be persuaded to take him without some Money being given with him." The Meeting, willing as usual in such cases to use all its resources, appointed a committee which included Samuel Powel, the "rich carpenter" who had become a wealthy landlord. The committee placed him with a Friend "to Learn the Trade of a Joiner," at a fee of ten pounds. The boy ran away, however, and went to sea! In two years he was back, again in need of assistance, which the Meeting felt bound to give in paternal fashion. As "the business of a Marriner" was the only employment he could "be persuaded to follow," the Meeting put his affairs in the hands of two prominent merchants, Israel Pemberton the younger, and John Reynell, to act as would "be most for his advantage," which they were well able to do.[23]

Apprenticeship was only a step toward a place in the economic world. After training, a young man needed capital. The case of another boy showed more of the whole process. The Meeting first helped him after the death of his widowed mother, when it arranged a settlement with his deceased father's creditors, in an attempt to save part of the estate. Four years later it put the boy out to learn the trade of a potter "and to get him taught reading, writ-

53

ing & Arithmetic." But his master died before the lad reached majority, and no other potter in the fellowship would take him. Somehow the Meeting surmounted the difficulty and lent him money to set up his own shop. Four years later an unspecified catastrophe made another loan necessary to fit him out again.[24]

In other ways, too, the Friends acted in place of parents, sometimes as the result of specific requests in wills. Meetings appointed committees to investigate complaints of ill-usage of apprentices, to act in the interest of orphans' estates in court, and to insist on the maintenance of the legal rights of children when their mothers remarried.[25]

So important did Friends regard charity to poor children that some of the larger legacies to Meetings were designated for the "putting of poor Friends' children to trades." The most notable such bequest was that of William Carter to Philadelphia Monthly Meeting, which at first yielded five pounds annually — enough to outfit and pay the apprentice fee for one boy. Though the income gradually increased, prices rose proportionally, so the legacy remained adequate only to help one lad. However, the needs were not so great as expected: in 1774, unused money from William Carter's annuity had accumulated to a total of £112 10s. 3d.; and by that time Philadelphia had been given another large bequest for the same purpose.[26]

William Carter, like other far-seeing Friends, made other gifts, including one for relief of the poor and another for the schooling of their children. Philadelphia Yearly Meeting encouraged gifts of this kind, and renewed its exhortations to bequeath money for educational uses when it resumed pressure on the lower Meetings to establish schools.[27]

The Meetings accepted bequests of another kind to be divided among poor Friends and others. A committee made a brief inquiry, drew up a list, and distributed the money. Some of these sums were large; one from George Emlen amounted to £50. Such legacies, which offer a marked contrast to the normally prudent approach to mutual aid, were in fact not part of specifically Quaker practice. Their antecedents were the "funeral doles" of the sixteenth century. The virtue of such gifts was scarcely to be found in their tendency to encourage the recipients to self-help or any other long-range benefit. Rather, it was the convenience to the executors of the will and the Meeting. When John Martin gave usable property and William Carter gave revenue-yielding real estate, their bequests required complicated legal arrangements and made the task of the executors longer and harder. Property required constant watchfulness on the part of the Meeting. To distribute a sum of money, on the other hand, was soon done for all concerned. Furthermore, small gifts were probably beneficial in many cases of temporary and acute distress.[28]

Though a Meeting respected the wishes of a donor who left money to be distributed to outsiders as well as Friends, ordinarily mutual aid touched only those within the Quaker circle. Children of insiders were important beneficiaries, though not truly in the religious fellowship. Meetings carefully avoided ambiguity on this point by referring to boys and girls who were children of Friends or had their education among them. By the middle of the eighteenth century, when the concept of birthright membership had emerged, it became possible to speak of children with such a right even though they were not yet old enough to participate in business meetings. However their relationship with the religious Society was described, when it came to charity Friends' children were within the fold even more than their elders.[29]

For adult Quakers, long-standing policy made the Meeting's assistance contingent upon good behavior. The Philadelphia settlers laid down the basic principle in 1684, that aid should not be given to "such as walk disorderly." But the sincere desire to help often led Friends to refrain from applying this rule strictly to members whose unacceptable conduct was under disciplinary "dealings" and offered some prospect of reform. As definitions of membership were written and made more precise, it came to be axiomatic that one who could not prove a right of membership or be accepted by a Monthly Meeting had no right to Friends' aid, though the Meeting might help him in any case. The use of the certificate system helped make membership a knowable thing. In one instance, Burlington Friends refused aid to a woman who they thought "was not Properly a Member" and instead sent a committee to ask her father what "Reasons he may offer for not Assisting of her." Four months later the committee reported that her father had done little for her and that she should be treated as a member because the Meeting had once given her a certificate. Aid was then forthcoming.[30]

In withholding assistance from the disorderly, the Meeting, in effect, used power to enforce discipline in a way which belied the strict voluntarism in the theory of church government. The ideal purity of the sect and the ideal bond of love between the members sometimes proved incompatible. Philadelphia Monthly Meeting refused to accept a tavern-keeper into fellowship on certificate (and hence become responsible for his welfare if he became poor) because it thought he should change his occupation. A man, and later his widow, were told that they must improve their conduct or "Friends will not think themselves obliged to Assist them as they have heretofore done or esteem them Members of our Community." The power to stop aid was used even to compel compliance with recommendations of the Meeting, such as moving to the country, which it thought would be of benefit to the recipient.[31]

But the conflict between the two ideals posed its greatest problem when slightly deranged individuals turned up from time to time. In the case of a certain Friend Sarah, a poor widow "under some disorder of Mind," the Meeting sent aid and offered to find her a place out of town. The next time she asked for help, a committee was sent to check on her right of membership. She had a right, but had been behaving "very disorderly" and had surreptitiously gotten into "one of our Almshouses," so the committee was sent to enquire further and oust her. The committee reported that her misbehavior was mainly due to her mental state and that she was a proper object of charity. But soon she was acting "in a very scandalous manner, which is thought to have been occasioned by vicious Inclination rather than a Disorder in her Senses," so a new committee, including a doctor, was sent to investigate. They learned that she wanted to go back to England, which the Meeting thought unwise. For a while she mended her ways, and Friends saw fit to pay her board, but her reform was incomplete. When the Meeting heard that she had "for a considerable time past been addicted to a lewd Course of Life & frequently drinking strong Liquors to Excess," it concluded at last that its efforts were not producing the desired effect and disowned her. In other instances, Friends followed the same criterion: when a slightly insane person became a positive scandal to the Society, the time had come to testify its disunity with him.[32]

The Meeting considered its good offices abused and the reputation of Truth neglected if those who sought relief had not taken all prudent measures to reduce the amount necessary. To reduce the family's living expenses the children had to be bound out at the earliest opportunity, a measure for which the Meeting was willing to pay. The Meeting also tried to find work suited to the abilities of the adults in its charge. Men who could not otherwise support themselves sometimes held a job as caretaker of a meetinghouse; women were hired to help with its cleaning. One man who had become lame prepared, with his Meeting's help, to take up school-teaching.[33]

Persistent zeal to keep the poor doing their best inspired a few long-range plans. Newport tried to establish a project to give Friends "in low circumstances" the productive work of spinning wool. A member bequeathed £200 to Philadelphia Monthly Meeting on condition that it "Erect & build a publick Work house for the use of Friends in this City," beginning "within three years next after" his death, it being his "Earnest desire to promote so useful and Excellent an Establishment in this City for promoting Virtue & Morality & stopping the Growing of Vice & Idleness." Inexplicably, the Meeting allowed the three years to elapse and then appointed a committee "to consider of some Method by which the Poor among us may be employ'd in suitable Work." Nothing further was done in this direction, however, probably because Quakers and others, in cooperation with the government, started an institution for this and related purposes that was open to the whole citizenry. But the most common method of encouraging self-help and preserving self-respect was to take a note or security in exchange for money supplied to the needy. (This procedure may have made a gift somewhat more acceptable to those such as one poor man who, when "Asked about his Condition as to yᵉ Outward he Said he never was so poor for to desire any Assistance from Friends &c.") [34]

The Philadelphia Monthly Meeting, especially, struggled to curb the growth of the budget for the poor. It urged them to go away, sometimes offering to pay for long ocean voyages in order to reunite them with their relatives. It insisted that they live in the country, where costs were cheaper; and it made arrangements through rural Meetings for places to board the poor. By the middle of the eighteenth century it began to enforce a kind of settlement law. Quakers who moved to the city were scrutinized for signs of pauperism. The Meeting no longer simply accepted certificates of poor Friends. In 1745 it began to refuse them, if the carrier seemed to need relief, until the issuing Meeting agreed to foot the bill. Others did not always agree with Philadelphia's interpretation of its obligation, and this disagreement led to unseemly controversies. Soon other relatively wealthy Meetings began to take Philadelphia's attitude. During the Revolution refugees fleeing Newport created such an expense for neighboring Meetings that New England Yearly Meeting had to guarantee to foot the bill. This emergency measure incidentally endorsed the rule that a Monthly Meeting was obliged to support only its own members; after the Revolution, poor members were accepted on certificate only if their previous Meeting would guarantee their support.[35]

The development of jurisdictional consciousness combined strict method with emphasis on the in-group. The unity of Friends all over the world was important, but the fellowship in the particular Meeting carried the obligations of charity farthest. The mutual aid of Friends in their tightly organized communities did not overflow casually into aid to others. The distinctions drawn between the Meeting's duty to Friend and non-Friend, the care taken to ascertain a poor person's right of membership, and the great importance of the Monthly Meeting unit, which grew greater still in the jurisdictional disputes, showed that mutual aid was a duty arising from religious fellowship rather than from solidarity of the species. In fact, for the Quakers to make a virtue out of humanitarianism, it would be necessary to overcome this aspect of charity.

The Monthly Meeting, however, trained Friends in methodical relief of the distressed. This effect was most conspicuous in Philadelphia; there Friends' Almshouse required meticulous planning from the time the Meeting decided to build small tenements rather than repair the Martin house. But to some degree mutual aid had to be systematic everywhere. In Meetings where the burden of cases warranted regular Overseers of the Poor, the business became a well-ordered routine of discovering the needy and figuring out what they should have. Meetings grew adept at recruiting the services of even the most prominent members for humble tasks — from arranging apprenticeship for poor boys to helping with the legal problems of widows and orphans. The Meeting developed ways of producing results with charity. The goals it pursued were usually the encouragement of the distressed to provide for themselves and the improvement of their conduct. But skill in methods served other ends as well.

Stress on method and results gave Quaker charity a worldly flavor hardly to be expected from its spiritual conception. By delving into the smallest material circumstance, Friends strove to keep the "reputation of Truth" unspotted. They received credit for the fact that no beggar was seen in Philadelphia in early years.[36] But that was not because of their behavior in Meeting, where they extended care to the members only, and sometimes withheld it from the disorderly. Friends were content as a rule to answer the query on this phase of their fellowship in such words as: "We are careful with regard to the poor among us." [37]

IV

Charity in Education

No SUBDIVISION of charity had firmer backing than the campaign to insure "that the Children of believing parents may walk in the way of the Lord" and receive necessary learning for life in this world.[1] Yet Quakers took less interest than other denominations in the kinds of education conducted in schools. Meetings did little about elementary schools before 1746 and founded no college before 1833. Even after their religious Society undertook to provide primary education, Quakers regarded moral and vocational training outside the classroom as more important, and accordingly Meetings in charge of poor or fatherless children put greater stress on these branches of education than on school work.

In the view of Friends, education, however it was acquired, had two aspects — one useful to the spiritual life, the other to the economic. In neither did the school predominate. The distinction was one of purpose rather than of subject matter. Both categories included training in such branches of virtuous conduct as honesty, diligence and skill in business, and self-restraint in consumption. Formal classes had only limited functions, deprived as they were of the role of preparation for higher learning. Friends denounced much of the liberal college curriculum of the eighteenth century as useless or corrupting; they doggedly opposed a professional ministry and the training for it. While law and medicine did not meet with the same disapproval, Americans entered these professions usually through apprenticeship rather than through a university. Science, though it met no moral objections, as yet offered no generally recognized career for which systematic preparation was available. So Quaker children went to school fundamentally to get basic learning useful to all. Entrusted with this limited educational function, schoolmasters continued for many years to rank in importance behind parents or masters and Overseers of the Meeting. In the first half of the eighteenth century, Friends put primary stress on the religious aspect of child training in the home before apprenticeship, which they dealt with mainly as a part of the application of the discipline to parents. The school gained importance after 1750 not because of any revision of ideas about what it could or ought to do, but because Friends decided to make the establishment and support of schools part of the business of their Meetings.

Early in their history Quakers put the various kinds of learning to a test of utility. Reading, writing, and simple arithmetic easily passed. These skills either had to be learned by children before they could qualify for apprenticeship, or, in some cases, were to be taught by the master in addition to his trade.[2] Beyond the three R's, modern languages and bookkeeping were useful to future merchants; geometry and trigonometry were necessary to surveying and navigation. Even Latin, though possibly studied for honorific reasons, formed part of the necessary equipment of a physician. The range of practicality recognized by Quakers was shown in the project for public schools advanced by Thomas Budd in 1685. In addition to Latin and modern languages, the schools would teach the boys "some Mystery or Trade, as the making of *Mathematical Instruments, Joynery, Turnery*," and the girls "*Spinning of Flax* and *Wool*, and *Knitting* of *Gloves* and *Stockings, Sewing*, and making of all sorts of useful *Needle-Work*, and the Making of *Straw-work*, as *Hats, Baskets*, &c." Quakers always included a practical side of education in schools founded in the seventeenth and eighteenth centuries.[3]

But their belief in a utilitarian curriculum was not of itself sufficient reason for Friends to set up schools for themselves; they had religious objectives in mind, also. Charity compelled the Meeting to provide schooling for orphaned, fatherless, or poor children of members.[4] In these cases an unusually large burden of moral training fell on the teacher; and the Meeting could hardly allow outsiders to take over a task so intimately a part of religious brotherhood.

The overriding motive, however, was to be sure that schooling did the child as much good as possible and as little harm. The experience had no necessary place in religious life. "In the Beginning was the *Word*," wrote George Fox. "Since the Beginning were the *Words*, and since the Beginning was *Babel*, which is the Beginning of *Tongues*, which is the *Priests Original*." But education had from time immemorial been a function of the church, and the Quakers continued this tradition without questioning it seriously, since they were convinced that learning to read the Bible was enough to give schooling a religious purpose. Fox himself, though the casual orthography of his letters makes the fact astonishing, gave his followers a speller which they used extensively. In it he included a dialogue between a scholar, who asked, "*Is the Light sufficient for Salvation?*" and a good Quaker master, who replied, "Yes." [5]

Still, there were suggestions in eighteenth-century writings that some steps taken by human will were of some avail. According to the generally accepted view, parent, guardian, master, Elder or schoolmaster, could encourage the young "as well by example as precept" to moral conduct and "frequent reading of the Holy Scriptures," and, where nature or the law gave authority to do so, restrain them from doing that which experience and the Bible had revealed would lead to wickedness.[6] This view of the matter persisted through countless rephrasings into the nineteenth century.

In guiding children, responsibility lay first of all with the parents, who had "the first and best Opportunity of making Impressions upon, and biassing the tender Minds of" their children. They were not to "awaken or indulge, but rather nip in the Bud those Seeds of Pride so interwoven with, and implanted in the fallen Nature of Man." Ministers and Elders were to "Embrace all Opportunities of encouraging and strengthening the Hands of the truly concerned *Parents*, suitably caution the Remiss," and "admonish undutiful and libertine Children, both by Precept and Pattern." The service of the schoolmaster in this work was that of the "necessary Coadjutor," but did not extend far unless he had students boarding with him.

62

He had responsibility for imparting practical learning which "(tho' within the Bounds of Moderation in a subservient Way, may be good and commendable)" was "a small part" of his charge in comparison with the stewardship "over the Souls and Conduct" of Friends' offspring. The schoolmaster had the obligation to make it his "indispensible Duty to labour with the utmost Sincerity, Application, and Integrity, timely to implant in [the young] . . . the Maxims and Principles of the *one true Christian Religion*," and strive "to rivet the Precepts" he gave by the life he led.[7]

All those in charge of children could take measures for their religious welfare. To begin with, the elders could give an example: they should wait "in *pure Silence*" in religious meetings, "to feel the Aboundings of that Life which Christ saith, he came to give to his People *more abundantly*." Not only would correct worship induce a merciful attitude on the part of God, but there was "no visible Thing more likely to prevail upon Children, and to set them on thinking on good Things, than to see the awful Sittings, and sometimes the overflowing Tears of their *Parents* and *Elders*, in their Devotion before the Lord in their religious Retirements."[8]

The next step was to bring the youngsters more fully into religious exercises. Parents should make a practice of taking "seasonable opportunity . . . to wait upon the Lord," with the children in their families; "to make them sensible of his witness and seed of life and grace in their hearts," because it was known that on such occasions they felt "the divine power break in upon them." When the children had been successfully induced to read the Bible often, parents should discuss its contents with them. In particular, parents were required to be watchful for those times which experience led Friends to expect wherein "[children's] spirits are (more than at others) disposed" to attend to spiritual guidance.[9]

The lives of the young might benefit also from even more stringent discipline. Scripture and common knowledge alike endorsed restraining the young "from falling into Temptations frequently presenting to Ensnare them" — specifically, from keeping frivolous company, "improper indulgences" in fashionable attire, gaming, horse-racing, non-Quaker modes of speech, "going to public places of diversion" (often "an inlet into grosser evils"), or "having or

63

reading any books or papers, that have any tendency to prejudice the profession of the christian religion," or stir up "the least doubt or question concerning the truth of the holy scriptures, or those necessary and saving truths declared in them." Instead, the young were to go to meetings for worship, read proper religious books and, by compulsion if necessary, behave as though living a sanctified life. Though no man could give children "the *Power* of Truth," nevertheless, all those in authority had the "Duty carefully to bring them up in the Form thereof, at the same Time humbly praying to the Lord to . . . interpose by his Grace in their Hearts," which would grant them that power.[10]

The observance of the form of Christian conduct brought "the *internal* Work of the *Spirit*" not by earning it as a reward, but by increasing the possibility that a child would give a favorable reception to "those secret and tender visitations of divine love, which the Lord has graciously afforded for the help and instruction of all." In each young frame was a circuit tuned to the divine frequency. Furthermore, God's holy spirit wrought man's salvation "sometimes instrumentally, by making use of exterior and incidental things . . . such as preaching . . . pious conversation, worship, mercies, distresses, &c." The prudent then would be ready to benefit from these instruments. Children, however, were by nature subject to "animal desire and animal passion" which increased with age. They were drawn to "Conformity to the world [in] . . . divers Ways and in divers Shapes." It was all too easy for parents and teachers to encourage children in vanity or wicked ways, which would raise passions and self-indulgence and interfere with the reception of the signals of divine love in their hearts. But a proper education disposed the children to "profess to another and better Way of thinking and acting," until cooperation with the forces for goodness produced a "Renovation" of their minds, and the religion of their education become the religion of their judgment. Despite all such efforts, some offspring might "prove *Prodigals* and *Libertines*"; but nonetheless good conduct on the parents' part obliged them to strive to awaken the child to his spiritual potentialities.[11]

In the light of this theory of the relation between education and spiritual life, the wise man took care to choose "school-masters who [were] . . . faithful Friends, and well qualified." [12] The church encouraged a parent to do his duty; but Meetings which took charge of educating poor or fatherless children had to set an example by preserving them as well as possible from the snares of the world and their own carnal natures. Since such children lacked a normal home, they were thought to be unusually susceptible to corrupting influences. The Meeting supervised their moral and vocational training, but also took pains to ensure that they went to the right sort of school. Before the middle of the eighteenth century Meetings thought it safe enough to pay tuition fees for poor children in classes run by reliable members; it was not then considered necessary for the spiritual welfare of any child that his school be under the control of a Meeting, or that the pupils be restricted to the offspring of Friends. Since little schooling was considered necessary for most children, the church could provide as much for the poor as most natural parents did.

Outside the larger towns a Quaker community could hardly count on having a qualified Friend hold classes every winter. The Meeting, with its special obligation to the poor and fatherless, tried to lure and keep masters by maintaining a schoolhouse. Compared to this basic problem of making approved teaching available, paying tuition for the poor was a minor problem; yet conscientious Friends left bequests to their Meetings for this purpose.

Even among cities with sizable Quaker populations, Philadelphia was unusual, but its educational projects were manifestations of more widely held ideals that also influenced similar, but largely abortive, developments in Rhode Island and West New Jersey. In the 1680's Friends in Philadelphia and Burlington expected government aid to develop schools. In West New Jersey an Assembly in which Quakers predominated gave an island in the Delaware to a panel of overseers, called the Board of Island Managers, as endowment of a school to be established in Burlington for the use of its inhabitants and those of some adjoining districts. In the civil laws for Pennsylvania agreed to in England, Article XXVIII had required that all children "be taught some useful trade or skill, to the end none may be idle, but the poor may work to live, and the rich, if they become poor, may not want." In the frame of government given by Penn in 1683, Article X had provided that "the Governor and provincial Council shall erect and order all public schools." Accordingly, late in the same year the Council arranged terms with a Quaker named Enoch Flower to be a schoolmaster, offering his services at established fees. The Councilors did not found a public school in the modern American sense — nor had Penn necessarily intended that they should; by directing the Council to "order" a school, Penn probably meant that it should regulate rather than operate the institution. Nevertheless, since he believed education useful to civil government, and since the early laws alluded to the public value of its economic purposes, he may have expected the province to take the initiative in starting and supporting schools.[13]

Thomas Budd, however, hoped for a more far-reaching program. He wanted the government to found schools, presumably to take in all children in their vicinity, not only to teach economically useful skills but also to guide the young to a religious life. He proposed to add to the regular school week a "Seventh Day" afternoon meeting where the masters would give "good instruction and admonition" to the pupils, who would return thanks to "the Lord for his Mercies and Blessings that are daily received from him." Then the masters were to make "a strict examination . . . of the Conversation of the Scholars in the week past," and give "reproof, admonition and correction . . . to the offendors, according to the quantity and quality of their faults." There was nothing narrowly Quakerly about the form of religious guidance, but Budd probably expected that the content would be such as Friends would approve. The government was to endow the school in each town with a thousand acres. The schools could finance free education to the poor and Indians out of the profits from the work done by the scholars while learning useful trades.[14]

Behind the creation of the Board of Island Managers, the appointment of Enoch Flower, and Budd's plan, lay the assumption that all children in West New Jersey and Pennsylvania could go to the same schools. Friends expected no interdenominational friction. Civil and religious interests harmonized; the institutional pedigree of the schools mattered little in a society in which Quakers predominated and others drifted into their fellowship. But when it became obvious that other religious groups were establishing themselves permanently and might take umbrage at a sectarian bias in schools sponsored by the government, Friends, who had always opposed any union of church and state, saw that they would be wise to abandon plans to use public authority to establish their schools. Nevertheless, when Philadelphia Quakers adopted the policy of creating their own educational facilities as private institutions, they regarded them as serving the public, not just their own religious community.

The change in policy was not abrupt. Friends in the city founded a school in 1689. They won the support not of the government but of their Monthly Meeting, which virtually underwrote the salary of the master, George Keith. The Provincial Council made one mysterious gesture to assert its authority: it required Thomas Makin, Keith's assistant, to bring evidence of his fitness and to obtain a license.[15]

Within two years Keith had quit the school and had begun his schismatic movement within the church, and soon went back to England. The school project did not revive until 1697. The Monthly Meeting then sent a committee to consult with two possible masters, Daniel Pastorius and Thomas Makin, and called a general gathering of Quakers in the city to talk over founding a "free school." From their deliberations came an institution which, as a subsidiary of a Meeting for its first quarter of a century, was unique in the colonial Quakerdom of its time. The Lieutenant Governor and Council were petitioned for a charter, and the Meeting agreed to sponsor a subscription and pay the two masters. A standing committee was to supervise the school; and the men and women Friends each devised charts of rules ("Orders to be observed") for the boys and girls.[16]

Early in 1698, Lieutenant Governor Markham issued a charter in the form of a proclamation, embodying the terms used by the petitioners about the benevolent intentions of the institution. The rich were to pay "reasonable rates," and poor children were to "be freely maintained, taught & educated in good Literature, until they [became] . . . fit to be put out apprentices, or Capable to be masters or ushers in the said school." The school was to be public, that is, to take in "all children and servants, male and female, whose parents, guardians and masters [were] . . . willing to subject them to the rules and orders," and who received approval of the Overseers.[17]

In 1701, with Penn's power firmly re-established, after its vicissitudes in the 1690's, the Meeting thought it wise to build a schoolhouse and to request a new charter from the proprietor that would make clear the Monthly Meeting's power to appoint the Overseers. At the same time, the new fundamental law of the province dropped the obligation of the government to provide for education. If the school in Philadelphia under its proprietary charter had the public character claimed for it, then it was not properly on the agenda of the business meeting of the religious fellowship. In 1708, still another charter for this school vested control in Overseers who filled vacancies in their ranks by co-optation among Friends. At once the new board discussed the wisdom of opening their ranks to outsiders, and the Monthly Meeting ceased to regard them as a committee, though it recorded no decision to that effect; in fact, it continued to accept legacies for the benefit of the school and gave permission to masters to conduct private classes in the building.[18]

The charter was revised in 1711 to permit the Overseers to co-opt persons of other persuasions. The purposes of their corporation were broader than those appropriate to the Meeting; they were charged with the public duty to cultivate religion and virtue and qualify children "to serve their country and themselves, by breeding them in reading, writing, and learning of languages, and useful arts and sciences, suitable to their sex, age, and degree." Quakers assumed the responsibility, intending to harmonize its fulfillment with their denominational needs. The Overseers continued to fill vacancies in their ranks with Friends, even though not legally required to do so, and the Meeting later made a point of asking that they co-opt no outsiders. The Quaker-controlled provincial government bowed out of the educational scene with a series of enactments of permissive legislation for Protestant congregations to own property and receive bequests for purposes of schools, thereby demonstrating its good intentions for full toleration. With Friends supplying large amounts of money, the schools under the Overseers flourished, maintaining and educating poor youngsters of all denominations.[19]

In Newport, Rhode Island, another large, compact, and prosperous Quaker community wrestled with the problem of operating schools during the same years. Various forms of church and private control were tried, as in Philadelphia, although the role of the Meeting was smaller and no device succeeded in establishing a permanent institution. In 1684 "Christian Loddewick" obtained permission to hold classes in the Newport meetinghouse. Like Keith, he soon gave up his school and went into opposition to Quakerism. After an interval of fifteen years the Portsmouth branch of the Meeting found another master to take the assignment. Newport tried again in 1710, with better results; it sent to England for a teacher and acquired land for a schoolhouse. But the building did not come under the Meeting's ownership until 1718, when the proprietors could no longer finance it by subscriptions.[20]

This transfer of control to the Meeting did not solve all the problems, however. "Disorders" broke out in 1727, and difficulty in getting a master persisted until William Lake took over from 1738 to 1749. Perhaps "keeping the School house glass in good Repair" discouraged him; in any case, he left the post, and the trustees gave up trying to maintain a Meeting school, renting out the building instead.[21]

In the interval between Keith's departure and the re-establishment of the Philadelphia school under Pastorius and Makin, the Monthly Meeting had turned to one of the two methods commonly employed by Friends in the eighteenth century to help take care of the religious essentials in education. It established a Youths' Meeting in 1696. The Yearly Meeting had suggested this expedient two years previously, and it was also tried in Maryland, New England, and New York. The plan was to hold four meetings a year at which ordinary Quaker worship was supplemented by reading statements, such as Yearly Meeting "advices," on the proper behavior for Friends.[22]

Although tried in many places, Youths' Meetings were not very successful. Sometimes attendance was too small; sometimes too many older Quakers attended, intent on instructing the handful of young. The frequency of these Meetings, never high to begin with, declined in some places. Newport and Portsmouth, Rhode Island, had originally planned to hold them every month; the interval lengthened to every other month, then to a year. Finally even this modest effort was abandoned. Exhortation, reading good precepts from the Discipline, and letting mature Friends present themselves before the youthful members in silent waiting on the Lord all suited Quaker ideas, but a few hours a year were too little to add much to the total program.[23]

A similar difficulty attended attempts to put Friends' books in the path of the youth by means of Meeting libraries. Even in Philadelphia it was necessary to appoint a committee to "consider of some suitable Method for encouraging our Members to read them." [24]

But such institutional devices as youths' meetings and libraries were of little help in the best of cases. To guide children it was necessary to influence them by more intensive and dependable means. Toward the middle of the eighteenth century it became clear that parents were not doing their part. All too often they neither gave their children enough moral training at home nor secured the services of Quaker schoolmasters, even where Monthly Meetings had provided buildings for classes. London Yearly Meeting had repeatedly called attention to the parents' duties, but to no avail before 1745. By that time, however, two developments on the American side of the Atlantic had predisposed Friends in Philadelphia Yearly Meeting to heed the call to reform. The Great Awakening, beginning in 1740, had stirred other denominations to zeal for education and a somewhat competitive effort to found schools; the Quakers discovered that they were lagging behind and would not only have to catch up but also give a sectarian emphasis to their schools comparable to those of their rivals. The second development was the acceptance, first officially acknowledged in England in 1737, of hereditary or "birthright" membership among Friends as the standard way of bringing new members into the Society. To cope with both the internal and external changes, the first goal in the campaign was to start enough schools to put a Quaker education within the reach of all Friends' children.

The relation between "birthrightism" and the campaign for sectarian schools was close but ambivalent. Obviously, once Friends had begun to regard their children automatically as members-to-be in the Meeting, it was more appropriate for the religious fellowship to devote its resources to their education than it had been before. Implicit in hereditary membership, however, was a new basis for apathy on sectarian training, since birthrightism diminished emphasis on the old criterion for membership, the active participation in the fellowship, and instead allowed membership to be assumed for Friends' offspring until their behavior deviated so notoriously from the Society's standards as to require disownment. By the middle of the eighteenth century Quakers on both sides of the Atlantic were so preoccupied with lineage (no doubt largely responsible for the acceptance of the concept of birthright membership) that they could easily tolerate a lack of positive attachment to the church on the part of their children rather than excommunicate them. Quaker schools could help prevent such a decay of the fellowship if they genuinely contributed to the spiritual nurture of young Friends, but could do just the opposite if they were regarded as a cure-all which would make it justifiable for parents to neglect their own share of the responsibility. London warned in 1747 that "virtue passes not by lineal succession, nor piety by inheritance"; only the constant care of parents could ensure that "the Almighty" would have "an especial and gracious regard" to their hopes for their children.[25]

Once zeal for a Quaker education had been kindled in Pennsylvania and New Jersey, Philadelphia Yearly Meeting in 1746 lent its support by sending an epistle to the Quarterly and Monthly Meetings under it, exhorting them to "encourage and assist each other in the Settlement and Support of Schools" to teach the children "at least to read and Write and some further useful Learning, to such whose Circumstances will permit it." The epistle, it should be noted, called for greater joint efforts by Quaker communities; it did not insist that their schools be operated by Monthly Meetings, though in later years a strong tendency appeared to rely on the church organization to solve the practical problems of creating educational facilities.[26]

In 1750 Philadelphia Quarter proposed that the Yearly Meeting adopt a recommendation of "some Method to encourage the settling of Schools in the Country, under the care of Friends." The city, of course, had schools under a corporation of Friends, but the representatives of the Quarter suggested that Monthly Meetings hire a good religious schoolmaster at a fixed salary to teach as many children "on behalf of each Monthly Meeting as the said Meeting might judge adequate to the Salary," and take no other pupils. In 1751 the Yearly Meeting, backed by London, urged action by the Monthly Meetings as "fully as their circumstances will permit." Two years later the Yearly Meeting recommended that the lower Meetings scan the funds given them for charitable uses to find some appropriate for educational purposes. The next year, apparently impatient for results, Philadelphia Quarterly Meeting appointed a committee and called on other Quarters to do likewise, the committees to meet together on the problem of directing Meeting moneys toward the support of schools.[27]

Nevertheless, progress remained slow. Although Philadelphia did all it asked others to do, even Burlington thought it beyond its resources to start schools at once, and instead petitioned the Governor of New Jersey to charter an endowed school. Goshen and Abington Monthly Meetings (which had owned land for a schoolhouse for many years) fell to work diligently, but Haddonfield, Middletown, and others were "of the opinion that the method proposed will not answer for the Friends who live remote from each other in the country." Friends in Wilmington started a school in 1748, with provision for the poor as its objective. But the more usual response was resistance to the new policy: in Falls, a committee reported its opinion that the best the Monthly Meeting could do was to appoint a school committee to spend the funds for the tuition of poor children. Gradually, however, Monthly Meetings founded vigilant committees and built up the resources at their disposal. The generation before the Revolution reaped a fine crop of legacies for educational charity, and in the territory of the

Philadelphia Yearly Meeting some rural churches accumulated enough money to set up schools.[28]

At the same time Friends broadened the range of their donations: Legacies often stipulated that the proceeds were to be used for poor children who were not necessarily Quakers. The Overseers of the school in Philadelphia, who already spent heavily on non-Friends, received permission to invest some money anew for the benefit of the poor. Among the better-known beneficiaries were children of the Acadians.[29]

But Friends continued to prosecute the religious education of their own children in the same old ways. New youths' meetings were set up, new care devoted to the libraries and the distribution of religious literature. More passages from the Discipline were read, and renewed exhortations were given "to Excite the Masters of Apprentices and heads of Families" to use "Circumspection & Care" in guiding the youth, which might be "a means to restrain them from falling into Temptations" they could not resist. The bare bones of charity — the care of the poor, provision of useful learning to their children and apprenticeship among Friends — were preserved fairly well, as many reports to Quarterly Meetings revealed. But the flesh and blood of charity, the religious nurture of young Quakers, could not be made to surround and animate them. The Meetings did nothing more than intensify the old expedients.[30]

In the Revolutionary crisis, laxity and disunity prevented the faithful discharge of existing responsibilities. Philadelphia Monthly Meeting lamented that "there is in the general a sorrowful neglect of restraining" the children "from such conversation & company as have a tendency to lead them into a deviation from the purity of our Christian profession." More care was needed "early & frequently to impress on their tender minds the grounds of our religious principles." The Yearly Meeting at Philadelphia implored members to revivify the ancient practice of visiting families in 1774 and 1775.[31]

When Friends assembled in the fall of 1777, they weightily considered "the important matters of instructing Youth" both in temporal and religious subjects, "of promoting a Reformation of Speech, Behavior, Apparel and Household Furniture," among other

73

deficiencies, so that "the Cause of Righteousness may be thereby advanced." This time Burlington, not Philadelphia Quarter, proposed that the Meeting set up and support schools "which should be visited and regulated in a Religious manner." [32]

The committee which undertook the task of making recommendations on this extensive subject produced a report to the Yearly Meeting of 1778, signed by two Philadelphia Friends, Anthony Benezet and Isaac Zane. They denounced the hiring of non-Quakers to teach members' children, reminded Friends of the Yearly Meeting Minutes of 1746 and 1750, and went on to attack the major problems of funds and teachers. They advised systematic gathering of endowments to enable Meetings to guarantee a salary to a master and to pay for schooling of the poor. They urged Meetings to provide teachers with a big house, stable, and pasture, in order to attract and keep married men; their households could decently receive boarding pupils. They put great stress on the moral character of masters, hinting that a sincere desire to benefit the youth was rather to be sought than ambition, and that uprightness rather than learning should be made the first criterion. The report concluded with a stern lecture on the doctrine of stewardship. If Friends had not been so intent on heaping up "riches for their offspring, contrary to our blessed Saviour's express command," if they had been more generous in the service of their fellow men, "the virtuous education of our youth, would not have lain neglected, for so long a course of years; after such pressing advices had been, so expressly, handed down from the Yearly Meeting." [33]

This plea elicited a good deal of action. Friends evidently approved the strong emphases on method and moral fervor in the report of 1778. Meetings at all levels appointed committees which did their best in the face of wartime disorder. Though many Quakers may have thought that the new policy on education was merely a stricter version of old ones, actually it was the first step in a decisive change. True, new schools would enable parents to put their children under an approved master and Meetings to give a safe education to the young in their charge; but more than in 1746 and 1750, the Society began to make the schools extensions of its corporate competence. The school was to be an institutional expression of the mutual aid and surveillance in the religious fellowship to the immature members; morally safe education was to be a joint endeavor of the Quaker community, not a matter of discipline imposed on parents.

It would be inaccurate, however, to describe the change of policy in 1778 as clear and simple. There was still no prevalent desire to transfer to the schools any of the parents' and masters' responsibilities for spiritual nurture of young Friends. Neither did Quakers want to carry out the ideal of sectarian education to the point of excluding outsiders from their classes; quite the contrary, during the Revolutionary period more often than ever before they were giving free tuition at Meeting schools to outsiders, both colored and poor white. Although the report of 1778 was recognized throughout American Quakerdom as an important revision of policy, it contained implications which were not fully accepted until later.

V

Charity among Meetings

CHARITY at its purest existed primarily within the Monthly Meeting, where the bond of friendship led the members to help and keep watch over each other. But their affairs, both worldly and spiritual, were not always confined to the territory in which the brethren in Christ could be personally acquainted. Charity extended to distant Friends rested on a conventional assumption of brotherhood, based on more or less direct knowledge of the status of the remote Quakers within the church organization. In long-distance transactions that involved persons who had met either at a Yearly Meeting or on travels in the ministry, mutual confidence was high and well grounded. More formally, the system of certification and the exchange of epistles among Meetings enabled the Friends to judge each other's standing in the faith.

Nevertheless, charity had to be conventionalized to apply on an inter-Meeting level, and being conventionalized gradually prepared the way to action by Meetings for the benefit of outsiders who by some other convention might merit their help. Charity to Quakers beyond the circle of the known religious community reduced the importance of the bond of friendship as the foundation of charity, and, by compelling the Meetings to operate through committees and remote agents, surrounded the help rendered to distant Friends with the air of business routine. Finally, charity on this wider scale led to the creation of organs of the Society of Friends, notably the Meetings for Sufferings, which later became useful in dealing with outsiders.

Charity within the world of Quakers became appropriate in a variety of ways. Fires, Indian raids, or invading armies might necessitate help from distant Friends. But less drastic occasions arose too; sometimes one Meeting served another by supplying information or by assisting in the performance of a specialized task, such as printing. Charity which involved the cooperation of persons in more than one Meeting in Quakerdom usually had another purpose, too: improvement of the good name of the faith, care for the "reputation of Truth."

Friends from a wide area joined resources to give aid to brethren who suffered great disasters, likely to draw the attention of outsiders and not the result of misconduct. Subscriptions to rebuild houses and barns destroyed by fire carried on an ancient tradition of "fire briefs" by which medieval popes had called for contributions to replace churches, and secular English authorities had authorized solicitations of funds to restore lost homes. Perhaps because of neighborly help in quenching blazes in towns, or possibly because city folk did not depend so heavily on their buildings to make a living, the calls to replace losses by fire were usually sounded for the benefit of country Quakers. After a holocaust a Monthly Meeting gave temporary aid, but it usually had to appeal to its whole Quarterly Meeting to raise enough money to rebuild the vanished property.[1]

In the late seventeenth century, Friends responded most sympathetically to the distress of captivity by Barbary pirates. Americans did not receive many appeals for ransom but were generous when they did. Quakers in Philadelphia and Chester Counties contributed "toward the redemption and relief of Captives at Masquenes in Turkey and more especially for George Palmer who is or was lately a prisoner there." They sent the money to brethren in London who had charge of a fund for such purposes between 1679 and 1709. When George Palmer wrote from captivity to ask his relatives to sell some of his Pennsylvania property, the Philadelphia Meeting tried to make other arrangements for him and to preserve his land.[2]

One classic episode of American Quakerdom involved Friends seized and taken to Canada by Indians. John Hanson was "a friend inhabitant in New England, who had his wife & several children taken Captives by the Indians and redeemed all save one." The cost

77

was "too heavy for the friend to bear, preserve his credit & support his family," so Quakers all over America gathered contributions for him. Friends along the Delaware raised over £180, of which almost a quarter was given in Philadelphia. This outburst of charity made it possible for New England Yearly Meeting to devote its resources to redeeming Ebenezer Downes, whose plight had not been so well publicized.[3]

In 1697 a crop failure reduced the "friends & other people . . . to the Eastward of Salem in New England" to "great Distress, and want of Provisions." Their Yearly Meeting sent word to New York and Pennsylvania. Philadelphia Monthly Meeting appointed Edward Shippen and Samuel Carpenter to get up a subscription and recommended the same course "to the Quarterly & Monthly meetings of Bucks & Chester." The Yearly Meeting, which assembled a few weeks later, endorsed the campaign and urged all Meetings to bestir themselves. Money-raising went on for over a year. Several years later, during Queen Anne's War, the Friends down East again found themselves in dire straits; the aid of fellow New Englanders then proved sufficient.[4]

On less dramatic occasions inter-Meeting cooperation solved problems which baffled individuals. Philadelphia, for instance, on application from "Ratcliff meeting near London" took care of a Friend's son who had been sent as an apprentice to the New World but by reason of some disease or accident which damaged his leg had become too lame to work. Ratcliff promised to repay the cost of passage to send him home, which was eventually done. The Men's Meeting in Dublin once sought aid from Newport, Rhode Island, to find a legacy and send it to an Irishwoman. Sometimes, when members had sold property located at a distance, Meetings could help get the purchasers to finish paying. Boys put out to non-Friends or ill-used by masters out of the range of their own Monthly Meetings got the attention of local Quakers and through them the application of suitable corporate pressures on the adults who had fallen in their behavior.[5]

The main service performed by particular churches for each other, however, was assistance in building meetinghouses. Among the Meetings in Pennsylvania and New Jersey, the first large-scale effort of this sort was the construction of the Center Square Meeting House in Philadelphia, intended to be a kind of Quaker Capitol. Later, money was gathered for meetinghouses at Germantown in 1705, Byberry in 1714, Shrewsbury in 1722, Horsham in 1724, and Chesterfield in 1725, to mention only early efforts. Once Friends in their Quarterly Meeting in Barbados sent "Effects" to the value of £50 as a contribution to the building of a meetinghouse planned by their Philadelphia brethren. In New England such inter-Meeting aid was quite common, with Newport and South Kingstown Monthly Meetings helping out poorer communities.[6]

Boston Preparative Meeting received unusual assistance for its place of worship. Contributions from the rest of New England helped finance a first building in 1695. Twelve years later new land was acquired for a new brick meetinghouse. The Yearly Meeting asked all American Friends to support "soe good a work in Building a meeting house in Boston wheare ou^r ffaithfull ffriends haue sufered marterdum ffor theare testamoney to ye Blessed Truth." Quakers in Pennsylvania, New Jersey, and even Barbados, agreed that a fine structure in the Puritan citadel would "be of a good sauour," and donated over a third of the amount needed. When the building burned down in 1760, Boston issued a new appeal to its neighboring churches and one direct to the Monthly Meeting at Philadelphia. Although quick with excuses and suggestions that Rhode Island brethren were at the moment much better able to pay, Philadelphia sent £100 without waiting to raise a subscription, consult the Quarterly Meeting, or even gain the concurrence of the Yearly Meeting which met about the same time![7]

Quakers, especially in Philadelphia, also gave care to preserving the outpost in Charleston, South Carolina. They raised money to aid sufferers from the fire there in 1741. The Quaker Community in Charleston dwindled to a single member by 1767, but still the Philadelphia Meeting for Sufferings thought it worthwhile to preserve First day meetings, as some of "the inhabitants there continue inclinable to attend our Meetings." So it appointed a committee to use its ingenuity to get repairs made to the meetinghouse.

79

(In a few years the Philadelphia Meeting for Sufferings took charge of Friends' property in Wilmington, North Carolina, as well.)[8]

Meetings also helped each other fight to eliminate the legal obstacles remaining to their religious liberty. New England Friends sent messages to the Governor and delegations to the General Assembly in Massachusetts to plead for an end to ecclesiastical taxes. They also raised money to pay for lobbying by London Friends and the Rhode Island colony agent against the Bay Colony's "priests' rates," against similar taxes in Connecticut, and in Massachusetts against the requirement of an oath of office with no provision for Quakers to take an affirmation.[9]

Meetings served the general good of the church also with defensive publications. At first the printing of Friends' books had necessitated preliminary consultations among various Meetings to ensure a market. In the second half of the eighteenth century, however, money was available to pay the cost of useful works. Meetings then corresponded about the needs to be filled and about the desirability of various texts. A series of subsidized imprints in English, German, and other languages flowed from presses at the command of the Meetings for Sufferings in Philadelphia and London, in order to draw Pennsylvania Dutch and Acadian "Neutrals," as well as English-speaking Americans, to Quaker beliefs. Other ventures, such as the printing of "Anthony Benezetts Books on Slave Keeping," influenced Friends and edified the general public.[10]

Meetings also helped in writing books. The desire to put the record of the Society of Friends before the world and to preserve the memory of early Quakers to their descendants inspired some complicated projects. Monthly and Yearly Meetings prepared accounts of their founding and subsequent events which they transmitted to Friends undertaking to write histories; the Meetings later checked details of fact. The Meetings for Sufferings helped by giving the authors advice on aspects of presentation.[11]

A duty of the Meeting for Sufferings in Philadelphia that was closer to its main purpose arose from the Indian claims to land occupied by Quakers at Hopewell Monthly Meeting, Virginia. The ground had been purchased by the provincial government at the

Treaty of Lancaster in 1744 from some Iroquois who claimed a vague right to it by conquest of the previous inhabitants. When the western Indians, uncontrolled by the Six Nations, became hostile to the English, Pennsylvanians feared that they would molest Hopewell Friends as receivers of stolen property. The people at Hopewell, though they had long before been urged to acquire the rights to their land in some orderly way, had not done so. After four years of conferences and correspondence, the Meeting for Sufferings persuaded them to settle up. But the closer they inquired into the business, the more difficult it proved to find any Indians who could claim descent from the aboriginal occupants. The objective of the Meeting for Sufferings slowly changed to a disciplinary one; Hopewell Friends must pay, not to right a specific wrong, but to be virtuous. By 1778 they had subscribed to pay £665 10s. in Pennsylvania currency to give to Indians — if not in exchange for rights to their land, at least "for the Service & Benefit of other Indians." [12]

The Hopewell case also had a bearing on pacifist principles. When Indian hostilities had threatened the Virginia frontier in 1757, Hopewell Quakers had behaved shamefully. They had "all of them been concerned in building a Fortification and dwelling therein for defense against the Indian Enemy." Chester Quarterly Meeting therefore decided that Hopewell Friends "could not reputably keep up a meeting for worship" under the Quaker name. The Meeting for Sufferings, which had the duty to uphold the dignity of the Yearly Meeting, defend the reputation of the church, and distribute relief to victims of Indian warfare, took over the whole touchy case when relief actually became necessary to the Hopewell backsliders. [13]

Charity which extended outside the Monthly Meeting was a consequence of solidarity among Friends and an exercise which made that solidarity real. Stories of captives in exotic places lifted belief in the whole brotherhood above an abstract level, while contributions to the ransom demonstrated the quality of good will on the part of donors who knew of the beneficiary only as a Friend. But if a concern for the welfare of individual fellow members at a distance ordinarily lacked any basis in the kind of sentiment which bound a Monthly Meeting together, it was easily equated with concern for the "reputation for Truth." Outsiders who heard about the case of John Hanson would learn that Friends took care of their own. In matters where personal hardship was not involved, inter-Meeting cooperation could, of course, be even more single-mindedly attuned to the impression that it would make on non-Friends. This was especially true in the efforts to preserve meetings for worship in Boston and in Charleston, South Carolina.

At the beginning of the eighteenth century the orderly hierarchical use of the Meeting structure had reached an adequate development for most kinds of inter-Meeting activities. Funds for victims of fire or the building of meetinghouses could be easily raised. Transatlantic negotiations between units of the Quaker fellowship could be handled. For the first half of the century the central institutions at London remained adequate to the coordination of the Society when direct communication between the constituent Meetings concerned in some pieces of business was insufficient.

The maintenance of Friends' position in the eyes of outsiders, however, soon required use of the organization in ways which did not follow the hierarchical pattern. The initiative taken by Philadelphia Monthly Meeting in sending aid after the "calamity" in New England in 1697 was autonomous because speed mattered. There was a cumbersome quality in the use of Quarterly Meetings, and the concentration of ready cash and influential Friends in the city far exceeded that in the country. Philadelphia had to agree to any decision; if speed was to be achieved, action had to be started by some unit in the Society which met often, and that meant in practice the Monthly Meeting, until Meetings for Sufferings were founded.

Nor did the structure of the church organization at first have organs for all its business. Inasmuch as outsiders were not under a Monthly Meeting, there was no clear institutional channel through which to supply the books to convert them. At first the Philadelphians who took an interest in this subject applied to the Yearly Meeting, which passed it to the Meeting for Sufferings of London. Time did not matter. But when the actions of the religious Society fell under close watch from outside, when a need arose for consistency between the actions and words of Friends in even the most remote places, when swiftness in relief or public statements became important at the time of border raids in the French and Indian War, inter-Meeting charity had to be put into the care of Meetings for Sufferings. They could use the orderly processes of the Meetings for business, or deal directly with problems which either did not suit the patterns of the organization, such as the Hopewell case, or required expedition, such as the relief to Friends of Exeter Monthly Meeting driven from their homes in the winter of 1757.[14] To these maneuverable central committees gravitated most business which involved the image presented by Friends as a people before the world.

Charity to Neighbors
Outside the Membership

I T WAS not accidental that charity which concerned outsiders received the least attention from the Meeting. The neglect was the outcome both of the concept of charity and of a prudent evaluation of the place of the sect in the world. But this quiet corner of the religious fellowship needs close attention to explain the rise of humanitarianism after the middle of the eighteenth century.

This sector of charity came to be regarded as insufficient in a few places because English practices adapted imperfectly to American conditions. Most colonial Quakers were humble folk residing quietly in the shadow of other denominations in whose ranks stood the high and mighty. But, in the provinces around the Delaware, Friends could shape social institutions and take the lead in public affairs. Though they seldom used their Meetings in support of this leadership, they stretched the limits of the proper business of the religious Society as it had been conceived in England. In Pennsylvania, moreover, they faced a people unknown to the Old World, the Indians. Friends in government had to make and administer laws about colonial Indian relations; in Meeting they had to decide how to apply the standards of virtue to personal dealings with the natives. The challenge of this primitive neighbor brought out some specific recommendations in the early years, but in broad terms remained unfinished business until border warfare renewed its urgency. While the concept of charity remained Friends' only guide, the challenge could not be met.

In regard to white neighbors of different religious views, Quaker ideas developed in England could usually be applied in America. Charity to outsiders consisted mainly of negative duties. Universal love for mankind demanded "a friendly and neighbourly deportment toward men's persons, in not seeking to ruin and destroy them, whether in life, liberty, or estate." Further, it required that there be no double standard: while Friends might take their business to each other when possible, they should not allow any difference between the economic ethics practiced toward those in and those out of their religious fellowship. Quaker tailors were not even to take orders for "making such fashionable cloathing as Tends to the Corruption of Youth, & breaking the good orders of Truth." Performance of obligations in this sphere was both individual virtue and an advertisement for principle. It was no mitigation of an offense if a member defaulted, cheated, or offered to sell vain "indulgences" to an outsider. No Quaker should make or sell what he disapproved of using. He must pay his debts and not launch "into business" beyond his "stock & knowledge in trade." He must not "keep a disorderly house, and sell strong Liquors to English and Indians, suffering them to drink till they are drunk," or even run a temperate establishment where "Play & Games" were "sett up, & carried on . . . to the manifest injury & corruption of such as frequented said Games" as well as "the reproach . . . [of] Truth." Of course, Friends in Meeting were "not so foolish," as to concern themselves with non-members; far less, with those who stood in opposition to them, "so as to reprove, instruct, or reclaim them, as Fellow-Members or Brethren." [1]

Significantly, in Pennsylvania economic morality early became more than a matter of individual virtue. The Yearly Meeting thought it necessary during one of its early sessions to exhort its members to give full measure and accurate description of goods which they exported, in order to remove a stain from the name of the province.[2]

Friends there also developed a different attitude toward their more positive duties to those around them. Quakers everywhere thought it right to applaud the good and deplore the bad in outsiders, and to attempt to draw them into the fellowship. But it was mainly in Pennsylvania that they tried to exert a good influence on the public through their religious organization. The Monthly Meeting in Philadelphia even reproved outsiders from time to time! It held itself responsible because of its character as organized voice of the historically first-ranking religious "people." It once sent Isaac Norris and Evan Owen "to speak to the particular schoolmasters of every society in this City that they discipline their scholars in sobriety and restrain them what they can from a rude & noisy behaviour, more especially on first days & times of religious worship." But this was as close as the Meeting ever went to reproving or instructing outsiders on a personal level.[3]

As a rule it confined itself to public pronouncements. The exhortation of others to mend their ways was a staple of Quaker service to others in the eighteenth century, since "a perfect Abhorrence was fixed in [Friends'] . . . Hearts against the wicked, unjust, vain, ungodly, unlawful Part of the World in all Respects." In 1730 Philadelphia Quakers protested against the "firing Guns and Revellings occasiond by the Classing together Nationally Numbers of People under Pretence of Keeping a day to their S^t called as St Patrick," which had not been customary in Pennsylvania, a province "chiefly setled by Sober People," and was a celebration likely to have "dangerous Consequences in several respects." The Meeting asked the Governor in the name of all the "Sober Inhabitants" of the city "as much as in him lyes to Discountenance such Doings for the future." Subsequent petitions for public morality or suppression of drama put even more stress on the Meeting's right to protest arising from the fact that Quakers had settled the province.[4]

In contrast to their predecessors, Friends during the first half of the eighteenth century seldom went out of their way to put their belief before the public to win converts. Meetings ordinarily left "convincement" of outsiders entirely to individual action. By 1748, however, Friends in Philadelphia had begun to think that the Meeting ought to take some responsibility in this field as an outgrowth of its control of publications. Yearly Meetings began to distribute approved reading matter suitable for persuading outsiders.

Quakers had not been officially blind to the possibilities of propaganda earlier. They often expected charitable acts to put their virtues and views before the public, at least as a secondary objective. Here again, Pennsylvania Friends had the greatest opportunities and exploited them most persistently. The educational benefits conferred on poor children surely inculcated their beliefs to some extent in all but the dullest waifs, though there is no occasion to denigrate the feeling of public responsibility behind this charity. Relief given to the nonresisting sufferers in a French raid on Lewes, in the Lower Counties in 1709, or to victims of Indian warfare in the Carolinas in 1715, and especially to refugees from the Pennsylvania frontier during the French and Indian War, while of service to the recipients also justified Friends' pacifism. Raising money to aid victims of a fire in Charleston in 1741 put Quakers in competition with other religious groups.[5]

The basic criterion for what the Meeting might do to benefit outsiders — protection of the "reputation of Truth" — ordinarily meant that the insiders held each other to standards of fair dealing and consistent support of the distinctive Quaker "testimonies." But as soon as the fair name of the sect became connected with the success of West New Jersey and Pennsylvania, this same criterion grew more demanding. So in the territory of Philadelphia Yearly Meeting, Friends began to use their religious organization in unusual ways to practice charity toward their neighbors. More and more often solicitude for the reputation of their faith led them to overrule the standing assumption that the fellowship should simply take care of its own.

The need to depart from established ways was clearer still in a world which included Negroes and Indians who could not be treated in the same fashion as Anglicans, or even Presbyterians. Negroes (often heathen) were imported slaves, while the aborigines were free and followed customs of their own. Yet, even when the possibility of Indian servitude arose, the presence of free relatives in the nearby forests, not to mention the ease with which a captive could escape to rejoin them, tinged the treatment of the natives with political considerations.

Of greater immediate interest to early American Friends was the fact that getting along with the Indians meant applying moral standards to relations with people of primitive culture. Such persons could not be relied upon to control themselves or drive a hard bargain as normal neighbors did. The virtuous white man, therefore, had to impose unusual limitations on himself. For many years Quakers could agree only on a few special kinds of self-restraint — notably in negotiations for land purchases and selling strong drink, areas where sensitive consciences in other denominations had already pointed the way.

The first settlers in Pennsylvania and West New Jersey found that the Indians drank "not to Moderation, but to Excess & Drunkenness," and to the "abuse of themselves and others." Yet the Meeting's disapproval fell on the sale of liquor to them rather than on their use of it. Penn entertained visiting chiefs with firewater during his first stay in America, and Quakers later countenanced the distribution of rum at parleys. But when the Monthly Meeting at Burlington asked if it "be Lawfull att all for friends" to sell "Rum unto the Indians," the Yearly Meeting in 1685 answered firmly that it was not, and two years later asked the Monthly Meetings to have their members affix their signatures to a minute on the subject. Philadelphia appointed a special committee to encourage good behavior, and the vigilance of Falls Monthly Meeting uncovered a loophole, which it promptly closed, in selling strong drink to Indians through an intermediary.[6]

This major subject for the Meeting's discipline quickly disappeared. As settlement spread in Pennsylvania, Indians and Friends saw less and less of each other. Specialized fur traders carried on the rum traffic out of sight of civilized communities, and it created a problem for the Friends who ran the provincial government only if they chose to see it.[7]

In the same way, other commercial dealings with the Indians became remote or matters for the government. In 1687 a Quarterly Meeting worried about members buying "Hogs Bells" which the natives might have stolen, but soon only the purchase of land by the Penns remained to inspire moralizing. At first Friends upheld no special standards; in New Jersey, Quaker negotiators once paid with the usual trade goods, including trinkets and rum. Such a bargain, of course, became unacceptable when the Meeting took a strong stand against selling drink to the aborigines.[8]

The sterile issue of proper payment yielded the stage, however, to a more fruitful topic for speculation. Going back to first principles, Thomas Chalkley in 1738 stated the case for full and fair purchase of native rights to the soil in abstract terms which provided the basis for more refined scruples later. The Indians, he argued, had a "natural Right" to the ground arising from their own and "their Fore-fathers . . . Possession of this Continent of *America*." So Friends must take care to acquire it equitably, for "no People, according to the Law of Nature and Justice, and our own Principle . . . ought to take away, or settle, on other Mens Lands . . . without Consent, or purchasing the same, by Agreement of the Parties concern'd." Had not Penn taken care to send a letter to the Indians the year before founding the colony, asking for their consent, and subsequently "by his wise and religious Care . . . settled a lasting Peace and Commerce with the Natives"? His enduring reputation among them proved his virtue and justice. It followed that when Indians raided colonial settlements the cause was to be sought by inspecting the record for violence against them or lapses from justice. By a further extension of this line of reasoning, a raid became *prima facie* evidence of injustice, especially in respect to land rights.[9]

The Meeting did not have to analyze the morality of detailed aspects of negotiating with Indians, however, for basically, as everyone agreed, buying their land was a task for the political authorities. For many years Quaker Meetings took without question the government's word about when a purchase had been made properly. Chalkley wrote on the moral fundamentals when he discovered that some Virginia Friends in Hopewell had settled on territory for which the Indian title had not yet been extinguished. Quaker consciences should not have been quieted in 1744 when Virginia bought from the Six Nations rights that rested on conquest. But no Meeting troubled the Hopewell sinners until the outbreak of hostilities in Pennsylvania in 1755 started a train of events which included the withdrawal of Quakers from control of the provincial Assembly and a search for the causes of war. Then Friends became "aroused as never before on the subject of Indian land purchases," and exhortations to blameless conduct began to flow from Philadelphia. At the height of the fervor, leading Quakers demanded a standard of justice beyond the consent of chiefs around a council fire; compensation must be adequate by the conscientious Quaker's abstract definition. Zeal in the cause led to a long effort to give compensation for the ground under the Hopewell settlers, though at first no Indians could be found who had claimed it at any time.[10]

A desire to rectify injustice in New Jersey also inspired a private organization of Friends there to give some land to Indians who had none. By 1764 devotion to rigorous justice had spread to North Carolina, where New Garden Monthly Meeting appointed a committee "to discover whether there could be any Indian claim against the lands on which they lived." The committee found only a small number of persons with a plausible claim to descent from the tribe which had been there when whites arrived. This purported remnant lived among another tribe, and the Meeting therefore decided to let the matter drop.[11]

In 1763 Philadelphia Yearly Meeting, probably mindful of the Indian uprising, reaffirmed the minimal rule of conduct. Monthly Meetings should refuse certificates of removal to Friends planning to move to lands not duly purchased by the government from the Indians. That this minute was not altogether too late was shown by the dealings of Philadelphia Friends with one of their members who had "been concerned in the purchase of Lands before the[y] were bought of the Indians," in 1771. Even after the Revolution, North Carolina Friends had a chance to enforce such advice and redress their ancestors' injustices. In 1787 they rebuked some of their number who had moved to eastern Tennessee. The accused pioneers protested their innocence, while the Yearly Meeting upheld the claims of some Indians. Fortunately, the United States prevented an unseemly deadlock by buying up the natives' rights.[12]

In Quakers' comments on the questions of land rights and the rum traffic, the dictates of abstract justice ordinarily received strong support from practical considerations. The natives were easily provoked to cruel retaliation for encroachments or chicanery. So it behooved a peace-loving sect to treat them well. Friends on occasion urged each other "to avoid giving them Occasion of Discontent" in more serious ways: taking arms against them and making slaves of prisoners. But the opportunities were rare. No Indian wars took place in colonies where Quakers had strong influence in the government between 1676 and 1755. In King Philip's War, Rhode Island resolved not to enslave Indian captives, but at the other end of this period of peace the possibility did not occur. In between, Philadelphia Yearly Meeting, while preparing a revised Discipline in 1719, saw fit to proclaim its desire "that Friends do not buy or sell Indian slaves." [13]

The prohibition of 1719 had little importance in itself, but marked a significant change. A generation earlier it would have been unthinkable to debate the morality of buying Indians; some of the emigrants to the Delaware Valley had dreams of living intermixed with the Indians in a developing civil and religious community, a hope raised by the earliest contacts between Quakers and Indians.

In the heroic days of the First Publishers, traveling Friends, in their determination to preach the Gospel to every living creature, had visited Indians and Negroes as well as white immigrants in the colonies. Often the missionaries were more favorably impressed with dignified natives than with the irate Puritans. But something had to be done after an apostle had given a throng of Indians a summary of Christian beliefs. Fox proposed a course of instruction to convince the redmen that "God doth pour out of his Spirit upon all flesh these days of the New Covenant, and New Testament," and that all must be "led by his good Spirit," and strive to be responsive to its motions within them. More in the normal Quaker fashion, meetings were held on several recorded occasions, including a few in Pennsylvania and New Jersey before 1685, where Friends explained "the principles of *Christianity*, and the practice of a true *christian* life" as well as the evils of too much drink. In 1687 Burlington Quarterly Meeting announced a special campaign to convert Indians. For the rest of the decade interest remained lively in this endeavor, and in 1689 Fox appealed to Meetings throughout the colonies to report to London Yearly Meeting every year on their progress in converting the savages. He had hopes that if Quakers could win over the "Emperors," "kings," and "cockaroofes," their supposed subjects would follow obediently. [14]

Indians gave some encouraging response to preaching, but ordinarily the effects of reform did not last long. Rarely did a man appear like Ockanickon, who saw the damage done by liquor and who became a devoted admirer of the Quaker settlers in West New Jersey. Even more rare was the response which George Fox reported after preaching for two hours to a band of Indians harbored by an early Friend on an island off Long Island. They "appeared very Loveinge" and "saide all was truth" that he had told them. He thereupon "sett up a meettinge amonge them once a fortnight," with their patron, "freinde Joseph Silvister . . . to reade the Scriptures to them." Nothing better could be achieved among the Indians than the rudiments of orderly church fellowship.[15]

Such slender beginnings heralded success in one of the missions of the Quaker colonists, who had come to "release millions from the chains of *Satan*, and . . . teach them their rights as Men, and their happiness [and] . . . glorious liberty" as sons of God. A certain number of the Indians would surely receive grace, be taken into Christ's kingdom, become "freemen of Christ" as others might become freemen of London, and be liberated from sin, which was a sign of bondage to the devil.[16]

The first successes of the religious mission to the Indians, however, suggested a more exciting idea. Quakers then thought of their church as the only true one, the nucleus for expansion to embrace all Christendom. If their beliefs were correct, all men had the seed of grace, and some everywhere and at all times had cultivated it and were properly to be counted in the invisible church. Moreover, God had stirred the hearts of these true Christians in ways they could feel and know. It followed, then, that among the Indians, who were out of contact with Hebrew antiquities and the historic Christian fellowships, the work of salvation and the knowledge of the cosmic order might well have been described in ideas and metaphors which Englishmen would have to search out and decipher. Even if the Indians were not actively familiar with the inspiration of the Inner Light, the revelations to earlier generations might have been preserved in traditional lore which would provide the Quaker with a basis for missionary success almost as good as recent experience of direction by the divine guide.

Discovery of illuminations to the heathen Indians by Christ's spirit, whether in the present or the past, would be a great prize to the missionary who could report them in Christian doctrinal controversy: he could bring proof, as from a controlled experiment, that the Inner Light operated as Friends claimed it did in all men, even among savages isolated from all earthly means of learning divine truths. This possibility tantalized a succession of traveling Quakers among the several who reported the willingness of Indians to agree with what they said about the spirit of God within.[17]

This essential doctrinal point was only the first on which the missionaries sought corroboration from the American natives. The Friends found common ground with the Indians in the manifestations of conscience, a phenomenon which the savages readily acknowledged, unaware of the theological constructions on it being fought over in England. There was further encouragement in the solemnity of the Indians at a treaty or impromptu meeting for worship; they seemed to out-Quaker the Quakers. William Penn and John Richardson probed farthest into the religious beliefs of the natives and interpreted simple or enigmatic information as best they could to agree with their own ideas. Richardson, in 1701, told some Indians in Chester County, Pennsylvania, not to steal, kill, be drunkards, or put away their wives for small faults lest "the great and good man above would be angry with them, and . . . bring trouble on them." When these exhortations had been interpreted to them, "they wept, and tears ran down their naked bodies, and they smote their hands upon their breasts," and through the interpreter told Richardson "all [he] . . . had delivered to them was good, and except the great man had sent [him, he] . . . could not have told them these things." When asked how they knew that his message was good, "they replied, and smote their hands on their breasts, the good man here, meaning in their hearts, told them [that it] . . . was all good."[18] Thereby the missionary received both confirmation of his faith in the Inner Light and the Quaker theory of ministry, and an earnest of success in his evangelical efforts.

At the Governor's mansion, in Penn's presence, Richardson asked some Indians through an interpreter what they knew of God and the future state. Told that they believed in a divine Being who sees all things and that people who do bad deeds go to a cold country without fat venison or blankets, while the rest go to a warm one well provisioned, he reflected that "as these poor creatures had not the knowledge of God by the Scriptures, as we have who are called Christians," they must have received information through other sources. Their understanding of God must have been achieved "by an inward sensation, by contemplating the works of God in the creation, or probably from some tradition handed down from father to son." They formed their ideas about a future state of rewards and punishments from the desirable and undesirable possibilities they knew in this world.[19]

Such speculation delighted men from England for whom the exotic experience of holding a meeting with Indians was an exciting incident on a missionary journey. Quaker settlers in Pennsylvania and New Jersey, who encountered the aborigines often on less solemn occasions, had a different view of these primitive neighbors until separated from them by settlements of white non-Friends. A few early Quaker colonists shared Penn's hopes that their people and the Indians would live together; and expected contact between natives and newcomers. Mixed juries, for example, were to try Indians' crimes, and Thomas Budd's plans for a school in West New Jersey had provided for both peoples. In the long run, however, the most important legal statements were the least specific: the reiterated metaphors and promises in the treaties which proclaimed English and Indians one people.[20]

These ceremonial declarations were easily ignored by the first generation of settlers along the Delaware. They managed to live on neighborly terms with the Lenni Lenape and for a while in Meeting supported projects to convert them, but they quickly saw how long the chain of friendship was and how deep the gulf it spanned. As early as 1700, Philadelphia Monthly Meeting politely ignored Penn's renewed pleas for enlightening the savages, even though accompanied by an offer to furnish the interpreters and call the Indians to conferences. Close daily acquaintance with Indians failed to draw them into the Christian community, and when the settlers thought about the failure they concluded that the Indians would have to learn to live in the manner of Englishmen as a part of "preparation for the gospel, which God in his season without doubt" would "cause to dawn among them." [21]

But the hour of sunrise had not yet come. The simple denizens of the forest whose solemnity had delighted Fox and Penn suffered a horrifying transformation when the rum went around. Nor did they have permanent homes, work industriously, and deny the carnal appetites. This was no people ripe for convincement! Since Friends' institutions had no way to establish missions, Quaker colonists settled down to await God's unpredictable next move.

Once the Indians had been pushed back into the more remote areas of the province by the flood of settlers pouring into Pennsylvania, the dreams which had excited Penn and Richardson once more caught the imaginations of some colonists. In 1706 Thomas Chalkley and a troop of Friends from Nottingham went to hold meetings with some Seneca and Shawnee at Conestogoe on the Susquehanna. They did not have to go far, but it was an expedition which required an inward drawing of the spirit. At the village, Chalkley explained the rudiments of Christianity and the function of the Inner Light as a guide to conduct, to which the listeners assented. Thus encouraged along the old trail blazed by Fox, he went on to explain the use of Holy Scripture. Although the occasion gave satisfaction to all concerned, and some of the travelers expressed a wish to go again, no sufficient inner prompting impelled them. Their Meeting made no other arrangement to improve the opportunity which the visit opened;[22] in the first half of the eighteenth century Quakers saw no possibility of dealing with the Indians unless as part of civil community and religious fellowship. The practical outcome of this exacting view was virtual paralysis. The aborigines, out of sight beyond the hills, required no attention from their professed "Friends."

But the danger of Indian warfare which suddenly loomed up in the 1750's changed the situation drastically, stirring up a tempest in Pennsylvania Quakerdom out of which came a new Holy Experiment, a new social role for the Society of Friends. The first departures from the old practice of doing nothing were only temporary deviations from long-held ideas. During the French and Indian War, Quakers formed two private organizations to benefit the troublesome natives, The New Jersey Association for Helping the Indians and the Friendly Association for Regaining and Preserving Peace with the Indians by Pacific Measures. The first was founded primarily to buy land to make a reservation for landless Indians. The second had larger aims, which it pursued by arranging conferences between various Indians and the Pennsylvania government, in which the Association acted as a mediating third party, giving advice and presents to the Indians and promoting a pure concept of justice in land cessions. Although they did so with only the unofficial backing of their religious Society, Friends in these two associations showed a willingness to organize to help Indians systematically. Even more important, the two organizations did not seek primarily to convert the natives and did not act only on detailed drawings of the spirit. To be sure, religious "opportunities" were taken at the treaties at Easton and on any other occasion which the activities of these associations afforded, but the restoration of peace and the equitable settlement of land claims were worthy goals in themselves, for which Friends might strive without any other justification than the secular benefits to Christians and heathen. Quakers gave up whatever lingering hope they may have had of living in one brotherhood with the Indians when they supported the establishment of special tracts of land for their villages.[23]

If the dream of practical brotherhood had died out, however, faith remained that God would raise up some members of the invisible church among the natives. Suddenly this faith was rewarded; the border raids proved to be the dark hour before the dawn. After the peace had been restored, the Indians were required to return their captives. Three prisoners, who had been taken by raiders but later acquired somehow by a village of pacifists, were returned to Philadelphia in 1760. The pacifist community was under a Delaware leader who had actually undergone religious regeneration as Friends knew it. When the Quakers learned about this man they took new hope in missionary possibilities among the Indians. The sanctified Indian, Papunahung, who came from the same region as some of the most terrifying raiders, showed that divine power could bring peace and holiness out of a land which to human eyes contained only violence and danger. Warfare had brought misery and hardship to both sides; restoration of peace had revealed God's way of defeating human evil. What better demonstration could there be of the worth of Friends' efforts to negotiate peace?

Though Papunahung had received some instruction from Moravians and had attracted attention for his religious leadership, he was an awe-inspiring surprise to Philadelphia Quakers. Anthony Benezet compiled two narratives, which he circulated in manuscript, relating the details of the Indian's conversion and later conferences between him and his followers and Friends. Benezet construed the conversion as a work of God unaided by any human Christian influence. He did not mention the Moravian teachings, of which he may have been ignorant, but eagerly recorded those aspects of the case which accorded best with his own sect.[24]

He found Papunahung's experience a close parallel to a normal Quaker pattern of regeneration. According to Benezet's account, the Delaware leader had been "a Drunken Man, but the Death of his Father bringing sorrow over his Mind, he fell into a thought full melancoly state." His eyes "were turned to behold the Earth and consider the things that are there on, & seeing the folly & wickedness that prevailed, his sorrows increased," thus taking him to the stage of religious development which Howard Brinton has called "The Period of Search and Conflict."

Like many Quakers experiencing a religious awakening, the Indian next received an insight into the "Great Power that had created all these things." Yet his glimpse of the Creator did not eclipse the sight and the horror of sin. "He forsook the Town & went to the woods in great Bitterness of Spirit, . . . but at the end of five days it pleased God to appear to him to his comfort," and to give him a new understanding, not only of the divine being but also of "the works of Nature." He passed over the sectarian steps of convincement of Friends' principles and adoption of their peculiar ways, of course, and reached "Conversion" with a curiously literal kind of "unfolding of Heavenly light." Not only did he receive the knowledge that of all creation man is closest to God, but also "a sense was given him of the Virtues, and Nature of Several Herbs, Roots, Plants & Trees and the different Relation they had one to another."

Finally, "he was made sensible of his Duty to God, & he came home rejoycing & endeavouring to put in practice what he apprehended was required of him." Still, he did not achieve sanctification so easily; like Quakers, "he was kept in an unsettled State" until at length he knew an end to doubt and embarked on a career of honor to God through universal love and approved only acts for the "mutual Benefit to Mankind," thus reaching the final summit.[25]

Among Papunahung's people there had been for some years "an immediate awakening," which increased when, still in the best Quaker pattern, he "apprehended himself called to preach to them, in which service he was some time after Joyned by two, or three more." They were "very earnest in promoting true Piety," which, like Friends, they believed to be an "inward work, by which the Heart is changed from bad to Good." They described this transformation as "the Heart's becoming Soft, & being filled with Good." Thus improved, they renounced war under any circumstances and forswore strong drink.[26]

The Indians in fellowship with Papunahung, when home from the hunt, held religious meetings twice a day, at which they behaved much like Friends. The silence was broken only when someone, usually their leader, felt moved to prayer or edifying discourse. The rest confined their expression to sighs, groans, and tears. They even shook hands with each other, Quaker fashion, at the end of meeting. In Philadelphia, when a Friend prayed at one of their gatherings, there was an unprecedented display "of the tendering Power of divine Grace," and when they left there was discovered "a string of wet where the Indians had sat from the plentiful tears they had shed." [27]

Roughly after the Quaker manner, the circle around Papunahung had "set off" another meeting under one of the converts, Samuel Curtis of the Nanticoke tribe. When he visited Philadelphia in 1761 he surprised everyone with a quarter-hour of preaching at a regular meeting for worship, and though he spoke in his own tongue, "his delivery was very much like that of Friends." [28]

The appearance of these religious natives at the end of the anguish of the French and Indian War had a great impact on the more pious Quakers. John Woolman met some of Papunahung's followers in Philadelphia in August 1761, and almost at once began to feel "inward drawings toward a Visit" to their village. He connected the impulse with a long-felt love "towards the Natives of this Land, . . . whose Ancestors were the owners and possessors" of the country where Friends dwelt, and had sold it "for a very small consideration." Woolman's renewed interest in the spiritual improvement of the Indians readily combined with concerns over fair payments for their land rights which he and other Quakers had developed in the period of the French and Indian War. He had joined the New Jersey Association to give farms to landless redskins, but the project — undertaken as much to prevent raids as to do justice — had been uninspiring. After the appearance of spiritual life among the savages, benevolent acts seemed more worthwhile. Woolman laid his concern before the appropriate Meetings, obtained a certificate, and left for "Wahalowsing" late in the spring of 1763, in spite of reports of Indian trouble brewing.[29]

A Moravian missionary who had regular duties with these religious Indians arrived before Woolman, but they got along harmoniously. The Quaker took care to present his certificate before proceeding to religious exercises with the Indians, indicating that he ranked the group with a Quaker Meeting. With the formalities out of the way there still remained the problem of language. Impatient with the interpreter, Woolman sometimes asked him to desist and trusted to the Holy Spirit to work "on Some hearts to Edification where all the words were not understood." [30]

At least his own heart had been wrought upon. Perhaps the most important result of his journey was his meditation, shortly to be published in his *Journal*, "on the Alterations of the Circumstances of the Natives of this land since the coming of the English." He understood the changes which the Indians had had to make not only in moving away from the more desirable coastal regions, but in their manner of living. It struck him that the English had a great advantage, "and a weighty and Heavenly care came over [his] . . . mind, and love filled [his] . . . heart toward all mankind." In this state, he felt an urgent hope that the Quakers would "attend to pure Universal Righteousness" and be obedient to the Lord while they still enjoyed his mercies. If they were faithful to

99

God, they would "give no just cause of offence to the gentiles who do not profess christianity, Whither the Blacks from Africa, or the Native Inhabitants" of North America. Characteristically, he at once began to ask himself what more he could do to live as a "Sincere follower of Christ" and avoid giving offense to the natives.[31]

Woolman's was not the only heart stirred. In 1762 the Yearly Meeting at Philadelphia reported to London that because Papunahung and his followers had been "immediately visited with the day Spring from on High, . . . the attention, and care of many Friends" had become "deeply engaged . . . that the Fruits of Life among them [might] . . . be rightly cherished in a manner suitable to their weak States, and that such proper notice & care [might] . . . be taken of them as their circumstances" required. The Meeting thought that peace with the aborigines and settlement of their land claims had already enlarged the opportunities to help them to true religion and hoped that the freshets of the "day Spring" would make it easier to keep the peace and restore the amity that had existed between Friend and Indian many years before.[32]

Still, the Quakers as a religious Society were not willing to provide resident teachers or any other form of continuous missionary service. They left the matter entirely to individual initiative. The fact that the Indians kept moving to more distant places made religious visits to them less and less easy. By the outbreak of the American Revolution some of the Delawares were building their campfires in what is now Indiana. Preoccupation with the events which led other Americans to rebellion cannot entirely explain the failure of Friends to act for the good of the Indians; the Philadelphia Meeting for Sufferings received several requests for various kinds of aid, including resident teachers of religion, and had the institutional competence to meet them. But it did nothing, even though the Delawares were appealing in their turn to the former solidarity between their people and Penn's, and recalling the old promises to make the two one. They even went so far as to ask to be brought into the same religion.[33]

Not until 1773, however, when an aged Friend named Zebulon Heston, with John Parrish as his companion, felt drawn to visit

Papunahung and some of the other distant Indians in a religious way, did the Meeting for Sufferings do anything. It officially sponsored their journey and sent a message explaining that it had hoped that "the love of God, through our Lord and Saviour Jesus Christ, would engage and constrain some of the ministers of the gospel to visit [the Indians]." But it renewed its previous advice to them to wait for resident teachers and, in the meantime, "to attend diligently to the instructions of the Spirit of Christ within" themselves, by which they might learn their "duty to God and one unto another." The enlightenment of the mind by Christ, not human wisdom, would give true religious knowledge. The Indian had to learn that "in a state of nature we are weak, blind, and miserable, and can never come to a state of true happiness without a Saviour." Even ministers sent by God could tell only what they had "tasted and felt" of Christ's love, and might be "instrumental to raise the feeling sense of it in those to whom they [spoke]," but they could not inject grace. "No man," wrote the Meeting, "can do this work for his brother, nor for his nearest friend." Understanding that the Indians wanted a basic description of Christianity, the Meeting promised to assist and encourage a "rightly qualified" teacher whenever one might be found willing to go.[34]

But Quakers shrank from the priestly and "outward" in religion, and put great faith in the power of Christ's spirit to instruct the soul according to its needs. In addition, their belief that religious fellowship was a prerequisite to, rather than a result of, benevolent oversight, and their inability to accept any hypothesis of instrumental means to grace beyond silent waiting, reading the Bible, exemplary conduct, and specifically inspired religious exercises, made this message from the Philadelphia Meeting for Sufferings the normal position of Quakers during most of the century.

Official ideas about what Friends ought to do, through the Meeting, for outsiders in the same civil society did not change significantly between 1700 and 1775. The Meeting expected honesty and innocuous deportment in members' dealings with non-Friends. Possibilities of change had arisen, however. In Pennsylvania, which Quakers thought of as their own — and in Philadelphia especially — they began to look on the Meeting as a tribune to safeguard public morality. Responsibility in government also led to an increasing number of situations in which the Society supplemented the exercise of power in government by taking an initiative in public improvements or going to the defense of Friends' principles when outsiders charged they were deleterious to the public safety. Specifically, relief to victims of war gave a philanthropic direction to the Meeting's techniques in preserving the reputation of Truth.

Indians received special consideration from the time of Fox until the early eighteenth century. Yet the effort to draw them into religious fellowship did not succeed. Pennsylvania's crisis in Indian relations between 1756 and 1761, however, opened new institutional possibilities for benevolence, and the appearance of Papunahung reawakened hopes that the secular benefits would have religious results. For a short time Quakers combined the effort to do justice to the Indians with respect to their lands with a program of religious encouragement. But the supposedly spontaneous perfection of the work of grace among the Minusings and Nanticokes brought emphasis back to the strictly religious side. The Meetings for Discipline found no role for themselves in positive good works for the Indians; even the Meeting for Sufferings could only hope for the appearance of men with an inward mandate to become missionaries. The bond between Friends and the American natives shrank steadily, until little was left but the old promises to be as one people made long before by Penn and the Delaware and Iroquois chiefs. The Indians had to remind Quakers of even this minimal, quasi-contractual tie. But the lingering intention to do something for the natives, whether in religious or in secular ways, kept presenting Friends with the prospect of benevolent acts for outsiders beyond the ordinary meaning of charity. The Yearly Meeting had come close to taking responsibility for promoting the Friendly Association in 1756, but had decided to do no more, officially, than give the private organization approving recognition.

VII

Charity and the Negro Slave

SLAVEHOLDING, even more than the problem of the Indians, broke down the limitations of "charity" to outsiders. Neither of these non-European peoples was Christian or had the ability to act in the fashion expected of English non-Quakers. The difference between Friends' dealings with Indians and those with Negroes stemmed from the different basic responsibilities which the Quakers felt toward them. In the case of the slaves, there was no primary contact implying equality of the parties. Consequently, there was no decline to a position of weakness and supplication as there was on the part of the Indians. Nor did the Quaker come upon the Africans in a social order of their own. Rather, he met them as slaves toward whom he acquired obligations as an owner, whether by purchase or inheritance.

From the start the Negroes were in servitude and, ideally, were linked by quasi-familial bonds to their masters. Even when the slaves lost their original place in the family along with their imputed status as the equals of other bound servants, their attitudes and ways of life were derived from the colonial milieu, not Africa. Quakers may have thought of their slaves as inferiors — certainly as outsiders to the religious fellowship — but they put themselves in a position of responsibility for them, and found that they could treat the "black People" as imperfect Englishmen when it came to education and economic skills.

At the beginning Friends accepted slaveholding as did their neighbors, whether in Virginia, Barbados, Rhode Island, or Pennsylvania. Their beliefs did not lead them to attack the institution. Missionary activity was strong among the early Quakers, with accompanying devotion to the universalistic features of their doctrine. "[Christ's] Blood was shed for all Men"; all had the seed of grace within them. But civil freedom did not appear as a prerequisite for religion. Friends made no theological distinction between the servitude for life which was the lot of the African and the servitude for a term of years which freeborn Englishmen entered, whether voluntarily or not. Servitude did not bar a man from church in the Old World. Why should it bar him from the meetinghouse in the New? [1]

The English servant, however, had been reared with some knowledge of Christianity, while the African was completely ignorant of the new dispensation and consequently had a great deal to learn as well as much to forget. It was appropriate that he be placed under the tutelage of a Christian whom he was obliged to obey. At any rate, such a rationale for the religious functions of slaveholding met objections to the institution itself.

American Quakers before 1689 left no record of their ideas about slavery. To judge from what others said, however, they saw no objection to holding Negroes in servitude and thought little about it. An early settler in New Jersey noticed their complacency on this subject and upbraided them with the shameful contrast between their attitude and that of a few English Friends traveling in the ministry who were troubled by slaveholding and formed the important seventeenth-century ideas about it which entered the Quaker heritage. With the possible exception of William Southeby, the men in early Pennsylvania who objected to slavery had been educated and grown to maturity in the Old World, where they had not been in contact with the institution. From their encounters with it came the foundation for later American anti-slavery campaigns.[2]

The shocks delivered by slavery to the consciences of European Quakers began with the visit of George Fox to Barbados in 1671. Finding Negroes treated in a fashion which hardly conformed to the patriarchal ideal, he tried to excite Friends there to greater consistency. He accepted the patriarchal concept and even the servile status of those born of slaves on the island. Therefore, he could indignantly repudiate the notion that Quakers stirred up slaves to revolt. He desired to provide for the spiritual welfare of the Africans, and accordingly, he preached to them at Quaker homes, instructed them in the outlines of Christian belief, exhorted them to love God and obey the Biblical commands about good behavior. He told their owners, in turn, to carry on instruction both in doctrine and morality. Probably on scriptural precedent, he urged putting a limit to the term of servitude of the Negroes, suggesting thirty years on one occasion. Since the African servants were part of the slaveholder's family, there was no need to wait for a specific impulsion from the spirit to teach religion to them any more than to children. There was no transgression of Christian liberty when masters instructed their families or had others do it. Quite the opposite, Fox argued, "it is a very Great duty incumbent upon them." It was a duty for which an account would be required from the masters "at the great day of Judgment." As long as Friends could look on the Africans as a particularly ignorant kind of bound servant, charity required no more.[3]

The first Quaker to take a stand against slavery was William Edmundson, apostle to Ireland and a primary theorist of charity and the self-consciousness of his sect. Yet at first he approached the needs of the Africans much as Fox had. So insistent was he in 1675 that the Negroes be given instruction in religion, that he tried to convince the Governor of Barbados that he had no quarrel with slavery but simply thought it *"a good Work to bring* [the slaves] *. . . to the Knowledge of God and Christ Jesus, and to believe in him that died for them, and all Men."* He even went so far as to argue that religion *"would keep them from rebelling, or cutting any Man's Throat,"* as the Governor feared. Edmundson claimed that any rebellion would be the result of the white man's policy of *"keeping them in Ignorance,"* oppressing them, and *"giving them Liberty to be common with Women (like Beasts) and on the other Hand starve them for want of Meat and Cloaths convenient."* Like Fox, he contemplated only two kinds of liberty for them: liberty to sin and liberty *"in that which God allowed and afforded to all Men, which was Meat and Cloaths."* [4]

After he left the West Indies, however, Edmundson began to worry about the Quaker masters, toward whom he had a greater responsibility than to the slaves, who were not fully his brethren in Christ. As part of virtuous behavior the slave-owners should rule their families justly and rear those under them into true religion. But there was a deeper lesson to be learned. The simple inversion of justice in Barbados, where masters were giving slaves "*Liberty in that which God restrained, and restraining them in that which God allowed,*" as Edmundson pondered it, suggested a comparison to the spiritual condition of the masters. As Penn later put it, "Christ's liberty," the liberty of the Christian, "is obtained through Christ's-cross; they that would be his free-men, must be his bondsmen, and wear his blessed yoke." The Christian is free "*from* sin, not *to* sin"; to do Christ's will, not his own. The Christian stood in the same relation to God's law as the slave to the master's. So when Edmundson used a variant of the scriptural phrase for having compassion — "make their condition your own" — he not only asked his readers to take upon themselves and act against the wrong done to the slave ("perpetual slavery"), but let Truth break the yoke of sin and make them freemen (in a mystical paradox, bondsmen) of Christ. It would be a good work on the part of the masters to let their slaves "feel, see, and partake" of Christian liberty. In this complex comparison, Edmundson recommended secular freedom for the slave primarily as a means to Christian liberty.[5]

Fortunately, Edmundson dispensed with mystical comparisons when addressing Friends around Chesapeake Bay. Permanent slavery was wrong; "which of you," he asked rhetorically, "would have the blacks, or others, to make you their slaves without hope or expectation of freedom?" As an act of virtue on their own part — not in the first place as benefit to the Negro — Friends ought to refrain from subjecting anyone to servitude for life. When Edmundson said that endless slavery was "an oppression on the mind" and anchored the slave's soul to the earth, masters who knew the immense gulf between their own and their slaves' concepts of religion, probably were not moved. The Blacks would hardly get anything more than "Liberty in that which God restrained" if turned loose in the foreseeable future; surely no one would want their masters to have the responsibility for sponsoring that kind of freedom.[6] It was unacceptable to practical Friends to put the enslavement of convinced Quakers by infidels on a par with enslavement of savages by Christians. While they believed that every man had in him the seed of grace, some required extensive training before any work of redemption could make headway.

By the end of the seventeenth century, Negro slavery had been clearly differentiated from white indentured servitude, and the distinction between the two institutions made it possible to apply religious ideals and social controls to them in different ways. Slaveowners were among the first to distinguish the Negro's lifelong, hereditary bondage from the indentured service of the European who was obligated for a fixed term of years. The slave was definitely inferior and not to rise out of his status. Accordingly, after Fox had called on Friends in Barbados to take Negroes to meetings for worship and give them schooling, the colonial government there forbade these practices, which were grounded on the assumption of moral equality between the races and were intended to reduce the actual differences between them. Friends occasionally disobeyed the law, as they did wherever they faced such restrictions, but they could no longer maintain the fiction that religious benefits to the Africans provided a serious amelioration of slavery.[7] Throughout the colonial world, moreover, the differentiation between slavery and indentured servitude made it possible for Quakers to attack the one without opposing the other. They based new arguments against Negro bondage on its origins in the obvious evils of capturing, enslaving, and selling Africans. However, Friends did not drop their original objection to the fact that the Africans were held in bondage without hope of release; in due time this evil provided a foundation for more direct attacks on Negro servitude itself.

For Quakers the proposition that Christ died for all men remained the anchor of opposition to slavery, assuming, as it did, some kind of moral equality which no observable inequalities could overrule. But it had to be reinforced by other propositions which dealt with tenets of right and wrong undeniably common to all men. It found this support in the argument that slavery led to separation of families, which was bad in itself, but in turn led to worse — adultery — for which the enslaver had to take the blame vicariously. By 1700 this and most of the other enduring features of Quaker arguments against slavery had begun their long course. The celebrated protest by Daniel Pastorius and the Friends at Germantown repeated Edmundson's objection to the enslavement of Africans on the ground that it was a violation of the command to "do to all men like as we will be done ourselves." [8]

But the German settlers thought it necessary to make it plain that the differences between English bondsmen and Negro slaves in no way altered the moral point. They did so by equating what Friends knew and condemned with some aspect of the slaves' experience. They appealed to recollections of fellow emigrants at sea when they saw "a strange vessel — being afraid it should be a Turk, and they should be taken and sold for slaves into Turkey." Being Christians, Pennsylvanians ought to be better than Turks. Africans, moreover, unlike indentured servants, were "brought hither against their will and consent" — that is, "stolen." The Germans could not believe that there was "more liberty to have them slaves," even though they were of a different race from white men. After all, there was no difference between the man who stole the African and the one who bought him, and no one would defend robbery or the receiving of stolen goods. [9]

For the Quakers the problem of violation of consent introduced a real dilemma: On what grounds could they object if their slaves were to conspire and take violent measures to regain their freedom? Would their self-styled owners discard their pacifist principles and "take the sword at hand and war against these poor slaves"? Did the Negroes not have "as much right to fight for their freedom" as the Quakers had to hold them in slavery? If Friends, who had committed themselves to obey the moral law of love, violated it in their dealings with the Africans, then the latter could not be bound to it except by consent, which they had not given. These considerations, in turn, suggested the damage slavery might do to Friends' corporate testimony against war. [10]

Slavery posed a threat even closer to the heart of the Holy Experiment: Continental Europeans who were inclined to emigrate to Penn's province might lose respect for the religion which sponsored it and prefer not to live among slaveholders. The road to temporal success and preservation of the good repute of the Society of Friends led through perfect adherence to the moral law of reciprocity. The stain of slavery must be wiped out. On the banks of the Delaware there was a "liberty of conscience, which is right and reasonable"; there "ought to be likewise liberty of the body, except of evil-doers." [11]

In 1693 schismatic Quakers under George Keith gave a new twist to the identification of slaves with stolen goods which well suited Friends' thought and later became a standard feature of the arguments against slavery. They claimed that slaves were captives of war and consequently came under the opprobrious classification of "prize goods." Friends upheld their "peace testimony" by refusing to deal in such merchandise. This argument became an accepted tenet among orthodox Friends, though in modified form, when Robert Pyle pointed out that buying slaves encouraged the wars in which Africans took each other captive. Those who bought the prisoners acquired a vicarious guilt for the war.[12]

The fundamental set of arguments against the slave trade and slaveholding remained the same until Woolman's time. Change took place in two areas — the ideas about what to do for the slaves, and the degree to which the Discipline required that Friends' conduct toward the Negroes harmonize with the antislavery view. For Quakers who expected to reside in America it was necessary to do more than formulate ideas about Negro servitude; they had to act on them and to live with the consequences. The ideas had therefore to be usable and create no danger to the unity of the religious fellowship. While there was no question that a master should give his slaves the benefit of religious teaching and of restraint from sin, the duty of the Friend who opposed slavery remained undefined for some time. There was little guidance from the revered leaders of the sect. Edmundson, beyond preaching the duties of masters as rulers of households, had urged only that a time limit be set to the Africans' service.

In Pennsylvania, where Friends were trying to create a purified civil community, they struggled with the Negro problem for over twenty years, without finding a solution. Thwarted by lack of agreement in the Meeting, they encountered opposition from outside the province which closed other possibilities for action. The Keithian schismatics made the first demand for the drastic step of immediately manumitting their own slaves and aiding the rest to escape.[13] But this extremist stand found no acceptance among Friends in the main society. It clearly repudiated the religious responsibilities to the Africans, though it might cleanse the masters' records of some injustices.

The closest approach to immediate manumission in orthodox circles came from Cadwalader Morgan, who urged the Yearly Meeting in 1696 to agree that owning slaves was wrong. Morgan told of his temptation to buy a slave in order to assure himself of labor on his farm and so be more at liberty to attend meetings. Not only did he realize in time that he wanted the slave for personal gain, which was wrong, but he found in himself an anxiety over the prospect of getting a wicked man who would need punishment or vicariously put the burden of sin on his owner's soul. So Morgan, resolved to do right, prayed to know the divine will in the matter, and presently believed that God opposed slavery. When, a few years later, he found that he was not alone in this conviction, he decided to publicize his views so that others could "consider this thing before the Lord, to know His will therein." [14]

Two years later Robert Pyle offered a version of George Fox's recommendation, a limit to the term of servitude for the Negroes. But he did not propose to make the system obligatory on Friends: let Quarterly Meetings fix the length of service for slaves owned by members who had scruples against keeping Negroes for life. He proposed, apparently to deaf ears, that the Meetings appraise what the slave owed the master for maintenance, what the master owed the slave for labor, balance the two, and determine a time in which the slave could work off his debt. This method of fighting slavery by proposing limits to its duration continued, although the manner of carrying it into practice changed. Before the end of the seventeenth century, Friends whose consciences were troubled by slave-ownership evaded the need to see the consequences of manumission by providing for it in their wills. By the middle of the eighteenth century, Friends were giving their adult slaves real freedom and fixing terms of service for young ones; and, by 1776, requiring manumission of all with provision for the training of the young under written arrangements like apprenticeship, support for the aged, and even compensation for past labor.[15]

The only aspect of the Negro problem with which Meetings could cope at all was religious duty to the slave. Though they were chronically remiss in their duties and did little to correct the situation — John Hepburn declared in 1713 that not one master in five hundred took his slaves to meetings for worship — Friends never saw their way clear to alter their original views on this point. Recognition of the fact of moral equality in which they believed made it necessary to consider the spiritual welfare of their slaves. When Edmundson exhorted the masters to remember that the Negroes could also enjoy "liberty in the gospel of Christ," he urged the owners to help their slaves to attain it by example, while they restrained them from sin; civil liberty to be given, if ever, only after a term of years. In the late seventeenth century, a Friend in Pennsylvania, George Gray, wrote a paper entitled, "Testimony for Family Meetings and Keeping Negro servants until they are in some Measure brought into a Christian Life which is the Duty of every Master and Mistress of families to Endeavor to Bring them so that they may be freemen Indeed." Though the text of the exhortation is missing, the title shows that the original program of Fox and Edmundson still had to be advanced.[16]

About the same time, William Southeby expounded his views on slavery to Friends in a paper of which not even the title survives. However, since he appealed to the authority of Fox's *Gospel Family-Order*, it is likely that Southeby called for the religious training of Negroes, and at most suggested that their servitude have a limit in time. In 1696, after hearing this and other documents, Philadelphia Yearly Meeting formulated an advice "that Friends be Careful not to Encourage the bringing in of any more Negroes." Otherwise, the Meeting reiterated old exhortations to restrain slaves from "Loose, & Lewd Living," give them religious training, and, if possible, take them to meetings for worship instead of letting them ramble abroad "on First Days or other Times." This advice probably reflected Southeby's paper directly.[17]

The Philadelphia Monthly Meeting, following William Penn's

suggestion, proposed to uplift the slaves spiritually by holding meetings for worship for Negroes once a month. Significantly, Southeby was asked "to give publick notice" of them. Masters were told to inform slaves in their families and to attend "with them at the said meeting as frequent as may be." (There was a striking similarity between the meetings for Negroes and those founded four years earlier for youths.) Penn also urged, as Meetings did every now and then, that slaves be taken to regular First day meetings for worship. Evidently Friends were remiss in the religious encouragement of their colored dependents in this respect as well as in teaching them at home. Their dereliction created the need for an institution for the good of nonmembers. Slaves, however, were part of the families of members; the Meeting helped owners by providing facilities whereby they might more readily do their duty. So the value of this early institution for the benefit of outsiders to the Meeting accrued primarily to the insiders.[18]

The special meetings for Negroes lasted only a short time and were not revived until 1756, when Philadelphia again decided that it was a proper function of the religious Society to sponsor such aids to the members in performing their obligations. By then the task could be given to another arm of the organization, the Meeting for Ministers and Elders. Philadelphia's example was soon imitated even in the Deep South. Before long such meetings were part of the process of smoothing the way to general manumission of Friends' slaves.[19]

The meetings for Negroes differed from those for youths in at least one respect: there was no expectation at first that the slaves would mature into full-fledged Christians. Even later, when the meetings were to prepare them for religious adulthood, the Negroes were not to be readied for fellowship with Friends. In Quaker families, the slaves were expected to attend First day worship and to be included in household religious gatherings, but in the first half of the eighteenth century Meetings required nothing further of the slave-owning members. True, masters were required to treat their Negroes well; some were even disowned for lapses into brutality. But Meetings would not oversee the behavior of slaves, and in other ways, such as refusing them burial in Friends' graveyards, were unwilling to regard them as brethren in Christ.[20]

There was a real difficulty in taking slaves into the fellowship, even apart from their unfree status. Robert Pyle mentioned the problem when he described the Negroes as "a people not subject to yᵉ truth, nor yet likely so to bee." Not that he would deny that they had "yᵉ witness of god" in them; but in order that "indevors used to convince them" might succeed, the colored people had to be trained more fully to follow the general pattern of life led by Quakers, beginning with the English language.[21] Pyle thus pointed out the general features of a program to benefit the Negroes which Friends began to follow in the middle of the eighteenth century. But when he wrote in 1698, most Quakers were unable to accept the need for such a roundabout approach to uplifting the slaves. Friends never claimed that leading a virtuous life was easy; they wrote about the difficulties both of adhering to their code of conduct and maintaining purity in worship. However, they regarded participation in their religious fellowship as requiring no special sectarian attitudes or training, only willingness to attend to the Light Within. They were brought to an impasse, consequently, when they found themselves unwilling to ignore the cultural difference and embrace the Negro slaves in the religious fellowship, and found the slaves mysteriously lacking the supposedly universal capacity to adopt Quakerism. The Friends had reached this stalemate in their attempts to define their religious duty toward the slaves as early as the 1690's, which may account for the failure of family instruction and Negroes' meetings from the start. If the religious care of Friends had a purpose, it was membership in the Meeting, and if that purpose was not to be allowed, the whole point of Fox's and Edmundson's fervor was lost. The ordinary ideas of charity did not supply a policy; Negroes were neither neighbors to be let alone, nor prospective converts, nor children who would outgrow their childhood and be raised into the church.

The long-range failure of Friends with the Negroes on the religious level was not solely the result of a cultural gulf, however; it was inherent in the institutions of slavery and the Society of Friends.

Slavery and liberty in Christ were incompatible. Penn had argued the case for religious toleration in ways that might have made the matter clear, but neither he nor many other Quakers applied the lesson to the Negroes. The prince (or slave-master) might rule the body, but Christ would have to rule in his kingdom — the heart, understanding, and will — and his government would take precedence over the earthly.[22] The life-long slave could not be subject to the will of Christ in all the ways which fellowship with Friends might require: in religious terms, slavery made him a child for life. Since he was not to grow to spiritual adulthood, religious restraint by his master had no more spiritual importance than other applications of the master's authority.

During the last two decades of the seventeenth century, proposals to alter slavery — either by insisting on religious training of the slaves or by reducing the term of servitude — gained a hearing without much protest in Friends' Meetings. Quakers would even listen to men like Cadwalader Morgan who opposed slaveholding altogether. Experience in slave-owning, however, exposed the obstacles to doing any more for Negroes than simply using them well. As these difficulties became more apparent, Quakers lost their missionary zeal and became more concerned for the harmony, solidarity, and purity of their religious fellowship. Not only did they become reconciled to leaving out those hard to assimilate, but also looked for ways to handle the situation created by conscientious objection to slaveholding without increasing animosity among Friends.

Although Quakers of Philadelphia Yearly Meeting never owned many slaves, by 1700 the minority of masters were putting up a strong resistance to attacks on the practice. Sentiment was polarizing for or against slavery; the attacks grew stronger, too. The fact that arguments against the capture and importation of Africans had been more successful than arguments against slaveholding itself, together with a desire to preserve harmony, made it possible for many years to maintain the compromise reached in 1696, when the Yearly Meeting opposed further importation of slaves and recommended good treatment and religious care for those already in Friends' households. In this way the Meeting avoided tampering with slave labor, but conceded something to the other side, and hoped by this compromise to minimize the problem.

By 1698 it was becoming hard to dispose of Negroes in Philadelphia. A paper endorsed by Philadelphia Monthly Meeting against "selling of Negroe's at the publick Markett place," set off a discussion of the rise of the colored population of the province. A special meeting was called the outcome of which is unknown, unless it was the letter to Friends in Barbados sent by the Monthly Meeting soon after, urging that no more slaves be included in cargoes destined for the Delaware River. The letter claimed that their importation might "prove prejudicial several ways to us and our posterity," but did not explain in what way.[23]

After this final attempt by the religious fellowship to control the size of the slave problem, Friends turned to governmental channels where decisions did not have to rest on the sense of the Meeting. The Pennsylvania government recognized the special status of the Negro population; it gave legal existence and definition to the institution of slavery by the "Black Code" of 1700, which imposed harsher penalties upon Negroes than upon whites for certain crimes. However, like the religious Society, the province remained willing to oppose the influx of slaves. The Assembly voted to put import duties on them in 1700, 1705, and 1710. In 1711 it decided to bar them completely and, when the law was disallowed, to tax them at a prohibitory rate — a measure which was in turn disallowed. The Assembly, in reality, had been attempting the impossible. The Royal African Company, in the interests of which the Pennsylvania laws were vetoed, had decided that the Quaker colonies were markets to develop.[24]

When the disallowance of the flat exclusion bill had become known, and the Negro problem had thereby been thrown back to the religious fellowship, the Yearly Meeting of 1712 wrote in its epistle to Friends in London that a "Concern" had rested on the "minds of some of [the] . . . Brethren for many years" about both keeping and dealing in slaves. It reviewed its actions in the past and, pointing out that a coordinated policy must be made, hinted that London ought to do something toward formulating one. It was no longer possible to handle the problem on a local basis in the Pennsylvania Assembly, where it could be treated as a matter of commercial interest and civil order rather than in terms of a moral absolute. The royal government itself was opposed to the exclusion of slaves, and persons of other denominations, over whom the Society of Friends had no jurisdiction, had poured into the province and markedly increased the total of Negroes. Any move against the slave trade would have to be by the Society, and that meant dealing openly in moral absolutes after all.[25]

Nevertheless, a principled decision against the slave trade, which would cast doubt on the morality of slave-owning, encountered greater opposition in 1712 than it had earlier. Indeed, events conspired to make of that year a period of crisis in the Negro problem, a fact recognized by at least one Quaker, John Hepburn, at the time. Special temporary circumstances, of course, merely added to conditions that existed both before and after the crisis, remaining until the middle of the eighteenth century.

The decline of zeal, even in Pennsylvania, to establish a purified civil community weakened one support for the anti-slavery cause. As the old ideal faded, the insidious attachment to personal gain grew. Cadwalader Morgan had seen this evil lurking in slavery and recoiled from buying a Negro; many other Friends did not. In New York City, Philadelphia, and rural regions farther south, some Quakers had come to appreciate the benefits of a Negro domestic in the household or a helper in the field or shop. They used colored servants just as other provincials did. The prevailing shortage of labor made slaves attractive; they could not quit as apprentices did. In the plantation areas a rich Quaker landlord could not compete with his neighbors unless he had access to a steady supply of Negroes. Whenever the conscience of a master troubled him, he could sell his human assets, which was an evasion of his religious duty to them, though for many years the Meeting silently tolerated it.[26]

Friends had also become involved in slave trading. As late as 1770, Newport merchants dealt in Negroes and owned ships which went to Africa to take captives to the sugar islands. With such a deep economic commitment, Friends involved in slavery may well have felt a reluctance to declare the institution too evil to touch, even when they could let it go without ruining themselves.[27]

Those who held the line against any tampering with slavery had power in the Meeting, and remained strong enough before and after 1712 to create a formidable problem of harmony in the church. They managed to push the issue to the highest institutional levels of the church, where it escaped the confines of any one Yearly Meeting and drew into the fray Barbadians and Carolinians as well as Pennsylvanians. The Discipline of one Yearly Meeting could not be changed to oppose slavery until most of the members who were directly involved assented. Slaveholders were not content to refuse, but insisted that even if one Yearly Meeting could unite behind the anti-slavery principle, it was necessary to forbear from a public pronouncement or from proceeding to disciplinary dealings until those in other regions were willing to agree. Religious Truth might grow, but not in different directions. If opposition to slavery did turn out to be morally necessary, and not just a passing fanaticism, it would have to pass the test of general acceptance by Friends.[28]

Nor should disputes on doctrine be permitted to inject dissension into the church. Doctrine was not the foundation of the religious fellowship; Friends had not been "gathered together by an unity of opinion," but rather, by pursuit of a "secret want," a search for "something beyond all opinion, . . . even the revelation of God's righteous judgment" in their hearts, a purifying fire "to burn up the unrighteous root and the fruits thereof." Having experienced this liberation from corrupt human will, "many came to be joined and united together in heart and spirit, in this one life of righteousness," and only after their union "in one body" they came "by degrees . . . to find themselves agreed in the plain and simple doctrines of Christ." This "external agreement as well on doctrines as in the practices necessarily following thereupon, became as one external bond and tie of their outward and visible fellowship obvious to the world." Agreement, therefore, was not the basis but the sign or result of unity, as Friends saw it. The spiritual community should not be sacrificed to "particular disquisitions of notions." [29]

If such ideal considerations needed reinforcement, a very practical side to the need for unity produced an emergency in 1712. Quakers required special conditions in law to achieve what they regarded as religious toleration. When the slavery issue first came to the attention of American Meetings, English Friends were still trying to persuade their government to sponsor legislation allowing them to affirm (rather than take oaths) in a form which would satisfy the consciences of English Quakers. An untimely attack on slavery as an institution might antagonize powerful commercial interests in the Royal African Company to a point where they could defeat the efforts of the London Meeting for Sufferings; it could also provoke a counterattack on the affirmation privilege in the Quaker colonies or on the proprietary government of Pennsylvania itself.

The necessity to deal with the Negro question in terms of the Discipline, then, did not free it from political considerations. In 1712 there were reasons to believe that the well-being of the church as an institution depended on avoiding an attack on slavery. An explosive political situation prevailed in England in the years when Pennsylvania Friends were presenting bills to the royal government calling for the exclusion of Negroes, with the campaign for the affirmation bill still incomplete. The machinations of the Tories, and the rise of a group of them to power as Queen Anne's ministers, accompanied by an upsurge of vitality in High Church circles which endangered toleration, the negotiations for the peace of Utrecht, the trade pact with France, the *asiento* of Spain, combined to make the political scene and the policies of those interested in the slave trade unpredictable. Would access to markets in the Spanish colonies make the Royal African Company more or less determined to keep its market in Pennsylvania? Would a rise in hostility to toleration make Friends' position worse or would it help them in the long run by restoring their alliance with other dissenters? The air was filled with a medley of hopes, threats, and uncertainties. In 1712 Penn confused the situation further by coming down with apoplexy, which wrecked his mind at the crucial moment in negotiations to sell the government of Pennsylvania to the Crown. That disaster stopped the sale, but deprived Friends of his valuable connections at court.[30]

London Yearly Meeting, apparently unwilling to make a decision during this turmoil, refused to lead the way in formulating a policy on slavery and told Philadelphia that it should have consulted other American Friends and then submitted a joint opinion. It is easy to understand this evasive and irregular act. London did not completely abdicate its leadership, however; it recommended that Friends stay out of the traffic with Africa. This reply and the disallowance of Pennsylvania's prohibitory tax provoked dissatisfaction in Philadelphia. Friends there had not been taking slaves in Africa and were, rather, trying to discourage both owning and dealing in slaves. The epistle to London called on the senior Meeting to use its influence to prevent the quashing of another such law and do its duty in consulting other American Yearly Meetings. London replied as before.[31]

The crisis had arrived, and the Quakers had not been able to cope with it. Instead of decision there had been paralysis in the highest institutions of the church. London sensibly advised American Friends, who had the Negroes, to propose a policy; Philadelphia told London to exercise its unifying supervision. American Friends who preferred not to give up their colored servants or saw no way of disposing of them that would answer all the requirements of religious and civic duty, strove harder than ever to throw a blanket of silence over the whole problem. John Hepburn of New Jersey decided he must publish his objections to slave-owning before it was too late. In *The American Defence of the Christian Golden Rule*, printed in 1715 and written in the two preceding years, he took American Friends to task for letting themselves be corrupted by the love of gain. Pennsylvania, he declared, had taken a fatal step in 1711 when the Assembly voted to support the expedition against Canada; at that moment they had "Sacrificed their primitive Innocence." When put to the test they had chosen ease and safety over purity. Before the "excellent souls . . . who came out of *Old England*, that [had] . . . kept their Integrity" and spoken against slavery had disappeared, Hepburn wanted to add an American voice to show that fidelity to Christian virtue had not yet died out in the New World. He was ignored completely.[32]

The treatment of Hepburn was mild at a time when the subject of slavery was arousing more and more bitterness in the Society of Friends. Protests against owning Negroes now became rare; those who made them found the opposition aggravating and were sometimes provoked to acts which earned their disownment. Still, though Meetings took up the slave question only with reluctance and disposed of most objections by sending them to other Meetings to get the views of Friends elsewhere, there remained earnest men throughout the northern colonies who challenged the slave-owners. Englishmen — especially those who had seen slavery for the first time in the West Indies — kept arriving on the mainland, where they stirred up flames from the lingering opposition to the institution.

The record of the Americans was not, in fact, quite as bad as Hepburn described it. William Southeby grew to outright opposition to slavery and spoke against it after presenting his paper in 1696. He made a vain effort to persuade the Pennsylvania Assembly to abolish slavery in 1712 and opposed referring the problem from Philadelphia to London Yearly Meeting that same year. He received support repeatedly from Chester Quarterly Meeting. At the Yearly Meetings of 1711, 1715, and 1716, the report from this Quarter reopened the question of Friends' duty in regard to the importation of Negroes. Each time, the Yearly Meeting refused to make its advice against the traffic a matter of disownment. Finally, it expressed impatience with the reiteration of a request made so often, conceding only a recommendation that "friends generally do as much as may be [to] avoid buying such Negroes as shall hereafter be brought in, rather than offend any friends who are against it." [33]

Chester Quarterly Meeting remained dissatisfied, but it sent no questions or requests on the slave trade for several years. The antislavery cause had come into bad odor by the insistence of Southeby, who had become so ardent an opponent of slave-keeping as openly to show disdain for the unity of the church. To him, being right was more important. If London would not lay down a rule, then Philadelphia should; if Philadelphia wished that he say no more about it, he would speak anyway. He went so far as to make his dispute with the church public and attacked the Friends who opposed him, in time to provoke a special phrase in a Yearly Meeting minute in 1715, which declared that Friends should "avoid judging one another in this matter publickly or otherwise." Although he repented and made his peace with his Monthly Meeting before the

Yearly Meeting sat again, when it refused to condemn slavery in 1716 he published another paper. After that he may have been dis-owned, and Chester Quarterly Meeting let slavery alone.[34]

In New England and New York Yearly Meetings, strikingly similar events took place about the same time. There was a center of opposition to slavery in Flushing Monthly and Quarterly Meet-ings in New York, and in Dartmouth and Nantucket Monthly Meetings in Massachusetts. William Burling, a leading spirit in Flushing, recorded his views in a paper which he wrote against slave-keeping and probably presented at the New York Yearly Meeting in 1718. He had become sure of the sinfulness of the prac-tice over thirty years earlier and had consequently *"thought it strange, that the Church did not exclude it, by her discipline, and fix the Judgment of Truth upon it."* Still, he found it necessary to remind the "Elders of the Church" that the topic ought to be con-sidered and pleaded *"that whatever Friend hath any thing from the movings of the Spirit of Truth to communicate to his Brethren, either by word or writing,"* should be allowed to speak, *"so long as he keep to the counsel and directions of the Holy Spirit, and there-fore delivers nothing but what is according to Truth,"* even if his audience should find what he said *"contrary to* [their] *. . . in-terest."* As if it was not strange enough that he had waited thirty years to write a paper on his opinions and felt constrained to plead for the right of any man to be heard on a prompting of the spirit, he conceded that even though he wanted a prohibition of slave-keeping added to the discipline, he would not seek to have it done, since the attempt would be so strongly opposed as to cause *"much strife and disorder in the Church, which is generally hurtful where-ever it prevaileth; therefore to be carefully avoided."* Burling was resigning his cause in the interests of the unity of Friends. He did so probably to enter a plea against condemnation of another man.[35]

In 1717 Horsman Mullenix and a "public Friend" from England, John Farmer, attended a Quarterly Meeting at Flushing, on Long Island, where they brought up the subjects of the slave trade and keeping Negroes for term of life. These matters were discussed and sent to New York Yearly Meeting for further deliberation, which took place in 1717 and 1718. Several members "declared that they were fully satisfied in their Consciences" that the practice of buying and keeping slaves "wass not Rite." Others were willing to obey the will of God on this question when he should divulge it. An exchange of epistles with London followed, very like that between Philadelphia and the English Yearly Meeting.[36]

Farmer went to New England, where the same two topics had been raised by Dartmouth Monthly Meeting in Massachusetts. It had sent a question to its Quarterly Meeting (Rhode Island), which referred it back to the constituent Monthly Meetings. They replied very differently. Nantucket condemned both practices, Dartmouth only the slave trade. Greenwich (on the west side of Narragansett Bay, where slave labor was in common use) only the importation of slaves, and Newport, most heavily involved in all aspects of slavery, made no reply. The Quarterly Meeting made the standard decision to wait until the sentiments of Friends elsewhere could be learned. Farmer's preaching in the spring of 1717 made all sides in the discussion more determined. Nantucket approved his antislavery views; Newport did not.[37]

The dramatic climax came when Farmer read a paper "Relateing to Negroes" to the Yearly Meeting of Ministers and Elders. The Meeting soon decided to demand "that he Cease to preach Reflectingly against frds" (probably those engaged in the slave trade), take no steps to make his essay public, and deliver his papers to its custody. He refused. When further persuasion and "labor" proved unavailing, the Meeting directed him to "forbeare to goe forth to Offer his Gift" until he had made satisfaction for his obstreperous conduct. When the Ministers and Elders issued a final command that he attend and bow to their disciplinary action, "he Refused to come." In spite of this ruckus, the Yearly Meeting for business, like Philadelphia, referred the slavery question to its lower Meetings and urged those of the members who were merchants to "write their Correspondants in the Islands and elsewhere to discourage their sending" Negroes. The opinions brought in from the Quarterly Meetings at the next session induced the Yearly Meeting to leave its advice of 1717 untouched.[38]

Farmer set out for Philadelphia when it became clear that he had failed in New England, reading his essay to any group that would listen. It was at this time that Burling gave up the attempt to prohibit slave-keeping by an addition to the Discipline in New York, but asked that any Friend be allowed to speak or write as moved by the spirit. He dropped the slavery issue, perhaps temporarily, giving the unity of the church first priority, a policy which was technically proper. Very likely, Burling's plea had some good effect for Farmer; at any rate, the English minister passed through New York without further penalties or incidents. He, like Southeby, held the view that Philadelphia should be the leading Yearly Meeting among the American six, and hoped to have New England overruled. When he arrived, however, he was treated as a problem of church order, and Friends testified to their disunity with him in every conceivable way — in a Meeting for Ministers and Elders, a Monthly Meeting for business, a Quarterly Meeting on appeal, and finally the Yearly Meeting. Farmer stayed in Philadelphia, developing into a crank, holding meetings to denounce slavery and lotteries to those who probably agreed with him already.[39]

The resistance to a stand against slavery on the part of the religious Society had led Southeby and Farmer, both formerly respected ministers, to devote themselves so ardently to their message that they put it above "love and unity" among Friends. However their defiance may have been provoked, they were disowned for sound cause. They took the crucial step of attacking Friends for dealing in or having slaves, not simply the evils themselves. In Quaker belief, the man moved to reprove his brother should labor to persuade him to reform, not condemn sin and sinner at once. The Meeting might disown an incorrigible sinner to remove the stain of his acts from the church, but only after an orderly exercise of brotherly care, and in the light of approved standards of conduct. But just as those who resisted *"care* and *order,"* by "any of the Lord's eminent servants," had always suffered "the mark of God's rebuke; so those that . . . opposed the wisdom of God in his faithful servants [had] . . . ever failed of their purpose, and been finally manifested to have been led by a wrong spirit." Nothing showed a wrong spirit so conclusively as publishing attacks on Friends. It was well known that "Jesus Christ under the Gospel" had "ordinarily revealed his Will . . . through the Elders, and Ministers of the Church, or a General Meeting." So unless it could be shown that these normal authorities were "decayed" and had "lost their Discerning," no individual would deny their judgments unless "being puft up," he would affect "Singularity" to attract attention.[40]

The last two men disowned for disorderly conduct in trying to impose antislavery views, Ralph Sandiford and Benjamin Lay, were amply endowed with singularity. Both were Englishmen who had been in business in the West Indies before taking up residence in Philadelphia. The disturbances they created brought to an end the ten-year interlude following the decision by the Yearly Meeting to forbid its members to "be concern'd in the fetching, or importing Negro slaves," during which the slavery issue was not raised. Sandiford, a man of phenomenal sensitivity, became so oppressed by the sight of slave auctions after less than a year's stay in Pennsylvania, that he fell ill and had to give vent to his feelings in a bitter attack upon Friends, in *A Brief Examination of the Practice of the Times* . . . (1729). The Quakers could have made their name glorious by forbidding slavery, he asserted, and thereby, perhaps, have stimulated the conversion of the Africans as well.[41]

While Sandiford relied on the usual arguments against slavery, he carried his logic to precisely the most explosive point. Slave-keeping, he declared, proved that ministers and elders had no true spiritual gift. He had asked permission from the Overseers of the Press in Philadelphia to publish his book, and, naturally, had been refused. When he proceeded anyway to make the most insulting attack in the most disorderly way, it was an act of forbearance on the part of Friends to maintain the semblance of unity with him for as much as a year. But he had succeeded in raising the old subject, and Chester Quarterly Meeting took the opportunity to make a request for its consideration.[42]

Chester Friends stated their opinion that since the Discipline forbade importing slaves, it was "as reasonable, that we should be restricted from buying them when imported." The Yearly Meeting in 1729 asked the lower Meetings to ascertain their views on this proposition. In the fall of 1730 they reported: two small New

Jersey Quarterly Meetings agreed with Chester; Bucks could not agree on any reply; Philadelphia thought no further addition to the Discipline or advices necessary; and Burlington proposed approximately the course which was adopted — an advice that "Friends ought to be very Cautious of making any . . . Purchases" of newly imported Negroes, though not making disobedience a matter of disownment. Monthly Meetings should see only that "Such who may be, or are likely to be found in that Practice, may be admonish'd and caution'd how they offend herein." [43]

Sandiford had already published a new and enlarged edition of his book, *The Mystery of Iniquity* . . . (1730), believing it necessary to improve his health as well as ease his conscience. After the Yearly Meeting of 1730, his disappointment wrecked his chances of recovery and he left his business to retire to the country and an early grave.[44]

Benjamin Lay, who visited Sandiford in his last days, continued the attack on the validity of the spiritual appointment of the ministers and elders who kept slaves. When he committed his accusations to print, in a book entitled *All Slave-Keepers, That keep the Innocent in Bondage, Apostates* . . . (1737), he defended Sandiford and excoriated all Quaker slaveholders, calling them "a Parcel of Hypocrites, and Deceivers . . . under the greatest appearance and Pretention to Religion and Sanctity that ever was in the World." He was most bitter, though, against the slave-owning ministers, "the choicest Treasure the Devil can or has to bring out of his Lazaretto, to establish Slave-keeping," because by their smooth hypocrisy they drew the unthinking to indulge in the evil. The printing of *All Slave-Keepers* . . . was by no means the only weapon in his artillery. Though Lay demonstrated an exemplary love for the Africans, it impressed Friends little in comparison with his denunciations of slaveholders and his bizarre actions to symbolize their wickedness, the most famous incident being the one when he appeared at a Quaker Meeting wearing a sword and military uniform under his Quaker coat. At the climax of his tirade, he dramatized his description of the slave-owner by throwing off his coat, seizing the sword, and stabbing what was probably taken to be a Bible, but actually was only the covers of a book enclosing a bladder full of red juice. As the mock blood spattered on the Friends sitting near him, he explained that it was no better for a master to run a sword through a man than keep him in slavery; either act was a murderous assault on Christ's gospel of love, befitting only those who had not renounced carnal strife. Lay kept going to Meetings after the inevitable round of "denials" and had to be forcibly ejected. It was not long before he took on additional crusades against such sins as drinking tea, eating meat, and charging interest on loans. In the antislavery campaign among Friends, the career of Lay reached the high-water mark of eccentricity and futility.[45]

From the time when Fox visited Barbados until Lay retreated from Philadelphia to live in a cave in Abington, Quaker hostility to the prevailing system of exploitation of Negro labor developed during unsuccessful attempts to overcome the opposition based on self-interest. At first, when the difference in status between the Africans and white indentured servants had not been formulated, it was possible to recognize no special moral problem in slavery. Fox and Edmundson, seeing the freshly imported Negroes of the West Indian plantations, called on the owners to do what masters of any other sort of servant should do: give them religious training and discipline, and use them "with humanity."

The morality of slave-owning as such did not become controversial until the slave had been given a clearly defined inferior status — that is, not until the 1670's in the West Indies and the southern mainland colonies, about 1700 in Pennsylvania, and later still in Rhode Island.[46] Once the social position of the Negroes had been made plain, the Quakers, who were becoming more attached to the fraternal relationship in their religious Society, gave up the idea of drawing the slaves into their fellowship. Still, if slaves were to be used, they should be in the owner's household, under his supervision, and subject to religious training. The early Quaker missionaries had also recommended some limit in time on Negro servitude. Though Fox and Edmundson realized it only vaguely, lifelong slavery ran counter to their beliefs about the duty of the owner, since it offered no prospect of completing his task of rearing the Negro to social and religious equality with white colonists.

Development of the case against slavery on moral grounds acknowledged by all Quakers proceeded in the late seventeenth century, though it heightened the conflict between the two main implications of charity to the Negro — if he was considered simply as a non-Friend, he should be freed; if as a member of a Friend's household, he should be educated. Inasmuch as most Quaker slaveholders did little or nothing for the religious nurture of their human property during the first half of the eighteenth century, the conflict tortured not the users but the opponents of slavery. The Quaker world reached a deadlock when political considerations sustained the desire of masters to put off the demands made by men like Pyle, Southeby, or Burling that they free their Negroes in order to uphold Friends' testimony against war, to preserve the sanctity of the family, or simply to observe the Golden Rule. Those who persisted in efforts to stir their fellow Quakers to reject slavery did not succeed in ending the old conflict of ideals and repeatedly lost the ear of their brethren by behaving in ways which demonstrated their lack of devotion to the solidarity of the religious fellowship.

VIII

The Victory of Abolitionist
Principles among Friends

THE prospects of the antislavery campaign in Philadelphia Yearly Meeting underwent a dramatic reversal between 1737 and 1755. Even while the eccentric Englishmen, Farmer, Sandiford, and Lay, had been making nuisances of themselves in the eyes of their American brethren, others had been opposing slavery in much more Friendly spirit. Success in their efforts required more than energy or a flair for publicity. Before the first goals were won there was a marked change in public opinion at large, a spiritual quickening and political crisis among Pennsylvania Quakers, and the appearance of zealots for the cause in the bosom of the church; among them was one of the most influential Friends of all time, John Woolman. There was also a resolution of the program to be pursued for the Negro.

Patient and anonymous American Friends, at work to fight slavery rather than slave-keepers, found a method to expand the Discipline against it. The method, which was successfully used in most parts of colonial Quakerdom, amounted to dividing the problem into steps, each of which could be taken after it had been rendered acceptable by association with a long-standing moral absolute. The association was ordinarily made by comparisons which had more validity on the level of sentiment than of logic. Each step could be subdivided further into a matter of advice and then a matter of discipline.

The first step — against participation in the procurement of slaves in Africa or their importation into America — had been taken when these activities were identified with theft, reception of stolen wares, encouragement of war, and dealing in prize goods. Philadelphia had made avoidance of these activities a matter of advice in 1696, of discipline in 1719. Virginia Yearly Meeting, in 1722, advised against these two practices as well as against dealing in American-born slaves, but did not make the prohibition permanently mandatory until 1768. London advised in 1727 and went the rest of the way in 1761. New England advised against importation in 1717 and 1744 and made it a disciplinary matter in 1760. Maryland Friends tried to go directly to a disciplinary stand in 1759, but had to back down in part the following year. New York Yearly Meeting apparently accepted the advice of London in 1718, but its minutes for several decades following were later destroyed and the first surviving minute to this effect was recorded in 1758. The Meeting did not make its stand stronger than advice until 1774. In North Carolina, the question of buying Negroes did not arise until 1768; four years later the Yearly Meeting advised against it.[1]

The next step was that urged at Philadelphia by Chester Quarterly Meeting in 1729 — the prohibition of buying or selling slaves once imported. This was an easy logical step at first, but a difficult social one, and in the South it was sometimes broken down into several parts. Once Negroes had entered commerce and changed hands a few times under the protection of the law, it was hard to call them stolen goods any longer, and especially so if, as was increasingly common, they had been born to slavery. Besides, in promoting such a prohibition its consequences had to be ignored. If selling men was as evil as buying them, an owner of considerable capital in the form of slaves could not reinvest it otherwise and would actually acquire more such property by natural increase, a mode of acquisition to which Friends made no objection. There was no ground for letting the slave question rest with a formulation that made it easier for an owner to continue using slave labor than to stop, and that sanctioned acquisition of slaves by one method and not another.

The moral axiom with which the prohibition of any traffic in slaves could be identified was that selling them broke up families and, by separating husband and wife, encouraged sin. This feature of the case was plainly recognized in North Carolina where the Yearly Meeting forbade members to deal in slaves as merchandise or to patronize slave traders. Efforts to clarify the application of this decision led to a curious reply of the Yearly Meeting to Western Quarterly Meeting in 1772, in which it was declared that Friends should sell slaves only to each other (so they would not be guilty of shirking their religious responsibilities or turning the Negroes over to harsh masters beyond the reach of church discipline) unless to prevent the division of families or for some other good cause which the Monthly Meeting of the seller had approved.[2]

Philadelphia Yearly Meeting advised with mounting vigor against buying or selling slaves in 1730, 1735, 1736, 1737, and 1758, but did not forbid it on pain of disownment until 1774. Elsewhere in America, advices were given and disciplinary decisions made in the years between 1758 and 1776. After London Yearly Meeting, in 1761, decided that dealing in slaves merited disownment the issue was hardly in doubt. In 1758 Philadelphia compromised between advice and disownment: it excluded those who bought and sold slaves from Meetings for business and from any other "service of Truth," including making contributions to the stock! This chastisement carried neither the weight of a threat of disownment nor any promise of continued contact between the Meeting and the offender. However, private "dealings" were to go on, and branding the money of slave-sellers as unacceptable to the church called their attention to the fact that the Meeting found avarice the only explanation for their misbehavior.[3]

In Philadelphia the campaign against buying and selling slaves actually became submerged in two others: one against owning slaves and one against compromise with worldly standards in the conduct of public affairs. Significantly, the halfway disownment devised by Philadelphia in 1758 was also applied to members who held public office, contrary to the Meeting's new principles. The dominant element in Philadelphia Yearly Meeting thought it right to stay off the bench and out of the legislature (which meant giving up control of the provincial Assembly to non-Quakers) and tried to pursue an Indian policy by private means. These new policies emerged from a religious revival which, as part of a general re-shaping of the religious community, endorsed virtuous conduct toward Negroes. The spiritual leaders looked beyond the issue of selling slaves to a goal of freeing them. The important step taken on the Negro problem in 1758 was the appointment of a Yearly Meeting committee which was to be joined by assistants designated by the Quarterly Meetings in a visit to all slaveholders in their jurisdictions. The adoption of this course of action owed much to the efforts of John Woolman and Anthony Benezet, though it was Benjamin Lay who had suggested the ideal to be followed on the treatment of slaves.

American writers — John Hepburn, Elihu Coleman of Nantucket, and as far as can be known, William Burling — had offered no program to prepare the Negroes for freedom. This deficiency had allowed the masters the comfort of believing they served the good cause of Christianizing their heathen slaves. Hepburn denounced this idea as hypocritical and added that even if religious nurture could be carried on under the slave system, it could not undo the wrong of taking the liberty of the Negroes in the first place. The Africans, he asserted, should be allowed to go back where they came from. The slaves held by North American colonials in the middle of the eighteenth century, however, were not really Africans, so proposals to free them had to offer some plan to deal with them as free men where they were.[4]

Benjamin Lay pointed the way to such a plan. In the "Ninth month," 1736, as he "sat in *Concord* Meeting House" at a session of Chester Quarterly Meeting, it occurred to him that if Quaker slaveholders had taught their Negroes to read and write and had endeavored "in the sweet Love of Truth to instruct and teach 'em the principles of truth and righteousness, and learn them some Honest Trade or Imployment, and then set them free," at the same time telling them that their masters intended "to let them go free in a very reasonable time: and that our Religious Principle will not allow of such Severity, as to keep them in everlasting Bondage and Slavery," several good results would have followed. It might have inspired "such Love and Tenderness in them, toward their Masters or Mistresses, and to the blessed Truth for their Sakes; that it might be a means to convince some of them." This was sound Quaker thinking, though out of step with the normal assumptions of charity, which expected the bond of love to follow rather than precede agreement on religion. If unity in love were extended, convincement might well follow.[5]

Lay added an attraction to the prospect which Hepburn, among earlier writers, had thought of: The convinced freedmen might "come under a concern and necessity, to go and visit their Brethren, of their own colour, and Country, and Language, and preach the Gospel of eternal Salvation unto them, from Sin and Captivity, both of Body and Soul." The special virtue of this possibility was not the enlargement of the flock of Christ, but the "compensation to God and Man," which the slave-owners could make "for being so long in a practice that [had] . . . so much Wickedness of it continually." Lay even attacked the belief in the inferiority of the "black People" and claimed that the status of slavery dimmed "their bright Genius." [6] He was, in short, couching the argument against slavery in the old terms of bringing the Negroes into the religious fellowship at the same time that he was making a sound suggestion about what to do in a practical way toward the release of slaves. His assertion that they must be educated for freedom in economic and civil ways as well as religious, and his confidence that they could learn, pointed to the path ultimately taken.

The contribution of Woolman to the abolitionist effort was far more significant than Lay's. He supplied one partially new concept to the antislavery point of view: that slave-owning, as a flagrant violation of the divinely ordained brotherhood of man, might bring God's wrath down on Friends for tolerating it. Yet the persuasiveness of his preaching came not so much from his ability to elaborate arguments as from his ability to use his whole being to convey them. By combining Burling's devotion to the unity of Friends with the love of Friend and Negro, which Lay preached but could not convey, Woolman could expound his cause without attacking his opponents. Moreover, he knew how to make the slave's condition his own in ways which would be affecting to Friends, yet not antagonize them. He refused the hospitality of slave-owners, not indignantly but sadly, leaving their homes and letting them find out why. In Meetings where the opponents of action against selling or holding slaves held forth, he suffered visibly but not ostentatiously. Far from being in a hurry to publish his views, he kept his writings private until the Meeting was willing to publish them, and quietly sought to persuade other Quakers to his beliefs.[7]

In his first published pleas against slavery, Woolman succeeded in so using the old arguments as to transform them. Under his treatment they acquired new urgency, practicality, and corollaries in duty. It was his gift to insist that Friends be pure from sin, and to persuade them to examine their motives in keeping their slaves in such a way as to concentrate on personal virtue, and not try to imagine the situation of the slaves. He was able to do what Cadwalader Morgan had attempted less skilfully: attach slaveholding to the root stock of all evil acts, self-will. He asked that each man look into his own heart; if he found motives of lust for gain behind keeping slaves, he ought to free them, for nothing would extenuate subtracting the individual from the love of God by submitting to private desire. He saw the proof of this proposition around him, especially in the South, where the slaves were ill-used and looked "like a burthensome Stone" weighing down those who had them. If the masters pursued material gain before the welfare of the slaves and did not "act Conscientiously toward them as fellow Creatures," the "burthen" would grow "heavier and heavier." Since slave-keeping alienated the mind "from its true and real Happiness," no plea for retaining the slaves in order to do a "Duty by them" could be accepted. This was Hepburn's and Lay's point cut down to useful size.[8]

As Woolman defined it, the duty of Quakers to their Negroes in the religious sphere was to use "proper Means for their Acquaintance with the Holy Scriptures, and the advantage of true Religion," prepare them for liberty in Christ as much as possible, but not necessarily draw them into the religious Society. This slight alteration of the old ideas had immense importance. It was well suited to a time when Quakers were making renewed efforts to bring their religious fellowship to a high degree of purity and consistency. Woolman exhorted Friends to purify their conduct by divesting themselves of slaves after giving them religious instruction, and not let their decisions to manumit or not be governed by the success or failure of the missionary effect on the Negroes. He buttressed the exhortation with a restatement of the plea that the Africans ought to have civil freedom. Like Sandiford, he postulated liberty as their natural right. It followed that Quakers should train their slaves avowedly for participation in society as freemen, as Benjamin Lay had told Chester Quarterly Meeting. Since freedom was a natural right, a Quaker did not need to feel qualms about letting his slaves loose to sin; he did right to free them if he had done his best to prepare them "to make a proper use of their Liberty." This approach to the Negro issue gained the official approval of Philadelphia Yearly Meeting by 1753, when a newly enlarged Board of Overseers of the Press decided to print Woolman's first essay, *Some Considerations on the Keeping of Negroes,* and the next year an Epistle drafted by Woolman covering the same ground but drawing conclusions mainly against buying and selling slaves.[9]

In this *Epistle of Caution and Advice* Woolman carried his points by the old method of making an emotional identification of certain aspects of his subject with accepted morality. He depicted the miseries of the "poor Creatures" in Africa being "stolen away, Parents from Children, and Children from Parents," amid "Scenes of Murther and Cruelty." The "barbarous Ravages" of the slave dealers tore the Negroes "from what they esteemed a happy Situation," and took them to places where they were "compelled to toil in a State of Slavery, too often extreamly cruel!" Thus he tried to awaken a horror of the sin as well as a consciousness of it. He not only carried further than had anyone before him the identification of slave-keeping with love of luxury and sloth, but declared that the methods used in managing slave labor tended to harden the master's heart and "render . . . [his] Soul less susceptible of that holy Spirit of Love, Meekness and Charity, which is the peculiar Character of a true Christian." [10]

But the ramifying evil of slavery would not remain an individual misfortune. Woolman scored a new point that had special urgency for Quakers embarking on a compaign of moral reawakening in their church: "Where *Slave* keeping prevails, pure Religion and Sobriety decline." If slave-keeping brought a man to damnation, it could provoke God to withdraw his favor from his "People called Quakers." Woolman told them to look back to the founding of Pennsylvania and New Jersey to see how God had prospered their ancestors, who in Europe had known "manifold Sufferings"; how he preserved them from the might of the Indians and made room among them for the settlers to clear "pleasant Fields" and enjoy their "civil and religious Liberties" in peace while wars raged elsewhere.[11]

The virtues of the earlier generation offered more than an example; they imposed a responsibility. Wise men, said Woolman, would see that the work of the pioneers and the help of God had not been poured out "to be buried in Oblivion; but to prepare a People for more fruitful Returns." Friends who gave this consideration due weight would be humble in their prosperity and strive to show a Christian benevolence toward their "Inferiors." However, if Quakers, "through a stupid Indolence," conceived "Views of Interest, separate from the general Good of the great Brotherhood, and, in Pursuance thereof," used slave labor rigorously to accumulate wealth for themselves and for their children, what would they do when God visited his displeasure on them? Woolman's insistence on the moral equality of all human beings as brethren in the sight of God had the implication of solidarity of the species. "The State of Mankind was harmonious in the Beginning," he wrote, "and tho' sin hath introduced Discord, yet through the wonderful Love of God in Christ Jesus our Lord, the Way is open for our Redemption, and Means are appointed to restore us to primitive Harmony." So whatever individual or corporate group caused another human being to suffer invited "the greatest of Evils." [12] This elaboration on the command to love thy neighbor as thyself carried a threat!

It is not likely that Woolman had a definite divine retribution in mind, but the events which followed the publication of his essay proved very pertinent to his argument. The Indians ceased to be content with the demographic arrangements merited by the early Friends and started retaking the land, or so it seemed. Friends in public office were denounced for leaving Pennsylvania defenseless, and the more conscientious ones withdrew to private life, still hoping to prove that pacifism was a practical policy and that some kind of violence by the white men had caused the violence by the Indians. John Churchman, a Quaker renowned for piety, came to believe that his fellow-Pennsylvanians had brought the French and Indian War on themselves by using slave labor. He could easily see the obvious link between the wickedness of the people and the "calamity and scourge" of the border raids. But one day as he walked along the street, still unsatisfied with this explanation, "it was said in [his] . . . soul, This land is polluted with blood, and in the day of inquisition for blood, it will not only be required at the frontiers and borders, but even in [Philadelphia]." He asked, "How can this be? since this has been a land of peace, and as yet not much concerned in war; but as it were in a moment my eyes turned to the case of the poor enslaved Negroes." No matter how little direct connection Pennsylvania slave-owners might have with the procurement of captives in Africa, they were "partakers in iniquity, encouragers of war and the shedding of innocent blood." [13]

Between the eloquence of Woolman and the logic of events, the antislavery cause had been attached to the reform movement among Friends of Philadelphia Yearly Meeting. It became part of the campaign against any compromise of conscience with policy, against impious attachment to power, place, or wealth.

Some of the terrors of disunity over the slave issue had been dispelled by advances into religious and educational benevolence toward Negroes by persons of other denominations. English efforts through the Society for the Propagation of the Gospel in Foreign Parts had been going on for decades. Cotton Mather had made a gesture toward educating Negroes. Colonists in Philadelphia — especially the Anglicans and New Light Presbyterians — took increased interest in such activities during the middle of the eighteenth century. The Quaker Benezet had, without provoking any trouble, begun an evening school for slaves' children in 1750. Doing good to the Negro, far from arousing suspicion, had come to enjoy a mild vogue. A shift in emphasis took place among zealots of several persuasions, from catechizing or other simple evangelical work to providing the Negroes with secular and religious educa-tion.[14]

Certainly, hope grew in Quaker circles that training the slaves for liberty could eliminate the old contradiction between granting them civil freedom and providing religious care. Quakers revised their ideas on the slave question in their own terms, however, some-times noting the good examples of outsiders, but not avowedly imitating them.

If anything, Friends had lagged behind other English sects in developing a stand against slavery. During the 1740's Thomas Hazard's conversation with a deacon of the Established Church in Connecticut revealed how well the Quakers had succeeded in stifling the issue. The deacon claimed the Friends could not be Christians because they held slaves, a novel idea to Hazard, pro-spective heir to a large plantation with a labor force of Negroes. Violently affected, he went home to Rhode Island convinced that neither he nor anyone else ought to own a fellow man.[15]

The difference between the day of Benjamin Lay and that of Woolman had been made by the Great Awakening and its quiet counterpart in the Society of Friends, quite as much as by the inex-orable process of facing long-potential corollaries of Quaker belief or by the appearance of the Christ-like Woolman, a man who could not be driven to disorderly acts. The singularity had gone from the cause, not from the pleaders. Two years before Wool-man's famous journey into Virginia and North Carolina, Samuel Fothergill and Israel Pemberton the younger, both prominent lead-ers of the Quaker revival, had traveled the same ground, vigorously preaching against slavery. Wherever Woolman went he found Friends who opposed slave-keeping and would admit it, or who would discuss the subject even if they did not. The weight of gen-eral opinion had ceased to back the few slaveholders in the church. All indications point to the conclusion that after the middle of the century Friends listened readily to antislavery preaching and with few exceptions wanted to be persuaded, not intellectually, but beyond all opinions, "in the love of God," which first made them "love one another." [16]

At last, the leaders of the church in Philadelphia Yearly Meeting decided that the time had come to take disciplinary action against slaveholding in the ranks. Monthly Meetings in Pennsylvania and New Jersey began to exert pressure on members to present papers condemning their purchase of Negroes and fix terms of service for those they still held even before the decisions of 1758, which only excluded purchasers from the "service of Truth" and instigated a visit to all slaveholders. The Minute of 1755 had offered some grounds for discretion to the subordinate Meetings, directing them to treat buyers of slaves "as they may be directed in the Wisdom of Truth." In 1758 the Yearly Meeting made the effort to end selling, buying, and keeping slaves a responsibility of all Meetings, but by means short of disownment. In addition, the Yearly Meeting's decision promoted attention to important auxiliary duties — reasonable treatment of slaves, promotion of their religious and secular education, and the limitation of their servitude. When the Meeting undertook to enforce these duties seriously (and the answers to queries gradually began to reveal that Overseers in the complacent days before the French and Indian War had been ignoring a good deal of laxity) and exclude those who bought or sold a slave, Friends made the Negroes' case their own in a corporate way: the Meeting took the well-being of the slave as its own concern when it meant opposing one of its own members; it was not enough that a Friend refrain from committing sins against the slave which would have been sins against anybody.[17]

In the years immediately following 1758 the Meeting strove for written commitments by slave-owners as to their good intentions. In one paper, which was accepted as satisfactory, a man who had "inadvertantly [!] purchased a negro Boy contrary to the advice of the Yearly Meeting," acknowledged that he had become aware that it was "not consistent with true Christianity to enslave our Fellow Men." To show his sincerity he promised to teach the boy "to read and write and train him up in the Principles of the Christian Religion, also to learn him a trade or bring him up to Business whereby he may be able to get a comfortable living." Moreover, when the boy reached the age of twenty-one, the repentant purchaser would "Leave it to Friends of the Monthly Meeting to judge when he ought to be free." In other Yearly Meetings, there was an increase in efforts to enforce these elements of good treatment. In Virginia, Woolman spoke on education at the Yearly Meeting in 1757. The following year Friends there and in North Carolina deliberated on all aspects of religious and secular duty toward Negroes, and Maryland Friends gave their attention to them a year later.[18]

Giving slaves religious and other learning — though Friends had long considered it the master's duty for other reasons — was justified after 1758 as preparation for freedom. Indeed, as the theory gained support that manumission of slaves was a necessity in justice, it became impossible to justify educating them except as a preliminary to liberating them. Negroes, as Sandiford and Woolman had insisted, had a natural right to freedom which should be honored. So, as a Friend should not cheat, he should not keep a slave. Since the best thinking among Quakers held that slavery hampered the development of the mind and receptiveness to the inward stirrings of the spirit, specific training for freedom was an obligation which justice imposed on the owner. The duty to provide religious education, however, was upheld on the assumption that it would not lead to unity with Friends.

Philadelphia Yearly Meeting, in its leadership in the slavery question, by 1758 had strongly implied that ultimately no solution could be reached except the compulsory manumission of all Friends' Negroes with reparation for wrongs done them. For a few years, however, the Meeting refrained from making a more forthright declaration. One reason was that the Society of Friends did not yet think it correct to take any formal institutional step which went beyond dealing with members; another, that Quakers were determined to preserve their sect in its bond of love and knew that Rhode Island and southern brethren might not concur in any further step. Philadelphia used its declared principles, however, as the basis of a campaign of ardent and active persuasion — but without threat of disownment — directed toward inducing slaveholding members to liberate their Negroes. At the same time, abolitionist sentiment grew in other Yearly Meetings, and discussions of the subject went on between colonies, with the result that on the eve of the Revolution virtually all American Friends were ready to proceed to the final declarations against slaveholding. By 1760 abolitionism had been accepted by the Quakers to the extent that they were considering no alternative. The formal prohibition of slave-owning, however, had to be put off until Friends were willing to back it with a more comprehensive campaign to persuade the owners to give up their claims and with a program, initiated by the Meeting, for the care of the freed Negroes. Both of these requirements were to be met as parts of the general moral reform which had begun in Philadelphia Yearly Meeting, but the means utilized to benefit former slaves came from a transformation of the special circumstances of Pennsylvania Quakerdom.

IX

Government, Benevolence, and the Quaker Revival

THE vigorous action by the Pennsylvania Meetings against slaveholding by the membership was part of a much broader attempt to purify the church. The leaders considered moral reform a revival of the strict conformity to Quaker standards of an earlier generation. Certainly the movement renewed emphasis on the distinctive dress and speech of Friends as well as on rigorous pacifism. But in the attempt to cleanse the church of the insidiously widening stain of worldliness, the reformers went beyond a return to the real or fancied "good old days." The campaign against slave-owning was still new. Increased regularity of church government and the introduction of written answers to queries were likewise innovations rather than restorations. The most conspicuous change, however, was a reappraisal of the proper relation between Friends and the government in Pennsylvania, occasioned by the onset of Indian raids in the fall of 1755, the same event which brought the reform movement as a whole to its first climax.

The reform campaign had its first center in Philadelphia and did not spread effectively until the political crises after 1764 brought to Friends in other Yearly Meetings trials similar to those of the French and Indian War in Pennsylvania. Yet even in the 1750's all Quakerdom shared in the campaign for reform, if only in relatively superficial or rudimentary ways, through the exchange of epistles and traveling ministers, notable among whom was the great English preacher of the revival, Samuel Fothergill.

In the long run, the fact that the revival movement in Pennsylvania had touched all American Quakers proved highly important. Beginning with Penn's Holy Experiment, Friends there had enjoyed the special experience of founding and operating their own government. Pacifism, as indeed any other aspect of a Quaker program, had to be treated not as a minority demand unlikely to be met, but as a policy to be implemented for a body politic. Elsewhere, Friends' attitudes on political matters were those of men who exerted no public power and who sought relief from religious oppression. Even in colonies like Maryland, where Quakers could hold office because they were allowed to make an affirmation rather than swear an oath, they had no sense of responsibility for the commonwealth as a "People." For most Friends, a few relatively simple political maxims — not necessarily consistent with each other — served well enough. In Pennsylvania, on the other hand, prolonged responsibility in public affairs tested Quaker ideas. The result of the first few decades was the abandonment of religiously oriented objectives by the Quaker politicians in favor of a strictly secular approach.

By 1755, when Friends in the Assembly were accused by the local opposition of rigid pacifist principles which made them unfit to hold office, many of them had long since become inured to accepting compromises on their sect's peace testimony and had reconciled themselves to all the artful dodging required by statecraft and political maneuvering within the British empire. These men had devoted their talents to controlling the provincial government through the legislature and had become what might be called Quaker *politiques*. Some of them surely retained scruples against voting for forts, military supplies, and aid to the king's campaigns, but with the single exception of a compulsory militia law, at which they drew the line, the Quaker majority in the Pennsylvania Assembly managed to do as much for warfare as the legislators in most other colonies. Some conscientious Friends tried to reconcile their principles to their practices: James Logan, Penn's secretary and occasionally acting chief executive of the colony, had, early in his career, declared his belief that defensive war was justifiable; others adopted this point of view, and a pamphlet advocating a colonial militia and fortifications was offered to the Yearly Meeting in 1741. The official stand of the Meeting, however, never wavered from complete pacifism.[1]

The peace testimony, however, became for Quakers the symbol of morality in politics, the position to be held at all costs to preserve the good name of their church. Most of them felt that it must be defended not merely in Meeting, but in public policy as well. In 1755 the glib suggestion by an English Quaker that Friends in Pennsylvania could simply shed their leadership in society and become outsiders to the control of provincial affairs met a cool reception. The past, and the possibilities it had opened up, could not be ignored.

But perhaps the whole history of the Quaker colonies had been a mistake? Not even the moral reformers wanted to think so. They searched the record to find clues to the goodness of Penn's Holy Experiment — clues which would enable them to revive virtue in politics as well as in dress and household order. The legacy of political theories from William Penn offered no explanation; not only was it inconsistent and sometimes materialistic in its implications, but it had continued to be the source of intellectual guidance while the decline from virtue took place. Nor did the specific laws and policies of early Pennsylvania reveal much; for the most part they had not been abandoned. The reformers, in effect, repudiated much of what had once appeared the foundation of the province when they found the key to its original virtue in a concept that probably would not have seemed so vital to the earlier generation — that of disinterested benevolence. The failure of Pennsylvania politics was far more extensive than the failure to avert war in 1755; it was a relapse from the cardinal virtue which could make government truly good into an easy life of worldly manipulations. To understand the significance of this analysis made by the reformers, it is necessary to examine the body of equivocal political ideas inherited from Penn and the disappointing course of his Holy Experiment.

Friends shared political ideas with other British subjects in the eighteenth century. Their controversial writings, petitions, and conduct in office showed that they had no distinctive approach of their own. Those who remained in unity never tried to convert religious institutional patterns to political uses. Men in authority, like Friends in Meeting, could wait to have "that principle of God" raised up in them to guide them and preserve them from selfishness. But to turn the system of Meetings into a political organization would have required either the abandonment of the "sense of the meeting" in favor of decisions by voting, or the development of a political unity before and beyond opinion such as the religious fellowship rested upon.[2] Instead of special ideas about the grounds of governmental authority and the forms by which it should be exercised, Quakers distinguished themselves by their policies, among which were religious freedom and absence of preparation for war.

William Penn, who gave political ideas more attention than any other Friend, supplied the formulations used by Quakers throughout the eighteenth century. As pamphleteer against religious persecution in England, however, he often developed ideas quite different from those he propounded as founder of Pennsylvania. Penn argued for toleration by reasoning from widely accepted premises to limited, predetermined conclusions; he did not speculate freely about society and government in general. Having had some training in law, he often argued that political liberty — the rights to hold property, to be governed by laws made by a representative body, to trial by jury — were parts of the inheritance of Englishmen rather than determined by some imperative in the construction of the universe. Englishmen, Penn claimed as a matter of legal fact, had an ancient right freely to elect the members of "frequent Parliaments." Using the same technique in Pennsylvania, David Lloyd made a plausible argument about specific matters of provincial law from rights and privileges which he believed to be afforded by the English constitution. The lawyer's approach, whenever used, virtually excluded denominational peculiarity in the theory of government.[3]

Penn and other Quakers also argued from the ancient axioms of Christian political speculation. Experience, Scripture, and observation combined to convince Friends of the proposition that government was instituted by God for the well-being of the governed, and "Magistrates may be looked upon as Ministers under *God*, invested with some branches of power, for the public benefit, *viz.* To be a terror and scourge to *evil doers*, and a praise to them who *do well*." Their ideal should be to distribute justice impartially, "with clean hands and pure hearts." The natural depravity of man after Adam's fall made government's repressive functions necessary. In fact, the magistrates, while they were "as Gods on earth," had to restrain the human passion to preserve political authority. For this reason, prudence required government to educate those under it as far as possible to reduce the amount of punishment necessary.[4]

The repressive function of government was only part of its usefulness. Echoing the morality of mercantilism, Penn asserted that it was the concern of good government "to curb and rebuke excess," and exclude "foreign vanities," since luxury would bring "effeminacy, laziness, poverty, and misery"; but temperance would lead people to improve native commodities for sale and ultimately to create a favorable balance of trade. Government, however, had still more basic utilitarian purposes: to make property secure, increase trade and population, prevent pauperism, and insure "true christian and civil liberty." All things considered, government was "as capable of kindness, goodness and charity, as a more private society."[5]

Friends more often called for severe limitation on the function of the state. They thought they should guard themselves from political power by elaborating the inner life of the religious community to a point where they could voluntarily reject governmental services, such as poor relief and adjudication in courts of law, which they thought the state should supply to others. Quakers wanted the state to keep the peace and to cease waging war, taking tithes, requiring oaths, and persecuting religious minorities. Frequently, they thought participation in the religious fellowshp inconsistent with participation in political life, even where they were not barred from it by law, and so they tended to do no more than preach to outsiders and call for the election of good men.[6]

The scope they envisaged for the government more or less coincided with liberal common sense of the times, though in economic matters hints of mercantilism appeared, somewhat inconsistently. The secular description of the state, however, was basic. In the absence of agreement on religion, which would be the best bond of a body politic, Penn advocated no attempt to force unanimity, but rather a resort to the principle that "civil interest is the foundation and end of civil government; and where it is not maintained intire, the government must needs decline." By "interest," Penn meant "'a *legal endeavour* to keep *rights*, or augment honest *profits*,' whether it be in a private person or a society." An independent government had an interest of its own: to maintain its sway and enlarge its subject population. It did these things best by serving or, more properly, harmonizing their interests and alienating none on such irrelevant grounds as religious belief. Sensible citizens knew that they needed civil rights and had to guarantee them to their neighbors to gain success. No man could conceive an interest in another's opinions, and since "*Interest* will not *lie*," and "*self* will always be true to its *interest*," the mutual advantages of civil society would prove a feasible bond of the parties. Indeed, the less the basis of association in the body politic, the larger the number of persons who could be peacefully brought into it; the bigger it became, the stronger its government in trade or international politics, and hence the more capable of serving the various interests! The more it reconciled the component interests, the more people would become industrious and use rather than store up their funds; so wealth "which, like the blood, that hath its due passage, [would] . . . give life and vigour to every member in the publick body." [7]

This description of the basis of civil society satisfied members of a persecuted religious minority, anxious to have everybody go about his business, and resolved to remain aloof from their neighbors. It became relevant to Pennsylvania when Friends became a minority. When Quakers gave foremost thought to the maintenance of group autonomy in the face of pressures from the "World" around them, they leaned on ideas about government which provided policies to deal with social entities as they actually were rather than to alter them. James Logan and Isaac Norris, opposing a paper-money scheme touted as an aid to the poor, extended the theory that conflicting interests would automatically promote the general good, to argue against government's seeking to determine the fate of individual interests in defiance of natural operations of credit. Penn argued that the art of constructing a constitution was one of tuning, or counterbalancing, the interests of the citizens who were to live under it. Robert Proud, defending Quaker consciences in Revolutionary Pennsylvania, claimed that the balanced assortment of virtues and talents among the population had been essential to the happiness of the province. The body politic, he said, like the human body, needed various members; if Friends pursued the arts of peace, they did their part as well as the soldiers.[8]

When under particularly severe pressure from outsiders, Friends often resorted to a view of the nation which was not secular. They always accepted the ancient idea that God prospered nations of virtuous people and punished those in which wickedness prevailed. Penn thought it a matter of historical fact as well as one of moral justice and revealed truth. Due regard for this belief should have ruled out sectarian aloofness on the part of Quakers; since the success of all in their secular endeavors depended on reducing sin, all citizens should contribute to a campaign for virtue. Friends, however, found it hard to believe that God would punish the good, the "saving remnant," no matter how wicked their compatriots. Among themselves Quakers talked of the nation's troubles as heralds of the horrible death agonies of wickedness which would be followed by a world of righteousness. To outsiders they prophesied the consequences of evil ways, using the conception of the nation as a moral unit to establish the relevance of their preaching against sin or religious persecution to other citizens. They did not insist that the others became Friends, since everyone already agreed on the eternal principles of conduct, the general good to be secured by observing them, and the need for officials to help repress such evils as the religious institutions could not.[9]

Friends appealed to another view of government, one which gave it even greater moral importance, when they embarked on colonization in the New World. While the settlers along the Delaware expected a political structure which would preserve them in freedom to cultivate their interests, they also had some hope of reordering society along ideal lines.

Particularly when working as founder of his colony, Penn developed a nonsecular political hypothesis. Government was "a part of religion itself, a thing sacred in its institution and end." Though it could not remove the cause of evil, it crushed its effect, and therefore was a lower "emanation of the same Divine Power" as religion. Government at its best resembled the "universal goodness of God, who dispenses his light, air, showers, and comfortable seasons to *all*, and whom Caesar ought always to imitate." Political obligation came from God's command, like that of children to parents; "divine right," Penn asserted, "runs through more things of the world, and acts of our lives, than we are aware of." [10]

The practical meaning of these ideas was not always consistent with Quaker morality. It was something of a paradox for Friends to believe the power of their governors to be divinely ordained and then refuse to comply with part of their orders. The authority of God indirectly expressed by kings always had to be given second place to direct commands through the Inner Light. The paradox was even more striking in view of Quakers' inability to reconcile the historical with the moral origins of political authority. Penington assured them they must not foment revolution, no matter how oppressive their governors, "for the Lord God Almighty, who with ease removed their enemies, . . . can with as great ease remove them, and put the power in another hand." This was part of the Lord's work, however, in which Quakers could not help without committing sin! [11]

Logical consistency in governmental theory, however, rarely mattered to colonial Quakers. Normally their purposes were served by one or more of the political ideas deriving from a secular theory of the state. Outside of Pennsylvania and West New Jersey, Friends did not take responsibility for shaping the government under which they lived. They gave attention to political matters mainly to ask in the name of justice and liberty of conscience for privileges to uphold their "testimonies" as a people without penalty. When their requests were denied, they asked forbearance in the inevitable distraints on their goods for taxes or fines. In the belief that the nation's fortunes depended on the collective behavior of the people, they sometimes responded to heavy demands for military service or financial contributions in time of war with critical analyses of the cause of the fighting. They ascribed New England border raids, for example, to the persecution of Quakers in the seventeenth century. As a rule, though, they did not parade denials of the binding nature of laws repugnant to their consciences. To Friends in Virginia, Maryland, New York, and Massachusetts, the government was always something run by and for others.[12]

In several colonies, because a few were wealthy and enjoyed high social rank, Friends attained public office or even political predominance, but outside of Pennsylvania there were few departures from the Quaker view that government was a secular matter, not to be guided by Friends' principles. Thus, in Carolina, John Archdale, a capable English Quaker who owned or controlled a share of the proprietary rights in the province, was governor between 1694 and 1696, but his administration exhibited no traits specifically derived from Quakerism. At his arrival the Friends alone among the denominations had organized a church, and many of them sat in the legislature, but after he left and other Protestant sects were organized, Carolinian Friends ceased to be influential in public affairs. Similarly, the English Friends failed to use their control of New Jersey in a way relevant to their religious views. In West New Jersey, where their numbers made the Quaker settlers politically important and where prominent Friends sat in the legislature and on the Governor's Council, they used their voice in public affairs only to oppose laws from which they suffered. Even in Rhode Island, where the Quaker fold included many leading inhabitants and an impressive array of colonial political and economic leaders, no distinctive policy came of their prominence in elective offices in the century after King Philip's War. Rather, they settled quickly into the custom of making the accommodations of principle necessary to the normal conduct of public business.[13]

The descendants of the Quakers who had founded colonies in West New Jersey and Pennsylvania took pains to perpetuate an explanation of the main motive that led the settlers to America. In fleeing persecution in England, they had chiefly in view "a Quiet, Moral & Religious Life." The early Friends had abhorred "fearfulness of sufferings," an emotion which did not enhance the reputation of Truth or lead to the proper obedience to God. Only when a campaign of persecution threatened to destroy them economically by outrageous seizures of goods to pay fines did they leave for the New World. They wanted liberty to be diligent in their callings as well as regular in their attendance of meetings; to lead a virtuous life to the full, not just the martyr's scope. In general, the immigrants wanted no novelties in government, no welfare state, though they probably thought well of the constitutional and judicial experiments of Penn and Byllynge.[14]

In most aspects, the constitutional arrangements and social regulations in Pennsylvania and West New Jersey before 1702 followed the patterns in other colonies or in England. For example, there were only slight limits on the power of the chief executives at Philadelphia and Burlington to declare war, raise a militia, and commission officers. However, the basic laws of the colonies contained strong guarantees of liberties, especially religious freedom and the right to trial by jury, and judicial practices in the Quaker colonies were marked by simplifications in procedure and a few innovations designed to suit local conditions or improve upon English models. The "Laws, Concessions, and Agreements" of West New Jersey (1676/7) forbade imprisonment for debt in order that debtors might continue to earn money to satisfy their creditors. Pennsylvania experimented with some reduction in the severity of punishments in the last two decades of the seventeenth century.[15]

A few unusual arrangements, though not strictly innovations, reflected Friends' special ways and interests. Pennsylvania courts appointed "Peace-makers" to settle "Differences betwixt man and man," much as Meetings appointed arbitrators if Friends failed to find their own. This procedure also showed traces of Quaker distrust of lawyers and distaste for dispute in open court, since the peacemakers aimed to resolve differences by private conferences and to avoid suits over small matters. The affairs of widows and orphans were put under the jurisdiction of Orphan's Courts, special sessions of the County Courts which performed the functions of probate courts when minor heirs were concerned. They saw to the apprenticing of children under their care. Though begun early, they did not prove their worth for many years. There was less devotion on the part of the settlers to a theory prized by reform-minded English Quakers, that prisons should be workhouses. A law to this effect was made by Penn and his advisers for Pennsylvania in 1682. They resolved also that (as in the jails of West New Jersey) there should be no fees for food and lodging. Eighteen years later Penn had to appeal to the Council of the colony in person to put the law into effect.[16]

Quaker government simply followed English practice in the system of raising money for sufferers from fire by a wide-scale, government-approved appeal for contributions (called a "fire-brief" in both England and Pennsylvania) and in the regulation of servitude and terms of "settlement" to qualify for public poor relief. In fact, in these areas, as in the use of a modified form of the "head-right" privilege in Pennsylvania and a version of the certificate system to check the character of prospective immigrants into New Jersey, even the slight hints of adaptation of methods used by Quaker Meetings derived from English and Virginia usages.[17]

Penn's constitutional laws specified that Pennsylvania take responsibility for education. The Council acted directly in 1683 only; thereafter, it waited until private initiative appeared and blessed the interest of the citizens with charter rights, a policy which Penn endorsed by imitation. As their recipients requested, the charters specified duties to maintain and teach poor children. In 1712 the legislature took a new approach to the schools when it passed the first of three acts to empower Protestant religious organizations to receive and hold property to help them carry on education, as they had already begun to do. In West New Jersey, after the endowment of the Board of Island Managers, the initiative in education also went to the religious societies, where it remained through the eighteenth century. Friends and non-Friends alike supported the policy in the two provinces.[18]

Relief to the poor in Pennsylvania followed a similar course. The Quaker government gave responsibility to county courts in

1682. Tax money for poor relief, though voted by the Assembly, did not always reach the public Overseers of the Poor; the religious societies did most of the relief work. Philadelphia had a disproportionate share of the burden, but the Assembly arranged taxation so that the country districts did not share it. For a few years the city left the poor to the charity of the churches, and to the Quaker Meeting in particular. In 1712 the town corporation finally decided to establish a place for indoor relief, but did not begin to build the public almshouse until 1729, when the Assembly lent it £1000. The institution remained the mainstay of relief administered by the city until the building of the Bettering House. The public almshouse was backed by Quakers in the city government, but their basic attitude was shown by the fact that the Monthly Meeting had created its own almshouse years before.[19]

Pennsylvania tried, though without novel measures, to protect both laborers and province by limiting the authority of masters and by controlling the importation of servants. The Assembly attempted to cut down the influx of convict and Negro labor early in the eighteenth century but its laws of 1705, calling for severe punishment of slave offenses and guarding against uprising, suggested that it acted solely out of concern for public order. Quaker government protected the peace and the interests of slaveholders by repressive legislation, and left the concerns which so exercised the Meeting — the place of the slave in the family unit — strictly alone.[20]

A strong undercurrent of utopianism, however, ran through the founding of the Quaker colonies. Some Friends responded to the opportunity to begin a new society in America by the determination to conduct a "Holy Experiment." The bulk of the experimental content of West New Jersey and Pennsylvania consisted of constitutional and judicial details, but some Quakers saw in the colonial venture an opportunity to create a reformed society, and they wanted to use the political authority as the agency for such efforts.[21]

For a while the religious and civil societies seemed to be merging in the Quaker colonies. The same men led church and state. There was a prospect that freedom of religion would prove freedom to respond to the spirit of God within. German and Welsh settlers with Quaker inclinations came to lodge securely in the framework of the Yearly Meeting. Until the Keithian schism and the formation of the Anglican congregation at Christ Church, all Philadelphians went to First day meetings. For a while, church and state used the same public buildings, and in 1685 Philadelphia Monthly Meeting actually considered the possibility of relying on governmental records of vital statistics, although it had been one of the time-honored tasks of Friends' Meetings to keep them. It was not odd that the unknown author of "The Planter's Speech" dreamed of improving the moral character of his neighbors to the point that association in the political unit would be possible on a religious footing. Free from the lusts and evil traditions of the Old World, subjected to benign customs, including vegetarianism and sobriety, colonists on the *"virgin elysian shore"* could enhance the bond of love and live in harmony, an example to all mankind.[22]

Thomas Budd entertained a similar vision. In addition to vigorous efforts by magistrates and heads of families to govern in the wisdom of God and strive to inculcate and enforce virtuous conduct, he wanted the government to establish public schools where trades, morals, and book learning would be taught to all children, including those of the Indians. He also proposed economic innovations: a private land bank and public warehouses that would facilitate commerce and give the basis for a paper currency. Few of the utopian schemes received much attention. Budd and five other men asked, but did not get, the encouragement of the Lieutenant Governor and Council in setting up a bank in 1688. Bills to require all men to marry by a certain age and to prohibit the ownership of clothing of more than two different kinds of cloth had already been proposed in 1683, but had come to nothing. A plan — seemingly more practical — by English backers of the Quaker colonies to offer land to poor men who would go to the colonies as settlers, aroused little interest among those who were already there.[23]

The utopian plans for the new colonies nevertheless had a firm connection with some ultra-rigorous manifestions of Quaker morality. Tendencies toward vegetarianism or quirkish asceticism in regard to clothing were often present in the notable spiritual leaders.

Woolman's singularity in dress was well known. The anonymous "Planter's" belief in 1684 that killing animals tended to enlarge the cruelty of the killer could also be found early in Woolman's life. The same convictions, along with hostility to drink and interest, were held by Joshua Evans, Benjamin Lay, William Southeby, Ralph Sandiford, Anthony Benezet, and others. Propensities to ascetic and business reforms were often apparent in those who had a special part in the development of humanitarianism. Other Friends, including many respected ministers, did not share these traits. For many Quakers, Budd's projects seemed unwise entanglements with the world and the "Planter's" techniques for gathering all colonists into a closer bond of love were unnecessary; their religious Society did well enough as it was. On the other hand, those prone to emphasize the bond uniting mankind found the intimacy of their church insufficient and partly in frustration turned to occasionally picayune means to make the moral truth a social fact.[24]

The most important side of utopianism in early Pennsylvania and West New Jersey was the effort to live peaceably with and convert the Indians, one of the aims of colonization as described both in Penn's charter and the "Planter's Speech." In both colonies the usual good intentions prevailed about buying lands justly from the natives and preventing unscrupulous trade with them. At first there was ample evidence of good personal relations between settlers and redmen, but laws, no matter how often passed or revised, did not keep white settlers from selling rum to the natives or straying onto unpurchased land.

Penn and the idealistic settlers wanted to bring the Indians under the provincial government by their own consent, as a result of a sort of social contract. The "Concessions" of West New Jersey predicated a partial subjection of the natives to provincial magistrates. The tribal authority was not entirely to be superseded: Indians were to be held responsible in the first instance by their own king for damages done to Englishmen, but when disputes went to trial, if either party was an Indian, half the jury was to be composed of his tribesmen. Such a body could dispense justice because even though particular customs might vary, the universal law of God was in all men's hearts. The mixed jury plan was applied first to Rhode Island under one of the Quaker Governors in 1673 and to Pennsylvania in 1681, although the "Concessions" of that year exempted Indians from Pennsylvania criminal law. Twenty years of colonial life did not develop the expected solidarity between Quakers and Indians; nevertheless, Penn, at the famous treaty in the spring of 1701, modified only slightly the sense of social contract and still obtained from the Indian spokesmen an agreement to acknowledge the English Crown and submit to the laws of the province.[25]

Justice to the Indians, together with their economic advancement, might improve the chances to convert them. Penn even tried to enlist the fur trade in this good work! He established a joint stock company which was to be run by virtuous men and to have a monopoly on trade with the Indians. The company's agents were not to use liquor and would draw the Indians to Christianity by showing them its values in virtuous conduct. The plan did not work; the Holy Experiment was a failure by 1705 and the business of fur trading, like other relations with the natives, became a secular matter. The clause in Penn's treaties binding natives and newcomers to be "as one people," having "one head and heart," was to be repeated in later agreements with the Delawares or Iroquois. But the Indians would take these declarations of solidarity more seriously than the successors of William Penn.[26]

The governments of the Quaker colonies reached a turning point in the early years of the eighteenth century, when a new generation arrived on the political scene. In 1702 proprietary government came to an end in West New Jersey without any noticeable display of anguish on the part of Friends, who were soon reduced to a permanent minority as a result of defections, the influx of outsiders, and the union with East Jersey. At about the same time the Quakers became less than a majority in Pennsylvania. The solidarity of the religious community had already been ruined by the Keithian schism and the Lloyd-Logan struggles. Though Friends retained a majority in the legislature for years and tended to smooth over their disagreements until there was one "Quaker Party," they gave up attempts to make government more than a means of manipulating interests.[27]

By 1705 Indian relations and the regulation of Negro servitude in Pennsylvania had ceased to be influenced by religious ideals. The failure of the prohibitory tax on slaves in 1712 was the last blow to reformism in politics, and the death of Hannah Penn in 1727 brought Quaker dominance in the Governor's Council to an end. During Queen Anne's War, even the policy of strict pacifism in the Assembly gave way before a sense of political responsibility or before pressure from London. Threatened by the loss of office if the affirmation privilege were ended, Quaker legislators voted for military supplies, and some even followed James Logan in his justification of defensive war. Pennsylvania government ceased to be a demonstration to the world of how different a state could be when conducted by men who were attentive to the Light Within. The rise of a Quaker element willing to compromise on the peace testimony saved the province for their brethren, who were spared persecution through tampering with the affirmation privileges, through tithe or militia exactions, or through interference with the legal standing of their religious Society and its affiliated corporations and endowments.[28]

The Quakers in the city government of Philadelphia and the colonial legislature escaped attack for several decades after the end of the early Holy Experiment. The aldermen of the metropolis virtually co-opted one another, and Quaker politicians felt no great threat from the non-Quaker opposition which gradually coalesced with the interests of the Penn family to form a Proprietary party, as the sons of William Penn deserted Quakerism. The Penns and their chief executives came to rely increasingly on Presbyterians, Irish "newcomers," and some of the Anglicans to oppose the Quaker politicians. The latter added to their voting strength by German support, used the Yearly Meeting as a ready-made caucus, and pulled together a set of interests that made them invincible at the polls.[29]

Political events revolved around such vital economic matters as paper currency and taxation. No question of social reform remained, nor even much sense of obligation to mitigate common forms of misery. Quakers in the Assembly, far from distinguishing themselves for benevolence, passed harsh settlement laws and required masters to give sureties of thirty pounds when they freed slaves in order to keep them from becoming a public charge. The lawmakers tried to put the burden of support for the poor on the users of servile labor, but succeeded in transferring it more and more to private charity. By the middle of the eighteenth century inadequate tax levies induced the legislators not to raise more money, but to authorize public Overseers of the Poor to receive private contributions. The drift away from governmental action proceeded to an extreme, under requests from philanthropic Friends, when the Assembly allowed a private association virtually to supersede regular officials in Philadelphia in 1766.[30]

Friends in politics did not pretend to do more than preserve liberties, especially in the religious sphere, in addition to carrying out their regular duties as legislators or judges. Often they were men of substance, born and bred to a station in society which naturally carried with it a political career; their power began to appear to them as a rightful inheritance from Penn and their ancestors. More and more they supported measures for military defense provided the purpose was veiled with vague descriptions; less and less often were they prominent in Meeting affairs. As Samuel Fothergill disdainfully analyzed them, they made "a profession of religion which was partly national, which descended like the patrimony from their fathers, and cost as little." Their compromise with the world and the pointlessness to which the Holy Experiment had been reduced stimulated a constant opposition to them among Friends, though the clamor for reformation remained muted until the middle of the eighteenth century.[31]

The sentiment against worldliness flared up dramatically during the Great Awakening and just at the time when French machinations in the west touched off new demands for military precautions. Among the younger men whom wealth and family position destined for political leadership there appeared some determined to bring compromise to an end. They believed that a day of reckoning approached. John Churchman, one of their coadjutors in the Quaker ministry, put their chiliastic tendency most plainly when he began to prophesy new onslaughts of persecution and wickedness, more terrible evils, after which a day of righteousness would dawn. The death of John Kinsey in 1750 removed the outstand-ing compromiser, who had been a power in the church as well. Is-rael Pemberton, the younger, his successor as Clerk of the Yearly Meeting, turned out to be a very different sort of man. Intense and passionate, an aggressive champion of virtuous consistency rather than a smooth-tongued master of accommodation, he earned the nickname "King of the Quakers." Yet he exerted his influence in politics almost entirely from out of office. He had unsuccessfully challenged Kinsey's leadership in 1744, years before his own single term in the Assembly (1750–1751), and once he had the prepon-derance of Quaker sentiment behind him, stopped running for election.[32]

Israel Pemberton's two brothers served as capable lieutenants in the campaign against compromise. James stayed in the Assembly steadily except when the French and Indian War made it impos-sible for him to reconcile it with his conscience. No tool of his elder brother, he followed his own judgment to different conclusions on many political issues, but remained faithful to the moral ob-jective. James became a notable minister in his later years, after the Revolution had ruined his political career. John Pemberton lacked his brothers' unconquerable itch to be in public affairs — he even lacked their acumen in business — and after a few only mildly successful ventures in trade, devoted himself to the service of his church, most conspicuously as Clerk of the Meeting for Sufferings at Philadelphia.

Israel could not follow either of the relatively simple patterns of life which his brothers traced. He could be neither the self-pos-sessed merchant-legislator nor the religious leader. In fact, the man who led the conscientious Friends to consistent pacifism and warmly backed the withdrawal from politics was a born fighter and politi-cal juggler. His inner turmoil was revealed in his letters. Occasion-ally he gave way to feelings which in theory he abhorred. In his business career he once sought a contract to supply the British navy vessels in North American waters; at an Indian treaty he vented his outrage on discovering that Lieutenant Governor Denny would not send some of his guard to drive away Indians molesting farms near Lancaster.[33]

Backing Israel Pemberton and his brothers were numerous capable Friends in various walks of life. Two Philadelphians played important parts in a surprising number of reform moves, John Reynell, a generous merchant, and Isaac Zane, father-in-law of John Pemberton. Anthony Benezet, Zane's collaborator in a report on education to the Yearly Meeting of 1778, had less to do with politics, but wrote pamphlets for moral reform and exhibited to his fellow Philadelphians a life of service to others and divorce from worldliness without any excessive displays of self-denial. The purity and consistency of his character stood out in sharp contrast to the paradoxes and turbulence of Israel Pemberton's. Three spiritual leaders, John Woolman, John Churchman, and Daniel Stanton, used their abilities to urge Quakers to stricter piety. Though Woolman's literary skill preserved his reputation far better than those of the other two, contemporary comments made it plain that they had at least as great an impact in Meeting or private "dealings." Among the English backers of the reform movement, John Hunt, a London merchant and member of the London Meeting for Sufferings, figured prominently, but was overshadowed by the Fothergill brothers. Dr. John Fothergill, a fashionable physician in London as well as a member of the Meeting for Sufferings there, used his professional acquaintance with the Penn family, Lord Granville, and other important people, to disentangle the Pennsylvania Quaker leadership from the webs of misunderstanding and misrepresentation of their actions in the imperial capital. Samuel Fothergill, whose career was less dramatic, possibly had even greater importance.[34]

In the spiritual adventure of his great American tour of 1754–1756 Samuel Fothergill joined his efforts to the Pemberton leadership. His role in the Quaker revival was similar to that of George Whitefield in the Great Awakening. In fact, Fothergill thought of his work as related to that of the great evangelist; he was inwardly drawn to travel to places where Whitefield had been or was about to go. Both men spoke strongly for rejection of pride, greed, and worldliness in general; Christians could hardly differ on such points. Both warmly endorsed practical piety in doing good to fellow men, even Negro slaves; both found the confines of a single denomination irrelevant to much of what they had to say and eagerly embraced opportunities to address audiences drawn from all the colonial sects. Whitefield, who received a warm reception from Congregationalists and Presbyterians but not from his fellow Anglicans, had to ignore denominational lines far more than Fothergill, who met only small and relatively silent opposition within his own church.[35]

Furthermore, Fothergill, unlike Whitefield, had a strictly sectarian mission to his fellow Quakers: to promote a stronger and more united church, more highly controlled by inner discipline. The Quaker threw his weight behind the reassertion, essential to the revival in his church, of the traditions and distinctive ways of Friends, the morality of *No Cross, No Crown*, and the quietism of George Whitehead. Like native reformers, who "began to be animated afresh to encourage one another in the great and necessary business, & to plead for the observance of the [Quaker] Law and the testimony, according to the strength & understanding they were favoured with," he decried superfluity in dress, furniture, and manners. He endorsed their campaign for sabbatarianism, sobriety, the strict use of Quaker speech, greater attention to the training of the youth, and a renewed tightening of the inner bonds of the religious fellowship, especially by the use of written replies to queries in Meeting and "the ancient practice of Family Visits." Since he recommended the same institutional measures wherever he went, in effect he strove for a new tightness in the organization of his church and for uniformity of institutional details throughout the American Yearly Meetings.[36]

In different colonies Fothergill found a wide variety of conditions in the church and had to labor for the improvements most necessary to each. "Maryland," he reported, "is poor; the gain of oppression, the price of blood is upon that province — I mean their purchasing, and keeping in slavery, negroes — the ruin of true religion the world over, wherever it prevails." A shrinking number, Maryland Friends had succumbed to the world in many ways, the most scandalous, because most unusual, being acquiescence in paying tithes. As a result, Fothergill wrote, "there is a great scarcity of ministers. I know not more than two in the province on whom is the heavenly stamp visible, and they are neither negro keepers nor priest payers." Virginia was almost as bad, and North Carolina was also falling into decay. South Carolina had only two meetings; one at Charleston, where there were "few who bear our name, and fewer who deserve it," though the other still kept the faith. Throughout the South Fothergill preached against slaveholding, and in Maryland against tithe-paying as well, in addition to making the more general call for devotion to God.[37]

In New York and New England, attachment to ease, wealth, and respectability were the obvious targets, but the fellowship also required organizational strengthening. In Long Island declining fervor in the older generation had led the large number of Friends into sorry straits, while in Rhode Island "this world has intercepted their prospect of a better, and greatly impaired that beauty which once rested on them, or their ancestors." Fothergill "met with few places more discouraging." "Divisions and contentions, the certain companions of the spirit of this world," spoiled the scene in Nantucket. In the rest of Massachusetts, "what open persecution could not effect, [had] . . . been too fully accomplished by the caresses and favours extended to Friends there." [38]

Fothergill accomplished little in New York, but he did manage to get a few rudimentary steps taken in New England. As a result of his efforts arbitration was started to end the dispute at Nantucket over paying a special tax in lieu of military services; he encouraged the leaders of all Monthly Meetings to define the membership, repair the long-standing neglect of records of births and marriages, and prepare publicly to deny the casual and unconscientious people who attended meetings for worship and were commonly thought to be Friends whenever they threatened to bring scandal on Quakerism. He urged a cautious approach to the whole business, but some Monthly Meetings began a general canvass of those either claiming or reputed to be Friends, expelling those with birthrights to membership who no longer lived consistently with the principles of the parents, and inviting those without any formal right of membership who behaved as Friends to apply for the Meeting's care. In the New England Yearly Meeting of 1755, Fothergill successfully promoted the use of written replies to the queries

in both business and select Meetings. In a burst of zeal the Yearly
Meetings registered several minutes in favor of greater dedication
to God and "reviual of Zion['s] Ancient Beauty" by renewed
strictness in adherence to Quaker ways. The revival did not catch
fire at this time in New England, however. Further signs of it did
appear in 1763, but a decade after Fothergill's visit, John Griffith
reported that the land was still "overspread with darkness." Though
there was much good ministry at the Yearly Meeting of 1766, he
warned Friends against deism. Furthermore, the business and select
Meetings were falling into corruption despite the use of the queries, for the youth remained prone to indulge in "undue liberties,"
and the elders remained attached to terrestrial things, "having so
much to do in government affairs, many of them got into offices,
friendships, and parties, as well as into the profits of this world." [39]

Throughout America, however, Fothergill found cause for hope
in "the rising youth," among whom were "some of the true Hebrew race, who have heard the alarm of the heavenly trumpet, and
come out of their dens and caves." The right-minded were most
numerous in the old Quaker colonies. In spite of much "chaff" in
New Jersey, the "valuable body of Friends" of true spiritual concern made Fothergill "trust [that] things are upon the revival."
But Pennsylvania afforded the exciting prospect of a game for
big stakes with a good chance of winning. There, "A noble seed,
of several classes respecting age, though too few of the aged
amongst them, [had] . . . kept their garments clean, and . . .
hands . . . strong." In spite of decline, generation by generation,
from the time of the first founders, in spite of ease, affluence, and
decay of discipline, "yet was there a noble remnant" . . . "here
and there to be discovered in the Country, not without individuals
in the great City, who united in Spirit and saw the necessity for
stirring & searching." Surely the hopeful condition of the church
owed nothing to human means. "As every like begets its like, a generation was likely to succeed, formed upon other maxims" than
true spiritual principles "if the everlasting Father had not merci-
fully extended a visitation, to supply the deficiency of their natural
parents." [40]

As a visitor of quite different kind sent to aid in this holy work,

Fothergill discovered at Philadelphia in the Eleventh month, 1755, that although he had expected to return to England, "It hath pleased the holy Master of our assemblies to clothe my spirit with a concern for the renewal of the discipline in his family." John Churchman and William Brown, he felt, were to join in his work, which would include a visit to every Quarterly and Monthly Meeting in Pennsylvania. The crisis of Indian border raids had just arrived and Friends were in turmoil, unable to agree on what to do.[41]

After the alarming portent of an earthquake on the eighteenth of the Eleventh month, Fothergill preached to "a vast congregation . . . on this awful visitation, with the sword new destroying upon their borders." His text was Revelations 19:5,6, and his words proved "memorably advantageous to some" and "melting to many hundreds present." His listeners were ripe for spiritual quickening. "Agitated with fear and horror, they felt . . . their want of a good foundation in this time of need": "Great is the perturbation of many, and plain the discovery now made, of the unprofitable professions many have made of religion, in this time of clamour and rumour of war; few know where to have recourse for a rock of defence, and a safe hiding." They had been relying too much on earthly means and political authority. To them Fothergill proclaimed, "Praise our God, all ye his servants . . . for the Lord God omnipotent reigneth." [42]

Translating this message of comfort into practical measures proved difficult. Fothergill and others could confer with the Quakers in the Pennsylvania Assembly to urge them to act more consistently with their religious profession, but no provincial policy could alter the geography of the imperial conflict between France and England. An Englishwoman thought everything would work out for the best if only the politicians "could be free to resign, and live in peace and quietness, minding their own business, as Friends do everywhere else." Quakers in Pennsylvania and New Jersey had already begun to think that they should wash their hands of public office. The trouble was that abandoning Pennsylvania to outsiders would bring neither peace nor quietness, but the heartbreaking indignity of compulsory militia laws and distraints for war taxes in the province that had once been their refuge. Nor were men like Israel Pemberton willing to admit they were unfit to govern and concede that their sect's ideals were visionary notions which would subvert the state if any fool or knave was allowed to put them into practice.[43]

While they doubtless liked having the legislature safe from Anglican or Presbyterian control, Friends officially could not approve either "fearfulness of sufferings" at the hands of their political enemies or the continuation of their brethren in office. In fact, the perpetuation of a "Quaker Party" run by Franklin and the *politiques*, flouting Friends' principles and making a name for itself largely by the ingenuity with which it thwarted the moves of the Lieutenant Governors, was especially repugnant to the moral reformers. The attitude of the spiritual purists came out in full force in a printed epistle "To Friends on the continent of America," issued by the Meeting of Ministers and Elders at the General Spring Meeting in Philadelphia, 1755, before Braddock's defeat or the onset of border raids. Although indirectly worded by the man who was probably its principal author, John Woolman, it aroused bitterness among Friends less devoted than he to absolute consistency.[44]

The epistle attacked participation in government as a way of inducing men to put their trust "in man" instead of "the Lord alone." It declared that Christ's mission had been "to repair the breach" between God's government and men "made by Disobediance, to finish sin & transgression, that his Kingdom might come." As a result, Friends had no rightful part in "National Contests productive of Misery & bloodshed." Rather, they should submit to God's rule, trusting their safety to him instead of a majority in the legislature, and partake in the spread of the "Spiritual Kingdom" which will "break in pieces all Kingdoms that oppose it." If, in order to help the establishment of the "peaceable kingdom," Christ "should give us to taiste of that bitter cup which his faithfull ones often partook of, O that we may be rightly prepared to receive it!" The conscientious Quaker politician must look to his own future safety and not shirk his obligation to prepare the way for the kingdom of Christ on earth by devoting himself instead to political or other worldly ease. It was clear that the establishment of the peaceable kingdom was not being forwarded by the Assembly of Pennsylvania. Perhaps, as the Ministers and Elders hinted, the salvation of religious liberty by staying in the government was a way to damnation by attachment to an unsanctified objective. Christ's freeman might have to be man's bondsman. He who bore no cross would receive no crown in glory.[45]

Friends' thoughts went back to William Penn and the hopes for a free and reformed society which had been entertained in the seventeenth century. Dominion could be rightly conducted, Woolman thought, only in divine love. In it "the Endowments of Men are so employ'd, that the Friend and the Governor are united in one, and oppressive Customs come to an end." But Quakers should not hold public office if they could not attain Penn's state through love of God and neighbors. It was wrong for political Friends to store up wealth for themselves, seek worldly honors, oppress the poor, practice cruelty to animals, and make government a clever juggling of interests (by definition, kinds of attachment to the world), as Penn the pamphleteer for toleration had demanded, and not a Holy Experiment as the Founder and Governor had proposed, as well as the "Planter" and Thomas Budd. Philadelphia Quarterly Meeting contrasted the Penns of 1755 with William, and gave praise to him not for his political sagacity, but for the quality which imparted virtue to his political career, his "benevolent and disinterested love of mankind." [46]

Most Quaker Assemblymen were not swayed by these strictures and, as 1755 went on, plunged deeper and deeper into compromise and amoral partisan maneuvering. They voted appropriations for military preparations to be paid with taxes so designed that the Lieutenant Governor would veto the bill. He performed as predicted. Border raids broke the stalemate in the fall, however; the Assemblymen accepted a deal with the Penns which permitted an appropriation to go through into law. Soon a noncompulsory militia law went on the books, and the province set to work building its first forts. Pennsylvania spent public funds on a larger scale and more openly than ever before to prepare for war within its borders. Friends faced the question of whether to pay their taxes or not. Many were willing to pay "mixed" taxes (partly to foot the bill for military expenses), but the thoroughgoing adherents to pacifism were not. Quaker judges waited on their benches for the day when they would have to order distraints on Friends' property to satisfy the assessments. The Yearly Meeting of 1755 could reach no generally acceptable stand and left the taxation problem to the deliberations of two committees. When they met in the Twelfth month, they could not agree after several sessions, and those who were willing to compromise with political necessity finally walked out. Twenty members (and Samuel Fothergill, with trepidation) remained to sign an epistle declaring their principles against paying the taxes and asserting that their stand was necessary for the preservation of their church. The implied slap at the compromisers could almost be heard. The legislators and magistrates, enemies to the peaceable kingdom founded on a unity in love with all animal existence, had proceeded to practice cruelty to Negroes by enforcing the slave system and to political opponents by wrangling over public affairs, until finally they had become willing to support war against their ancient brethren the Delawares, to oppress their fellow Quakers, and thus to attack the church, the body of Christ, itself. These deserters from the Truth were making their political affairs more important than morality and the unity of their religious Society. The reformers, if their first pronunciamentos may be put together, had managed to link an enlarged benevolence to all animate creation with strict pacifism and sectarian solidarity.[47]

The militia law, offensive as it was to Quakers, was disallowed in England at the instigation of the Penns, who wanted a compulsory military requirement like those in other colonies. Proprietary politicians had urged that the affirmation privilege be wiped out by Act of Parliament, to drive Friends out of office. In the face of such drastic possibilities, Dr. John Fothergill, aware of the sentiments of his brother Samuel, Israel Pemberton, and the moral reformers generally, reached an understanding with Lord Granville, President of the Privy Council. Doctor Fothergill, essentially speaking for the Meeting for Sufferings, agreed to use his influence to persuade Quakers to resign public office in Pennsylvania if Granville would do his best to stop any measure to close such offices to them permanently by abolishing the affirmation privilege. The

Meeting for Sufferings sent John Hunt and Christopher Wilson to convey the message and apply their persuasions to the officeholders to reinforce those of Samuel Fothergill, Woolman, and the rest of the reformers on the western side of the Atlantic.[48]

Immediately after news of this arrangement reached Philadelphia and after the Lieutenant Governor proclaimed hostilities against the Delaware Indians, James Pemberton led a group of six Quakers who resigned from the Assembly. Their departure gave seats to more compromisers and Franklin-led Anglicans. Other Quakers refused to stand for re-election when their terms expired, but those who kept their seats thereafter, including Speaker Isaac Norris, refused to budge, even after the arrival of Hunt and Wilson. In 1758, after some Friends in office had compromised the reputation of Truth on a grand scale by backing Franklin's wagon caravan of military supplies to the West, a business which successfully tempted many rural brethren to earn a little money by carrying equipment for war, the Yearly Meeting finally took a stand, making persistent officeholders ineligible (like the slave-traders) to participate in business Meetings or contribute to the stock. It appointed a committee to persuade officeholders to resign. A series of advices, minutes, and paragraphs in epistles followed in later years, expounding and enlarging the disapprobation which the Meeting felt for those who would not withdraw. In 1760 the new Meeting for Sufferings of Philadelphia Yearly Meeting appointed a committee to labor with the Quakers in the Assembly, again without success. Instead of acting as the lever to pry them out, the Meeting for Sufferings became in effect the liaison between the Yearly Meeting and the semi-excluded politicians, the powerful but not untainted Quaker *politiques*. The Meeting had to do its best to avoid ill repute to the church arising from the acts of those whom neither it nor Monthly Meetings could do much to control.[49]

This convenient arrangement, by which the Yearly Meeting kept its good name by renouncing the Quaker Party, yet made the best of its success at elections for the benefit of religious freedom, could not satisfy the reformers indefinitely. It smacked too much of "fearfulness of sufferings," not to mention deviousness. Above all, it accomplished nothing toward reasserting Quaker policies in the goverment of Pennsylvania. The moral reformers had proposed benevolence, justice, and indifference to worldly success as principles on which to ground new positive actions. Under the leadership of Israel Pemberton, the strict Friends tried to put together a program which would meet these requirements and preserve the church at the same time.

X

Coping with the Crisis of 1755

THE French and Indian War brought a crisis to Pennsylvania's Quaker community which had as a people taken responsibility for public affairs. It was true that Friends had sat out wartime emergencies successfully before. In 1755, however, the situation had two new features: the Proprietary family, the Penns, for the first time used their power vigorously to oppose pacifism and the Quaker Party; and even more important, the fighting broke out inside the province. Since the French, who had recently seized control of the upper Ohio River valley, incited and equipped the hostile Indians, the war in Pennsylvania was part of a general imperial conflict between France and Great Britain, and consequently could not be dealt with as a military problem purely on the local level. Friends confronted an unavoidable decision: either they must adjust principles to temporal facts, as James Logan and the *politiques* had done, and contribute to the military success of the British empire; or they must depart from the traditional political course. Since the bulk of Friends, acting in the religious Society, denounced any step toward compromise and called for a revival of sectarian strictness, the religious fellowship came under external attack as never before, while experiencing at the same time internal strains from the dissident minority. The few Quakers who chose to be "realistic" and remain in office included a large part of the rich and powerful element in the church.

The split between the compromising and the strict Friends broke apart a combination of political and economic power with a large, highly organized religious body which had insured the primacy of the Quaker community during the first half of the eighteenth century. Some possibility existed after 1762 that the old combination might be restored. James Pemberton himself sought and won election to the Pennsylvania Assembly again. But the moral revival excluded the compromisers forever from leadership in Meetings, the Quaker politicians remained susceptible to the same split as in 1755, and the crises that led to the American Revolution created new occasions for division. No matter where their political sympathies lay, strict Friends could not conscientiously back measures which plainly tended to produce rebellion.

In the years after 1755 the leaders of the moral revival and the withdrawal of strict Quakers from political office had to propose measures to protect the religious Society from internal and external threats. They also remained determined to preserve as much as possible of their sect's heritage of primacy in Pennsylvania and to justify their political morality by some course of action which would demonstrate its practicality to the public at large. No clear body of ideas or precedents guided them, for they had exhausted the possibilities in the old theories and observed what a hollow ruin the first Holy Experiment had become. When the Quaker leadership had split, wealth remained fairly equally divided, and the men who would have expected to take positions of authority in the province if they had not supported the withdrawal hoped to enjoy power still. They tried to accomplish all of their objectives by a combination of measures which foreshadowed the course later to be found acceptable in Pennsylvania and ultimately in the rest of Quakerdom as well. The Pemberton policy substituted the united power of the religious fellowship for the strength lost by squeezing out the compromisers. Energies spent in earlier years on public affairs, as such, began to operate inside the religious Society, making it — very cautiously at first — an agency by which Friends could influence the province. This result, of course, had to be achieved outside public office, and largely outside the formal structure of Meetings. But by closely banding together behind a program inspired by benevolence, justice, and the moral revival generally, Friends could protect their religious fellowship, make its inner unity better than ever, and perhaps even turn the tables on their political adversaries.

To protect the religious fellowship, Friends created the Meeting for Sufferings of Philadelphia Yearly Meeting. The name obviously came from the old London Meeting which had been set up under similar circumstances to cope with persecution under Charles II. But the word "suffering" carried additional meaning in the moral revival. Benezet, like Woolman, thought Friends in general had become too much attached to property and wanted to keep political power to preserve it. Instead, he said, they should obey the teachings of Christ, imitate his example, and "*resist not evil*, but rather suffer wrong and thus overcome evil with good." If they did so, they would find "the only way to true rest and peace," though they would "often become a prey." However, they should "not only . . . rejoice thereat, but even . . . shout for joy," and not succumb to the temptation to limit this to suffering "in what is generally called religious matters." There was "no distinction in Christianity between civil and religious matters," for those who followed Christ should lead pure, holy lives for his sake. They must renounce interest "and suffer matters to go contrary to" their judgments, for human wisdom could not judge correctly and should defer to the truth in the great mystery of "God becoming man, letting the whole power of hell spend its wrath upon him, and being finally made perfect through suffering." The wisdom of God had made this "the means ordained" by which to root out sin and evil.[1] Hell was spending its wrath on the frontiers. The religious Society, through the Meeting for Sufferings, took on itself as the mystical body of Christ, the distress of its members and became more nearly perfect in compassion and aid to other pacifist sufferers.

The new Meeting was set up very cautiously. From the start it was an agency of the Pemberton leadership, and many Friends suspected that it might become too powerful. The first steps toward its creation were taken at the Yearly Meeting of 1755, which occurred between Braddock's defeat and the beginning of border raids. This was a time of apprehension which gave the moral reformers a sudden advantage over the less zealous Friends. Israel Pemberton marked the occasion by setting down an unusual minute commemorating the "Divine Condescension & favour extended to us thro' the several Sittings of this Meeting." He followed it with one even more unusual, setting the adjournment to the regular time the following year "if the Lord permit." It was plain that perilous months lay ahead. The Yearly Meeting directed a committee on the accounts to confer with a committee to correspond with Friends in England and visit the Monthly Meetings, the two to deliberate on further measures to meet the emergency.[2]

Out of their conferences in the last month of 1755 came the controversial epistle on mixed taxes. At the following Yearly Meeting time, they reported that in view of the "distressed State of the Frontier Settlements of these Provinces" and the likelihood that outlying Quakers would be exposed to danger and need help, the Yearly Meeting should call for an unprecedented £1000 addition to the stock. To advise on its use a committee should be created, composed of twelve men chosen by the Yearly Meeting from among members living in or near Philadelphia, and four men to be chosen by each of the six Quarterly Meetings. The report proposed that the "Relief Committee" should direct where the money should be spent for the benefit of sufferers from Indian raids; and in addition, the committee would correspond with the London Meeting for Sufferings and represent Philadelphia Yearly Meeting in all matters except disciplinary cases. These extensions of the "Relief Committee's" powers showed clearly that it was to be no ordinary arm of the Yearly Meeting. To study these proposals, the Meeting in 1756 appointed a new committee, which officially pulled the cloak off the proceedings by firmly recommending the establishment of a Meeting for Sufferings according to the specifications for the "Relief Committee." The Yearly Meeting accepted this report, stipulated that the new Meeting might not make any decision on faith or discipline, and required that it present its minutes twelve months later, when the question of its further existence would be decided.[3]

The twelve members of the Meeting for Sufferings appointed by the Yearly Meeting were nominated by the representatives of the Quarterly Meetings. They were to be the active part of the new Meeting. The four men from each Quarterly Meeting were to guard against any sinister domination of the Yearly Meeting by a city oligarchy, but were not expected to attend very often. The Meeting was to sit at least once a month, and more often when business required it. Among those appointed to the active core were the stalwarts of the moral reform movement, John Reynell, Isaac Zane, Israel Pemberton, Anthony Benezet, Daniel Stanton, Owen Jones, and the first Clerk, James Pemberton. The same twelve were appointed again in 1757 by the same process; thereafter, the formality of an annual renewal of the Meeting for Sufferings was gradually dropped.[4]

The new Meeting went to work hearing appeals for help from Quakers and others who were attacked by Indians or who left their homes to avoid raids. It sent money and clothing, and offered to place children of refugees in foster homes or apprenticeship in safe parts of Pennsylvania. It was a short step to move on from relief to an inquiry into the causes of Indian hostility. The Meeting negotiated with the Friends of Hopewell Monthly Meeting to compensate the erstwhile native owners of the land and offered to help locate the claimants.[5]

The Meeting's objectives expanded quickly, for it supplied English Friends with information useful to the defense of the sect against the machinations of the Proprietary family. Significantly, the Meeting for Sufferings prefaced its minutes with a collection of documents relating to the withdrawal from the Assembly, an event which had occurred before its creation. Later, it tried to persuade Quaker legislators and judges to resign, though with little success. It transmitted regular reports to its London counterpart explaining what it regarded as the truth behind the latest attacks on Quakers in Pennsylvania.[6]

The emergency passed with the successful negotiations with the Indians and the departure of the French from Ft. Duquesne. The Meeting for Sufferings, with its main work reduced to getting a few displaced Friends back on their farms, turned to procuring religious books to explain Quaker beliefs, in their native tongues, to Pennsylvania Germans and deported French Acadians. It also assumed a duty which for lack of a more appropriate agency had in the past devolved upon Philadelphia Monthly or Quarterly Meeting, the task of presenting statements of Friends' views to provincial officials when the Yearly Meeting was not in session. The Meeting for Sufferings soon found an occasion to call on Pennsylvania to prohibit stage plays for the "good Order, Morals, & Prosperity" of the colony.[7]

While spokesmen for the Quakers called for improved public morality, the Monthly Meetings set out to purify the religious community itself. The safety of the church depended, in the long run, more on the members' faithful adherence to their common standards than on donations of cash to refugees from border farms. Church government had to be strengthened at all levels. The Yearly Meeting distributed to the subordinate Meetings many copies of Robert Barclay's *Anarchy of the Ranters, and other Libertines*, an old treatise endorsing tight organization. Without resorting to novel techniques of discipline, Meetings could make extensive changes simply by closer attention to standing rules. Minute books were brought up to date, revealing unfinished business. Friends were urged to attend mid-week meetings for worship. The Overseers of conduct began to act more vigilantly. The preparation of written replies to the queries on behavior of the membership was a device used to stimulate a thorough inspection. A good deal of opposition to written replies turned up for several years after the Yearly Meeting had first called for them, but all the Monthly Meetings eventually fell into line. Cases of improper conduct were discovered which had remained unnoticed for years. Dealings were begun more promptly on new cases.[8]

The ardent reformers devised or promoted other improvements in the routine of loving mutual surveillance. Meetings developed the use of committees to visit some category of the brethren — parents, to urge greater diligence in holding their children and apprentices to the form of Truth; slaveholders or those who remained in office, to convince them of the evil of slavery or the inconsistency of officeholding with charity; or even the entire membership, to prevent backsliding and reinforce spiritual qualities before weakness made deeper inroads. The Yearly Meeting, partly inspired by exhortation from England, renewed recommendations of the "ancient practice of Family Visits" for many years after 1751. Earnest Quakers, mindful of their conviction that a minority of the pure in heart had failed to save the early Christian Church from a general apostasy, were determined to prevent a repetition of this tragedy in the Society of Friends by using the "saving remnant" of the "truly concerned" to fullest advantage in the committee work.[9]

Inevitably, programs of visiting raised the question of defining membership. The answer was renewed emphasis on conscious adherence to Quaker principles as qualification for membership. As a rule, the Monthly Meeting's care extended to members only, but since lists had not been kept, and the assumption had become widespread that children of members had a birthright to be considered Friends, the rule was hard to apply. It became harder as the campaign for consistency, and the temptations to misbehavior presented by the political events between 1756 and 1783, resulted in entire or partial disownment for more and more Friends. Children of couples, one of whom had lost his or her right of membership or had fallen from good standing to the point of being excluded from the service of Truth under one of the minutes of 1758, were in an uncertain position. Philadelphia Yearly Meeting decided that such children should be under Meeting care only when they themselves, or one or both of their parents, made formal application. In this way fellowship with Friends became more a matter of positive belief and less one of hereditary or "ethnic" affiliation.[10]

Paradoxically, the attempt to draw the line of membership to leave out the lukewarm led to some extension of surveillance to those who had been excluded. Its interests required the Society of Friends to keep an eye on those whom it would not embrace but who were commonly considered Quakers. Obdurate officeholders who took the affirmation instead of the oath were generally regarded as Friends even though barred from the service of Truth or wholly disowned. The behavior of such brethren, or even the acts of their children with cloudy birthrights to membership, reflected on the reputation of Truth. The Yearly Meeting therefore advised Monthly Meetings to "have a watchful Care over them," giving such advice and caution as might be necessary, and to proclaim their lack of membership when their conduct threatened to bring reproach to the Society.[11]

The reformers strove for greater consistency in behavior on the part of all their brethren — use of the second person singular pronouns and of numbers instead of names for days and months; elimination of unnecessary ornamentation in dress and household goods; and refusal to take oaths or doff hats before magistrates. Strictness in "dress and address" became a more significant indication of spiritual growth than ever before; it proclaimed a will to reject attachment to the world which had been far less positive in the lax years of the 1730's and 1740's. Further, adherence to the externals of Quaker behavior meant putting on a uniform, like that of a soldier or monk, which both Friends and non-Friends could readily identify and which committed the wearer to make his acts a standard by which the public would judge his religious Society.

Conspicuous sectarian uniformity would conduce to the welfare of the church by fostering faithfulness to the discipline. But it could brighten the Quaker name even more if it made the Society a moral force for the good of the whole community. The events of 1755 posed a challenge: how to apply such a force to a state which was going to war, when strict Quakers were preparing to yield their strong positions in public office. Friends again proclaimed the moral unity of the body politic and called on it to repent and reform both collectively and individually. Philadelphia Monthly Meeting, in one of the increasingly common manifesto-like petitions, told the Representatives in the Assembly in 1761 that "Righteousness exalteth a Nation & sin is a reproach to any People," and went on to point out some kinds of "Profaneness & Vice" which lately had been on the increase, and which the legislature should do something about so as to avert a new visitation of divine wrath.[12] A petition was a feeble gesture in itself, however. To find better ways to exert a force for good in politics it was necessary to go back to fundamentals.

Disinterested benevolence and justice were the basic requirements of virtue in government. By comparison, legal and constitutional niceties mattered little. Selfishness and love of ease had enslaved too many Quakers to false interests. If they were to turn aside the tomahawk from their own scalps, they would have to revive the ancient virtues of their sect. Though this remedy was enough in Virginia and Massachusetts, it did not suffice in Pennsylvania, where Friends had tried to conduct the government and were being given the blame for the province's misery. They had to make a positive, unified program out of individual rectitude. They must turn to "true charity . . . the love which was in Christ," and if it prevailed in them, they would promote "practical Christianity," deny self in order to "relieve the oppressed," "bind up the broken-hearted," and try constantly to honor God with their "Substance." Benevolent acts and the whole program of moral rejuvenation inside the church would prevent future calamities like the Indian warfare which had begun in 1755.[13]

For the benefit of the church and external society alike, individual Quakers could take a consistent stand on their relationship to the government. The issue of "mixed" taxes which had proved so divisive to the leaders of the sect was an opportunity to reassert the primacy of divine law, as when Woolman in 1758 discussed his refusal to pay taxes for support of war with a Quaker Justice of the Peace in Pennsylvania who believed in the social contract theory. Civil government, the magistrate argued, was an "agreement of free men," by which they obliged themselves "to Abide by Certain Laws as a Standard." Refusal "to Obey in that Case" was therefore the same "as to refuse to do any particular act which we had Covenanted to do." Woolman replied with several reasons: that no man should bind himself to agree to the orders of any persons in advance, but if he did so, ought not to obey orders to work evil, since "an active Obedience in that case would be Ading one evil to another." He should, rather, take the contracted penalty.[14]

More characteristic of Woolman's distinctive Quakerism, though, was his belief that rational argument would be far less effective to win over his adversaries than means which would not start a contest of wits. Accordingly he held that when a Quaker refused to obey governmental authority, his life should be such as to make it plain that his motives were not wicked, and the refusal should be made in such a way as "may tend to put men a thinking about their own publick Conduct." As introspection would be the surest way to bring divine guidance to political life, a responsible citizen should encourage it in public officials, both to do his duty toward them as fellow men and to bring the standard of disinterested benevolence to prevail in the affairs of the civil community.[15]

Woolman's way, however, was not Israel Pemberton's. Although the saint from Mt. Holly pointed the direction to effective techniques of persuasion and although private societies to do good offered a means of influencing the civil community without entanglement with worldliness, the strict Quakers who gave up constitutional political power wanted to find a way to carry on their public policy by other means after 1755. Under Pemberton's leadership they resorted to an organization neither private, public, nor part of their religious Society, but something of all three, the Friendly Association for Gaining and Preserving Peace with the Indians by Pacific Measures. Through this formidable society the strict Quakers hoped to redeem Quaker pacifism in government by stopping Indian raids without military measures, help the frontiersmen and secure the release of captives, embarrass the Proprietary government and take policy-making out of the hands of the Lieutenant Governors. If consistent Friends were to bear the opprobrium for the defenseless state of the province, they would have to have a voice in the executive functions in order to show that, properly carried out, their legislative program would work. Anything less "would be a Concealing ye Testimony we ought to bear to the World." In their efforts to seize control of negotiations with the Indians and in their use of the provincial archives, the leaders of the Friendly Association went beyond the possibilities open to the legislature.[16]

This grandiose adventure in pressure politics did not enjoy the open sponsorship of the Society of Friends. The Yearly Meeting of 1756 deliberated taking such a step, but decided against it, partly because of the civil nature of the Association's activities. The Meeting merely expressed an "Approbation of the Design" and recommended that Friends in general help to carry it forward.

In spite of this decision the Friendly Association and its business of "a civil Nature" occupied the Meetings for Sufferings of Philadelphia and London steadily for several years. Proprietary officials sent charges to England against the Quaker organization; so as to protect the reputation of Friends, the Meeting for Sufferings in Pennsylvania — in its words, "to obviate the Prejudice of our Adversaries against us" — decided to have "an impartial Account" collected and put in the hands of the London Meeting for use as it might see fit. At one time, the London Meeting presented an address by the Friendly Association to the Proprietaries, though the more usual line of communication between the Pennsylvanian society and the English authorities was one outside organizational channels, through letters from Israel Pemberton to Dr. John Fothergill. If the Friendly Association was not strictly a part of the Quaker church organization, it had an advantage not given to other private societies, the services of the Meetings for Sufferings.[17]

This semi-official connection could not be duplicated when the Friendly Association dealt with the provincial government. Yet it had to achieve something more than the role regularly open to private citizens. The primary purpose of the Association was to mobilize the generosity of individual Friends to force the colonial officials to make peace with the Indians. Therefore, from the start the Friendly Association had to get permission from the provincial government to carry on its activities. Consent was won or extorted by a variety of tactics, but the total result was that the Lieutenant Governors could not hold treaties without members of the Association attending and imposing on the unwilling officials their ideas of how the business should be carried out.

The Pembertons and their colleagues plunged into efforts to steer the executive branch of government in April 1756, when Lieutenant Governor Robert Hunter Morris set scalp bounties on the Delaware Indians. Willing to suffer mixed taxes, though not in silence, strict Quakers reacted to the imminent declaration of war by sending Israel Pemberton and Samuel Fothergill to Morris with a statement protesting the policy as neither expedient nor humane. The remonstrance having had no effect, the Friends returned to declare their willingness to spend money freely to help the province pursue a peaceful course. After Conrad Weiser, an experienced provincial interpreter and agent, recommended an attempt to negotiate, Morris allowed the Quakers to hold conferences at Israel Pemberton's house with Indians at that time in Philadelphia. Messages then invited Delawares living in the Susquehanna Valley to a parley. Israel Pemberton first planned to make his sect mediators between the province and the hostile natives, and pay the bills for the conferences, but Morris, in a panic, tried to go in all directions at once — to rearrange the Quaker-sponsored conference immediately after declaring war, probably hoping to win the political advantages of making peace for himself. This offended Sir William Johnson (the British official whose business it was to conduct Indian relations north of Virginia), who also had been trying to negotiate an end to Delaware attacks on Pennsylvania. It soon became clear to the Pembertons that they would have to find better ways to manipulate the Lieutenant Governor.[18]

On July 22, 1756, before Lieutenant Governor Morris went to meet the Delawares at Easton, Israel Pemberton called a meeting of interested Friends. To the enthusiastic crowd he disclosed a plan to raise a large sum of money to be invested, the proceeds to be used to give presents and perhaps other benefits to the Indians in order to ensure their friendship to the province. Over £2000 was subscribed, some of which was soon spent on gifts to the natives gathered for the parley or "treaty." Since the Lieutenant Governor had very little to give, having nearly run out of funds by the time the conference began, he had to present the gifts and mention the donors, even though he would not let the Quakers who accompanied him bestow them in person.[19]

At Easton, Israel Pemberton found a Delaware spokesman, Teedyuscung, whose talents for public speaking and braggadocio made him potentially useful and whose mingled admiration, envy, and hatred of English colonial society made him highly susceptible to the overtures of the Quakers. The Indians were accustomed to the standard procedure which always put them on a level inferior to that of the British negotiators. Tribal representatives had to acknowledge themselves "children" to the father, the king of England. They had to put their marks on papers — meaningless to them — which recorded their latest concessions. They had to make various gestures of deference to royal officials. The Friends at Easton, however, went to call on the Indians and received them as equals when they repaid the courtesy. Provincial officials, and later Sir William Johnson, found this subversion of protocol highly annoying. Visiting back and forth, however, turned out to be merely the start of efforts to raise the Indians to a level with the whites in negotiating peace.[20]

The first treaty at Easton arranged no more than a tentative armistice. The dignitaries sent belts of wampum to "ten tribes" in the hinterland, urging peace. By the time the Indians congregated for the second treaty, several new developments complicated the situation. A new Lieutenant Governor, William Denny, had succeeded Morris. Denny was a more pliable man, a fact that worked to Israel Pemberton's advantage. But Sir William Johnson, and the new military commander for North America, Lord Loudoun, ordered Pennsylvania to stop independent negotiations for peace. (Johnson had persuaded a Susquehanna Delaware chief to make peace with the British Empire on behalf of his fellows even before the first treaty at Easton.) Fortunately for the Quakers, the Proprietary officials did not want to surrender Pennsylvania Indian relations to anybody, even to the king's officers. On the advice of his Council and Assembly, Denny decided to go to the second treaty, though Johnson's opposition imperiled his authority there. Seeing that things were going as well as he could expect, Israel Pemberton called a meeting which converted the rough organization of Friends and their Indian fund into the Friendly Association. Quakers, who had been discovering a "multitude of difficulties . . . to excuse their pockets," took renewed enthusiasm when official wrangling made continued Indian negotiation doubtful. So at the last minute, though there was no time to attend to the formalities of choosing officers and making by-laws, the contributors to the fund agreed to form a permanent society.[21]

With his backing thus improved, Pemberton rushed to Easton to confer with Teedyuscung, who was to have a special role in carrying out the program of the strict Quakers. Operating on the theory that the Indians' friendship depended on strict justice in all dealings, but especially in land sales, Israel Pemberton found a way to eliminate the importance of the French in stirring up the warfare. The actions of a foreign power, after all, were beyond the control of anyone in Pennsylvania; but if grievances against the colonial regime had impelled the Indians to side with the French, then righting the old wrongs should win them back. Thus the imperial conflict between France and Great Britain could be ruled out as an excuse for military action by Pennsylvania. It remained to find out what frauds and misunderstandings lay behind the border raids. So Teedyuscung — once Pemberton and Franklin had induced Lieutenant Governor Denny to ask for the causes of the Indians' hostility — was to reply with a catalogue of injustices done to his fellow tribesmen. Between his own powers of persuasion and the gifts (including liquor!) purchased with £500 from the Friendly Association, Pemberton brought Teedyuscung to cooperate.[22]

The Delaware's grievances included a surprising list of alleged land frauds, some of which were charged to New Jersey. Among the more important ones, he claimed that a large tract beyond the Kittatinny Mountains acquired by the Penn family in 1749 from the Six Nations of the Iroquois had not been theirs to sell. But the claim that quickly became the symbol of all the rest was against the so-called Walking Purchase. On this point Israel Pemberton's prompting had been seconded by that of an influential Delaware, Nutimus, who had protested the Walk much earlier. The purchase itself had been negotiated in 1686, though the Indians were left in possession of the ground until such time as the Proprietor might have use for it and mark the limits. The transaction was reconfirmed in 1737, after some slick diplomacy, and the crucial dimension of the tract, a day and a half's walk, was forthwith stretched as far as cleared roads and champion walkers could make it. The few Delawares whose lands were transferred to the Penns by the Walking Purchase, had thought the original cession extended less than half as far along the Delaware River. They were angry in 1737 and remained so for years afterwards. Nevertheless, when Teedyuscung protested the injustice and claimed that it was one reason for the Indian raids, there had been eighteen years for the swindled Delawares to cool off. The Indians' spokesman introduced one new dimension to the complaint: he went beyond the cavils over details of the walk and claimed that the papers produced for reconfirmation in 1737 had been forged and did not represent the agreement of 1686.[23]

The resurrection of the controversy over the Walking Purchase fitted well into the Quakers' interpretations of the cause of the border raids. As they did not fail to point out in 1756 and later, there had been scalping parties on the land swept into the Walking Purchase, as well as on one of the other tracts about which Teedyuscung charged injustice. It was probably no accident that the wife, son, and daughter of the man who performed the walk in 1737 were slaughtered in one of the raids. Those of Teedyuscung's followers actually displaced resented sales made by the Iroquois sachems after the early years of the Holy Experiment. For several decades after the final departure of William Penn, Pennsylvanian officials had accepted and relied upon the Six Nations' control over the natives of the province. As the power of the Iroquois weakened, the politicians at their capital, Onondaga, had become increasingly willing to sell land they could not dominate south of the New York border. Shuffled around by New Jersey, Pennsylvania, and the Six Nations, scrambled with remnants of other eastern tribes and the Shawnees farther west, many Delawares whose families had lost their rights to hunting lands had finally been driven to hostility against both the English and Iroquois. The antagonism erupted into warfare when the French seized control of the Indian trade in the Allegheny and upper Ohio River valleys. But it was the land question which supplied the point at which the desires of the aggrieved Indians and the strict Quakers met. Teedyuscung's complaints, then, were something more than political contrivances — though they did not account for the actions of all the scalpers — and had been put into terms dictated by the interests of Franklin's Quaker Party and the moral statecraft of Israel Pemberton.[24]

Lieutenant Governor Denny tried to meet the complaints in the usual way, by giving additional compensation and wampum belts to the Indians, who would then put their marks on documents. Teedyuscung refused to accept such a solution, however, advancing considerations which may have been suggested by the Quakers.

He said it was too late to satisfy the Indians by more trifling gifts; the land had increased in value and the payment been delayed, so "Interest is to be added." Furthermore, he could not arrange terms until all other Indians involved had been consulted. So this treaty, too, failed to bring the business to an end.[25]

For Israel Pemberton and the Friendly Association it was merely the beginning. Disputes raged over the Walking Purchase for six years. At a meeting held in Philadelphia after the second treaty at Easton, the Association adopted its proper title, The Friendly Association for Regaining and Preserving Peace with the Indians by Pacific Measures, agreed on a method to choose officers, and took care of other formalities. The leaders of the Association began to broaden their operations almost immediately. They wrote to enlist the aid of pacifist German congregations. They began thinking of longer-range benefits to the Indians, making a modest start by agreeing to find a master wheelwright to train an Indian boy who would also be sent to school for four years at the Association's expense. By spring 1757, they explained to some Mennonites that if land were allotted to the Indians and the proper people were encouraged to assist them in settling together, "not only a foundation may be lay'd for the future welfare of many of them by impressing on their Minds by Precept & a corresponding Conduct the great Truths of the Christian Religion, but they may be as a hedge to us to prevent ye incursions of French Indians." (Evidently they were not to be taught pacifism!) [26]

But Israel Pemberton had no intention of letting the political advantages won by Teedyuscung's grievances go unimproved. In January 1757, he and William Callender asked the provincial secretary, Richard Peters, to let them inspect the records on land purchases. If common knowledge supplied a few good subjects for complaint, perhaps inside information would reveal more. Peters refused, and for the time being the Quakers could do nothing. Sir William Johnson and other imperial officials, while in favor of a negotiated peace, were exasperated with the Friends' behavior at treaties, which they considered an infringement on the royal prerogative to conduct relations with foreign powers.[27]

If the Indians were foreign powers, however, they could certainly keep their own records of peace conferences and the agreements reached at them. Accordingly, in July 1757 leaders of the Friendly Association stepped into new roles at the third treaty of Easton — as agents for the Indians! After consulting with Israel Pemberton, Teedyuscung demanded his own clerk and chose Charles Thomson, a master at a Quaker school. Thomson (presumably with assistance) reduced the Indian's vague list of alleged land frauds to a carefully worded document. Then Teedyuscung demanded that the Proprietary officials produce their documents for public inspection, presumably by his Quaker friends (in other words, to meet Pemberton's earlier request), before transmitting copies of them to King George for his impartial adjudication. The Quaker on the Governor's Council, William Logan, argued for letting at least the deeds be produced. Added to the threats of the Indians, who went on a binge while the Council deliberated, the persuasion of Logan led to the disclosure of the deeds, which Thomson copied. Only one imperfect specimen (a copy of a deed made in 1718, with some blank spaces left at crucial points) could give any pretext for new charges of fraud. The Indians, many of whom were from places outside the disputed areas, found this inspection of records tedious and time-consuming when they had come fully intending to conclude peace. Teedyuscung therefore had to agree to end warfare and restore prisoners, while Israel Pemberton pursued his own policy, demanding to see the Proprietary correspondence on the land purchases. In fact, he believed the Proprietary officials "perfidious" in their revelation of only part of the documents and their promise to do justice to the Indians. He kept trying to unearth further evidence of fraud until 1762, at one time offering to exchange secrets with Councilor Logan.[28]

Though Israel Pemberton's political manipulations became more extensive and devious, the Friendly Association, guided by the ambitions of Teedyuscung, took a small but forthright part in carrying out some agreements reached at the third treaty at Easton, which opened a door to private benevolence. Teedyuscung had presented a plan for a permanent Delaware preserve that had roots both in his own desires and in Quaker ideas of proper Indian relations. Wishing to solidify his control over his followers by introducing English ways among them, he asked that Pennsylvania set aside a large tract in the Wyoming country on the upper Susquehanna to be theirs forever, build a suitable town of permanent houses, and send several Christian missionaries, teachers, and advisers to coach them in the new way of life. Provincial officials hoped to make the settlement a buffer against tribes farther north and west while Quakers looked forward to making the Indians Christians and civilized men.[29]

The provincial Assembly appropriated money for the buildings and sent a team of men to get the work done. Winter halted operations by the end of November 1757, and the Friendly Association appointed a committee to make sure that work would be resumed as soon as the weather permitted. Nevertheless, delays occurred, and finally, after Teedyuscung had gone to Philadelphia to demand action, it turned out that the government had no funds to send a new expedition to build the houses; so the Friendly Association lent money for the purpose, and at last, in May, a party of men went back to the Wyoming country. Although many Friends declined to go on the grounds that the workers had been given protection by a troop of militia, Isaac Zane set out after the main expedition to see that the work got done. Several alarming incidents presently stopped it, however. First, one of the masons was killed by a hostile Indian. The timely arrival of Zane and some overdue supplies kept the remaining workmen from leaving, but after fresh manifestations of opposition by neighboring tribes, the men could not be induced to stay any longer. They finished only eleven houses and cleared and plowed some fields on which the Indians planted their belated crops. Nevertheless, construction of the village came nearer to completion than the rest of Teedyuscung's plans. The teachers of civilized ways were never even chosen, though the Friendly Association searched for suitable candidates to offer to the Pennsylvania authorities.[30]

While this unedifying example of provincial ineptitude was being displayed, the Assembly addressed itself to regulating the Indian trade, a more important question, and one that could be decided without money in the treasury. The business was put in the hands of a board of commissioners, headed by John Reynell, treasurer of the Friendly Association, charged with the duty of licensing traders, keeping liquor from the Indians, and setting up stores to be run at a profit for the province. Prices were to be set at a reasonably low scale which independent traders would have to match, while the provincial stores earned money to pay the expenses of Indian treaties and hire schoolmasters to go to the natives' villages. This system, while copied from that of Massachusetts in several particulars, nevertheless embodied the wishes of the Friendly Association and drew the praise of Sir William Johnson, who knew that the allegiance of the Indians would not be held unless they could count on being able to buy the coats, blankets, kettles, knives, and ammunition they needed.[31]

All things considered, the Friendly Association was working out well in the spring of 1758. It could claim an essential role in preventing war on the Delawares, stopping the border raids, introducing the ways of civilization to some of the Indians, and fostering a wise trade policy. For the time being, Sir William Johnson had a good word for Pennsylvania's course of action, and Brigadier General John Forbes, the new commander sent to oust the French from the forks of the Ohio, soon had an opportunity to applaud Israel Pemberton's information and his recommendations for employing Indians in the campaign. On one occasion Pemberton had the satisfaction of sitting with the Governor's Council while Forbes insisted on following his advice against the will of the Proprietary officials.[32]

But Pemberton's newest policy of bringing Indians from farther north and west — especially the pro-French elements in the Six Nations — to a conference to make peace with Pennsylvania led to the reversal of the Association's fortunes. A general treaty, the first in a series, opened in late September 1758, at Easton, while Forbes neared Ft. Duquesne. At once the Lieutenant Governor stole the Quakers' thunder by canceling a particularly noisome land purchase made from the Iroquois in 1754. This proved the first step in re-establishing the pre-war policy of cordial dealings with the Six Nations and reliance on them to manage the Delawares. Pennsylvania no longer needed Teedyuscung to stop the border raids, and he was quickly relegated to a minor place, and with him his Quaker advisers. He tried to shore up his own prestige by demanding royal adjudication of the Walking Purchase. The officials in London, however, preferred to send the matter back to New York and put it in Sir William Johnson's hands. That official was ostensibly to hold only a primary hearing, but everyone expected that his verdict would be merely rubber-stamped on the other side of the Atlantic. Teedyuscung refused to agree to a hearing by Johnson, who he feared would take a stand to please the Six Nations. Thus the land fraud claims steadily became even more of a side issue than they had been in the summer of 1757. Teedyuscung reiterated his demand for a large permanent reservation, but Pennsylvania could not allow his request without denying the Iroquois' claim to the land. There was no point in doing that *after* the summer of 1758, since the western braves had deserted the French and would no longer be apt to strike Pennsylvanian farms by traveling down the Susquehanna.[33]

The time had come for the Friendly Association to shift its emphasis to pacific measures which would operate on a routine basis independent of the particular diplomatic strategy employed by Pennsylvania. The Assembly had opened the way to such useful services as trade and teaching when it had passed the legislation favored by the Association during the previous spring. But the Association showed surprisingly little inclination to undertake the work, even though suitable Friends declared their desire to serve as traders or teachers. Israel Pemberton could not persuade the Quaker organization to spend money from its treasury to stock the provincial stores even when the commissioners, who lacked adequate public funds, appealed to it for help. First at Ft. Augusta, on a small scale, and then at Ft. Pitt, in a much larger way, Pemberton used his own resources to enter the Indian trade. Part of the Friendly Association was willing to back the Ft. Pitt venture, but a stand against any project which looked toward profit prevailed after Pemberton and his agents, James Kenny and Samuel Lightfoot, had set out. A message instructed Pemberton that the £1500 worth of goods which he was trying to convey to Ft. Pitt might be used only as presents, if General Forbes should want them for that purpose, or as a stock for the provincial store (which had not yet been set up).[34]

Forbes thought trade much more urgent than gifts and approved Pemberton's plan to go into business at the forks of the Ohio. Pemberton reimbursed the Friendly Association and continued to conduct trade at the fort for the "honour of God & the good of Mankind." After clearing a modest profit, he retired from the field when an appropriation enabled the provincial commissioners to establish the government's store. Lightfoot hoped that the sight of honest men would convince the Indians "that happiness consits [sic] more in doing good to than destroying Mankind." Doubtless to help impress this message, Kenny, like Pemberton's agent at Ft. Augusta, remained to operate the provincial business. A pious and benevolent Quaker, he did his best to inject morality into the trade, to the great disgust of private operators, who probably were responsible for undermining the government's efforts by getting its shipments of goods between Ft. Pitt and the east bungled repeatedly.[35]

Influenced by the views of Forbes and General John Stanwix, and the excited interest of John Hunt in fostering an honest Indian trade, the Friendly Association soon repented of its opposition to Israel Pemberton. It did not, however, take any steps to safeguard the operation of the provincial stores. It satisfied itself by offering to send schoolmasters to teach Indian children at Ft. Augusta and by acting on a suggestion by Kenny that the time was ripe to supply instructors for the Indians on the upper Ohio. The Association had no Quaker to offer, but paid for the services of an eminently well-qualified Moravian, Christian Frederick Post, who soon departed for Ft. Pitt. The Indians proved less ready than Kenny had thought. Post soon concluded that "whan one come in thear contry, wear the Devell has his sead [seat] amongst them, & his scheaf governemend amongst them, it is som wad worser then to go in hoeal [hell], for ther the ar in schean [chains], & ounder govermend, boud her the leave as Lous Sperits, & The ar Beter annymis ageanst all wat god cammeands." Post's mission ended soon after it began. Kenny, too, despaired of accomplishing anything worthwhile and returned across the mountains.[36]

The Friendly Association had fumbled its most promising opportunities in the establishment of Teedyuscung's village, the trading posts, and the mission to the Ohio country. This failure may be set down, in part, to formidable opposition, but also to the return of Quaker apathy on Indian affairs after the border raids had stopped. In a more fundamental sense, it may also be ascribed to a failure of vision and to submission to worldly considerations. Certainly the Association kept providing money generously to redeem prisoners, to entertain Indians who visited Philadelphia, and to supply gifts at the various treaties held between 1758 and 1762; ultimately, it could boast of spending for these purposes "about Five Thousand Pounds . . . for the Service of the Public." These were simple acts to meet the requirements of the day. The Quaker leadership, however, had formulated its long-range policy in a way which proved too vulnerable to the diplomatic reverses which began at Easton in September 1758.[37]

In keeping with the original conception of the Friendly Association, an organization to give Pennsylvania an Indian policy which would ensure lasting peace, the Quaker leadership came to believe that probity in land transactions would not be enough; for the future the natives must be made secure in their holdings. The Ohio Indians opposed the establishment of English power at Ft. Pitt, fearing with good reason that it would lead to white settlement, no matter what the officials said. Pemberton favored both giving the Delawares a permanent preserve in the upper Susquehanna valley and ensuring the western lands to their natives. Without meeting such basic conditions, the dispatch of honest traders, missionaries, and teachers of European agriculture were no more than futile gestures. The western Indians, though slightly comforted by the Pennsylvanian laws and proclamations forbidding settlers and private traders to enter the trans-Allegheny region, developed little receptivity to white man's civilization. Teedyuscung himself delivered the last two blows to the Friendly Association's long-range plans: in 1761 he conceded to the Iroquois their former supervision over his Delaware followers and gave up his dream of an independent principality; in 1762 he yielded to Lieutenant Governor Hamilton and Sir William Johnson, who arranged a sizable gift in return for the withdrawal of charges of fraud in the Walking Purchase.[38]

Thereafter the Friendly Association was reduced permanently to giving gifts to Indians who visited Philadelphia and making kindly gestures to Papunahung and his Christian brethren. Although the British government in 1763 — perhaps on the suggestion of Israel Pemberton sent to imperial officials by Dr. John Fothergill — did establish a policy of preventing white intrusion into Indian territory, the prohibition did not prove entirely effective and failed to pave the way for missionary work. The Indian uprisings in 1763 and 1764 ruined the future for Quaker policy and put pacifism in lower repute than ever.[39]

The Friendly Association, without intending to do so at the outset, had attached its projects to the success in replacing Pennsylvania's policy of working with the Six Nations by a policy of dealing directly with the Indians inside the province. The substitution was indispensable to the Quaker program: there was no hope of abstracting Indian affairs from inter-empire conflicts while they remained in an imperial framework. In 1756, however, neither the difficulty nor the magnitude of the substitution could be seen. Then it was a question of getting the raiders to bury their hatchets, whoever they were or whatever the cause of their hostility. In the emergency, a private pressure group could induce provincial officials to set aside long-accepted practices. When the raids stopped and imperial officials began to act more effectively, the leaders of the Association found themselves tied to Teedyuscung and his projects, which, however well they fitted Quaker ideas, ran head-on into opposition by Johnson, Loudoun, and Forbes as well as the Proprietary interest in Pennsylvania. So the Friendly Association found itself in the thick of politics, working closely with the compromisers in the Assembly. The more useful possibilities for such benevolent acts as sending teachers and honest traders to the Indians, which Forbes and the Assembly offered the Association, became less important in its estimation than winning the big battle over policy, which seemed like a necessary preliminary to further endeavors.

As the public expression of the Quaker reform movement, the

organization which was to give social value to the revival of sectarian strictness and strengthening of the church government, the Friendly Association failed. The effort to inject morality into public affairs by controlling provincial policy had done nearly the opposite of what had been intended. Under the leadership of Israel Pemberton, the Association had dragged itself into sordid wrangling and political manipulation; it had made the strict Quakers join hands with the obdurate officeholders in the Assembly; it had become paralyzed when confronted with opportunities to do good to the Indians; in short, it had become hopelessly entangled in worldliness. When Teedyuscung submitted to Sir William Johnson in 1762, there could be no doubt that the leaders of the Quaker revival had suffered major defeat. Yet to those less personally committed to the battle than Israel Pemberton, it was a salutary humbling, a "taiste of that bitter cup" which would prove a purifying draught.

Private Societies to Do Good

A FTER the whirlwind of the Friendly Association had died down, strict Quakers realized that they had been hearing a still, small voice. It was possible to enhance the reputation of Truth and influence public affairs through private societies which did not depend for success on control of the government. Less power could be wielded in this way than by seats in the legislature or by an organization like the Friendly Association; but he who exerted worldly power was subject to its corrupting effects. Purity of motive, devotion to benevolence and justice, could survive only when men remained free to respond to spiritual direction from within themselves or their church.

When the Quaker reformers had smashed the barriers between the civil and religious spheres which had enabled Friends in public office to pervert the first Holy Experiment into an ordinary secular government and drag the name of Quakerism into amoral political disputes, the reformers had sponsored the withdrawal from public office. This step was necessary in 1756, but it was intended to detach Friends from an infectious legacy, not to remove them from the public arena. Some of the historical developments which had led to the political crisis of 1755, notably the decline of Friends to a minority in Pennsylvania, had earlier encouraged them to experiment with the voluntary society as a means to reach private ends. Though Quakers in Pennsylvania and New Jersey resorted to this form of social action at first without any ecclesiastical strategy in mind, by 1750 some of them had begun to see the usefulness of benevolent institutions to shield their sect from the mud flung by its enemies. Out of this perception the zealous proponents of purity of the church produced a second Holy Experiment to replace that which they believed had been hopelessly undermined. Friends could influence public affairs as private citizens through voluntary organizations, which were at first strictly separate from the religious Society, though some ultimately became its subsidiaries.

The novelties of the new Holy Experiment came out of, and greatly enlarged, the scope of charity in the private capacity. The old ideal appeared in the testimony of appreciation issued upon the death of Thomas Chalkley by his Monthly Meeting in 1749. His life had exhibited charity in many ways, in and out of Meeting, for in his spiritual awakening, "the Love of God influencing his Heart, and opening his Understanding, he became concerned for the general good of mankind." Though also "a Lover of Unity amongst Brethren, and careful to promote and maintain it," he showed "the Example of a Meek Courteous, and Loving Deportment, not only to Friends, but all others." [1] Chalkley had taken an interest in the Indians, spoken against slavery, and gone out of his way to help fellow white men during a long, adventurous life. Even outside his services in the church he had exemplified charity in his behavior beyond the demands of religious duty made upon Quakers of his day.

In the first half of the eighteenth century, charity, outside the church and the political arena, required chiefly individual, not group, action. Duty clearly called on a Friend to practice neighborly kindness, visit jails to pray with the prisoners, and give aid to the poor. By their nature, however, such actions left few traces. It is probable that Friends behaved much like their fellow-citizens — some were generous, some not. Though their principles endorsed personal acts of charity, and Meetings praised them, other Christian sects had approximately the same views, and Quaker devotion to in-group solidarity for years overshadowed concepts of duty to outsiders while the Meeting's help to needy insiders obviated the necessity for much private aid in the fellowship.

There is, moreover, little foundation for the idea that Friends were more systematic or calculating in private charity than others.

Israel Pemberton, the younger, sought out the poor and gave money or tuition to some whom he considered deserving. He took extraordinary pains to follow Penn's advice "to avoid *ostentation in our charity*"; little is known, therefore, of his far-flung benevolences except what appears in his correspondence with Friends who acted as his agents. Pemberton inspected the merits and needs of the poor before he gave aid; however, his practices in this respect hardly differed from those of non-Quakers, such as Cotton Mather.[2]

Another attitude was exhibited by Friend John Smith who could be very generous for thoroughly studied acts of charity, yet remarked in 1747 that he had never sent a beggar "away Empty handed." Smith's explanation of his policy of indiscriminate almsgiving fitted quite as well with Quaker beliefs as did entirely contradictory policies proclaimed by other Friends. He declared that "a fellow feeling of the Infirmities and wants of our Brethren — as all mankind are — is a duty, and not sufficiently practiced, without Administering Relief when in our power." Without justifying it on such lofty grounds, William Penn took a similar position in his handbook of piety, *No Cross, No Crown*, in which he advocated that Christians find recreation by going out to "relieve the necessitous, see the sick, visit the imprisoned, administer to their infirmities, and indispositions, endeavour peace amongst neighbors." Penn's secretary, James Logan, and Isaac Norris, on the other hand, warned Pennsylvania against encouraging the poor in "luxury, idleness and folly."[3]

Logan, as did others, liked the cautious course of making his benefactions in cooperation with the Meeting. At one time he gave a regular sum to a poor man as supplement to that paid by the Philadelphia Monthly Meeting from the stock. There were occasions, also, when Friends performed charitable acts for which their Meeting agreed to reimburse them. Especially after 1750 a few bequests of money to be given to the poor, regardless of their religion, were put in the hands of Monthly Meetings for distribution, and after the revival of concern over education, it became appropriate to make bequests for the use of schools or the education of the poor to be applied by a Meeting.[4]

Such developments, however, had slight significance compared with the entry of American Quakers, by the middle of the eighteenth century, into private societies to do good. In many respects they acted in this field, as in others, like their neighbors of different persuasions. The eighteenth century was a time when such undertakings enjoyed a vogue in the colonies as well as the mother country. Ingenious men devised many projects for the benefit of the community or merely the self-improvement of a group of club members, yet did not want or could not expect the sponsorship of existing religious or political institutions.

As a device for getting things done the voluntary association had a greater range of usefulness in the colonies than in England, though under more challenging conditions. In the Old World ancient foundations with rich patrons, endowments, and often charters of privileges from the crown, floated in a misty region, not plainly either private or public institutions, but examples to inspire and guide imitators. In the New World, however, all societies for social service had to start from scratch, with less reliance on old wealth or on the government. Leadership came from men whose standing in the colonial scale might be high, as in the case of Cotton Mather, or modest, as in the case of Benjamin Franklin, but who could never tap the money or prestige available on the other side of the Atlantic. In Boston and Philadelphia wide-open fields but undependable monetary resources awaited the groups of young men of education and substance, or just high civic spirits, who gathered to found a library, hospital, or club to stamp out vice.

Private initiative was not necessarily in opposition to governmental sponsorship in America, although it tended to become so. The voluntary societies undertook projects not because it would have been improper for the state to do so, but because disputes prevented political action, or because money could be more easily raised by private solicitation, or because they thought they would act more vigorously. Probably more important, by erecting a category of private projects, colonials could at least make themselves independent of the alien political control inherent in the British imperial structure. It was better, for instance, in Massachusetts, to establish voluntary fraternities to suppress vice than to rely on the ancient method which used the church and magistracy, when the latter fell to a clique centered around an Anglican royal governor and ceased to be subject to the moral pressure of the established Congregational churches. Colonials who sought private channels of action and tended to minimize governmental supervision drew confidence, inspiration, and even financial encouragement, from Englishmen with similar aims. In the mother country Dissent inclined toward "liberal" political theories which gave narrow scope to what government might legitimately do, after a rabidly Anglican Parliament had insisted on measures to enforce conformity. Dissenters were excluded from the universities, which were part of the old set of public institutions susceptible to control by government in just such matters as their religious requirements for graduation. Nonconformists founded private academies and charity schools, institutions amenable to the category of "private" as the political situation induced them to define it.[5]

Although Englishmen and colonials learned to prize the freedom to act without interference by the government or established church, they also discovered the power of private institutions. Corporations in England had long wielded public authority. Various political functions often rested in the hands of companies, by virtue either of traditional right or charter grant. Such community business as fire protection and the water supply frequently remained fields for private enterprise. Voluntary societies could undertake many projects which no political or ecclesiastical authority would carry out, without becoming enmeshed in the plainly governmental machinery.

As Pennsylvania Quakers acquired scruples against holding public office they found in lobby-like groups and benevolent institutions satisfactory alternative means to impress their views on governmental affairs. They had no desire to retreat into a sectarian shell. By the time the crisis of 1755 forced strict Quakers to stop running for election, complex and comparatively undramatic developments had opened a wide field for private societies.

Several changes since Penn's day had already encouraged Friends to think of governmental power as sharply defined and unsuited to deal with a large number of public purposes. Broadly speaking, these developments included the passing of a dominant Quaker element with its own program and the inability of the Pennsylvanians to eliminate control over their affairs from England. Long before the crisis of 1755 the main lines of change had been unmistakable. The Proprietary family ceased to serve Quaker sectarian interest after the death of William Penn's widow in 1727. Royal disallowance of provincial enactments and special instructions from the Penns to Lieutenant Governors injected exterior considerations into Pennsylvania affairs. Germans and non-Quaker British elements increased rapidly in the province, diluting Friendly influence as their numbers were felt in politics. Finally, party divisions and city-country disputes cut across religious lines, reducing the common interests among Quakers and hampering efforts to use the colonial government to foster social services.[6]

The rural-urban contrast was especially marked in the field of voluntary organizations. Most Quakers lived around Philadelphia in the countryside, where they remained in a healthy majority until the middle of the eighteenth century. Like other country folk, they took no interest for many years in social organizations other than in churches and schools. As a rule, to keep schools in session for more than an occasional winter was beyond their means; they had few ambitions that generated a demand for other private societies. These remained the concern of city-dwellers, who saw the need to build markets and wharves, put up street lights, fight fires and vice, or establish libraries. They wanted legal rights to do these things and only rarely could get money or privileges from governments controlled by the rural element in the legislature. In such projects, unconnected with religious affairs, Philadelphians had explored the potentialities of the private society as a technique of social action before Quakers turned to them for sectarian purposes.[7]

Friends had joined in such endeavors enthusiastically from the start. A distinct minority of the city's population from early in its history, they nevertheless held top rank as one of the "Peoples" composing it and took pride in the fact that some of their number had made, or at least seconded, numerous proposals for civic betterment. Friends were to be found among the members of Franklin's Junto, the founders of the Philadelphia Contributionship for the Insurance of Houses for Loss by Fire; in the various organizations for the advancement of useful knowledge which led up to the American Philosophical Society; in the Academy of Philadelphia, the Library Company of Philadelphia, the Union Library Company, Association Library, and, across the Delaware in the old capital of West New Jersey, the Burlington Library Company.[8]

In none of these organizations, however, was the denominational flavor as strong as it was in the case of the Union Fire Company. Until the middle of the eighteenth century fire-fighting had been simply a duty of the townsfolk, who were expected to cooperate informally to help put out fires, save movable property, and pull down the hopelessly consumed structures to prevent spread of conflagration. They had used the city's small fire engines if they could not afford their own. But community spirit had waned to the point where the carelessness of the firefighters required the city to make large outlays not for additional equipment but for the repair of what was on hand. This state of affairs continued until responsibility for fire-fighting had been assumed by several volunteer companies. The first of these, the Union Fire Company, was founded by a group of men, mostly Friends, in 1736. By 1750 several others had been formed, most of them also drawing their members from a single denomination or a national group such as the Scotch-Irish. The citizens apparently formed these private clubs because of the absence of a feeling of responsibility simply as a body of citizenry. In 1749 the fire companies began to cooperate in inspecting equipment and the water supply; by 1755 the Union Company began to give equipment to the city; and in 1770 several societies jointly hired a man to care for the privately owned engines. Civic unity had been recaptured to some extent through a confederation of societies, none bearing a responsibility except voluntarily, many representing a People.[9]

In the case of the Union Fire Company, the connection between Quakerism and the voluntary society came not from a religion, properly speaking, but from the church community which the faith drew together. In regard to other organizations the situation was less clear. In some cases, certainly, civic projects had no conceivable denominational relevance and appealed to an assortment of men who did not all belong to the same church community. The scientific societies attracted some notable Quakers who were abandoning their old beliefs and may have found in the new associations the door to new social circles. In at least one instance — when the Free School was disconnected from Philadelphia Monthly Meeting — the emergence of the separate organization diminished the activity of a religious organization in order to allow participation by persons of other persuasions. But quite possibly Friends received at business Meetings a special training for harmonious participation and for reaching joint decisions in clubs and societies.[10]

The more usual case was that illustrated by the Philadelphia libraries. At their founding, a group of diligent and prosperous tradesmen and craftsmen, bent on self-help, gathered funds to start the collection. The second and third of these societies were formed when the price of joining those already established rose beyond the reach of such men. The conditions of colonial life compelled them to use their own ingenuity and left them free to act. Even the opening of James Logan's library to the public, in accordance with his will, did not create a public institution which satisfied the thirst for books. The economic, rather than the religious, similarity among the men who established private libraries was decisive. The fact that in a given instance a number of the founders were Friends, was due to the likelihood of there being several Quakers among the diligent but not well-to-do tradesmen from which all were drawn, the likelihood of their knowing each other, the mutual trust which sprang from the religious fellowship, and, to a lesser degree, to their similar attitudes toward group action.[11]

Out of this background of experience in private societies without close ties to the Quaker religious fellowship came an understanding of what individual citizens could do which was applied in organizations of Friends to do good for outsiders. One of them was the New Jersey Association for Helping the Indians, a strictly

Quaker venture founded in Burlington in 1757. A New Jersey counterpart of the Friendly Association, it was mainly a philanthropy of a wealthy family named Smith which put up £119 of the total stock of £170, and supplied much of the effort expended. The objective of the Association was to buy a tract to be kept by a Board of Managers for the use of Indians native to the province who had no freeholds.[12]

The New Jersey Association had hardly organized before it found its plans short-circuited. The leading Jersey Indians formed part of the following of Teedyuscung, who presented some of their grievances at Easton in November 1756. The claims were examined at a conference at Crosswicks, but the Indians remained unsatisfied and appealed to Israel Pemberton in the spring of 1758. He wrote his cousin, Charles Reade, a prominent New Jersey Quaker, then secretary and chief adviser to Governor Francis Bernard, saying that New Jersey must settle the claims or expose the colony to further raids, and urging that the arrangements be made at the forthcoming general treaty at Easton. After General Forbes seconded the proposal, Governor Bernard adopted it, and both at the treaty and later spoke the language of the Friendly Association which Reade wrote into his speeches, calling for "Justice & benevolence" to the Indians and "to all Mankind." Governor Bernard then stole the thunder from the New Jersey Association by arranging with the Indians to use the money agreed upon in settlement of their claims to set up a trading post and buy a 3000-acre tract for them near Evesham. The Association therefore did nothing further about a reservation and died soon afterwards, another casualty of the cooperation of the Friendly Association and the Quaker officeholders.[13]

Less formal but more productive of results was the private relief given to the Acadian "Neutrals," people of French ancestry who had been deported from Nova Scotia in 1755, after they had refused to take an unqualified oath of fidelity to George II. The quota assigned to Pennsylvania arrived near the beginning of winter, with no prospects for self-support and facing a serious risk of epidemic. The circumstances of their coming as well as their condition on arrival made the provincial government the appropriate agency to take care of them, but the Assembly adjourned for two months without taking action. The Governor's Council chose the Quaker Anthony Benezet to act for it in supplying the deportees' immediate needs for food. He continued to attend to their wants as a more or less official representative for several years. The Assembly, still with a Quaker majority, met in February 1756, voted to reimburse Benezet for "reasonable expenses," and authorized use of public money for the Acadians' subsistence. It put them in the care of the public "conservators of the poor," with the understanding that they would be housed in an unused barracks. Four months after the Neutrals had landed, however, the expense of maintaining them (and a wish to comply with the original plan of deportation — to resettle them in permanent homes scattered in the provinces south of Nova Scotia) led the Assembly to adopt a scheme similar to those tried in other colonies, to distribute them among the four long-settled counties with the very practical aim of settling them on the land in the spring. Commissioners were appointed for each county and empowered to rent farms and buy suitable equipment for the Neutrals.[14]

The Assembly's decisions did not please the Acadians, and Benezet overruled the legislature with the aid of private backing from philanthropic Friends. Rather than require the Neutrals to live in the barracks, he gathered contributions for new buildings on land lent for the purpose by Samuel Emlen, later a noted Quaker minister. Nor would the Acadians disperse and leave the city to take up farming as intended by the legislature, but asked instead to be treated as prisoners of war. In some places the local Overseers of the Poor were unwilling to have them come. Inevitably, the Neutrals required more relief to go on living in the city, and money had to be advanced by generous Friends. It was not the intention of Benezet and his associates, however, that private funds alone should be used in this work. The Assembly continued to reimburse him until the end of 1762, although not to the full extent of the outlay.[15]

The Assembly tried to reduce the burden of expense and break down resistance to its policies by ordering the children of such

Nova Scotians as were unable to support them to be bound out to learn a trade and literacy in the English language, leaving only the aged, sick, and maimed in the public charge. Resistance by the Acadians was quieted by the arrest of five ringleaders. The new law, however, was not faithfully executed by the public Overseers of the Poor. Behind the scenes Anthony Benezet went on helping to frustrate the plans of the government by encouraging the Neutrals in their resistance to dispersal; at the same time, he expected the government to continue paying for their livelihood. When the Assembly finally refused to supply any more funds, and many Acadians were being supported by the city of Philadelphia, he gave new interest to teaching them how to earn their living, and gathered money from Quakers to help them as late as 1779.[16]

The Acadians' cause may have been a good one, but the efforts of Benezet and other Friends to promote it went beyond merely filling a gap left by government: Benezet aimed to preserve them as a separate group until the policy of deportation and scattering could be reversed. To secure the reversal Benezet and his associates obstructed the official policy as best they could. The only step they took which followed the methods generally accepted for private citizens was to collect money to help leading English Friends with influence in the imperial government to smooth the way to consideration of the Acadians' memorial to the king asking to be returned to Nova Scotia or to be sent to France.[17]

A less involved project, one in which no opposition to public authority arose, was the aid to refugees from Indian depredations late in 1755. Joseph Spangenberg, a Moravian bishop and missionary, sent a request for assistance for those at Bethlehem to Anthony Benezet, who had a number of relatives in the Moravian fold. With Friends Joseph Norris and John Pemberton, Benezet quickly raised £200 and spent it on clothes, bedding, and other necessities.[18]

The three Philadelphians put distribution of these supplies into the hands of Bishop Spangenberg, requesting only that preference be given to those "who have no resource at all but in ye Lord," that special pains be taken to seek out and aid a certain "Family of Quakers," and that the project be so managed "that it may be in no Degree to prevent or lessen the Assistance which you & your distressed Neighbours are to receive from the Governmt. in common with ye rest of the suffering inhabitants." Among the refugees were a number of Indians who had been converted by the Moravians and had settled with whites of the same persuasion at Gnadenhütten. The wagon-load of supplies, which was later augmented, had been intended to help these Indians as well.[19]

The solution of the refugee problem, of course, was not in a series of gifts. Benezet had two practical recommendations for the future: to gain the ear of the government by applying to Benjamin Franklin, and to resettle the dispossessed in safe territory. He suggested that either the government or "some of our Gentlemen who have considerable Tracts of Land between Bethlehem & the Mountains" could furnish the ground at low rent, and perhaps the province and its "charitable Inhabitants" could give money to buy equipment.[20]

The activities of the New Jersey Association and Benezet's projects for the Acadian Neutrals and the refugees from border raids were, like those of the Friendly Association, efforts to use private charity to influence the public and produce specific modifications of official policy. Unlike the Friendly Association, however, they did not depend on Friends virtually seizing control of the government. They were undertaken during the French and Indian War, when Quaker control of the Pennsylvania Assembly was being destroyed by the political efforts of old enemies and the upsurge of hostility on the part of rank-and-file Friends toward any of their brethren in office who sanctioned warfare or worldly political compromise. It was also true that these three charitable efforts were to aid non-Quakers, and the Meeting resolutely concerned itself with members only. Private organizations were the proper media for those Friends who thought it their duty to carry out virtuous policies until the government could be induced to adopt them. While meticulously refraining from illegal obstruction or the symbolic manifestations of defiance, the Quakers set projects afoot which treated government, and even imperial policy, with a kind of disdain. They created object lessons and took initiatives in a fashion that was, formally speaking, quite as "disorderly" as Benjamin Lay's.

These private projects, though undertaken by groups of men rather than by individuals, carried out Woolman's suggestion of how a Friend should treat public officials and the laws, and did so much more satisfactorily than the Friendly Association had. The Quakers who formed these groups hoped to serve purposes which were inappropriate to their religious Society, and had resorted to a new method of action by using voluntary associations, but remained firmly within Quaker tradition when they refused to let government determine their obligations to it as it pleased.

The private societies, created by men of "an upright Uniform life," inspired by motives of disinterested justice and benevolence, took the initiative in following better policies than the officials adopted. The laws might have been made constitutionally, but virtuous men should proceed to carry out their own program as best they could until their example led the government to mend its ways and reimburse them or supplement their efforts. Strict Quakers repudiated in government that devotion to the formalities of decision-making which they prized in Meeting. Indeed Benezet's behavior toward the provincial authorities in the case of the Acadians would have led to disownment if practiced against the Meeting.

The Quakers who took leading positions in the founding of the Pennsylvania Hospital and the Philadelphia Bettering House had more respect for formalities than Anthony Benezet. The older of these two institutions, the Hospital, was even more deeply entangled with the political fortunes of Quakers than the affair of the Acadian Neutrals. The Hospital was established as a reply to attacks on Quakers and their political party. In addition to its merciful work for the sick, it was to advertise the philanthropy of Friends, though non-Quakers, and even anti-Quakers, had much to do with its success. In the early years of both Hospital and Bettering House, an effective combination was made of Friends' devotion to the substance of morality in the benevolent act and the political, persuasive, and legal skills of men like Franklin, Richard Peters, and Chief Justice William Allen, Pennsylvania's leading lay Presbyterian.

The Pennsylvania Hospital, chartered by the provincial government in 1751, originated with Dr. Thomas Bond, who had been disowned by Friends in 1742 for taking an oath. He was put on the path to success by Benjamin Franklin, without whose help "there was no such thing as carrying a public-spirited project through," and who had himself never been a Quaker. Franklin raised money for the hospital by declaring to a reluctant Assembly, in which Quakers were a majority, that individuals could be persuaded to give a total of £2000. Opposition came from country members who did not believe that such a sum could be raised and voted to give the same amount when private contributions had passed that mark. This promise made it easier to open the purses of the citizens, and £2750 was soon subscribed. A large part of the money came from Quakers, and as the contributors of £10 or more, under the charter voted by the Assembly in May 1751, elected the Board of Managers, seven of the twelve first chosen were Friends in unity.[21]

The legally declared purposes of the institution were the "publick Service" of "restoring useful and laborious Members to a Community," the humane and "religious Duty" of "Relief of the Sick Poor," the segregation of those with contagious diseases, and the treatment — or at least the confinement — of dangerous lunatics. Further details of the hospital's splendid record of achievements, which surpassed the hopes of the founders, need only be alluded to here. It became the scene of medical instruction in accord with the best methods practiced at the time, collected a notable library and museum, acquired well-designed buildings, and maintained a good dispensary.[22]

Quaker participation in the support of the hospital had political and denominational motives from the start. Even though it had taken Franklin's maneuvering to line up Quaker votes in the Assembly for the charter and promise of financial aid, Friends soon claimed that this political support, like their generous contributions as private citizens, showed that their faith made them liberal backers of projects they could approve. In 1750 some bitterness had arisen over the refusal of the Assembly to vote money for defense of the frontier. So the hospital was to be a standing remonstrance against provincial opinion which might demand more of Quakers than they were conscientiously able to do for what was thought to be the public good. The new institution, which "remained in Quaker hands throughout the colonial period and for many years thereafter . . . became a sort of headquarters and rallying-point for the Quakers, as the College of Philadelphia did for the Anglicans." [23]

Philadelphia Friends expected that contributions would be obtained "from the several parts of the province," and were "not without hopes of some assistance from abroad." Gifts came from London and the West Indies in time to be mentioned in Franklin's "Brief Account" (1754). The prominent London Friend, Dr. Fothergill, for example, was in an excellent position to help and did so with "three Cases containing Eighteen different curious Views of various parts of the Human Body in Crayons framed & glaized; three Cases of Anatomical Castings, & one Case containing a Skeleton & Foetus," worth some £350, which formed the nucleus of the museum. A further gift of a book, which was later supplemented by the libraries of two native Quaker doctors, began the library. Fothergill undertook to collect contributions in England to pay for medicines purchased at the Quaker firm of S. K. T. Bevan. A London merchant and colleague of the doctor in the London Meeting for Sufferings sent the hospital a small fire engine in 1763, which supplemented donations of equipment by the Union Fire Company, and was later kept in order by the joint donations of several fire companies.[24]

In its organization and purpose, however, the institution was in no sense denominational; it was simply a hospital offering its services to the general public. The Presbyterian Chief Justice contributed heavily, as did the Lieutenant Governor.[25] The hospital, under the Contributors as a body politic, enjoyed a public trust and never deviated from its duty nor alienated the support of non-Friends after that support had been won.

As soon as the Managers were organized, however, they showed skill and spirit in making their business politically provocative. Their choice of a location for the building quickly fell on a lot owned by the Penn family as Proprietaries, and the Board dispatched a request that it be given the hospital as a gift. Lieutenant Governor Hamilton opposed the Managers in public and private, advising the Penns against the donation, which he thought would be unfairly used by Friends to improve their sect's reputation. The Proprietaries then offered to give land to a corporation, under a charter issued by them rather than by the Assembly, in order to prevent Quakers from having unrestricted control. The Penns planned to reserve to themselves, or, in their absence, to two of the three chief provincial officials, the veto of any by-laws made by the corporation. The Penns' version, furthermore, required that accounts be available to any of the subscribers or to four Proprietary emissaries at virtually any hour and to the public in an annual report printed in a Philadelphia newspaper. The feature which drew most open objection, however, was the proviso that if the property granted to the hospital were to be used for other purposes, title would revert to the Proprietaries. The Penns tried to use the occasion to defeat their opponents in the Assembly by making their cooperation conditional on support of a request for the repeal of certain Acts of the Assembly, and, as a last blow, substituted for the lot originally selected one in a location earlier granted to the town of Philadelphia as a park.[26]

The Managers respectfully declined this offer and opened their hospital in temporary quarters, the house of the late John Kinsey, former Chief Justice, provincial Attorney General, Speaker of the Assembly, and Clerk of the Yearly Meeting. There were several reasons for this choice, not the least of which was the fact that Kinsey, who had died with unimpaired reputation, left a scandalous legacy. His executors found that as a trustee of the provincial General Loan Office he had misappropriated over £3,000 of public money for his own purposes, fifteen times his annual salary as Chief Justice. The executors, who included the elder Israel Pemberton, frantically tried to salvage his good name by clearing a trackless financial jungle, demanding payment of every old debt and selling every asset they could find. To preserve the house from a sheriff's auction by associating it with an unexceptionable benevolent institution seemed like a good stroke for a reputation so near that of Truth. In addition, the move gave time to the executors to collect more cash and to let the scandal cool down before they had to announce how far short they had fallen in their efforts to meet the estate's liabilities. No doubts need be cast on the suitability of the house to the purpose, as no one involved — philanthropic doctors, charitably disposed donors, or Quaker politicos — wanted anything but success for the hospital. After giving it a trial, the the Managers took the mansion on a three-year lease, while the first wing of a permanent structure was under construction.[27]

For the first ten years of its existence, the hospital continued to be involved in provincial politics. As the early years went by the institution found itself forced to make more and more requests for funds from the government. Seventeen men addressed the Assembly of Pennsylvania in 1754, asking for the job of signing the proposed issue of "Paper Bills of Credit," an onerous task which had to be done by hand. They intended to donate whatever they earned to the hospital. No issue was made that year, so the new institution's political favor remained untested. Subsequently, on eight occasions before the Revolution, the legislature allowed wellwishers to support the hospital in this way. Such governmental favors became routine after 1762, but while the Managers remained in the thick of political warfare during their first decade, they had to endure a severe trial. In 1759, with Franklin unable to use his influence because he was in England on provincial business, and with antagonism between government and Quakers at a new peak, the Managers found it necessary to appeal to the Assembly for money. The legislature, no longer with a Quaker majority, gave only a small amount in the form of fines which might be incurred under acts to prevent the sale of adulterated flour and the export of "unmerchantable" timber. This evasive move threw the Managers into jeopardy, for by their charter they forfeited their rights if they alienated the capital given them by the province in 1751. As they had had to do virtually that already to keep going during the French and Indian War, the denial of subsidy opened them to suit by anyone with a grievance who was willing to risk his reputation by bringing one.[28]

The Managers, following Franklin's example, published an account of the hospital's history, together with an appeal for funds, in the *Pennsylvania Gazette* of July 12, 1759. They called attention to the utility of the institution, and advised the "humane" citizens of the "real and lasting Satisfaction" they would experience after giving money and being able to reflect on "having made such a social Use of the Favours of Providence, as renders them, in some Measure, Instruments which open a Door of Ease and Comfort to such as are bowed down with Poverty and Sickness." The good work of the hospital was also advertised as increasing the population and as particularly helpful in treating victims of recent fighting, as well as those who would inevitably be injured in a bustling trading center like Philadelphia. All these services together made the hospital "immediately tend to the Honour of the Christian Religion, and the Happiness of Mankind," in which good endeavor it had to rival the work done elsewhere. The appeal for donations received a reply which, though direct evidence of premeditation is lacking, suggests malice inspired by wit. Shortly after the Meeting for Sufferings had presented its unsuccessful petition against the founding of a theater for stage plays, and a few months after the Assembly's refusal of a subsidy to the hospital, a company of actors from London staged a performance of *Hamlet* for the benefit of the institution. The Board of Managers could not very well welcome the gesture, but, unwilling to see needed funds elude them, gave their enemies the satisfaction of reading an explanation of the terms of their charter in which it was revealed that the Managers had been given no liberty to refuse contributions! [29]

The hospital's troubles continued as long as the strict Quakers remained in politics through the Friendly Association. As soon as the Proprietary officials had secured the upper hand in Indian treaties — that is, once the Six Nations had re-established supervision of the Delawares, and Teedyuscung had withdrawn his charges of fraud — the hospital ceased to be the victim of the Proprietary politicians. On the contrary, the Penns suddenly gave it land and an annual contribution. Dr. Fothergill, who had grown critical of Israel Pemberton's policies, showed his relief at the collapse of the Friendly Association by making his first sizable benefactions to the hospital at the same time, though he had, two years earlier, plucked what became its biggest financial plum in the colonial period — the right to funds in the hands of trustees from the sale of assets of the Pennsylvania Land Company which might still remain unclaimed in 1770. Through the remainder of the eighteenth century the Managers continued to receive grants from Pennsylvania, private individuals of all persuasions, business firms, and the Penns, in spite of the fluctuation in the political fortunes of the "Quaker" Party. Essentially, the institution had accomplished its ends, in its benevolent and merciful business as a hospital, its function as a center of medical learning, and its demonstration of Friends' public spirit and true interest in the preservation of mankind.[30]

So great was the success of the hospital that when in the years after 1762 the city of Philadelphia needed new funds and services to provide for its poor, a similar organization was set up to supplement the work of the public Overseers. The Assembly granted a charter in 1766 to a corporation, to consist — as in the case of the hospital — of all persons who might contribute £10 or more, and have as officers a board of twelve Managers and a Treasurer. This corporation, too, consisted largely of Quakers. It was to take over the old city almshouse, build such additions or replacements as might be necessary, put up a workhouse, and supervise the operation of these facilities. The Overseers of the Poor were to collect poor rates and put the money, with all other revenues they received, in the hands of the Treasurer of the new corporation. The "divers persons, charitably disposed" were to raise £1500 by donations and subscriptions, supplement this sum by a loan of £2,000 on the old almshouse property and by further loans, if necessary, on other security. Unfortunately, the Managers undertook projects which required more money than came in from all these sources, and the province had to rescue them from embarrassment with large subsidies or special taxes in 1767, 1768, and later.[31]

Though the new agency did not, as planned, banish the financial burden of poor relief, it did get useful work done. The Managers opened a much needed new almshouse the year after their incorporation. This "Bettering House" held a large number of inmates of various sorts. About half did spinning, sewing, or picking oakum to earn most of their keep. As a philanthropic venture, it was a success from the start and grew better by constant elaboration of its services. It contained a school for orphans among the inmates. It developed a function as a hospital, in association with the institution which inspired it, specializing in maternity cases, thereby further enriching the city's resources for medical education. Happily, by the generosity of citizens (mainly Friends) and the fire companies, the "Contributors to the Relief and Employment of the Poor of the City of Philadelphia" got ahead of their bills and even reached a point where the Treasurer could supply funds to the public Overseers for their tasks of outdoor relief. The Bettering House, by the time of the Revolution, had also managed to enhance the reputation of the sect which backed it.[32]

By 1776 Philadelphia Friends were participating in projects to aid prisoners with provisions or loans (if jailed for small debts), restore the freedom of "Negroes Unlawfully Held in Bondage," or provide fuel for the poor.[33] Informal or at least unincorporated, associations for carrying out charitable projects inappropriate to the Meeting, had become a common feature of Quaker benevolence.

The appearance of this kind of activity has long evoked the name of Franklin, one of its outstanding exponents, who was a leader of the Quaker Party in Pennsylvania for several years after 1754. He put at its simplest and clearest the view that virtue consisted not in orthodox adherence to some standard, but in doing good to one's fellow men in a disinterested way.[34] His ingenuity, gregariousness, and methodical bent combined with this idea to find an outlet in societies to accomplish service or charity. He took a firmly antisectarian stand and supported Presbyterian, Anglican, and Quaker projects. But Friends found his spirit congenial. Perhaps more successfully trained than others for committee work — surely so in corporate responsibility for continuous attention to

charity — they met Franklin's organizational and methodical pro-
clivities with more enthusiasm than his ethics. While they did not
approach societies to do good in quite the way that Cotton Mather
had done — as a means of regaining control over a population
which was drifting out from under a particular religious influence
— there was some similarity.

In Pennsylvania the Quakers were turned into a minority by im-
migration first in Philadelphia. They responded by preserving civic
leadership in education (their endowment of a school, wrote an
Anglican competitor in 1698, "is in effect to blast my endeavors" [35]), turning a Meeting-founded school into an independent
chartered institution rather than close it to children of non-Friends.
Several years later, when the heterogeneity of population had
sapped civic solidarity to the point where it would no longer support a general willingness to lend a hand in fire-fighting, Quakers
took the lead in forming volunteer companies, usually based on religious or national patterns of association, to assume the public duty
of controlling fires.

On a province-wide scale, the shaken predominance of Friends
in the government led to efforts to found large charitable institutions to embody positive social purposes which Quakers thought
government ought to support instead of military preparation or
war. In the French and Indian War, further alienation of Quakers
from the good will of provincial society led to private activities
which had the effect of thwarting governmental enterprise. After
the war crisis, however, Quakers found in organizations to do good
a solution to the problem of retaining the kinds of leadership in
society which they wanted and thought it right to exert. They
learned to rely on public good will rather than on the kind of political contention that plagued the hospital in its early years. In these
philanthropic associations they could assume responsibilities but
not run the risk of being placed in a position, as a result of pre-
sumed covenanted unity with non-Friends, which would oblige
them to accept decisions in which they could not conscientiously
concur. The voluntary association similarly afforded an opportunity for them to have solidarity with society — either by joining with outsiders, as in the Pennsylvania Hospital, or by acting

213

side by side with like organizations formed by persons of other groups, as in the case of the Union Fire Company.

Societies to do good taught by example — that is, they taught non-Friends how to do good and think well of Friends. Having tried in the hospital venture and in the relief of the Acadians to influence the political system more directly, Friends brought harmony to society by resigning their attempts to control, a fact signified more by the donations of the Penns to the hospital than by the withdrawal of Quakers from the Assembly. The fact was symbolized in the seal of the hospital, received for use in February 1754. It showed the Good Samaritan, a man of a people whom the Jews despised as semi-alien and imperfect worshippers of Jehovah, turning the wounded stranger over to the innkeeper, with an inscription derived from Luke, "Take care of him, and I will repay thee." [36] In the parable, the Samaritan's mercy qualified him as a neighbor to be loved. The praises lavished on the hospital and Bettering House by visitors to Philadelphia in the Revolutionary period were the compensation for the defeat of the hospital Managers in 1759.

To some Quakers their new subordinate role was a humiliation, no doubt. Nowhere except in Pennsylvania — not even in New Jersey or Rhode Island — did Friends regard themselves as the social leaders by history and inheritance. Exactly because they believed they held this position as a people, however, the Pennsylvania Quakers remained determined to exert public leadership when the combination of their own increasing scruples and the hostility of the other peoples persuaded them to relinquish governmental responsibility. It was hard to stop striving for public honors, such as John Kinsey had won, and start wielding social influence by ostentatiously trundling wheelbarrows of food to the prison.[37] But the important thing was that Quakers found a feasible method by which to continue influencing the public, even though it meant giving up power and being content with persuasion and remonstrance. To make the change it took the pressure of circumstances, an upsurge of spiritual zeal, and the leadership of several extraordinary men, notably Anthony Benezet, Israel Pemberton, the younger, John Churchman, Samuel Fothergill, John Woolman, and Benjamin Franklin the non-Quaker.

The new role for Philadelphia Friends nearly left religious ends behind. The private societies supported by Quakers tacitly accepted Franklin's idea of virtue in the benevolent act, as well as his religious toleration. To care for the poor, sick, and imprisoned was not to serve the cause of Quakerism directly. The major attempt to advance distinctive Quaker ideals through a private society, the Friendly Association, had embroiled its promoters in provincial and imperial politics more than the hospital did, with much less satisfactory results. When Friends in Pennsylvania adjusted their aspirations and methods of participating in public affairs to the fact that they had become, like Quakers elsewhere, a minority in the body politic, they redirected their efforts to influence society at large into private organizations. In this form they brought forth a new Holy Experiment which could be carried on by other American Friends.

XII

Justice to the Negro

Out of the moral revival in Philadephia Yearly Meeting and the new version of the Holy Experiment came a set of conditions which enabled Quakers to make and carry out the final decisions to forbid slaveholding on pain of disownment. The changes in church government produced new ways to deal with slave-owners and a willingness to undertake a suitable program of care for the Negroes to be freed. Yet the forces which pushed Friends to their final stand against slavery did not arise exclusively from within their community or from its ordeal of 1755–1758. Outside help came from the political philosophy of natural rights, which entered a fruitful partnership with the ideal of justice that Friends had invested with such great importance in connection with Indian lands. From this union were born the ideas which gave Quaker opinion on slavery its final form and earned the widespread approval of outsiders.

The campaign to end slaveholding drew its zeal and techniques of persuasion from the general reform movement. The reformers' hostility to love of property and power extended to the anti-slavery movement. The renewed determination to preserve Friends' sectarian peculiarities made the "oddness" which could be charged against the man who adopted a new ascetic practice, such as eschewing slave labor, less painful. Or perhaps it made him glory in the pain. In either case, the positive duty of benevolence and "practical Christianity" which the reformers preached when decrying luxury, gambling, or unprofitable conviviality, could be readily interpreted to support measures to relieve the oppression of the Negroes.

216

The committee of visitors was among the instruments for moral revival which aided the antislavery campaign. First to labor with the slaveholders, later to see to the welfare of the freed Negroes as well, these servants of the religious Society took its decisions to those whose lives they affected. The study of membership rights contributed even more toward getting the campaign going. The reformers stressed full intellectual commitment to Friends' principles as a prerequisite to good standing in the Meeting. But even the extension of the Meeting's care to disowned officeholders, to guard the reputation of Truth against the slurs occasioned by reputed (but not actual) members in politics, worked to the advantage of the antislavery zealots. It was not so hard thereafter to contemplate extending the same care to a Negro non-Friend who had passed out of the Meeting's indirect jurisdiction by manumission from a member's household.

The political crisis in Pennsylvania which sparked the moral revival altered the Quaker community in ways which also facilitated the antislavery movement. Those most inclined to go along with the world's ways were deprived of influence in the Meetings, leaving the reformers and their hostility to worldly interests in control. The campaign against slave-owning and in favor of strict Quaker ways drove out still more. The intensification of the group activity of the church and the development of private benevolent associations increased Friends' tolerance for departures from established ways toward systematic action for others as a corporate rather than an individual concern.

At first, the antislavery campaign required a great deal of ordinary disciplinary labor. After 1755, and especially after the decision of Philadelphia Yearly Meeting in 1758 to bar from the service of Truth those who bought or sold slaves, the visits to slaveholders began on a full scale. Woolman's *Journal* recorded his efforts to persuade masters to free their Negroes. He had occasion to "bow down before the Lord," who helped him preserve "Calmness under Some Sharp Conflicts, and begat a Spirit of Sympathy and tenderness in [him] . . . toward Some who were grievously Entangled by the Spirit of this world." [1] Armed with the minute of 1758, and a less saintly approach, the Monthly Meetings began, by means of the usual "dealings," to bear down on all those who bought or sold slaves.

Strictly speaking, Meetings were empowered to bar such members only from the business Meeting and from contributions to the stock. When dealings failed the committee on the case applied the penalty by delivering to the recalcitrant brother or sister a copy of the Minute of 1758. Zealous committeemen, however, brought greater pressure on an offender. They often discovered other evidences of misbehavior which warranted disownment. Those insensitive to Friends' opinion on selling slaves were casual about older branches of the Discipline as well. Woolman had argued that slave-owning dulled both sympathy and the moral sense, and produced a general decline of godly conduct wherever it prevailed. At any rate, those who bought and sold Negroes led lives sufficiently independent of the religious fellowship to keep other derelictions unnoticed until transactions in slave property invited special scrutiny. In some cases, such persons were disowned for marriage by the priest, drunkenness, blameable insolvency, or often a collection of offenses, including some almost never mentioned alone, such as lack of attendance at Meetings for worship or "Vain Conversation." Sometimes the subsidiary sins were cleared up, but not slave-buying; "dealings" were often protracted.[2] The case of one Philadelphian evoked all the talents of his Monthly Meeting. He had enjoyed the business of stabling horses for traveling Friends or for those who came from out of town on Truth's service. When the Meeting learned that he had bought two slaves it became dissatisfied with his behavior in general, instructed a formidable committee of antislavery stalwarts to audit the accounts he presented for reimbursement, and took steps to provide other quarters for the horses. The malefactor pretended to undergo a quick change of heart, but the Meeting stayed with the case for months and ultimately disowned him for excessive use of strong spirits, after he had proved intractable on the slave issue.[3]

Ingenuity and reformist zeal suggested extensions of the Minute of 1758. To right himself with the Meeting, the offender had to voice his approbation of Friends' principles, his intention to live in accordance with them, and his hope that his acts had not hurt the reputation of Truth or drawn others into wicked ways. Written declarations, however, showed a greater commitment, Friends believed, and deeds were more satisfactory still. Philadelphia Monthly Meeting began to insist that if it was to credit the slave-buyer's change of heart he must free his new property, or, if he had bought a young Negro, arrange for his education and fix legal terms of indenture. The Meeting wanted a formal document in one instance, giving the exact terms of servitude, with the buyer's promise to abide by them, the name of the Negro, as well as a full "declaration of being convinced of the iniquity of ye practice of Buying & keeping Slaves." In another case, after vigorous dealings over an addition to his troop of slaves, a member satisfied the Meeting by agreeing to free them all by his will. Thus, the decision of 1758 was converted into the beginning of Meeting action to require Quakers to free their Negroes.[4]

When slaves were sold, demonstration of reform was more difficult. The Meeting began to require repurchase and manumission, with appropriate guarantee of education or support in old age, if at all possible. When one Quaker, as executor of an estate, sold a slave to another contrary to precautionary advice by Friends, the Meeting arranged a resale and took up the offers of neighbors of the deceased master to lend the Negro money to buy his freedom. Members sometimes disposed of bondsmen to raise cash for immediate use, or to get a thieving or unruly person out of their households. When the slave was sold to another colony, it was often impossible to undo the transaction. The Meeting was usually satisfied by sincere regrets in written form, but in one case urged the sellers of a Negro to seek him out and do what they could to "contribute to his relief." [5]

The practices pioneered in Philadelphia quickly spread to New England Yearly Meeting, together with more abstract antislavery commitments. John Woolman, on his northern tour in 1760, probably carried word of what was afoot in his home Meeting's territory. But the declaration of Richard Smith, one of the few Connecticut Quakers — but a member of South Kingstown Monthly Meeting in Rhode Island — had revealed three years earlier a receptive spirit in southern New England. Smith gave the

Meeting a paper announcing his inner revelation that slave-keeping was evil and his "Intention to free his negro girl." [6]

Other members shared Smith's new convictions and lost no time in acting on them. Without mincing any words, the South Kingstown Meeting decided in 1760 to disown Samuel Rodman for buying a slave, though there was merely an advice against the practice in the Yearly Meeting discipline. His appeal to higher Meetings brought a reversal; South Kingstown Friends finally proclaimed the disownment in 1762, but in view of the deficiency in church law, they added to the grounds of the denial Rodman's persistent justification of his action. The Meeting's next case, that of Joshua Rathbone II and his son Joshua III, was handled more deftly, though with disappointing results. Joshua II, after dealings, declared himself convinced that "makeing slaves of our fellow Creatures" was wrong, and agreed to rear and free a colored girl he had bought. This pleasing promise he soon violated by giving the girl to Joshua III, who said he would manumit her in due time, but then sold her out of the colony! The outraged Meeting insisted that Joshua II do everything in his power to get the girl back, and, if all else failed, bring "an action at common Law against his son for the Recovery of Damages upon a promis made by his said son to him." The suit was necessary since the Meeting had just disowned Joshua III (the Yearly Meeting having recently provided the necessary addition to the discipline) for selling the girl, refusing to make any reparation to her, encouraging the practice of enslaving mankind, and breaking his promise. Joshua II, however, refused to go to court, and was thereupon expelled from the church. South Kingstown was compelled to disown several others for refusing to "comply with the advices of Friends respecting Slaves," and had to send a committee to persuade the members who freed their Negroes to sign proper papers of manumission in 1773. Once this was done, however, the remaining members united in strong opposition to every aspect of slavery. [7]

Elsewhere in the northeast determination to fight slavery developed more slowly. In Newport, after a private session with John Woolman, several Quakers manifested a "Concern" to change their wills to manumit their Negroes. But although Woolman joined the committee to revise the discipline, the Yearly Meeting would do no more than strengthen one of the queries in favor of giving slaves religious training and teaching them to read. Not until twelve years later did Friends in Boston, Lynn, and Salem begin to use the Meeting's authority against slaveholding. In New York, Flushing Monthly Meeting, as late as 1765, accepted a simple apology for importing slaves, without so much as a pious wish by the offender to repair the damage he had done. At about the same time Friends in the rural areas of the state began to favor eradicating slave-ownership by members of the church, but New York City brethren prevented the necessary changes in the discipline.[8]

Zeal in the crusade against slavery spread as part of the general Quaker reform movement. By 1760, when Woolman exerted his powers in the northern colonies and London began to experience the revival which had earlier caught fire in Philadelphia, local resistance in New York and in the southern colonies to extensions of the discipline against slavery was doomed. Nearly every year between 1760 and 1784 brought some fresh evidence that Quakers thought the sacrifice of a few obstinate brethren a low enough price to pay to purify their church and right the wrong done to Negroes in America.

In 1760, Philadelphia Yearly Meeting reported to London that all American Yearly Meetings were growing more ardent against slavery. Confirmation came that year in the epistle of South Carolina Friends to Philadelphia Yearly Meeting. The southerners expressed concern over keeping slaves and sought the views of the leading body of American Quakers. Philadelphia recommended that Friends demonstrate their "sympathy" for their Negro "fellow creatures" by refusing any part in fitting ships for the slave trade, but declared that it would be even more of a blow to slavery if Friends would stop keeping slaves. The next year, at Quaker instigation, Pennsylvania imposed an import tax on slaves which did much to discourage the traffic. Yearly Meetings waited to obtain general agreement, however, before forbidding members to buy or sell Negroes on pain of disownment. Maryland and Virginia had to abandon attempts to make strict declarations under pressure of adverse laws and opposition within the ranks. Nevertheless, these

Meetings managed gradually to expand the strong advices against the sale and purchase of slaves into a ban on slaveholding altogether, following the lines in Philadelphia Monthly Meeting.[9]

The abolitionist point of view required a final development, however, before it could prevail in the colonial world of the 1760's and 1770's. The abhorrence of greed and the devotion to benevolence furnished by the moral reform movement were not quite enough. Again following the leadership of the Quaker metropolis, Philadelphia Yearly Meeting made a part of its official terminology the set of concepts which finally carried the antislavery movement through its last stages. The language and ideas were partly drawn from contemporary radical rationalism in politics, and, as Benezet pointed out, related hostility toward slaveholding on moral grounds to some of the liveliest ideals of the day.

The new point was that justice required Friends (and all men) to give slaves their freedom as a natural right. Although Woolman and Richard Smith had earlier framed similar thoughts, and Philadelphia Monthly Meeting had used them in its minutes in 1760, not until 1765 did the Yearly Meeting adopt them. Then it urged further efforts (of persuasion only) to eradicate from the religious fellowship the buying, selling, and keeping of slaves in order that all members might "acquit themselves with Justice, and Equity towards a People, who by an unwarrantable Custom," had been "Unjustly deprived of the common Priviledges of Mankind." New York Yearly Meeting endorsed this view of the matter when it affirmed in 1768: "We are . . . fully of the mind that Negroes as rational creatures are by Nature born free." In the case of the colored slaves, as in that of the Delaware Indians, the idea of posing the moral problem as a matter of justice appealed to Friends.[10]

The strength of the appeal came partly from its invocation of the long-held belief in the moral equality of individuals and partly from its denunciation of "custom," which Quakers readily equated with corruption in religious life. On this point Friends shared the attitudes of the thinkers of the Enlightenment and their American disciples, who blamed custom for upholding oppression and irrationality in human affairs. But, most important, the appeal to justice provided a corollary which delighted the Quaker judgment:

If Negroes had been deprived of natural liberty not only when they had been forcibly transported from Africa, but every minute they were held in bondage under whatever pretext, justice required that the God-given freedom be "restored." In this light a master conferred no boon when he liberated a slave; he gave belatedly what he had hitherto "withheld" and simply ceased to "detain" a person who was, and always had been, free. This idea soon pervaded official Quaker language and provided Friends with an unfailing encouragement to fight slaveholding in the "world" at large. Ending a wicked usurpation of control over a man's life was as clearly a public duty as saving him from drowning, an obligation so positive as to relegate the spiritual or economic preparation of the slave for freedom to a position where it could not rightly control the decision to manumit or not. Quakers assimilated the Negro's woes to "oppression" in general, a concept familiar to the colonial scene in the 1770's.[11]

The invocation of "natural" liberty demonstrated that Friends had adjusted their views to ideas that were prevalent during the Revolutionary period. Previously, when Quakers had said "natural" they had ordinarily meant "unregenerate." Except in the sense that the unregenerate man had a God-given right to occupy and use the world, he enjoyed no liberty. He was a slave to innately wicked passions and impulses from which he could be freed only by accepting the guidance of Christ's Spirit within himself. If he did so, he enjoyed true or Christian liberty, a freedom from sin. In the unregenerate state, though he might make a legitimate use of the world to supply his physical needs, the important thing was that his innate depravity led him surely to sin and suffering. It did not greatly matter whether other men restricted his actions or not; absence of restraints might even leave him freer to sin. To bring virtue into man's life, the natural condition had to be reordered by divine power; "natural" thus stood in contrast to "redeemed."[12] When Quakers in the 1760's began to speak with favor of "natural liberty" they used implicitly a contrast between "natural" and "artificial," or man-made — a contrast between the divinely ordained circumstances of mankind, designated as "natural," and distortions of the plan made by imperfect human will. Since God had created man, sinful propensities and all, in a condition of freedom to enjoy the world and to accept the guidance of the Inner Light to a life of virtue, any human restriction on this "natural liberty" was wicked, whether motivated by greed or merely a misguided desire to observe oppressive laws and customs. Slavery was a prime example of society's violation of natural liberty: the institution obviously prevented the slave from enjoying the world to the best of his ability; Lay and Woolman had successfully argued that it also prevented him from developing a capacity to accept the benefit of the Inner Light. While the ideas behind the old and the new uses of the word "natural" were not logically incompatible, the new use ended the old emphasis on wickedness and misery as the results of the unregenerate man using his God-given right to occupy the world. In effect, the unregenerate condition came to be estimated more hopefully; as long as human restrictions did not prevent him, man could pursue his temporal and spiritual happiness with a reasonable prospect of success if he went about it in the right way. The opportunity to try was something which all men should help each other to enjoy.

Friends' concept of natural liberty stimulated them to action to remove human interference with the divinely decreed freedom. The old emphasis on natural depravity had encouraged patient waiting for supernatural intervention to improve human life, as was shown in the views of some Quakers at Philadelphia Yearly Meeting of 1758. Speaking against strong action to benefit the slaves, they "appear'd concern'd, lest the meeting Should go into Such measures as might give uneasiness to Many Brethren, alledging that if Friends patiently continued under the exercise, the Lord in time to Come, might open a way for the Deliverance of [the Negroes]." [13] As the new concept came to prevail, this sort of argument lost its force. Believing individual freedom good in itself and an essential condition to virtuous life, Friends could readily see that where man had tampered with it, man had the power to undo the damage. Reformers could proceed to restore natural liberty without waiting for inward "transformations" which would make the freed worthy of their freedom, or to combat social injustice instead of waiting for divine interference to correct it. Furthermore, convinced that natural rights existed apart from the will of the civil community, or even in the face of contrary laws, the Quaker reformers who asserted their obligation to promote virtue in politics by any means short of armed rebellion could use a right to liberty as grounds for defying a legal protection of slavery.

In the activist frame of mind engendered by the concept of natural liberty, Philadelphia Friends expanded the techniques of group action. Philadelphia Yearly Meeting posed more problems than could be found farther north. Virtually a microcosm of American Quakerdom, it included not only the Friends of the trading communities along the Delaware River, but also numerous farmers of a type common in the North, who rarely used or even saw Negro labor, and plantation owners from Delaware and the large parts of the Chesapeake Bay colonies which before the Revolution remained outside the jurisdictions of Baltimore and Virginia Yearly Meetings. Philadelphia, then, contained a generous share of both zealots and heel-draggers on the slavery problem — those who could see it as an abstract question of virtue and those for whom manumission meant a change in their control over a labor force which would expose their community to the hazards of a large population of freed slaves.

To keep its diversified membership diligently going in the right direction, at the same time allowing some local variation, the Yearly Meeting called for the creation of Monthly Meeting committees to visit the slaveholders individually and persuade them to free their Negroes. In 1770 it asked for a general report on slaveholding after a round of such visits. Four years later, after directing the Quarterly Meetings to help persuade owners to manumit slaves, it took the unusual step of asking that the names of the recalcitrant be brought in at the next sitting. Gradually, standing committees took shape in Monthly Meetings to labor with those who kept slaves, to inform them how to take the legal steps to manumission, or to report hopeless obduracy to the Meetings.[14]

From the committees working with actual cases, moreover, came continuous demands for more specific and inclusive statements of policy from above. Thorny problems arose over slaves who formed part of estates. Should a Friend, as executor, sell them to pay the deceased's debts? Could he free them without instructions to do so in the will? Could he conscientiously manumit them to the damage of heirs? Could he encumber the estate with the sureties required by law to be posted by those manumitting slaves? Could he fix terms of service and education for underage slaves? Could he give them away in an effort to get rid of the problem without actually violating the letter of the advice in the Minute of 1758? Perplexity over the last problem induced Falls Monthly Meeting to call for clarification by Bucks Quarterly Meeting in 1773.[15]

Further difficulties arose in connection with buying slaves for laudable purposes — as, for example, reuniting families. Meetings tended to tolerate such acts, especially if manumission was immediately insured; Virginia and North Carolina Yearly Meetings made such toleration official in 1772. Philadelphia was not inclined to do so, however, perhaps because several claims to excusable motives for buying slaves were found to have been made in bad faith.[16]

But problems most closely connected with the smooth working of church government led to the formal call for expansion of the discipline against buying and selling slaves. Could those guilty of such practices who had been barred from the Meeting under the terms of the "Minute of 1758" be dealt with further for other offenses? Was the Meeting still responsible for brotherly care and surveillance after it had barred a member from sitting with it or contributing to its stock? Could it leave the slave-trading offense unfinished business and disown the offender for something else? Falls Monthly Meeting wanted these points cleared up in 1773. Could a Meeting issue a certificate to, or accept one from, a man under this partial disownment? The answer to be drawn from institutional precedent seemed to be that the Meeting could, provided the certificate mentioned the disciplinary action against him. If that was the case, though, Friends in Philadelphia Monthly Meeting decided in the spring of 1774 that it was time to devise new ways to promote and maintain their testimony against "the iniquitous practice of buying, selling or keeping Slaves." After taking a month to reflect on the matter, they asked Philadelphia

Quarterly Meeting to put the subject before the Yearly Meeting.[17]

The Yearly Meeting could not evade its duty to clarify the regulations of the religious Society. Solutions to the numerous problems connected with slavery must be sought, moreover, only by further restricting Friends' contact with it. At the Yearly Meeting in 1774, Friends were well aware that coreligionists elsewhere favored stronger measures against slavery; in New England they had already taken some, and non-Quakers were growing enthusiastic in the cause. It was time to spur on the visiting committees by some sweeping statements of principle and to arm them with harsher penalties for those who defied the collective opinion. When Philadelphia and Bucks Quarterly Meetings raised the issue of clarifying the rules, the Yearly Meeting put the matter in the hands of a large committee (several leading opponents of slavery were omitted — most conspicuously, Anthony Benezet) which presently returned with a lengthy report which the Meeting approved. It made any act by which a slave was transferred from one master to another a matter for disownment, and forbade Friends to serve as executors or take out papers of administration for estates which included slaves. The Meeting also required its members to treat colored servants exactly as the law directed them to treat white ones — that is, to fix a term of years, give appropriate instruction, and provide certain minimums of clothing. Sounding the trumpet for a new campaign against slave-owning, it gave Monthly Meetings authority to bar obdurate masters from the service of Truth, and explained that in this state of partial expulsion they remained eligible for all other disciplinary dealings.[18]

The next year, although the campaign had not proceeded with the speed called for, the Yearly Meeting further expounded the positive duties of Friends toward freed Negroes. Quakers were to "Assist and Advise them as their Circumstances & Stations in Life may require," "both for their Spiritual & Temporal Good." That year and the next, Friends could take satisfaction in the large numbers of their "Fellow-Men, of the African Race, and others" (mulattoes and slaves with some Indian ancestors), who had been restored to their "natural Right to Liberty." In 1776 the Quarterly Meetings presented detailed enumerations of such persons, resplendent in language supplied by the new amalgam of Quaker morality and the concept of natural rights. Convinced that the issue of slavery was a matter of "common" justice thwarted by self-interest, the Meeting approved its committee's report recommending disownment for persistent slave-keepers and use of Quarterly Meeting committees to get the business done more rapidly by adding the weight of higher authority than the Monthly Meeting. In the Revolutionary turmoil it was the duty of Friends to reaffirm the Golden Rule and their belief "that Christ died for all Men without distinction," and to urge each other to practice "impartial Justice & Judgement, to Black, & White, Rich & Poor." Monthly Meetings were directed to record manumissions of members' slaves and make a list of those to whom Friends had a special obligation for care. The women Friends backed the new policy in their Meeting.[19]

Reports began to come back from the Monthly Meetings that they were clear of slavery. Many rural Meetings in Pennsylvania and New Jersey had had virtually no problem anyway. By 1779 the Yearly Meeting could survey a satisfactory scene, including some striking progress in plantation areas, but not until years had passed, and most of the Monthly Meetings south of Mason and Dixon's line had been turned over to Baltimore and Virginia Yearly Meetings, could Philadelphia claim to be purified of the taint of slaveholding. As late as 1804 a New Jersey Meeting was still working on a difficult case.[20]

Other Yearly Meetings followed roughly the pattern of Philadelphia: growing strictness against transferring slave ownership, and finally resort to disownment for slaveholding as well, after a period devoted to attempts to persuade members to manumit their Negroes. New England Yearly Meeting exhibited a sudden new fervor against slavery in 1763, when the moral revival set in. Among the "Breaches" which worldliness had "made in our Sion" (as New England reformers liked to call their religious fellowship) was the common neglect by Friends of the religious education of the Negroes "which they do Clame as there property." Six years later, Rhode Island Quarterly Meeting carried a question on slavery to the Yearly Meeting, at the instigation of South Kingstown (long militant on the subject). The Quarterly Meeting asked, purely rhetorically, if it was not "inconsistent to possess" colored people in the same way "as the brutal part of the Creation and yet use them well Or [hold them] as Slaves & at the same time bring them up in the true Religion." A committee to consider this problem in logic recommended changing the query on slavery, but not until a Yearly Meeting visiting committee had done its best to persuade masters to give up their powers. The next year Friends were forbidden to buy or import slaves. In 1771 the committee announced that most owners would set their slaves free, but "a few others which we have with sorrow to remark were mostly of the Elder sort manifested a disposition to keep them still in a Continued state of Bondage." Before another year had passed some of these owners had been disowned.[21]

In 1773 Rhode Island Quarterly Meeting proposed to forbid Friends to own slaves, though it was to be understood that "the Aged & Impotent and also infants & those in their nonage [must] be provided for brought up and instructed." The following year the Yearly Meeting added a recommendation that Monthly Meetings keep records of manumissions even though they should also make sure that towns kept them too. With the program thus laid out, New England acted decisively in the early years of the Revolution. Salem Monthly Meeting, which had done little previously, earnestly labored with its slave-owning members to prepare proper documents, one of which was signed at Meeting in 1775. A few months before the Declaration of Independence, "John Basset of Lynn" offered a paper to the Meeting stating his belief that all nations "are made of one Blood" and that "all men are by Nature eaquely free." He explained that he had held a slave only "through Inattention to the Righteous Law of doing to Others as I would thay should do to me," but having thought about it, "in a sence of Duty" released all claim in the pretended property. By early 1778 all the slaves held by Quakers in Boston, Salem, and Lynn had been liberated. The Yearly Meeting committee that year reported that slave-owners remained only in Newport, Rhode Island, where the church was not finally cleansed of the evil until 1782.[22]

In New York Yearly Meeting, where the moral reform caught

fire only on the eve of the Revolutionary War, the Yearly Meeting began the process of preliminary persuasion by a committee appointed in 1771 to urge members to manumit their slaves. At the same time it forbade members to sell Negroes without permission from their Monthly Meetings. After two years it threatened disownment for buyers and sellers of slaves, and in 1775 called on Monthly Meetings to stimulate owners to give religious and secular training to their Negroes and set them free at a proper age. Still cautious, the Yearly Meeting of 1776 decided to exclude unpersuadable owners from the service of Truth, but Monthly Meetings soon decided to apply the penalty of full disownment. Some masters converted slavery to regular apprenticeship or indenture. Others were excommunicated. But the church in New York was free of slave-owners by 1787.[23]

South of Philadelphia, Yearly Meetings strengthened their rules on slavery almost as fast, but they worked with a less tractable situation. For many Friends slave labor was an indispensable part of the economic system; moreover the size of the Negro population made the prospect of wholesale manumission frightening. Belief in a natural right of liberty therefore failed to inspire southern Friends. Maryland Quakers resorted to an unusual device in gradualism when they barred slaveholders from service as elders in 1770. They ultimately decided to disown slave-owners in 1778, but to meet resistance in the church they had to reaffirm and enlarge the decision in 1781. Virginia Yearly Meeting, proclaiming the need for impartial justice in words copied from the Philadelphia Meeting of three years earlier, in 1779 urged Friends to restore their slaves to freedom as they valued their own salvation. But even though Monthly Meetings might use all their power to persuade slave-owners to free their Negroes, legal obstacles, including a requirement that the freedman be removed from the state, stood in the way of manumission until the law was liberalized in 1782, partly as the result of Friends' pressure. Thus, Virginia waited until 1784 to require members to rid themselves of slaves. Within a decade they had nearly succeeded.[24]

In North Carolina the Yearly Meeting still dwelt on the evils of the slave trade in the years just before the Revolution, but it went along with Friends elsewhere in the face of great local opposition and decreed disownment for determined slaveholders in 1781. It had followed the usual steps of giving official sanction to abolitionist publications and sending committees to persuade masters to liberate their Negroes. But it had encountered an obstacle in laws forbidding manumission except for meritorious service. Friends, after futile application to the legislature, decided that they must not accept less than virtue because the lawmakers refused to make their path easy. Yet when freed Negoes were seized by government officials and resold into slavery, manumission was *not* a step toward justice for the Negroes. To solve the problem, the Yearly Meeting assumed the sins of its members. It appointed trustees in 1808 to receive ownership of Friends' slaves who were then allowed to live as free men.[25]

Quakers, however, could not satisfy their consciences merely by turning their colored servants loose. As Friends finally conceived their obligation — not simply to save their own souls, or to shun prize goods, or as an application of the rule of reciprocity, but to undo a wrong — manumission itself was merely a dramatic moment. They had to repair the injustice as well as behave toward their Negroes *in loco parentis*. Natural liberty might be an abstract right, but people had to be educated to enjoy it. If, as Woolman and Lay claimed, slavery stultified the minds and moral senses of the slaves, it might be necessary for Friends to tolerate shiftlessness or misbehavior on the part of freedmen which would have rendered them improper objects of care if they had always controlled their own lives. A very Quakerish conviction also gained acceptance that colonial America owed a great deal to the labor of the Negro people, while whites enjoyed the benefits and should be willing to go to great lengths to repay them. This idea, as clearly stated by Philadelphia Yearly Meeting in 1778, was promptly quoted by Virginia Yearly Meeting at its next sitting.[26] These considerations, reinforced by sureties to the state or by the manumission records kept by the Meeting, combined with revival of conscientiousness, gave durability to Friends' determination to see to the spiritual and temporal good of members' former slaves.

A realistic appraisal of what white ex-masters might be expected to do on their own, plus a heightened sense of the collective responsibility of the Meeting, led Quakers to a momentous step. The religious Society, as such, undertook the good work for ex-slaves although it had previously been only lukewarm in its requirements of members' duties in this regard. A special bond between Quakers and emancipated slaves and their descendants would go beyond the obligations arising from the brotherhood of man. All Yearly Meetings willingly underwrote the obligation, based as it was on ancient Quaker ideals about the treatment of young slaves. It was no more irregular than the "tender regard" and "watchful care" which Philadelphia and New England Meetings had decided to give the nonmembers who were commonly considered Friends.[27]

At first, the Quakers spoke as though they were merely reviving faithfulness to old standards. Meetings not only decided to stress obligations to give rudimentary religious instruction, but, surprisingly enough, in Virginia Yearly Meeting as early as 1767, training to operate as free labor. In cases where individual conscience so dictated, and in New York at the behest of the Yearly Meeting after 1781, Friends put their Negroes on a free labor basis retroactively, compensating ex-slaves for their labor, deducting costs of their keep. Meetings took Negro outsiders under their care in these respects, not so much to protect the reputation of Truth as to do justice and let members assist each other in virtue and benevolence.[28]

In carrying forward this view of what justice demanded for the Negro, ardent proponents met an almost silent resistance. They had the full backing of their religious society, so slave-owning members could not justify a refusal to free their Negroes on principle; at most, the reluctant masters could say that they did not yet feel fully convinced of the moral obligation to manumit. They had to sacrifice capital in slaves to prove their beliefs, a test not put to the sensitive soul who had never owned a Negro. But considerations of "temporal Gain" could take many forms which persuaded owners not to manumit slaves. A man hesitated to give up a dependable labor supply and rely instead on employees who were free to work or quit as they chose. Occasionally, slaves constituted the only repayment a debtor could offer. In the South, the commitment to a slave labor system by the populace at large operated in two special ways to paralyze the will of Quakers. Liberating slaves meant an end to high social rank and plantation life for well-to-do Friends. Many in Maryland and North Carolina, especially, left their land for cities or to settle in the West. Furthermore, the sureties required, as well as other legal obstacles, made a master shrink from manumission if he had many slaves, or little additional wealth, or if his slaves were apt to commit crimes or unlikely to provide for themselves successfully. Yet these realities of the slave-owner's position could barely be hinted at to the Meeting. Only the barriers erected by law bore even obliquely on the single moral argument against manumission that carried any weight among Friends — one based on the quasi-familial responsibility of owner to slave.[29]

A program of Meeting action was needed both to translate the assertions of responsibility for freed slaves into practice and to undercut the resistance of owners to manumission. Philadelphia Monthly Meeting led the way in several important respects. To take the spiritual care out of the hands of owners, Philadelphia revived its quarterly religious meeting for Negroes in 1756 and shortly thereafter put it under the care of the Meeting of Ministers and Elders on a permanent basis. This technique spread, along with hostility to slavery, until it assumed a new aspect. Instead of being a means of giving special attention to spiritual savages, it became a means of preparing slaves for moral living and an independent religious life. By 1758, three such meetings were being held in North Carolina, and the Yearly Meeting there had a committee to help Monthly Meetings with them. By 1764, there were a few near Baltimore.[30]

The practice of holding Negroes' meetings spread in Philadelphia Yearly Meeting, especially after 1778, when it was embodied in a wider program. That year, when Philadelphia Quarterly Meeting requested a stronger advice on Friends' duty to their former slaves, the Yearly Meeting recorded a minute recommending that Monthly Meetings establish committees for that service and consider what methods might be used. The following year the Yearly Meeting heard that most Monthly Meetings had appointed committees for the former slaves' "improvement in the Knowledge of Truth, and the practice of Piety and Virtue," and that in some places religious meetings were being held to "engage them to attend to the Teachings of Divine Grace, as their most profitable and best Instructor." Such meetings soon were being held in Burlington, Salem, Haddonfield, and Evesham, New Jersey, in Wilmington, Delaware, and in scattered places in rural Delaware and eastern Maryland. By 1791, Burlington had increased the frequency of its meetings from the usual four a year to twelve. It should be noted, though, that Meetings still found these efforts insufficient to promote the spiritual education of the freedmen.[31]

Manumission and Negroes' meetings were both managed in such fashion as to accord with the Friends' long-standing reluctance to draw Negroes into their religious fellowship. After leaving a Quaker's service, a Negro ceased to be part of the family group, and hence no longer under the indirect discipline of the Meeting. Not until 1796 did Philadelphia Yearly Meeting grudgingly concede that Negroes were eligible for membership. Few joined, however — perhaps because most colored people found Quakerism uncongenial. Their religious attitudes occasionally drew the scorn of Friends. One Meeting which was very diligent in the care of freed slaves noted that they had "but little savor of true religion." The Negroes' meetings were to inculcate the basic elements of Christian piety and virtue, not sectarian refinements. Friends expected the colored people to find their own way to church fellowship without the Meeting's aid. It was not long before the Society of Friends found itself in the astonishing position of having promoted its own intensely close fellowship and brotherly service to the point where its acts turned into service to nonmembers and religious ways at variance with those of the Society![32]

The resolution to aid ex-slaves in their temporal affairs produced several regular features of Meeting business. Monthly Meeting committees kept records of manumissions and vital statistics and gave close attention to their family affairs, especially to help them to be self-supporting and well-housed. Advice on earning a living and training children to useful trades, the sort of help given to members of Monthly Meetings in the name of Christian charity, was extended to Friends' ex-slaves by reason of the special obligation Quakers felt toward them. Instead of exerting pressure on members to perform these services, the Meeting undertook them as part of its corporate business. Such help, naturally, served as another way to cut the ground from under slaveholders who feared the risks of manumission.[33]

Care for Friends' former slaves also stimulated Meetings to further innovation in organizational practice. While the Meeting expected masters to educate young Negroes until the term of their service had been fulfilled, it was less easy to teach the three R's than a useful trade. From the Revolutionary years on, the impetus to establish Meeting schools gained support from the need for facilities to educate children of former slaves.[34]

Philadelphia Monthly Meeting faced this problem first and produced a solution of great importance, though, as experiment proved, it could not be imitated in many other places. Philadelphia established a school for free Negro children in 1770. The priority given to children of *free* Negroes was an inducement to masters to manumit their slaves, with the promise that the Meeting would take over their educational duties and enable the young to fit themselves for freedom. As it turned out, the intended clientele did not fill the school, and slave children were also taken as pupils; their masters were allowed, but not required, to pay tuition. The school, finally, had the purpose of proving that Negroes had the "Capacity & Inclination for receiving Instruction," a point which needed proof even though in some cases well-disposed Friends had already been sending their slaves' children to school.[35]

The idea of starting such a school was offered to Philadelphia Monthly Meeting near the beginning of 1770. Anthony Benezet has often been given credit for it, but Daniel Stanton and the Pemberton brothers had a great deal to do with the project. In this, as in many other benevolent activities, the Friends who were the prime movers preferred to let their roles be forgotten. After two months, the Meeting approved the plan, set up a committee of seven to hire a suitable schoolmistress, locate a room, and gather subscriptions to a stock.[36]

Instead, the committee found a master, Moles Patterson, who

opened a school within a few months. For several years Friends backed the school faithfully, convinced that it would do good, even though the response of the Negroes was not warm enough to prove this belief. Philanthropic Quakers fairly showered money on the project at first, and the committee soon built a schoolhouse on part of the lot occupied by Friends' Almshouse. Financial difficulties appeared only when the Revolution disrupted the currency and the fortunes of the subscribers. For a few years the school could not keep a suitable teacher — Patterson found a better job, his successor died suddenly, and the third was inexperienced — but beginning with the hiring of John Haughton in 1777, the teaching was better handled and turnover slower, as masters ordinarily took the post as a result of a specific sense of religious obligation.[37]

The real problem of the school was one of keeping pupils! Even a free school in which books and papers were supplied was expensive to families who lost the earnings of their children by sending them there. Not only did a smaller number of free Negroes attend than expected, but they, the slave children, and the poor white children taken in after 1775 proved so irregular in attendance that they made slow work of learning. The members of the committee inspected the school frequently and examined the pupils. Two or three dozen was a large number for any given day. Nevertheless, the school kept going. Under Haughton, the attendance increased somewhat; about two hundred and fifty pupils, including adults, were registered during his five-year term, and he visited their parents and guardians "to excite his Scholars to a diligent attendance, with a faithful religious Care," that pleased the committee. When he felt his duty discharged he resigned and was replaced by Anthony Benezet, who had been teaching Negroes since 1750 and had a "Concern . . . of taking the School whenever John Haughton should relinquish it." [38]

Haughton and Benezet secured the success of the school in its intended work. On Benezet's death, the committee found other teachers willing to take over the task, among them Sarah Dougherty, who began to hold a school for girls and little boys. By 1787, when the committee wrote to David Barclay in London to thank English Friends who had turned over to the school £500 left from funds intended for relief of Quakers in the Revolution, the institution was in a thriving condition. Though attendance by the hundred registered pupils was undependable, some progress was made. Girls learned the feminine arts of sewing and knitting. All studied reading, writing, and arithmetic, and some attained skill sufficient "for the common purposes of Life." The committee expected the results of education to grow more visible year by year in the Negroes' "more orderly deportment, and more reputable mode of gaining a Living." [39]

Other Meetings tried to imitate Philadelphia in training colored children. Ambitious plans were proposed in several cases, but ordinarily the financial burden was impossible for a small Meeting, especially when its territory contained a scattered rural population which needed more than one school. So in the years 1778–1780 the practice grew up of collecting Meeting funds to pay the tuition of free Negro children at any convenient established school. This probably meant that, outside of Philadelphia, educational benefits to Negroes at Meeting expense were apt to be confined to the children of Friends' ex-slaves, though in Salem, New Jersey, Monthly Meeting the committee on service to Negroes planned to give help to all children who needed it, whether slave or free. Some difficulties arose in southern areas where teachers were hard to find even for free white children, but a good degree of success crowned the integrated classes in Wilmington, Delaware, and generally in New Jersey and Pennsylvania.[40]

The business of seeing to the education of ex-slaves' children was often put in the hands of the same committee that saw to the schooling of young Friends. The committee sought contributions and bequests with good results, frequently collected an endowment, and in some cases used funds to arrange apprenticeship of Negro children as well as pay their tuition at schools and provide them with books and clothing. In Salem, New Jersey, the committee had the duty of exercising loving surveillance over the Negroes' morals and conduct and of visiting schools where they attended to inspect their behavior and improvement in learning. As early as 1782, Burlington Monthly Meeting took satisfaction in hearing its committee report that among the Negroes under their care, "there are several Families . . . who maintain themselves with Reputation, and some of them attend to their Childrens Learning." [41]

No matter how much Monthly Meetings did to care for freed Negroes, the legal support given to the institution of slavery by colonial governments compelled Quakers to direct their efforts to alter public policy. Quakers in Maryland, Virginia, and North Carolina carried demands for liberalized manumission laws to legislatures or went to protest re-enslavement of persons whom they had freed. To carry out their moral convictions it became necessary for Friends to convince society at large of their rightness. Furthermore, Friends began to believe that a whole-hearted opposition to the slave trade required that they go to the public officials to ask for laws against it. Good communications between the Yearly Meetings kept their efforts coordinated and served to bring the influence of Quakers in London and Philadelphia into harmonious support of such measures wherever possible. Thus, the campaign to tighten the religious fellowship and rid Friends and their church of the taint of slaveholding led to results which, far from being a simple turn from earthly concerns to eccentric, ingrown pietism, brought Quakers into new kinds of contact with the world around them. Moreover, the formulation of their convictions and the injection of them into political lobbying did not simply set them against the world's ways but brought their ideas into a degree of harmony with the revolutionary radicalism of the times.[42]

The effort to do justice to freed Negroes and cajole reluctant Friends into manumission extended Monthly Meeting care to non-members in need of special help and gave rise to institutions and practices designed solely for their benefit. Absence of a desire for religious unity between Negroes and their former masters put the care extended to freedmen outside the old boundary of charity. Consequently, the decision to establish the school for free Negro children in Philadelphia was a step of the greatest importance to the future of the organizational life of Friends; the school was the first institution set up by a Meeting for the direct benefit of non-members exclusively, even though it was designed as an aid in enforcing the Meeting's opposition to slave-owning by members. At this school, the existence of facilities not fully used by the intended beneficiaries easily led to their use by others — poor whites under the Meeting's care, other free Negroes, and children of slaves, who, of course, could not be owned by Friends in good standing after 1776. Similar extensions of Meetings' philanthropy were soon to be seen elsewhere. By 1783, Wilmington Monthly Meeting in Delaware came into possession of a bequest from David Ferris of "one hundred and thirty three . . . pieces of Eight . . . for the Schooling of poor children, White or Black, that has no right in any Religious Society." [43] The effort to purify the religious Society had converted it into an acceptable agent to do good to non-Friends, with less and less need to find special obligations by which members might justify giving help to those who needed it.

XIII

American Quakers and Social Service during the Revolution

THE campaign to give justice to the Negroes and the transformation of the Holy Experiment enabled American Quakers to respond creatively to the American Revolution. The war itself and the disturbances leading up to it subjected Friends in all the colonies to an ordeal comparable to that of the Pennsylvanians in the French and Indian War. First in New England, then in New York, and very mildly in the South, the Quakers reacted to adverse political conditions by joining the moral reform movement. But the three-part program devised in Philadelphia Yearly Meeting between 1755 and 1762 elsewhere required changes in established practices that were unnecessary in Pennsylvania. In their effect, these changes probably were more extensive than the surrender of Pennsylvania as a Quaker preserve, though there was no single displacement of tradition which could match it. In some parts of Quakerdom the Revolutionary crises brought departures from accustomed ways; in others it brought Friends as a united body into public life for the first time. As a sect, Quakers had to examine the nature and purpose of their religious fellowship as never before in the eighteenth century. They had to do so, moreover, on an unfamiliar plane of abstraction, in order to find a place for themselves in a world which heatedly discussed political ideas and forged new political institutions.

The Revolutionary movement brought new attacks on Quakerism and new threats to the order and solidarity of the religious Society. The main events in American public life between 1763 and

1782 almost invariably gave anguish to Friends. As in the Pennsylvania tax question, some Quakers kept trying to adjust their principles to the pressures of the times, but the majority which refused to accommodate itself carried its principles into action in ways which provoked the distrust and hostility of patriots and revolutionary governments. Pacifists could not comply with the new demands for taxes and militia service, and amid the general upheaval the old reasons for disobedience did not completely satisfy anyone. To meet the assault from their neighbors, Friends tried further to enhance conspicuous conformity to their ancient testimonies, to strengthen their church government to meet the attacks, and to counter the hostile opinions of outsiders by new benevolent projects and by explanations of their sect's role in the world.

Friends fell under suspicion as early as the Stamp Act crisis. On principle they condoned resistance to government only when that resistance was conscientious and passive. Plainly, they had to condemn threats of mob violence and illegal assemblies. Although some of the leading Quaker merchants who were most strict in their conduct publicly joined in the boycott of English goods in 1765, as a sect Friends appeared lukewarm in the American cause. Many outsiders began to regard them as enemies of patriotic intransigence after Franklin had compromised the anti-Proprietary, or Quaker, Party by securing the appointment of one of his lieutenants as stamp-master and enlisting another's support for acceptance of the tax. James Pemberton, who allowed himself to be elected to the Pennsylvania Assembly again in 1765 followed the only reasonable course for a Friend in public life. Generally in favor of resistance to British policies, but opposed to violence, he stayed in the popular movement to moderate it. The London Meeting for Sufferings commended the actions of the Pembertons and Whartons as restraining influences in the Stamp Act controversy and gave them credit for the good reputation of Pennsylvania in Parliament.[1]

But efforts to restrain extremist zeal became unpopular; agitators for colonial resistance described them as subversive. The leading Quakers, after lengthy dealings by their Meetings, gave up the attempt to reconcile opposition to violence with taking a part in the opposition to British imperial regulation when enforcement of the Nonimportation Agreement of 1768 fell into radical hands. The next year, the Monthly Meeting of Philadelphia directed a committee to advise members not to attend "the frequent General Meetings of the People of this City, on the Subject of Public Affairs, and to keep in stillness & Quietness." Since Friends took their stand against revolution and war, those who participated in public agitation, even to oppose violence, could give outsiders the mistaken idea that they were willing to support illegal acts. Consistent Quakers regarded any public demonstration as the prelude — or at least an invitation — to a riot. To them it was growing clear that "Asserting and Maintaining the Civil Liberties of the Colonies" might presently bring on a rebellion.[2]

The Meeting's stiffened attitude against opposition to British laws brought only a minor schism. The bulk of the membership united behind the morality of the withdrawal of 1756, and the dissident element in the Revolutionary period included no such group of wealthy and powerful men as those who had favored compromise during the French and Indian War. Some Friends, however, were deeply committed to the patriotic cause. A few joined in military preparations, held office in extra-legal governments, and took up arms against Great Britain. Ultimately, those who did not leave their faith entirely formed "Free" Quaker groups in Pennsylvania and New England, and followed Friendly ways except that they justified defensive war and payment of military taxes, opposed disownment on most grounds, and fought for American independence. Like-minded Quakers existed, unorganized, in New Jersey and Maryland.[3]

As the division of Americans over the issues of the Revolutionary period became apparent, conscientious Friends proclaimed their opposition to party strife as well as to armed conflict. Both originated in greed, envy of the rich, ambition, and other "Fruits of the Depravity & Corruption of the human Heart." As Philadelphia radicals discussed ways to go to the aid of Boston, suffering from the closing of its port, the Philadelphia Meeting for Sufferings, on July 30, 1774, recorded a minute against participation in the public disturbances and sent copies to be read in every meeting for worship at the close of some First day gathering. In this way alone could the unity of Friends be preserved and their ancient testimonies upheld. Regularly from then on, the Meeting for Sufferings sent letters of advice against participation in Revolutionary "Commotions." [4]

Consistent with its stand, the Meeting declined to sponsor any contribution "to the Relief of the distressed People of Boston," lest it should cause Friends "to be considered as approvers of their Conduct," though "on the Principles of Benevolence, & Charity" they might give aid later. For the time being they redoubled their protests of loyalty to George III. Especially in the Pennsylvania Assembly, Quakers had been devoted to legislative supremacy, but as the specter of revolution approached their descendants refurbished the older side of their history, which made heroes of English kings. They remembered Charles II and James II as rulers who had protected Friends from the religious persecution which Parliaments had sponsored. They remembered the favor shown to Penn at court by the last Stuart monarchs. In January 1776, just when the Revolutionary patriots were turning against the Crown, and again in September, following the Declaration of Independence, the Meeting for Sufferings and Philadelphia Yearly Meeting issued proclamations of their loyalty and determination to prevent smuggling and refusal by the members to pay taxes. In other Yearly Meetings official policy stressed the wisdom of attempts to stay apart from worldly strife, but largely accepted Philadelphia's unswerving loyalism. Indeed, no other policy was consistent with Quaker beliefs.[5]

The morality of declaring independence, however, was only one of the problems raised by the Revolution. More practical was the problem of actual government in the American provinces. As radical revolutionary regimes took control of them, whether proclaiming loyalty to the Crown or not, the application of Friends' testimonies produced dilemmas. American Quakers in 1776 believed they should obey whatever government prevailed where they lived; they clearly should follow Isaac Penington's advice to let God overturn as he chose, and "be still and quiet . . . and wait for righteousness" to prevail. However, there was no way of knowing when a new regime fighting to oust an old one had won the claim to be the established government which they should obey.[6]

As long as uncertainty remained over what authority was to be accepted, Friends should take no part in a revolutionary regime, not even accept its paper currency; they should refuse to pay its taxes and fines, and, as always, they should shun trade in materials for war or prize goods. If they should not obey a new regime, did it follow that they should still obey the old? If there were no officers of the crown conducting business, and insurrectionaries effectively governed, was a Quaker merchant to stop trade rather than smuggle when he could not pay duties to the king's treasury? Philadelphia Yearly Meeting, no more able to produce a simple answer to this question than to determine when good conscience ceased to require fidelity to George III, advised its members to practice economy and be prepared to give aid to sufferers from the fighting, outsiders as well as Friends. If "a Spirit of Benevolence, & true Charity" prevailed among them, and they preserved themselves as the right-minded and inevitably scarce peacemakers, Quakers would be of such worth to society as to merit the thanks of all their neighbors for the increased "Favours" which God would shower on them all.[7]

"Practical Christianity" was an acceptable program, but on a private basis only. A spirit of benevolence could not justify holding even the innocuous offices which had been retained by Quakers in 1756. When Pennsylvania fell under an insurgent regime, Friends refused for the first time in its history to serve as public Overseers of the Poor. They suffered distraints for £20 fines levied against them rather than "actively Comply with the New and Unsettled Authority, apprehending such voluntary Complyance contrary to the Advice of the Yearly Meeting and dangerous and ensnaring in its Tendency." [8]

The principled loyalism of the Yearly Meetings reflected the sentiments of most of the members. Friends' official view that the Revolutionary War, like any war or calamity, was a visitation of God's wrath on a sinful nation, aggravated the suspicions of those who thought it a heroic struggle against tyranny, thereby meriting divine aid. Although Quakers gave no aid or information to the British army, the insurgent Council of Pennsylvania in 1777, on vague accusations and suspicion of leadership in the anti-Revolutionary cause, arrested and exiled to Winchester, Virginia, twenty-two leading Friends, including the chiefs of the Meeting for Sufferings, the minutes of which were also seized. Nothing damaging was found in the minutes, and, after some protests, the exiles were allowed to return, without the satisfaction of either trial or hardship.[9]

Wherever the contending armies went, Quakers suffered. In New York and Philadelphia their meetinghouses were taken for military purposes, and their furniture smashed into firewood. The British occupation of Newport cut off communication between Friends there and on the mainland, except as word got out with the flocks of refugees who sought temporary homes with coreligionists in the rest of the state. New England Yearly Meeting was removed to Smithfield, Rhode Island, for three years. In New York City and Long Island, the British authorities vainly asked Quakers to do their share of supplying goods and standing watch. But whether their meetinghouse or personal property was requisitioned, Friends everywhere held principles against accepting compensation. Unwilling to engage in the profitable types of wartime trade, they felt the pinch on their private fortunes, which was made more severe by their refusal to take what advantage they could find of the currency situation. When they used Revolutionary paper at all, they expected fellow Quakers to repay any debts to full sterling value.[10]

Public hostility to Friends went to extremes in Pennsylvania. Members were charged double taxes, and many were jailed on political charges. A law requiring loyalty oaths to the new government on the part of schoolteachers caused the closing of Quaker schools in Philadelphia for a brief time. Attacks on the Meetings for Discipline occurred regularly in the Pennsylvania Assembly, some started by Free Quakers; the Society had to be defended against charges that it maintained uniformity by evil coercion and was incompatible with American liberty.[11]

Yearly Meetings made no overt decisions to recognize the authority of Revolutionary governments, but tacit acknowledgments appeared as the ability of the new regimes to govern and exert their will became evident. The conclusion is inescapable that the Meetings bowed to force. The New England Meeting for Sufferings virtually admitted this in 1780 when it approved a recommendation — based on the unexceptionable authority of Edward Burroughs — to avoid "Disputing whether the Authority in itself be absolutely of God or not," and to obey the regime which actually exerted power. In New England and the Hudson River Valley, country Friends accepted the new governments before the Yearly Meetings. Early in 1777 South Kingstown, Rhode Island, Monthly Meeting consented to cooperate with the Revolutionary authorities by testifying to the good standing of its own members, to enable them to avail themselves of the legal exemption from militia duty and requisitions. In 1780 Meetings in upstate New York sent contributions to the stock in Continental currency, which their Yearly Meeting refused. In the same year New England decided to keep a clause in the eighth query against depriving the king "of his duties," though the Clerk added a note saying that since for the time being the query was useless, Friends were advised "to suspend Answering." After the Meeting had fled to Smithfield again in 1781, while the French garrison braced for a British attack on Newport which never came, expressions of loyalty disappeared from the Meeting records.[12]

Philadelphia Yearly Meeting abandoned loyalism speedily after the leading members had felt the power of the Pennsylvania Council. Soon after the return of the exiles, the exemption of Quakers from the Test Act, and the death of Israel Pemberton (1779), the Meeting for Sufferings began to speak in words which indicated that it accepted the Revolutionary government. Near the beginning of 1780 the Meeting sent an epistle to its London counterpart phrased to indicate that the Americans considered their nation one separate from, and better than, Great Britain. The British failure to subdue the colonies according to the Meeting's new analysis, had been brought about by divine wrath at English avarice in the slave trade, an evil from which America was turning.[13]

Even after Friends had tacitly accepted the new civil authority, during the remaining war years, they did not ingratiate themselves with it. They could not easily live down their original stand or the fact that they were contributing nothing directly to winning American independence. Although the refusal of Pennsylvania Quakers to join in public thanksgiving for American victory in 1781 accorded with one of their long-standing customs, it nevertheless emphasized their desire to keep a distance between themselves and the rest of the community. They could not approve the public "Tumults," including the war, they explained, and had always refused to engage in "voluntary Humility and Will-Worship" by thanking God on command of human rulers.[14]

Quakers had intended all along to remain aloof from the "tumults," and detached from mundane interests. As events in the larger community made it harder for them to pursue their lives unmolested, they took increased determination to improve sectarian strictness and make themselves a people apart. Not surprisingly, this new extension of the Quaker revival broke out first in New England, where opposition to the mother country flared up most violently. Religious fervor among New England Friends had risen before when events in the world at large had challenged their faith. During the Great Awakening, at a time when war with France threatened to become intense, the Yearly Meeting had observed that "Truth seems to spread & Prevail in several quarters and a Religious disposition seems also to Increas in many Parts." But little had come of this happy condition except an unusually large amount of preaching in meetings for worship, some soul-searching on slavery, and a determination to bring the minute books up to date. Another false dawn had appeared at the beginning of the French and Indian War, encouraged by epistles from London favoring "a general reformation . . . of life & manners" and by the visit of Samuel Fothergill, who preached the revival of strictness and improvement of church government.[15]

The revival movement in New England had really begun in 1760. That year, when John Woolman visited the Yearly Meeting, he persuaded it to take a stand against the "prevailing Evil" of lotteries; perhaps more significant, however, was the resignation of Thomas Richardson, who had served as Clerk for almost forty years. As in Philadelphia when John Kinsey died, the change in New England Yearly Meeting was symptomatic of the passing of a generation which had grown accustomed to getting along with the world. The installation of a zealot for reform took place seven years later when Isaac Lawton began his tenure of the office. By then the Meeting had already appointed a committee on purity of conduct, such as existed steadily in Philadelphia during these years. As New England Friends explained to London, they took this step when a zealous minority feared the "Spirit of the world" had become too widespread. The committee found that there seemed to be "a Little Remnant in Every place," though too many were "at Ease in a Careless Luke warm State Contenting themSelves with Dwelling in the outward Court." Neglect of attendance at all kinds of meetings, weakening of love and unity in the fellowship, failure of parents to rear their children in Quaker ways, as well as laxity in duties to Negro slaves, gave the committee deepest concern. Some Monthly Meetings discovered special weaknesses of their own: in Salem and Lynn, of all places, parents were allowing their children to engage in promiscuous courting without serious intentions.[16]

Rigorous enforcement of the discipline spread in Monthly Meetings, together with a renewed effort to mark clear boundaries to the membership. Clarity on this point at first had meant no more than a negative exclusiveness; after a few years it was further improved when Meetings began to seek new members and admit them by a formal process. As in Philadelphia Yearly Meeting for decades prior to the onset of the moral revival, New England Meetings had paid little attention to "convincements." But in the 1760's, Monthly Meetings reported them steadily. In 1763 South Kingstown saw fit to clarify the procedure for determining a convert's fitness to join by emphasizing the intellectual commitment to the sect's "testimonies." A committee visited the prospective member to give him a copy of the queries and to ask if he "approved of them." If he stated that he was "willing to be inabled to Comply with the terms of said Queries" by the disciplinary action of the Meeting, the committee recommended that he be admitted. It was not long before the Yearly Meeting proudly reported to London the influx of new members. Even in 1778 it could say that though "darkness seems to hang over the Land, Yet . . . Divers have been Added to Our Society by convincement Since last year." When the Yearly Meeting defined the rights of membership in 1774, it followed the same logic implicit in South Kingstown's procedure: the person with anything short of a clear birthright from both parents had to make a declaration of principles and put himself under the Meeting's care. Thus, New England reached very quickly the practices worked out in Philadelphia.[17]

After 1770, Quarterly Meetings began to take proposals to the Yearly Meeting which increased exclusiveness and the systematic quality of church government still more, in ways which brought New England into uniformity with Philadelphia and London Yearly Meetings. Stricter procedures, adopted in 1772, for certifying a Friend's "clearness for marriage" or his Meeting's approval for a journey in the ministry, helped ensure that only true members would go under the Quaker name. Discontinuance of all the yearly meetings for worship, except that at Nantucket, made New England practice conform to that in other areas, as did the renewed interest taken in the writings of Robert Barclay. In 1774 the Yearly Meeting distributed to the subordinate Meetings copies of his book on church government, *The Anarchy of the Ranters, and Other Libertines.* Of broader significance, though, was the project recommended by Sandwich Quarterly Meeting to reprint his *Apology.* As the Clerk pointed out, the Yearly Meeting endorsed this idea unanimously, a comment made on no other decision in the eighteenth century. A committee was put to work to find a suitable printer. The book had been reprinted at Newport over forty years earlier, so it was hardly a fresh import. But this time the Yearly Meeting probably intended to encourage its members to learn the theological justification of their faith as part of the emphasis on intellectual commitment. Certainly, after this time New England Quakers began to use the word "Light" to designate the spirit of Christ within, as Barclay and all Quakers elsewhere had done.[18]

New England, however, did not match Philadelphia's sweeping condemnations of officeholding issued during the French and Indian War. Like James Pemberton, the Quaker magistrates in Rhode

Island regarded withdrawal as a temporary policy while the government waged war. Only during the Revolution did New England Friends extend the list of public responsibilities they would not perform beyond the standard peacetime avoidance of administering oaths and civil marriage ceremonies. Monthly Meetings and the Meeting for Sufferings urged members not to take any public duties, a policy that was generally followed, although the Yearly Meeting saw fit to make no recommendations on the subject until 1787, when it advised all its members, but especially ministers, elders, and the men in the Meeting for Sufferings, not to accept public offices.[19]

On the eve of the Revolution, New England Quakers became quite explicit about altering their religious fellowship to make it like other Quaker communities. In troubled times, Friends should exhibit "a uniform Conduct" to preserve their "Religious Testimony." Hearing that southern Yearly Meetings were sending men to confer at Philadelphia about how to achieve this goal, the New England Meeting for Sufferings sent three men to join the conference. The purpose in this emergency was to arrive at a common formula for pacifist behavior by which the man acting on Quaker principles would be distinguishable from one motivated by political disaffection. But in 1782 the Yearly Meeting expressed a more comprehensive view of the matter when it declared that the North American Meetings would "add Strength to the practice & exercise" of the discipline if they could agree on uniform rules. Accordingly, the Meeting for Sufferings, when it was given the task of revising the New England Discipline, consulted the rules of London, Philadelphia, and New York Meetings.[20]

The moral implications of the Revolution had become increasingly clear to New England Quakers. The Yearly Meeting which convened half a year after the Boston Tea Party wrote to London: "The commotion arising in the Brittish Dominions as they are in their Consequences outwardly Calamitous, may be feared are marks of Divine Displeasure." Hoping for God's aid in the adversities to come, the Meeting gave thanks for "the offers of mercy & Salvation being Continued to the Inhabitants of our Land," and lamented the "too evident . . . declention in the Society from the

Life purity & Power of Religion as possessed by our predecessors."
Lukewarmness in the ranks soon convinced the Meeting that it
must "prepare for a tryal both within & from without which will
shake the foundations of all who are not Established on the Sure
Rock." By 1776, when it reported that "there is a Cloud of Confusion & Calamitous distress . . . Surrounding us whereby many
are tossed to & fro as upon the waves of the Sea," one of the few
things inspiring hope was the "remnant in good measure preserved
from the defilements of this delusive World who are under a living Concern that our Discipline may be kept up . . . as a hedge
about us." While armies of worldly powers marched in their country, Quakers must remember "that they have Enlisted themselves
as soldiers under The Prince of peace." [21]

By that time a few Friends in New York Yearly Meeting, among
them, Elias Hicks, were discovering a passionate concern for the
order of the Society and the restoration of the ancient purity of
the brotherhood. The tribulations of the Revolutionary War years
stimulated similar concerns in others. When peace returned, New
York Yearly Meeting had directed the Monthly Meetings to put
their own committees to work for moral reform and had begun to
revise its Discipline, in consultation with Quakers elsewhere.[22]

In no other branch of church government was the answer to
the Revolutionary challenge clearer than in the founding of Meetings for Sufferings in all territories where they did not exist already.
This development took place even in the southern Yearly Meetings
where moral reform had touched only lightly. New York, in 1758,
had been first to follow the lead of Philadelphia, where the Meeting for Sufferings had dealt with problems arising from the French
and Indian War. The Meeting had languished, however, and had to
be revamped in 1778. Other Yearly Meetings established such interim committees during the Revolution: in New England in 1775,
in Maryland in 1778, and in Virginia in 1782. North Carolina created
similar bodies in its eastern and western Quarterly Meetings in 1757
and 1778. In New England, as earlier at Philadelphia, the establishment of the Meeting for Sufferings inspired meditation on the
mystical meaning of suffering. It was the duty of the Meeting to
see that Friends should not "wound the Cause of Truth, Loose the

reward of suffering for Righteousness sake, and bring reproach on our holy profession," nor fail to preserve themselves "alive to a feeling of the Suffering & Afflictions of their fellow Men." [23]

In addition, of course, these new central organs of church government carried the enlarged burden of inter-Meeting business and supervised Friends' public pronouncements, often in consultation with each other. They made the Quaker community more of a unit in its dealings with the world. They also found time to carry forward some business which grew out of Friends' desire to be understood and their belief that the safety of the religious Society depended on a firmer intellectual appreciation of it by the members. Since many in the rank and file had no religious literature, not even the Bible, the Meetings for Sufferings gathered subscriptions for printing various "Friends' books." Some copies were to be given to poor members, who were also to receive the Scriptures if they lacked them.[24]

Friends began to show a wider interest in the history of their sect, re-examining their past to discover new applications of principle and to set their ideas and achievements before each other and a critical world. Meetings for Sufferings arranged the reprinting of existing works, such as William Sewel's *History of the Rise, Increase, and Progress of the Christian People called Quakers,* as well as the compilation of new ones. After drifting along for decades, the project of assembling a history of Delaware Valley Quakerdom finally came to fruition in the Revolutionary period through the energy of Samuel Smith of Burlington, Robert Proud, and the Philadelphia Meeting for Sufferings, although what finally emerged was not a history of the various Meetings, but of Pennsylvania and New Jersey as colonies. Proud, especially, devoted much of his work to explaining Quakerism, expounding the virtues of the founding Friends, and praising their strict adherence to the sectarian testimonies.[25]

While seeking to arouse a sense of connection with the past, the moral reformers also became increasingly concerned with carrying their traditions on into future generations through the training of young Quakers. Reformers exhorted one another to join the "saving remnant" and bring up the youth "in that Exemplary plain-

ness, and Moderation which Adorns the Profession of Christianity."
To men imbued with religious zeal there is no such thing as a satisfactory level of virtue. To those convinced that their ancestors had
set a model of conduct, laxity in their own day constituted a grave
declension. Even the efforts of "well concerned Parents" did not
always raise proper Friends. Too many of the young preferred
"vain" books to the Bible. Too often they married outsiders, and
their parents, far from stopping improper courtship in time, let
their children keep company with non-Friends until late hours.
The youth spent time idly on First days and evenings, sometimes
at taverns or fairs where they might indulge in gambling or be
tempted into horse-racing. In order to improve the example set by
the adults, Meetings denounced superfluity in "Household Furniture," the use of tombstones, and the breach of the Sabbath during
haying season. Anthony Benezet recommended sobriety and religious attitudes for all harvesting, "a business which, under the
Mosaic Dispensation, was particularly enjoined to be carried on
with humiliation and thanksgiving, and ought by all means, to be
observed as such under the gospel." But such refinements of virtue
hardly could claim first priority when it was necessary to call for
more regular attendance at Meetings, especially those for Discipline and the week-day meetings for worship, and to fight the
"Drowsy Spirit" among Friends once they had assembled.[26]

More had to be done if the rising generation was to keep the
faith. The revival of youths' meetings was not enough. Eventually,
all Yearly Meetings came to rely on a network of subsidiary
schools. In Philadelphia, zeal redoubled between 1746 and 1778.
New England echoed this development. Newport Monthly Meeting kept a school open from 1749 to 1767; but not until Moses
Brown took up the cause and the report by Benezet and Zane to
Philadelphia Yearly Meeting had been read to New England in
1779 was there a widespread desire to have every Monthly Meeting
establish its own educational facilities. There were not enough
qualified masters, however. To train some, the Yearly Meeting
decided to establish a central boarding school like the one which
had been founded at Ackworth, Yorkshire, by English Friends.
The Meeting for Sufferings pushed the project until it succeeded

in opening a boarding school at Portsmouth, Rhode Island, in 1784. The effort was premature and lacked financial backing sufficient to enable it to perform all the good work intended, and it closed after a short career.[27]

In 1779, the Yearly Meetings of New York, Baltimore, and Virginia also seconded Philadelphia's advocacy of Monthly Meeting schools. Some Meetings in New York managed to carry out the recommendation in spite of such difficulties as the commandeering of schoolhouses by British soldiers. Thirdhaven Monthly Meeting appointed a committee and by 1781 opened the first Friends' school in Maryland. In Virginia, Fairfax Monthly Meeting managed to have classes held for a short time beginning in 1779, and South River for two or three years after. In North Carolina Yearly Meeting, nothing was done about schools until later. The trouble throughout the South was the "thin and dispersed situation" of Quakers and the difficulty of finding schoolmasters. Some steps were taken, however, to gather funds and set up committees in order to be able to start schools at a future date.[28]

In the territory of Philadelphia Yearly Meeting every effort was made to overcome the obstacles posed by rural life. Annually the Meeting urged the good work on committees at the local level. As it was hard to find suitable teachers, Anthony Benezet and John Todd offered to serve as a central placement agency in 1783. Under the circumstances many Meetings did well, either keeping schools going during the war years or starting them before the end. Burlington Quarterly Meeting in New Jersey could report that of twenty-one schools needed, nine were already there in 1779. In the twenty years following, Monthly and Preparative Meetings made a great deal of progress in raising endowment funds, acquiring land for schoolhouses or masters' homes, and putting schools in operation.[29]

Most Meetings insured a Friendly education to the children of poor members. Often this was the foremost purpose of the school funds, which were augmented, both before and after the stern words in the Benezet-Zane report, by bequests from charitable Quakers. Most donors expected their gifts to help Friends' children, but there were several bequests explicitly to pay for the instruction of outsiders in the Meeting schools.[30]

Next to the campaign for Monthly Meeting schools, most conspicuous in the moral revival during the Revolutionary period was the mounting disapproval of liquor. The temperance campaign was expected to benefit outsiders. Quakers in the past had remained loyal to an ordinary ideal of moderation, sometimes warning each other against unseemly conviviality on ceremonial occasions. By 1759 Philadelphia Quarterly Meeting deemed it wise to inaugurate a campaign against "giving or receiving Drams or other strong Liquor at Vendues, or Burials." Not only was drinking at auctions illegal, it was also "pernicious," and Friends should obey the law both for their "own Benefitt & good Example to others." In 1762 and 1763 the Meeting requested the government to curb drink, particularly by reducing the number of licenses to dispense liquor. The Meeting did its best toward that end; three men had been "under dealings" to persuade them to stop keeping taverns, because such places were "already farr too numerous. & become a Snare & temptation to many of the Youth and others." [31]

The campaign against hard drink lagged until the eve of the Revolution, when Anthony Benezet revived it in 1774 with a pamphlet he entitled *The Mighty Destroyer Displayed*. Attacks on tavern-keeping resumed, and a widespread agitation to augment the discipline began. The justification in Philadelphia for the new sally was abhorrence of using grain to make whisky. Having taken this stand, it was only reasonable for Friends to insist that they should not be "concerned in Distilling, or Selling Grain to be Distill'd into Spiritous Liquors," or "buying the Liquor when Distill'd." If antipathy to the "destruction" of grain had begun when there was a food shortage at Philadelphia during the British occupation, it would have been simple to explain. However, the increasing production of Pennsylvania rye whisky, the first liquor made from native materials, probably made it a prime target for moral objections, while an ignorance of chemistry allowed a strange concept of distillation to prevail. Benezet believed that whatever was contained in hard drink, including the intoxicating element, had been present in the raw material, while distillation merely broke up a benign combination. In what "the Almighty" had made, "the fiery property" was "so clothed and united with the earthy and balsamick parts, as to cause it to be quite friendly to our nature, and not liable to intoxicate; as the spirit alone will, when separated by distillation." So although the Meeting phrased its standards against whisky, the moral hostility to perversion by man of naturally good vegetable products applied as well to all other hard drink. After endorsing the stand against whisky taken in Philadelphia and Falls Monthly Meetings, the Yearly Meeting tacitly extended its strictures to other spiritous liquors. Elsewhere the official frown fell on "all kinds" of liquor immediately.[32]

Appeals to man's better side could stop the corruption of those products of the earth that were by nature good. Quakers were to spread a standard of abstinence "to the Nations." Tavern-keepers in the ranks damaged the reputation of Truth; Friends were to prevent liquor from bringing "Disgrace, and Ruin, both spiritually & temporally" to those "who from habit, may have acquired a thirst and inclination after it." Drink had "greatly tended to the Corruption & Depravity of the Morals of Mankind, thereby increasing Guilt on [America]." As a public service, those who saw this truth were to do everything in their power to help the less perceptive. Meetings required their members to set a good example and shun business which provided liquor to consumers, and in a private capacity Quakers carried propaganda for total abstinence to outsiders.[33]

Benezet's pamphlet, the outstanding literary weapon, elaborated the case against hard drink in a fashion harmonious with the Quaker revival, but with lurid testimony by physicians that liquor would "tear the tender vessels of the lungs in pieces," "rot the entrails," impoverish the blood, harden the stomach "somewhat like leather," and kill the drunkard by "a kind of dropsy, nervous convulsion, flux, if not a fever, or phrenzy." It warned of God's displeasure falling on those who allowed this havoc to continue and appealed to "all, who have any bowels of pity for their fellow-creatures, more especially the governors of the nations, as guardians and tender fathers, to guard the people committed to their charge from this *mighty destroyer.*" Since drink "heightens the passions of men and depraves their morals," benumbs "the feelings of the mind," and renders the user insensible "to the healing influence of religion," the abstainers had to act, for the drunkards would not. Benezet urged higher taxes on liquor, but thought individuals could accomplish much by avoiding the business, by giving no hard drink to hired laborers, and by teaching the benefits of the God-given natural beverage, water. He offered a few recipes for man-made potables to ease the transition — coffee "with a little milk to soften it," or better still, green tea, to "cleanse the alimentary passages, and wash of[f] the scorbutick and urinous salts" — but he reserved highest praise for a plain and simple diet. In early Pennsylvania, where people drank little, Dr. Benjamin Rush said the diseases had been "as few and simple as those of the Indians," while religion kept people's passions curbed and their benevolence enlarged. The idyllic past could be recaptured by a return to water-drinking.[34]

Benezet, like Woolman and the Yearly Meetings, linked liquor with the evil of slavery. Drunkenness, like slaveholding, contributed to moral callousness. "It is, in a great measure, through the introduction of those infernal spirits, that the poor negroes have been as it were bewitched, and have [been] prevailed upon to captivate their unhappy country people, in order to bring them to the European market"; while North American trade with the sugar plantations had simultaneously whetted an appetite for lucre and carried the raw material for rum to a once virtuous Pennsylvania. This vicious complex of unscrupulous commerce had caused alienation from Christ and abandonment to "Vice, Immorality & great Corruption." Drink and the slave trade, like slavery itself, were undoubtedly among the Grand Causes of the divine wrath which finally took shape as the Revolutionary War.[35]

Therefore, while Friends carried on their work to give justice to the Negroes whom they had held in bondage, they had to extend their efforts outside their own religious Society to persuade outsiders to give up the slave trade. Since the evil touched national morality so vitally, Friends, like other citizens, addressed themselves to the colonial, and later state and national, governments. Quakers presented petitions to legislatures for laws against the slave trade in Pennsylvania in 1761; in Maryland in 1771 and 1773; in Virginia in 1772; in Rhode Island in 1773 and 1784; and in England, 1783. They also developed a closer degree of cooperation between Yearly Meetings, especially through the Meetings for Sufferings, exchanging news, techniques, formulation of petitions and supporting evidence. The new organs of the religious Society enabled it to act as an international lobby.[36]

But just as the temperance crusade required Friends to do more than was appropriate to the Meeting's agenda, so their heightened zeal against slavery led to activities which could best be carried on by private societies. Attempts to re-enslave colored people inspired Quakers to take leading roles in the formation of two such organizations, The Pennsylvania Abolition Society, organized in 1775 as The Society for the Relief of Free Negroes, Unlawfully Held in Bondage, and reorganized in 1784; and the Society for Promoting the Manumission of Slaves and Protecting Such as Have or May be Liberated, organized in New York City in 1785.[37]

The Revolutionary War years, however, produced the most significant development of Friendly benevolence in war relief itself, directed both to members and outsiders. Friends found it unsatisfactory to their consciences to maintain complete nonparticipation in the war. Their first obligation was to help each other, though Philadelphians hesitated to do even that for brethren in Boston in 1774, fearing that by sending money they would appear to join fervent patriots rushing to thwart the purposes of the Boston Port Act. London Friends, however, assured the Philadelphians, and through them, New Englanders, that the possibility of misunderstanding should not keep them from their duty in the religious fellowship. The Clerk of Philadelphia Meeting for Sufferings, John Pemberton, then traveling in New England, inquired about what needed to be done and sent reports back to brother Israel. He discovered that Friends at Salem and Lynn could supply the needs of their brethren in Boston Preparative Meeting for the time being. If contemporary surmise was correct, Nantucket Quakers sent money to the committee of revolutionaries supervising relief in the city. They made the donation anonymously, probably to avoid seeming to take sides against the Crown.[38]

The need for relief in Boston in 1775, as in all New England during the Revolution, arose chiefly from interference with importation and from the caution of merchants and other businessmen who thought it prudent not to buy goods or hire men. During the siege of Boston, as later when the British occupied Newport, large numbers of people fled to the countryside, where they ordinarily had to live on someone's bounty. But actual shortages created hardship in the cities after they had been cut off from food and wood supplies by the Revolutionary armies. Similarly, in Nantucket, shortages became acute when the contending forces interrupted the island's imports of supplies as well as its exports of products of the fisheries. The object of relief, ordinarily, was to put money in the hands of those who needed it, until their lives could revert to normal.

After the Battles of Lexington and Concord the interior of Massachusetts began to suffer, too, as some 5,000 refugees rushed to rural towns. New England Quakers organized to help each other, took Philadelphia's advice to form a Committee (later Meeting) for Sufferings to supervise the business, but had to accept the aid offered by the Pennsylvanians. The Philadelphia Meeting for Sufferings, however, had resolved, with encouragement from Moses Brown of Providence, to do more than give charitable help to fellow Quakers; in the summer of 1775 it called on the Quarterly and Monthly Meetings in its territory to contribute for the "Relief of the Necessitous of every Religious Denomination" in New England. Perplexed, the New England Committee inquired how far the donors wished it to go in helping outsiders. Philadelphia thought it wise to supply aid to noncombatants only, in order to propagate pacifism and give no one cause to accuse Friends of supporting either side in the warfare. By way of precaution, the Meeting asked that records be kept of name, location, and religion of all who received money from Friends. Having £2,000 to send, with more available, Philadelphia was sure they could afford to help non-Quakers outside Boston as well as in the city. Even though the New Englanders found their efforts misconstrued as serving partisan ends, Philadelphia hoped that the distribution of money would reduce prejudice against Quakerism in New England and even lead to the "convincement" of some people there. If that happened, it would be a sign that the relief project was "an acceptable service to the Lord." [39]

When the money arrived from Philadelphia, the Committee for Sufferings appointed five members to distribute it. Moses Brown and his four colleagues left Rhode Island in December and kept at the work intermittently until the following summer. Unable to gain access to Boston, they passed a note of credit (worthless, as it turned out) across the lines by courtesy of the sheriff and gave money to many refugees in eastern Massachusetts and as far north as Casco Bay. Accompanied by selectmen, they went from house to house in Marblehead, Salem, and Cape Ann, distributing cash to enable the poor to pay the high prices for food and firewood. On the way back they distributed money to evacuees from Boston waiting out a twenty-one-day quarantine at Point Shirley. Then, as later, small pox in the city complicated the problem of relief. Subsequent expeditions took cash to many towns, some as far west as Worcester. By spring, help was needed in southeastern Massachusetts, Nantucket, and even Newport, where a British blockade stopped trade for several months. By September 1776, Philadelphia Meeting for Sufferings totaled up the results of the program with some precision. Almost £4,000 had been spent, most of it provided by Philadelphia Yearly Meeting; between 5,000 and 7,000 persons had received help, a great majority of them non-Quakers. [40]

After 1776 Friends' war relief followed the shift of the main scene of military events to the Middle Atlantic States and the South. Quakers helped alleviate distress at Norfolk, Virginia, in Westchester County, and in New Jersey. People on Nantucket Island also continued to suffer, "their whaling business being Stopt & the Cod-fishery from the shores discouraged for want of Salt." The New England Meeting for Sufferings sent wood and beef in 1778. The following year, money, fuel, and provisions were sent to Friends and others reduced to want by the British occupation of Newport. [41]

When the British and Continental armies reached New Jersey, Philadelphia Monthly Meeting anticipated work in its own territory. By the end of 1776 it appointed a special committee on victims of "the present Calamities." The committee spent £75 9s. 10d. out of the Meeting's stock "for the Benefit of our Members" and went on to get subscriptions to another fund out of which it expended £92 18s. 6½d. on relief of outsiders — "Persons who by their Conduct, and Appearance were supposed to be such as fell under our Notice." The Philadelphia Meeting for Sufferings had been taking steps to apply money left over from the aid to New England to the relief of Friends and other neutrals who fled to New York State from their homes in Rahway and Plainfield, New Jersey. Shortly afterwards, however, the war struck much closer. British soldiers entered Philadelphia and in December chose to use the Bettering House as a barracks. Friends thereupon housed the public poor in the Fourth Street Meeting House.[42]

When General Howe occupied the city in September 1777, the Continental army and militia took out as many supplies as they could. Until General Clinton evacuated Philadelphia the following June, the city was largely cut off from its usual sources of food and fuel. Isolation of the city also meant cessation of jobs for many city-dwellers and loss of markets for many farmers. Hindered by depreciating currency, nearby Monthly Meetings managed, with difficulty, to take care of Friends in their territory. In the city, however, it could not be done. Philadelphia Monthly Meeting and the Meeting for Sufferings appointed committees to raise money with which to aid the distressed. The pressure of need broke down the standing limits of charity; in the "Time of General Calamity," the Meeting declared, Christian love should extend "beyond the Bounds of" the religious "Community." But the rich Quakers who were willing to give supplies to their poor neighbors had none to give. The Meeting for Sufferings enlisted the aid of Meetings outside the city, asking them especially to send provisions, "if [the] way should open" to get such relief into Philadelphia. As far as possible, Friends pursued this objective, but accomplished little.[43]

The situation gave English Quakers an opportunity to help. In response to an appeal from a semiofficial committee of the Philadelphia Meeting for Sufferings, a group of prominent Bristol Friends sent a cargo of provisions to Philadelphia. Their ship containing £2,100 worth of goods was captured and taken to Boston. Another group of Friends dispatched £5,000 worth "of Flour and other Necessary Articles," but the cargo had been improperly stowed, and what had not been damaged by heat on the way to Philadelphia was soon reduced in value by the reopening of commerce between town and countryside after the British evacuation. The wealthy Quakers on the committee in Philadelphia agreed to make good the full value. A part of the provisions was turned over to the Monthly Meetings in the city to be paid for out of the stock and used for the relief of Friends and outsiders.[44]

Aid to Philadelphia from overseas opened the way to more effective efforts. Communications between London and Philadelphia remained good enough to allow English and Irish Quakers to begin a project for the relief of persons suffering from the war. The Irish National Meeting authorized a group of Philadelphia Quakers to draw up to £2,000 against its credit to be used by the Meeting for Sufferings to help Friends throughout America. An English contribution, intended for outsiders as well, was put at the disposal of an *ad hoc* committee like that formed to receive the cargoes of provisions. Keeping the aid to non-Quakers outside the Meeting for Sufferings in this instance — even more than before — was a mere formality. The committee of Philadelphians consisted largely of members of the Meeting, their business was partly carried on through the Meeting's correspondence, they reported to the Meeting on everything they did, and called on Meetings for Sufferings elsewhere to act as their agents. The funds available to American Friends from the two sources across the Atlantic ultimately amounted to more than £6,000 sterling, though not all the money had been used by 1783. The bulk of it was spent in Nantucket, Rhode Island, and North Carolina in 1780 and 1781.[45]

Toward the end of the war hardship became most widespread in the South, and relief to non-Friends became an ever larger part of the project. Some £500 were spent on the frontier areas of North Carolina, South Carolina, and Georgia. As soon as the British evacuated Charleston and Savannah, a committee of North Carolina Yearly Meeting rushed in to give money to the distressed poor. Some Quaker refugees from the back country were lodged in the Charleston Meeting House. As most Monthly Meetings could care for their own members, funds were available for such extraordinary services as the release of thirteen captives held by Indians. The last contribution to North Carolina was made in 1784, with £200 from the fund raised in Ireland. The donors had expected to help only Friends and felt some annoyance on learning how much had been spent on others.[46]

This slight friction was soon smoothed away, however, partly as a result of a new charitable project. A group of loyalists in dire straits was discovered in Nova Scotia. The women and children among them were Quakers, though the men were not — probably because they had been disowned for fighting. The Philadelphia Meeting for Sufferings sent books for their spiritual comfort, to be conveyed by a Friend traveling that way on business who was to send word about other needs which Philadelphia could supply. The London Meeting for Sufferings resolved to help, too. When the severe winter of 1786–1787 created a fresh emergency, Philadelphia sent two men with provisions bought with some of the remaining Irish funds. But the Americans thought the importation laws made it more economical for Friends still in the British Empire to send aid, and as, as a result, Quakers on both sides of the Atlantic cooperated to help victims of the conflict between their nations. The only outsiders given relief in Maritime Canada were some "free Black People" in Nova Scotia and New Brunswick whose "distressed Situation" came to the attention of London Quakers, who contributed about £200 in 1788 for salt and clothing.[47] This final project in war relief constituted a broadening of the philanthropic purpose, a willingness to let it be detached from the specific emergency. This modification manifested itself even more clearly in the disposition of the remaining funds gathered in England for war relief. In 1787 the donors consented to requests from Philadelphia to give the bulk of what remained undistributed to the Monthly Meeting's school for free Negro children.[48]

This transaction illustrated on a small scale much of the transformation of Quaker benevolence during the American Revolution. Wartime distress had been the occasion for an ambitious project to aid the public and protect the reputation of Quakerdom, but when the emergency was over Friends felt it was appropriate to give the remaining unused funds to a philanthropic institution with a value quite independent of the war. The two purposes were interchangeable because the religious fellowship had taken a responsibility to do good to the civil community around it. Throughout the American Yearly Meetings — though less so in the South than in the North — the Society of Friends had reshaped itself to make possible this revision of its role in the world. Paradoxically, the Quakers had achieved the enlargement of their Society's role in the world by withdrawing as individuals from older kinds of contact with the world to seek greater uniformity and stronger organization among themselves. They dug a deeper canyon between their church and the community around them by establishing schools to insulate their children from corrupt associations, by insisting on their distinctive behavior in the face of a suspicious or hostile public, by denying themselves glory or profit from the Revolution, and by imposing on themselves new self-denials by rejecting officeholding, liquor, and slave labor.

Yet these measures did not burn all bridges across the gap. Quakers believed that all men could purify themselves and achieve sanctification. They needed to demonstrate their conviction by their own lives, both to reassure themselves and to edify outsiders. If Quakerism had a value, as its adherents were sure it did, it needed all the protection that separateness could give to preserve itself in the Revolutionary turmoil. The religious Society, newly solidified and rebuilt, was to be a place of strength from which action could be directed to the world for the common good. The primary objective, it is true, was defense. Moral attack was the best defense against the opprobrium heaped on Friends for what they regarded as their virtues — pacifism and orderly self-discipline. Yet even before the war, they had begun to follow the leadership of Pennsylvania to find ways to influence the general public for good without compromising themselves.

Under pressure from other Americans, Quakers learned better how to stand as a united body, to use private societies and their Meetings to exert a counter-pressure. Between the network of Meetings for Sufferings and Monthly Meeting schools, they added greatly to their institutional equipment. Almost from the time of their creation these new corporate arms offered help to outsiders. With specialized subsidiaries, begun by the Philadelphia school for free Negroes, these innovations in church organization made service to non-Quakers a pursuit sponsored by the Society of Friends at its summit as well as in its local branches.

Acting as a united phalanx, Quakers advanced a process which had been under way for other reasons, the leveling of the membership. Not only did they expel those unable to act in concert with the group, they gave less prominence to individual leaders. The ranks no longer contained as many of the rich and powerful as had been there in the days of the Kinseys, Logans, Norrises, and Rhode Island Wantons, and those who remained lost the importance in the Society that they had already given up in the state. At the brink of the Revolution, the Pemberton brothers were Clerks of Philadelphia Monthly, Yearly, and Quarterly Meetings, and the Meeting for Sufferings. With their near associates — the Smiths, Drinkers, Anthony Benezet, Isaac Zane, and John Reynell — they continued to perform the most important work of the Society throughout the Revolutionary years. Thereafter, tenure in Clerkships began to grow short, and Philadelphia followed London Yearly Meeting in changing Clerks often. The new members entering the highest circles, moreover, tended to be persons of no great standing outside the Society, such as Isaac Lawton, the schoolmaster who presided over the moral revival as Clerk of New England Yearly Meeting, or men like John Pemberton or Nicholas Waln, who renounced the main atributes of success in the world when they took positions of leadership among Friends.

As the Society became more homogeneous, it became increasingly easy for Friends to use their organization for denominational ends in the public scene, and correspondingly harder to further those ends as individuals. It was the Society that petitioned Lieutenant Governor Penn against dramatic performances; the Society sent deputations with Memorials and Addresses to legislatures in Rhode Island, Pennsylvania, Maryland, Virginia, and North Carolina. It gave aid to refugees from Boston and victims of war on the

Carolina frontier, and obtained the release of illegally re-enslaved Negroes.

The Society publicized and cultivated the benevolent character of its work. Having offered "Acts of Benevolence & Humanity to our Fellow-Creatures in Distresses of many kinds" as an alternative to theatrical productions, it pointed out near the beginning of the Revolution that Friends had learned from Christ "that Meekness, Patience & universal Love to Mankind will be rewarded with Peace, passing the Understanding of the carnal Mind." But universal love to mankind had to be carried into conduct in an active way, and amid efforts to do so, Friends pointed out that their religious ways were particularly conducive to such good works. In the aftermath of the British occupation of Philadelphia, the Monthly Meeting recommended systematic frugality to its members in order to finance relief to the poor while cultivating virtuous self-restraint.[49]

Friends expected the good will of the public in return for benevolence. When their schools were attacked by requirement of a teachers' oath, they replied that they had always educated without charge the poor of other persuasions. When criticized for their relations with the Indians, they pointed to the "real Concern for the deplorable Situation of our fellow Subjects," as well as the Indians, which led them to give relief through the Meeting for Sufferings and contribute to the good projects of the Friendly Association. When baffled in an attempt to repair the lack of payment to Indians for lands occupied by members of Hopewell Monthly Meeting, the Meeting for Sufferings directed that the money gathered for that purpose be used "for the Service & Benefit of other Indians." When aid was given to sufferers from war in New England, Friends hoped that a good impression was made "by the uniform tenor of our Lives and Conduct, and the disinterested practice of doing good and communicating of the blessings imparted to us." When Friends' Discipline was attacked in the Pennsylvania Assembly, the Meeting for Sufferings could reply, "Our religious Meetings were instituted for the laudable Intention of inculcating in our fellow-Members Worship to Almighty God, Benevolence to Mankind, and to encourage one another in a sted-

fast upright Conduct according to the Principles of the Gospel."
Friends found their place in a hostile world from which they did
not want to withdraw completely by perfecting their own behavior — denying self in rank, display or power — and uniting in
their Society to preach reforms to others, lobby for better laws,
and do good for those around them.[50]

XIV

The Society of Friends in Post-Revolutionary America

At the end of the Revolutionary War, the devout Quakers realized that they would have to make greater efforts to purify the Society if it was to fill the role they had chosen for it in the community at large. They feared that the end of the special difficulties which beset them during the fighting would mean a relapse into "Lethargy of Soul" and a delusion of "false Security." New England Yearly Meeting lamented that "a people whose ancestors accounted nothing near or dear when it came in competition with their religious Testimonies, and who profess themselves bound by Divine conviction faithfully to maintain the same," should so "flagrantly" deviate from the example of the older generation! Surely it was inexcusable "in this day of Light wherein we have liberty to attend to our respective religious concerns, Unmolested." A few years earlier, while earthly dangers besieged the Friends, the Meeting for Sufferings had assured them that their tribulations had great worth. If Quakers persevered in "holding up of the light According to our Measure, in progressive steps," their sufferings would be "an acceptable offering" to God; they could even brace themselves with the conviction that partaking of Christ's "Cup of Affliction" in the form of the Revolutionary turmoil would lead to their own salvation and the welfare of the whole civil community, "for it is through Tribulation that the Righteous in every age enter the Kingdom" and learn to alleviate the woes of others. But in 1788 it was necessary to urge even the ministers and elders to refrain from holding public office; "rather let us by our peaceable lives &

good Conversation evidence to the world our Attachment to the real Welfare of our Country, & by a pious Uniform Labour for the Discouragement of Vice & Immorality be instrumental to the promotion of that Righteousness which Exalteth A Nation." [1]

Nor was the danger confined to New England. In the Territory of Philadelphia Yearly Meeting the same threat of relaxation arose once the war was over. In Pennsylvania renewed temptations to seek public office had to be fought. The Yearly Meeting detected too many hearts "secretly defiled and departed from the Love of God, and inordinately bound in their affections to perishing Treasures and sensual gratifications." Similar troubles prevailed in Virginia and North Carolina. [2]

To some degree these lamentations were conventional repetitions of the calls for improvement begun by the moral reform movement, which could hardly have continued with unflagging zeal in the Middle Atlantic states for over thirty years. Yet the pious felt a renewed sense of urgency in the good work in the North, and at last the corporate sense of sin and horror of sin came awake in the South. By 1788, among those who carried on the campaign in Philadelphia and New England Yearly Meetings, were many reared since the original outburst of fervor. Their freshest memories were not of the days when Friends had ranked among the high and mighty of Pennsylvania, New Jersey, and Rhode Island, but rather of the political trials and tempests which had begun in the middle of the eighteenth century and of the long struggle to reform their religious Society. In the post-Revolutionary years Quakers saw no way to prevent the spread of corruption in the church except by uniting the members in a tightly organized, highly uniform Society of Friends. [3]

The reformers of New England and Philadelphia, with the lengthening record of efforts to restore the ancient purity of the fellowship behind them, had to explain the lack of success and find new methods to maintain the structure of their religious Society as it had been reshaped during the troubled years. They tried to analyze the persistence of worldliness more carefully than before, to discover how it entered and kept its place. They began to give more attention to psychological explanations. One year Falls

Monthly Meeting, summarizing the advices from Philadelphia Yearly Meeting, set down the "Declention from the Life and Virtue of Truth" to "the enfeebling benumbing and stupefying effects of . . . a Love of and conformity to the Spirit and Maxims of this world, the Deceitfulness whereof leading from under the wholesome Discipline of the Cross & into a light estimation of the lowly innocent Simplicity of it." Thus, Friends neglected to attend religious meetings, or, if they went, were "unprepared by a right concern" for their duties there. Worse still, the parents' "Declention" exposed "unguarded Youth and others . . . to further Deviations from the several branches of [their] . . . Christian Testimony," thus promoting a general increase of depravity under which, among other evils, the enslavement of their fellow men had taken place. New England Yearly Meeting could find only an original fault of will to explain the failure of so many of its members to observe the restraints imposed by Friends' discipline. Once they had allowed their minds "to be . . . drawn aside and given up to the influence of the adversary of [their] . . . Immortal Souls," they exposed themselves "to the inundations of folly and vice, whereby their minds [were] . . . alienated from the principles of Piety and Virtue." [4]

It was a continuing challenge to the pious, however, that notwithstanding the repeated "advices" and visits by committees that had impressed the members with their obligations, there still remained many in the Society whose lives were "so far from being circumscribed by the Truth we profess, as to . . . unfit them for the immediate service of and usefulness in the Church." In New England the Yearly Meeting of Ministers and Elders concluded somewhat gloomily that restoring the church was "a gradual Work" that required "Many Overturnings of Every building on us Which our own hands may persume to Erect." Perfect restoration could not be expected at once, for only after every man-made structure had been demolished would "that building Whose foundation is the Rock of ages be Established in Glory and prosper in the Beauty of holiness Over Every Cunning Workmanship of man." It behooved every Friend to beware of the "Danger of Formality" in maintaining the church; but at least the rightly concerned could devote themselves to the good of the organization and not "under the specious Pretence of more extensive Charity," rush off to engage in worldly affairs, thus "blending the Precious with the Vile, and thereby lay[ing] Waste the Heritage of our God."[5]

Friends discovered no important new ascetic practices to improve their sect in these post-Revolutionary years. The southern Yearly Meetings continued to cleanse themselves of slaveholding while those in the North insisted that members avoid the use of products of slave labor and reimburse former slaves. With the new strictures against liquor, Philadelphia Yearly Meeting proceeded from stronger minutes of caution against tippling and dealing in strong drink, to appointing a committee to deal with offenders, then fixing a penalty for persistent violation. At worst, the Friend who used or sold liquor could be barred from "Truth's service," but a new query put the subject in the list of faults which Quakers encouraged one another to avoid. New York inserted a query against drink in 1783. Virginia Yearly Meeting threatened to disown distillers as early as 1782, though North Carolina did not take such a stand until a generation later.[6]

New England followed roughly the course of Philadelphia against liquor, inspired by the hope that Friends' temperance would presently become universal and be imitated first by "all Denominations of Christians," then by "Mankind in General." As with the signs of moral decline the Yearly Meeting sought the key to effective action against drunkenness by asking the members to look carefully at their motives for "using, . . . distilling, importing, trading in or handing out to others" any "Spirituous Liquors." Since intemperate drinking led "from calmness and innocency to . . . many evils," and might become habitual, Friends would serve alike the well-being of their religious Society and their neighbors by "holding up a Standard" of sobriety.[7]

Perhaps the leading trait of the post-Revolutionary reform spirit was its increased devotion to simplicity. Absence of ornament no longer satisfied the moral requirements. Ideally, even the plainest "luxuries" had to go. The virtuous Friend turned his back on the enjoyment of wealth as well as power in favor of a standard of living attainable by any industrious self-supporting man. More than ever before in the eighteenth century a social equality in the religious Society became feasible. As George Churchman observed: "More liberty than formerly, is graciously opened to some of mean, and of low estate . . . This prospect and experience of more liberty in Spirit, has at times been attended with a large expansion of heart towards the Brethren of all Classes, in every place" — as well as more widespread humility in the members when evaluating their own spiritual renovation.[8]

Simplicity abetted godliness. Plain living guarded the pious from worldiness and conditioned their souls for attachment to God and his church. Quakers did not discard their belief that regeneration was a result of the Light Within, but the reformers of the 1790's no longer had the sense of assisting a miraculous rebirth of piety in the church, such as Samuel Fothergill had felt in Pennsylvania in 1755. Instead, they hoped to sustain the revived moral fervor by better control of the human means which fostered godliness or wickedness in the psyche. More confident than their ancestors of man's ability to shape beneficial institutions, the post-Revolutionary generation sought to build into the church government the means to perpetuate the Society of Friends into future generations.

The clearest necessity was to start instructing young Friends at the tenderest age. Youths' meetings were carried on for several years, but toward the end of the eighteenth century they frequently were discontinued. Meetings made new efforts to put proper literature before the growing children, but the major emphasis had to be on schools. The development of facilities to educate children under the Society's care proceeded in all Yearly Meetings, though not with equal determination or at the same pace. Friends in New York did fairly well. In New England there was less general acceptance of the ideal of Meeting schools than elsewhere. Dartmouth Monthly Meeting in Massachusetts actually opposed it. Quakers in Smithfield, Rhode Island, could see no need to take their school under Meeting supervision. Newport Monthly Meeting operated a school for a few years prior to 1800 but then decided to use its educational funds to support a large number of institutions outside its control which served non-Friends as well. New Bedford Quakers preferred to back an Academy operated on a private charter. Nantucket alone managed to keep open a Meeting school, begun in 1784, and by 1803 decided to pay all its expenses out of the Meeting's stock and throw its doors open to all Friends' children free of charge. However, for a time the school employed a non-Quaker master! Elsewhere in New England nothing was accomplished.[9]

In Philadelphia Yearly Meeting most local units were successful in gathering endowment funds, buying necessary property and opening schools for the children of members, and sometimes for poor white non-Friends and Negroes as well. In some rural Meetings, however, it proved impossible to get Quaker children out of "mixed" schools, since country Friends were too widely scattered to attend the same day school and could not afford to board elsewhere during school sessions. Such Meetings charged their committees on education to exert some influence for the sectarian good by visiting schoolmasters patronized by Friends, even if the masters were not members. In southern and western Pennsylvania, especially, some "langour" on the subject of proper schooling was noticeable. The Yearly Meeting kept exhorting more care in every session from 1783 to 1787, and renewed the pleas in 1789. Although reports from the Quarterly Meetings had mentioned difficulties in finding proper masters or too great a tendency to rely on "private Subscriptions of Friends and others in their Neighbourhood who have youth to educate," by 1792 a satisfying amount of activity was reported. Year by year, Quarterly Meetings brought in details of new educational activities. By 1798 even remote Cattawissa Monthly Meeting could say that it had set up a school.[10]

In the South both the concern for setting up Meeting schools and success in doing so lagged behind Philadelphia. Maryland Friends took some interest in the business in 1783 and the later 1790's, but Baltimore Yearly Meeting did not push it until 1816. In Virginia, the Yearly Meeting drew up a plan for the establishment of a school in 1785, but there were few members, and only two of the Monthly Meetings managed to maintain schools, and those for only about three years at the most. In North Carolina many members were leaving for the West, and the urgency of the Yearly Meeting's plea to start schools in 1785 brought no response. The only evidence of concern came in annual complaints of grave deficiencies. Quaker teachers conducted classes as private ventures in several parts of the state, however, so many parents could patronize the next best thing to institutions under the Society's supervision. When the campaign to found Meeting schools had achieved nothing by 1829, the Yearly Meeting decided to lower its goal to the creation of Monthly Meeting libraries to enable members to protect the minds of their children from contamination.[11]

Meeting schools required heavy contributions by the members. To a large extent this meant intra-Meeting charity only. In New England there was no effort to offer schooling to children of outsiders at less than full tuition. In the territory of Philadelphia Yearly Meeting, however, unless poverty prevented them, Monthly and Preparative Meetings often made provision for poor children of white outsiders and for free Negroes. Friends readily accepted the task of aiding the colored children, and especially after 1789 were willing to add poor white non-members. Such youngsters had to accept the rules set down by the Meeting for its own scholars, which sometimes included attendance at Friends' religious worship as well as Quaker deportment. Evidently they were willing to conform, for during the 1790's white children outside the Society attended its schools in many places in Pennsylvania and New Jersey. The urban community which poured the most philanthropic energy into this work was Wilmington, Delaware. A series of gifts and bequests, culminating in the 1790's in the formation of a standing fund to receive small donations and subscriptions, brought the Monthly Meeting, by 1813, a capital of $2690.31, which it used to send the poor of all races and faiths to schools run by the Meeting or by individual Friends. Clauses in wills leaving bequests to swell this total revealed a strong insistence on the purpose of aiding non-Quakers.[12]

Quakers soon realized that the philanthropic use of Monthly Meeting schools defeated their main purpose. It was convenient to carry out the corporate concern to care for free Negroes by putting their children at the feet of Quaker schoolmasters; it was laudably benevolent to teach poor white children; but the Meeting schools had been intended to insulate young Friends from dangerous associations. As early as 1789, Philadelphia Yearly Meeting advised caution; it was unwise for Western Quarterly Meeting to take under its care a school partly financed and patronized by outsiders.[13]

To guarantee an education to the members' children that would be sectarian beyond all question the Yearly Meeting turned to the establishment of boarding schools exclusively for Quakers. The new method was not entirely antithetical to the objective of Monthly day schools. When New England Yearly Meeting first decided upon a boarding school it was partly to train masters to be hired by Monthly Meetings. To the local aspirations, however, was added the encouragement of English Friends who had started a boarding school at Ackworth and recommended that Americans set up similar institutions. The special training in silent waiting, the rigid insistence on Quaker dress and speech, could best be carried on in classes away from home and worldly neighbors. The New Englanders looked favorably on a "temporary weaning of Children from their expectations of parental indulgences." The Yearly Meeting operated the school at Portsmouth, Rhode Island, from 1784 to 1788, when it closed for lack of sufficient financial support. The Meeting for Sufferings continued to accumulate a fund to reopen it, but interest in sectarian education among New England Friends languished for many years.[14]

In Philadelphia, however, enthusiasm ripened quickly for a similar project. Discussion on the subject was brought to a focus by a pamphlet by Owen Biddle, who reviewed the solution to the educational problems of English Quakers in the Ackworth school. He quoted generously from Dr. John Fothergill on the advantages of the new institution for starting habits of Quaker behavior in the young, training them in silent waiting for the manifestations of the Inner Light, and replacing the world's false ideals of aggressive manliness with a laudable courage in virtue and sensitivity to the troubles and consciences of others. He added some suggestions of his own for modifying the plan of Ackworth to suit Pennsylvania conditions, recommending particularly that space be allowed in any American boarding school for resident "artificers and husbandmen" who would teach the scholars all the practical arts.[15]

Philadelphia Monthly Meeting appointed a committee to confer with Biddle. On the basis of its favorable report, the subject of a Yearly Meeting boarding school was taken up the ladder of Meetings. In 1794 the Yearly Meeting had the satisfaction of hearing from its committee on the project that interest existed throughout all the Quarterly Meetings, and Friends had already subscribed the £5,000 basic fund. Money-raising continued, some donations being offered specifically to pay for the tuition of poor Quakers' children, and the school was opened at Westtown in 1799. It succeeded admirably.[16]

Other Meetings began similar projects. While Philadelphia was still getting ready, New York Yearly Meeting opened its Nine Partners Boarding School in Dutchess County in 1796. Friends at Plainfield, New Jersey, apparently not satisfied to patronize either Westtown, Nine Partners, or the new institution run by the Monthly Meeting at New York City, wanted to start their own boarding school in 1801, but did not find enough support for the project.[17]

In Southern Quarter of Philadelphia Yearly Meeting (Delaware and the Eastern Shore of Maryland) the boarding-school plan recommended itself as a solution to the chief difficulty thwarting the establishment of Meeting day schools, the scattered residence of the members. The Quarterly Meeting kept a boarding school in session for four years at Duck Creek Cross Roads, Delaware, drawing not only local patronage but Friends of Virginia Yearly Meeting as well. The financial burden of the school, however, exceeded the willingness of the Quarterly Meeting to bear it. Opening the doors to outsiders failed to solve the problem, and after a group of members had struggled to keep classes going for several years as a private enterprise, the school was allowed to close.[18]

In New England the first permanent boarding school achieved a quite different record, but one equally disappointing to proponents of a strictly sectarian education even during the dozen years while it remained a Quaker institution. The Friends' Academy at New Bedford (now located in North Dartmouth, Massachusetts) was founded in 1810 as a private institution and soon received a charter from the state. The announced aim was the same as that of West-town, to educate young Quakers "without endangering their moral and religious principles," although from the start it was expected that the institution would be open to those outsiders who might be "usefully and safely admitted." The founders, most of whom were closely related to the whaling magnate William Rotch, first President of the Board of Trustees and leading donor, had a desire unusual among Massachusetts Quakers — to give their children an extensive scientific and literary education. Their interest in instilling the rules of Quaker behavior in the young may even be questioned. The first master, like many after him, was a bright young Harvard graduate without known leanings toward the Society of Friends. When most of the Trustees in 1823 joined a dissident element in the Society, dubbed "New Light," and as a result had to leave their Monthly Meeting either by resignation or disownment, they formally suspended operation of the Academy for four years, but kept their control of it, and reopened it in 1827. During the intervening years, the New Light Friends, almost to a man, had joined a Unitarian congregation. Under their supervision, whatever strictly Quaker character the institution may have had soon disappeared.[19]

Before that had happened, however, New England Yearly Meeting had managed to start its boarding school again, this time in Providence, Rhode Island. With the aid of donations of land and money from Moses Brown, together with contributions from as far away as England, the Meeting for Sufferings accumulated funds sufficient to put the institution on a secure foundation. The school, which is now the Moses Brown School, opened in 1819, the same year that Baltimore Yearly Meeting started its Fair Hill Boarding School.[20]

North Carolina Friends, unable to support local Meeting schools, looked with hope on the idea of boarding school. As early as 1801 Eastern Quarterly Meeting planned to establish such a school at Little River, but did not succeed until 1834. In 1831 North Carolina Yearly Meeting adopted the boarding-school plan, and opened the New Garden Boarding School six years later.[21]

At a time when many Quakers were taking increased interest in projects to do good for outsiders, and when the hostility of the public no longer served to keep the sect apart, the new schools helped reinforce the sense of separateness which Friends wanted to maintain between their religious community and the outside world. The possibility of recruiting new members through the Meeting schools had never impressed the older Friends; though they took new enthusiasm for carrying their religious message to outsiders, they preferred to use their educational facilities to insulate their children and to ensure that their religious Society would endure without loss of its distinctive traits.

In the light of Quakers' traditional belief that their religious life was the only correct one, and their determination to act toward the Negroes on the theory of equality among men, it would have been logical for them to take advantage of the domestic tranquility after 1783 to convert outsiders, but their behavior toward freed slaves showed most clearly that they felt no compulsion to do so. Many Negroes liberated from Quaker families had at least a rudimentary acquaintance with the religion of their former masters and could have been brought into the church fellowship; Monthly Meetings had formed committees charged with the spiritual and temporal welfare of these people. Yet the committees were not intended to recruit them as members, and the Society of Friends did not welcome them.

Although there may have been a few Negro members during the colonial period, this fact has not been proved. One colored woman had been granted membership in Maine in 1794, but the first known to have joined the Friends in Philadelphia territory was Abigail Franks, who applied to Birmingham Preparative Meeting in Pennsylvania in 1781. Her case was unusual, however. Of her great-grandparents, only one was a Negro and three were Indians; her complexion was light. The local Meeting was sure of the sincerity of her convincement, but in passing her application to the Monthly Meeting, raised the question of her ancestry. In 1783 the case reached the Yearly Meeting, which decided over strong opposition that her sincerity should determine the action of the lower Meeting. The episode continued to disturb leading Friends, including James Pemberton, who expressed himself in private, and Joseph

Drinker, who prepared a paper in 1795 stating his regrets that Friends were the only religious group opposed to taking colored persons into their ranks. The general issue was not regarded as settled by the decision of 1783, for not until 1796, when the application of a mulatto woman for membership in Rahway and Plainfield Monthly Meeting was brought to the Yearly Meeting, was a general rule laid down. A committee of the Men's Yearly Meeting, after consulting women Friends and visitors from other Yearly Meetings, produced a statement saying that they understood that it had always been Friends' intention that applications for membership be considered without regard to nationality or race. The Meeting accepted this view, and the woman became a Friend. A similar incident in North Carolina led to the same decision there in 1800.[22]

The formal minutes of the Society of Friends did not tell the whole story, however. John Hunt, a New Jersey Friend, recorded in his diary after the Yearly Meeting decision of 1796 that many Negroes and mulattoes had sought fellowship with Quakers for more than twenty years past, but had been refused because of the "spirit of prejudice which had been imbibed on account of colour." After the decision had been made to accept them, however, very few joined, and Friends did not seek them out. There were separate benches for colored persons in some meetinghouses even after color had ceased to be a test for membership. The comment which perhaps revealed most honestly the reluctance of Friends to extend the hand of fellowship was one made by the committee of Chesterfield, New Jersey, Monthly Meeting, that only a few freed slaves attended the meetings, "having but little savor of the true religion." "They are generally ignorant as to reading and writing — both old and young." They simply did not fit into the intimate church community which, after the Revolution, was more homogeneous than ever.[23]

The same objection could easily apply, though less obviously, to all white outsiders, too. Still, at the end of the Revolution, Meetings exhibited an interest (unprecedented in the eighteenth century) in winning white converts. Philadelphia Meeting for Sufferings inaugurated a veritable campaign in 1782 with an epistle to inform

Quakers in other Yearly Meetings that it had begun to compile a list of books to be made available to outsiders, and urged that the brethren everywhere join in the good work. There were "many . . . looking towards Friends, from whose Example as well as Doctrine they seem to expect some light and encouragement." Those able to dispense these benefits should "hope . . . to be instrumental in ministering a little Food to those hungry seeking souls." New England Quakers joined eagerly in the project.[24]

As time went on, efforts to enlarge the Society of Friends by convincements became less assertive and less grandiose. In 1790 the Philadelphia Meeting for Sufferings told London: "As new Settlements are forming in remote parts, & the prevalence of an enquiry into the grounds of our Christian testimony & principles is more manifest among persons not in profession with us, than at any former time; the expediency of our being attentive to encourage & promote it, is obvious, & we hope will be continued." With the help of the Londoners the Meeting arranged to get suitable pamphlets printed, including some in French and German. There were efforts to make Quaker religious exercises more accessible to the public. In 1794 Chester Monthly Meeting permitted meetings for worship at a new location, partly to make room for persons of other persuasions in that neighborhood. Friends in the ministry, as usual, expected to draw audiences that would include outsiders. Meetings took greater care to report convincements. But there was no return to the evangelical zeal of George Fox and the First Publishers. Above all, there was no intention to modify the standards of behavior so as to allow new Friends to work into the fellowship easily; the newly convinced had to be prepared to merge with the group.[25]

Rather than finding new ways to expound their doctrines to outsiders, Quakers put emphasis on making their conduct, both as individuals and as a church, a good example to the rest of the world. The better the example they could offer, the greater the influence they could exert and the more they could hope that "enquiring Beholders" would want to join them. But even without making converts, the example would have a beneficial effect on outsiders by "the more extensive spreading of the Light & Knowledge of

[God's] . . . blessed Truth in Places where it's Lustre hath not hitherto been so fully seen," and by "advancing the Doctrine of the Prince of Peace, against the dark & defiling Spirit which is prevalent in those Kingdoms & Nations involved in the cruel & desolating strategems of war." The Society of Friends, as one of the "families of the Earth," should serve the rest by maintaining its special traditions, preserving itself basically as a hereditary organization, and improving its discipline.[26]

Quakers after the Revolution began to accept diversity of denominations among Christians. Meetings tacitly and individual Friends explicitly adopted the view that their sect was not the one true church destined to embrace all the souls truly united to God. Even though the Quaker community was the purest and freest from superstitious observances, its members, while proclaiming divine Truth, need not try to wean less enlightened outsiders from their denominational affiliations. William Savery, one of the most renowned public Friends of the post-Revolutionary period, often found that his ministry was for outsiders. On one occasion he spoke on the theme that the invisible church — the totality of souls united to God — included some "in every name and among every nation," who were already brethren in Christ. He believed it unnecessary to draw them all into the Society of Friends; they could join in religious communion and receive the benefit of Savery's preaching without leaving their various denominations. Robert Proud explained that religious diversity arose from differences in customs, education, individual capacities to understand God's message, and different "situations in the world." Religious uniformity need not be expected while the facts of life remained which created diversity. But the general religious duty to honor the Divinity and obey his laws was well known to all men, and Friends had always maintained that it was logically necessary that God in his goodness had made the means of salvation available to everyone, and had done so by the Light Within. Friends thought their understanding of God's Truth clearer, their church purer and more conducive to right conduct, than others, but they acknowledged that the difference was one of degree, not of kind, and that a religious life could be led by men of other persuasions.[27]

Acting on these ideas, Quakers in the post-Revolutionary years offered examples of good works and proclaimed their religious Society's usefulness to the public. Occasions for such statements were particularly abundant in the years when state governments were being revised and national institutions set up. The Friends had reconciled themselves to the system of popular participation in choosing officials and laying down fundamental laws. Having shelved the old axiom that they should take no part in setting up governments, Quakers wanted to demonstrate their special capacity to advance the public welfare by calling official attention to basic moral truths.

Meetings had earlier petitioned legislatures for laws which would enable Friends to carry out their distinctive testimonies unmolested. When they required manumission laws, they asked, in effect, for benefits to Negroes, though the immediate purpose was to enable Friends to free their own slaves. The more general aspect of these laws did not escape the petitioners, however, and it was an easy next step for them to ask for laws against the slave trade or for compulsory manumission, which they had begun to do even before 1776. After the Revolution, when Meetings requested such laws, they usually took care to speak not only as a religious sect but also as a part of the sovereign people, justifying the demands by appeals to the Declaration of Independence or other official statements of principle. Philadelphia Yearly Meeting began this practice in 1783, in an "Address" to the Continental Congress asking action to stop the slave trade, but it soon was imitated in other Yearly Meetings. When New England, for example, asked the Commonwealth of Massachusetts to discourage the slave trade, it called on the General Court to make its laws consistent with the "declaration of invasion of civil Liberty" issued before "the great revolution of this Country." [28]

The requests made by Friends to the Federal government for measures against slavery earned them the hostility of southerners, who called them dangerous fanatics and questioned their loyalty during the Revolution. Their petitions, however, expressly emphasized the Quakers' acceptance of the political theory of natural rights and their devotion to supra-denominational principles of

Christianity, the constitutions of the several states, and the national welfare. They advised their compatriots that the well-being of the United States would be jeopardized by the continued existence of slavery: the institution was a "gross national Iniquity . . . whereby, in a christian View at least, additional national Guilt is daily accumulating, the Virtue, & of Course the Happiness of the People laid Waste, and the Youth, educated under the debasing Influence of so inhuman a Tyranny, exposed to great Corruption of Principle, & consequently dissoluteness of Manners." The slave trade alone was enough to endanger the gains made in the American Revolution by opening the door to "the evils which now [1793] over Spread those Countries with which we have been most connected." The very fact that Quakers did not stand alone, but were joined in their crusade against the iniquity by persons of many other denominations, afforded proof that they were right, since God governed all hearts. The petitions against the slave trade and the work of lobbying which went with them deliberately minimized sectarian peculiarities and emphasized instead Quaker participation in the body politic.[29]

The same emphasis could be made in even broader terms. Friends managed to present their religious fellowship to the public as a part of the civil community with distinctive and useful virtues, able to hold a guiding torch before the rest of the body politic. Philadelphia Yearly Meeting in 1789 sent an address "To the President Senate and House of Representatives of the United States," declaring that "Unfeigned Righteousness in public as well as private Stations is the only sure Ground of hope for the divine Blessing; whence alone Rulers can derive true Honour [and] establish sincere Confidence in the Hearts of the People." Moreover, the rulers whose "Minds" were "animated with the ennobling Principle of universal good Will to Men" would find "Success attending the Exercise of a solid uniform Virtue; short of which the warmest Pretensions to public Spirit, Zeal for our Country and the Rights of Man, are fallacious and illusive." The Yearly Meeting called on the first President to use his popularity to suppress "Vice, Infidelity and Irreligion and every species of oppression on the Persons and Consciences of Men, so that Righteousness and Peace . . . may prevail." The following year the Meeting for Sufferings, in phrases echoing the Declaration of Independence, stated its opposition to a national militia on grounds quite different from the traditional appeal to the long record of Quaker pacifism. Instead of a sectarian peculiarity, their "Testimony" was traced as "proceeding from the Catholic ground of universal good will to Men," which should be proclaimed whenever an opportunity presented itself.[30]

More urgent reasons for Quakers to tell the nation its duty arose when marks of divine displeasure with the United States appeared. The yellow fever epidemic in the capital city, Friends asserted, was one of the "diversified judgments" by which "the Almighty [brings] . . . down the loftiness of Men." The provoking wickedness on this occasion was the re-enslavement of freed Negroes in several of the states, no doubt aggravated by horse-racing, gambling, the theater, and other immoral or corrupting practices which the Continental Congress by resolutions passed in 1774 had promised to suppress. A petition on the re-enslaved Negroes demanded that the national promises be honored to avert further calamities. It was "very obvious that the God of the Spirits of all Flesh" had raised up the Quakers as advocates to plead the cause of the oppressed colored people. As the chosen people for this and other parts of the Lord's work, their efforts would be "of good Savour among the well disposed of all Classes of Men, & owned by the divine Witness of Truth in their Hearts." As a virtuous religious corporation they had the duty to be grateful for God's mercies during the Revolution; when peace returned, it was in the nature of a reward for their correct attitude, a trophy which they had won for their nation. Others should understand their triumph and "be brought to confess it is through the Love of God shed abroad in our Hearts, and under the Authority thereof, that we labour to promote Peace on Earth & universal good-will to Men, that we are afflicted with the Affliction of the Poor, and oppressed by the Oppression of the Stranger among us." Small wonder that an exasperated southerner in Congress asked, "Is the whole morality of the United States confined to Quakers?" [31]

Looking back on early Pennsylvania during the post-Revolutionary years, Robert Proud saw a demonstration to the world of the "possibility of a still superior bliss, and more exalted felicity, than is commonly experienced in the world." Though political power might not be the means to continue such demonstrations, Quaker Meetings remained institutions for "the Promotion of universal Righteousness" and the furthering of "benevolent purposes," and on at least one occasion a Friend under a concern to pay religious visits in a community went to all the families, not just the Quakers. While carrying on such activities, Friends had to maintain conspicuous uniformity and emphasize the role of their religious fraternity as a whole. If they were to carry its spirit to the world, they had to purify their lives so well and commit themselves so strongly to their sect's unusual ways, that the spirit of the world could not touch them. Mindful of this belief in their obligation to the community at large, Philadelphia Yearly Meeting could reconcile the post-Revolutionary re-emphasis on sectarian exclusiveness with the new role of the Society of Friends in the United States. Even the boarding school designed to insulate young Quakers from the company of other children would produce "an encouraging increase of Lights and way-Marks in the World, which must eventually prove highly beneficial to Civil and religious Community in General." If the Society benefited the nation by its solidarity in virtue and its services as a corporate preacher to the public at large, it served the nation well by the strictest system it could devise to ensure a new generation of Friends.[32]

XV

The First Flowering of Humanitarian Concerns

Quakers, fortified by their stricter, more uniform, discipline and their exclusive educational facilities, could safely undertake a wide array of projects for the benefit of outsiders without risking pollution from the world. Indeed, by their social value such benevolences could demonstrate the goodness of the religious community more fully than petitions. In the post-Revolutionary years the Friends fulfilled the claims which Robert Proud made for their ancestors — that they were "ever among the first, *in works and institutions of charity*, where they lived, according to their abilities: so that in contributions of this nature, they were observed mostly either to be among the introducers or promoters of them, or otherwise distinguished for their liberal donations." [1] Proud referred to private efforts, but after 1783 Meetings showed a willingness to back some of the same projects, and also undertook some highly significant new ones on their own. The further work to guide free Negroes occupied Monthly Meetings, while Yearly Meetings carried petitions to state legislatures and the United States Congress protesting the slave trade and the laws under which freedmen were re-enslaved. The most important expansion of Meeting action, however, came in the missions to teach the habits of civilized life to Indian tribes. These institutions were run by permanent committees which several Yearly Meetings established at about the same time as their boarding schools. The synchronization made manifest in a striking way the largely unconscious ecclesiastical strategy of intensifying group solidarity and entering the public arena *en bloc* to demand national virtue or carry out a useful program.

By the time the new institutions to help non-Quakers were successfully in operation they had become subjects of controversy among Friends and had contributed to the tensions in the Society which led to the schisms over the doctrines of New York's Elias Hicks and New England's John Wilbur. But the outpouring of philanthropic zeal after the Revolution and the pattern of development which led to the establishment of Yearly Meeting boarding schools and Indian committees were culminations of eighteenth-century history, whatever their relation to nineteenth-century experience.

The traditional barriers in the Quaker concept of charity to the operation of social service programs through Meetings did not yield completely under the impact of the Revolution. The extent of the breaches differed from place to place, but nowhere did Friends include every philanthropy that found support from members of their Society among the proper functions of the church. Justification of Quakerism by good works did not require that much! The field left to private organization for such projects consequently varied. But for the first time in America there were many Friends eager to organize, whether inside or outside of their Society, for reform, civic improvement, and aid to the downtrodden or ignorant. The widespread eagerness showed more about the character of Quakerdom than the careers of a few paragons of philanthropy. The outpouring of effort in activities not sponsored by the religious Society displayed the scope of social service which benevolent and public-spirited Friends thought worthwhile. To understand the undertakings of the Society as "corporate concerns" it will be helpful to examine them in comparison with the range of possible activities revealed by private projects.

Many American Friends responded to the end of wartime adversities much as John Bellers had asked English Friends to do when religious toleration had been won in their nation — they set out to promote reform by example as well as precept. In private societies — some of them consisting entirely or mostly of Quakers — or as individuals, they pursued a wide variety of objectives.

In some instances, organizations independent of the Society performed work which the church would not do. Several groups, for example, provided gifts and services to the poor, regardless of denomination. In Burlington, New Jersey, the Friendly Institution, founded in 1796 by Quakers, set out to discover and help the needy whom public officials neglected, a plan which individual Friends had followed previously, though their Society had simply recommended poor outsiders to public authorities. The Institution later took on educational charities and broadened its membership to include outsiders.[2]

In Philadelphia, New York, Flushing, Long Island, and Wilmington, Delaware, women Friends started societies to relieve the poor, especially of their own sex. The Philadelphians opened Aimwell, a free school for poor girls, in 1807, but they had earlier been holding regular classes for Negro women. They had also formed "female Societies" to assist "a certain class of poor women, who are sometimes neglected, although they have always the best claim to a charitable notice; those . . . who would be industrious, if they were provided with employment adapted to their strength & talents." The young women of the societies explored "the retreats of poverty in search of the most Deserving objects, among their own sex." They gave money or medicine when appropriate, "but to most of them materials for spinning, sewing, knitting, and other employments for which they are deemed best qualified." The Quaker women of Wilmington had a similar Female Benevolent Society, while those in the vicinity of Providence formed the Smithfield Female School Society to teach reading, writing, numbers, and religion to suitable beneficiaries.[3]

The most successful of the charity school organizations was that backed strongly by men Friends in New York City. Discussing ways to enlarge their projects, a group of Quakers, including Thomas Eddy, better known as a prison reformer, decided in 1805 to seek the support of outsiders. The augmented body was incorporated as the New York Free School Society and with the aid of government subsidies expanded its operations to an extent that it could perform the services of a public school system until it surrendered its charter and turned over its buildings to the city's school department in 1853.[4]

Elsewhere, Quakers participated in the founding and operation of schools which were not primarily charitable, and in various civic improvements, often in cooperation with persons of other religions. In Providence, for example, Moses Brown joined non-Quakers in a committee to develop the city's schools. In the Deptford Free School in New Jersey and the Friends' Academy at New Bedford, Quakers promoted institutions mainly for themselves. In addition, they backed a number of civic projects, including fire and library companies, and their names appeared among the sponsors of societies to provide Bibles to the needy.[5]

Support of medical institutions remained a matter for private philanthropy. The Pennsylvania Hospital continued to enjoy Quaker generosity, and other medical facilities had the support of various Friends. In New York, Thomas Eddy served for years on the Board of Governors of the New York Hospital and, inspired by the example of English Friends who had started the York Retreat for the insane, persuaded others on the Board to start a similar asylum at Bloomingdale.[6]

Prison and penal reform drew the interest of Quakers, though not promoted through their Society. Leadership in the penitentiary movement earned Eddy fame as the "Howard of America." Philadelphia Friends, however, had backed the cause before him. Some of them had been interested in prison reform prior to the Revolution and kept the Philadelphia Society for Assisting Distressed Prisoners going for over a year before the British occupation. Persons in jail were expected to pay for their own food and clothing, though they often could not afford it. The Philadelphia Society supplied these necessities. After the war, some Quakers resumed the service, but they wanted the injustice of the situation rectified by state support of prisoners. Friends also began to oppose imprisonment for debt, and both as individuals and in societies supplied money to secure the release of persons incarcerated for their inability to repay small sums. After the Revolution, the prison reform movement, with strong inspiration from Beccaria, Montesquieu, Howard, and the experiments in various European cities, acquired broader objectives. Some Quakers readily agreed to the ideal of reforming criminals and training them to take an effective part in the economy. The advantages of making prisons self-supporting at the same time that they became educational, by putting the convicts to work, appealed to Friends as moralists and taxpayers. The policy of solitary confinement to keep prisoners from encouraging each other in wickedness and to isolate them with their consciences met a ready response from Quakers, who had long believed that detachment from terrestrial things would lead to attention to the spiritual stirrings within.[7]

In company with many outsiders, Friends in 1787 formed the Philadelphia Society for Alleviating the Miseries of Public Prisons, later the Pennsylvania Prison Society. Caleb Lownes and Roberts Vaux were among the prominent Quakers in the organization, which secured legislation setting up the "Walnut Street Jail," in which the penitentiary plan was tried. The Prison Society also lobbied, with some success, for various experiments in administration and prisoner labor and for changes in the penal code to conform to advanced theories. The Pennsylvania reforms gave the Walnut Street Jail international fame between 1790 and 1799, but the movement flagged for several years until the building of Eastern State Penitentiary to try the solitary confinement plan.[8]

Friends in Delaware and New York joined men of other denominations to lobby and petition for prison reform. In Delaware the movement met success with the establishment of a penitentiary in the 1820's. In New York, Thomas Eddy, together with fellow Quakers and influential men of other religions, persuaded the state legislature to change the penal code in 1796 and later. The same men also promoted the establishment of reformed prisons by both state and city.[9]

Private associations enabled Quakers to combine forces with outsiders to carry out projects which the church would not undertake or which it wished to discontinue. When Meetings became convinced that accepting poor white students in schools established for the sectarian training of young Friends impeded the main purpose of these institutions, Quakers formed independent organizations to set up free schools for poor white children or to pay their tuition in existing schools. Although the official change of policy did not strike down with equal vigor the teaching of free Negro children at Meeting schools, some Quakers evidently saw a need for more benefits to Negroes than their fellow-members could agree to support. The opportunity to supplement the Society's efforts in this direction frequently took the more zealous Friends into partnership with outsiders, usually in the abolition societies.

These organizations sprang up in many parts of the United States after the Revolution. Quakers took part in them in Rhode Island, New York, New Jersey, Pennsylvania, Delaware, Maryland, and North Carolina. The abolition societies turned their attention first to regaining the freedom of colored persons who had been claimed as slaves, kidnaped, and sold into slavery, or even re-enslaved under the law (as in North Carolina). Quakers, who predominated in the organizations in Philadelphia and New York, took great interest in this work. A Baltimore Friend, Elisha Tyson, made himself famous for his daring rescues. Toward the end of the eighteenth century the abolition societies began to put stress on persuading legislatures to change the laws. They asked more stringent measures against kidnaping Negroes to re-enslave them, against the importation, sale, or bequest of slaves, toward equalizing the treatment of Negroes and whites, easing of manumission requirements, and even outright emancipation. The societies also began to educate the free Negroes.[10]

Sometimes — as in Philadelphia — the abolition societies sponsored schools for colored people, and sometimes gave financial aid to smaller clubs formed for that purpose. For example, the abolition society after 1793 paid the master of Philadelphia Monthly Meeting's school for free Negro children to hold evening classes with the assistance of Friends in the Association for the Instruction of Adult Colored Persons formed in 1789. The Meeting contributed only the use of its schoolhouse. Members of the Association took turns assisting the teacher and held classes on Sunday afternoon for those who could not attend evenings. The abolition society continued its support for several years. Quakers in Burlington, New Jersey, however, failed to make a similar arrangement with the local abolition society, though it recommended "the subject of Education" to the attention of the abolition societies elsewhere in the state.[11]

The little clubs of Quakers who set out to give education and moral training to the free Negroes ordinarily had to operate on their dues, enthusiasm, and very little else. The stock was ample in Philadelphia, where the Association of Friends held two classes for a time, charging no tuition, though allowing masters of bound servants to pay at a fixed rate if they chose to do so. The Quakers even held weekly evening sessions during the summer of 1790 "to prevent our scholars from forgetting what little they have learned." Ultimately the members of the Association decided to hire a permanent assistant teacher to supplement their own work in helping the regular master. The women in the Association similarly held classes for colored persons of their own sex. They became virtually autonomous in 1795, but discontinued their efforts after 1802, when they decided that other organizations were doing the good work. Another group of Quaker women revived the school in 1810. In all classes held under the Association and its ladies' auxiliaries the pupils were taught religion as well as reading, writing, and arithmetic. The women's sessions were "frequently attended by Friends engaged in the ministry, and appear to have been seasons of Divine favor."[12]

The example and precept of the Philadelphia Association guided similar organizations on a smaller scale elsewhere. They kept up correspondence, by which the Philadelphians encouraged the others when they became disheartened by the arduous labor, the irregular attendance, or the failure of the pupils to learn. A small club started by William Thompson and Walter Pierpoint in Baltimore taught an evening school which took in slaves, even without their masters' consent, and won the good will of the masters to such a degree as to assure their financial support as long as the club members did the work. After several seasons of dwindling enthusiasm, the members turned the project over to their Monthly Meeting. This happy remedy did not save the good work in New Jersey and Rhode Island. The Burlington School Society for the Free Instruction of the Blacks kept in operation for over three years, when it languished for want of zeal or sufficient funds. It was revived, with a women's branch, however, in 1797.[13]

The clubs in Providence and Newport were ephemeral. The moving spirits were Obadiah Brown, son of Moses, in Providence, and Benjamin Hadwen in Newport. The Rhode Islanders were inspired by the prospect of proving to the world that Negroes were men "of the Same species" as themselves, "possessing the same Capacities," and that only education created the "Apparent Contrast" between them. The Burlington Society had also felt "insensibly" united to the whole Negro "People" and thereby to "all mankind as Brethren." They, like the Philadelphians, believed that when Negroes had been educated as well as other Americans, the whites would lose their prejudices against them, would look on them as fellow rational beings, and be more disposed to give them their natural liberty.[14]

In the South, where educating Negroes posed the biggest problem and encountered the most stubborn local resistance, not even Quaker efforts could accomplish much. Robert Pleasants of Virginia, an outstanding philanthropic Friend, in 1784 sought to enlist the support of outsiders by circulating proposals for a school to be established in his state. In spite of the lack of response, he started a private institution on a plantation named "Gravelly Hills" which he donated as an endowment. Before he died the possibility of nonsectarian support had appeared so dim that his Monthly Meeting, White Oak Swamp, took over the school and kept it running at least until 1824. In North Carolina, with the ranks thinned by westward migration, Meetings tried to teach local Negroes, but without success. A group of young Friends made brave efforts to keep a Sunday afternoon school open at New Garden in 1821, but the best results were those of the Manumission Society, in which Quakers were active, during the 1820's.[15]

The role of the church remained limited. Only rarely were Meetings willing to undertake social services to white outsiders; at no time did they back reformist causes like the penitentiary movement. Wilmington's generosity in educating poor children was the most striking exception, and it did not establish any new institution. Corporate action by Meetings paralleled private efforts of the members almost exclusively in doing good for the Negroes.

Throughout Quakerdom the corporate concern for Friends' former slaves continued. Monthly Meeting committees made loans to Negro tradesmen, arranged apprenticeships for their children, and gave advice on temporal and spiritual matters. In Wilmington, Thirdhaven Monthly Meeting, Maryland, Westbury, New York, and in several other places, meetings for worship were set up for the colored people. After the Revolution Friends made one important change of policy on aid to the Negroes: Meetings began to offer help to all colored people, no longer just to those liberated by members. Philadelphia Yearly Meeting in 1788 advised all committees to do as some had done already — visit all free Negro families in their territory, whether manumitted by Friends or not. In 1790 the practice spread from Pennsylvania and New Jersey to Maryland.[16]

Attention to the spiritual welfare of the former slaves, however, did not mean trying to draw them into the Society of Friends. The Negroes' meetings were to inculcate the rudiments of the religious life. In Philadelphia the Free African Society, founded in 1787, held some promise of becoming an independent colored man's Society of Friends. At first it devoted itself mainly to charity and mutual aid, but its meetings, held at the Monthly Meeting's school for free Negro children, with the master of the school, a white Friend named Joseph Clarke, as Clerk and Treasurer, took on ecclesiastical functions, including mutual encouragement to virtue. By 1790 the Free African Society was holding meetings for worship, but soon thereafter its members drifted either into Methodist or Episcopal organizations. The Quakers, in the surprising position of godparents to organizations of a character very different from their own, showed no dismay. On the contrary, the Monthly Meeting in 1805 concluded that there was no longer any purpose in holding meetings for Negroes since they had found their way to their own religious bodies.[17]

But the corporate concern for free Negro education continued. Ordinarily this work was entrusted to the school committees and thereby integrated with the campaign to establish Monthly Meeting schools. In the Middle Atlantic states many education funds grew large enough to pay the tuition not only of poor Quaker children but of free colored as well. In North Carolina, however, public hostility to integrated classes gave added support to those who opposed any education for Negroes. Shortly after 1787, when Friends committed themselves to the policy of providing schools for whites and Negroes under their care, success had seemed possible. Committees were set up to work on the problem in Piney Woods Quarterly Meeting in 1787, and generally throughout the Yearly Meeting after 1809. Only at New Garden Monthly Meeting, however, was a school opened, in 1816, giving instruction to Negro children two days a week. Since segregated schools were impractical, and many Negroes requiring Friends' assistance were nominally slaves owned by a board of trustees set up by the Society to relieve the members of the burden of owning them, the Quakers had to resort to informal teaching, often as part of apprenticeship. This practice received the endorsement of the Yearly Meeting in 1817 after thirty years of discouraging efforts to send children of Friends' former slaves to regular schools.[18]

Elsewhere in the South similar problems existed. In Virginia and Maryland the Yearly Meetings sent advices urging education of the Negroes. Virginia pointed out that the education of slaves liberated by Friends would help all Negroes, since it was designed to "elevate their minds, and improve their habits . . . and thus contribute to . . . soften the prejudices that have obtained against that destitute class of people in the publick mind." But the exhortation was to no avail. Though Monthly Meetings formed committees, apart from the Gravelly Hills school the main results of the campaign were achieved in the homes of individual Quaker families where free Negroes were given instruction.[19]

Actually, the ideal solution to the problem of educating the Negroes remained segregated classes according to the pattern set by Philadelphia Monthly Meeting in 1770. The old institution there continued to thrive, with increases both in endowments and number of scholars. By 1800 the schoolhouse, newly enlarged, was filled to capacity, but the committee in charge of it did not choose to make any additional expansion of its facilities. Only in New York City did similar institutions have comparable success. Chester Monthly Meeting in Pennsylvania ran a school for Negroes for a few years after 1785, Baltimore took over one from a private club, and Wilmington started one in 1798 primarily for adult colored folk. None of these, however, acquired the firm foundations of the model in Philadelphia.[20]

The projects of Quakers to enable the Negroes to take their place in American society as free men complemented the efforts of their Yearly Meetings to destroy all the manifestations of slavery. Speaking as a dissident minority, though one determined to be part of the body politic, Friends in their religious Society attacked the laws and customs sanctioned by their fellow citizens. If protecting free Negroes, stopping the importation of slaves, and gaining liberty for those already in the United States meant combating settled opinions and vested interests entrenched in society at large, the Quakers insisted that they were saving the nation from the inevitable consequences of its own errors. The cause of the Negroes was the cause of people widely considered by the civil community to be "outsiders," but Friends believed that justice required white Americans to accept Negroes as equals.

For fifteen years after 1783 the Quakers vociferously attacked slavery and the slave trade. They knew that a "renewal" of the slave trade was under way, and, since it was the most vulnerable aspect of the evil institution, they fought it with the greatest ardor. In 1783, following the example of London Yearly Meeting's application to Parliament, Philadelphia addressed Congress, requesting action to stop the trade. In an effort to be persuasive and patriotic, the Quakers called the attention of Congress to the inconsistency of slavery with its own declarations about the universal right to liberty. Subsequent addresses and memorials were delivered to Congress, and to the legislatures of Pennsylvania and New Jersey. In 1786 New York Yearly Meeting joined Philadelphia in its appeal.[21]

Elsewhere, Friends backed other efforts to persuade legislatures to alter the laws on slavery. In Rhode Island, slaveholding was abolished after a long campaign climaxed by a final Quaker petition. In Pennsylvania a gradual abolition law had received the moral, if not the political, support of the Friends. But in Virginia, Delaware, and New York their first goal was to secure liberalization of the manumission requirements. In New Jersey and Delaware, Quakers made futile requests for legal equality of free Negroes with other citizens. In Maryland the Friends applied to the state legislature for a more stringent law when a number of free Negroes were kidnaped and sold in the West Indies.[22]

For two years, beginning in the summer of 1787, Yearly Meetings campaigned for state laws to forbid the fitting out of vessels for the slave trade. New England Yearly Meeting began the work with memorials to Massachusetts and Rhode Island, and the Meeting for Sufferings appealed to Philadelphia to give a push by persuading the Pennsylvania legislature to act first. As it happened, Massachusetts, Rhode Island, and New York all passed the desired laws before Pennsylvania. After a similar triumph in New Jersey, the Meeting for Sufferings at Philadelphia recommended that its techniques of petitioning and lobbying be employed in Maryland. Nothing was accomplished on the other side of Mason and Dixon's Line, but the New Englanders presently gained another victory in Connecticut and planned a barrage of pamphlets to "prepare the way for a prohibition of said Trade" in New Hampshire, after it was discovered that vessels were going there which had previously frequented southern New England ports. In Delaware, lobbying by Friends and non-Friends and by the local abolition society persuaded the state legislature to forbid the sending of ships for the slave trade in 1789. The Delaware River was finally closed to slavers.[23]

The climax — and greatest failure — of the campaign against the slave trade came in efforts to get action against it by the new Federal government. Persuasion failed to influence the Constitutional Convention; the example of the states, the high hopes for similar action by England in 1788, the backing of non-Friends, interviews with representatives and senators, three years of intensive effort, mainly by members of Philadelphia Yearly Meeting — all of these failed to move the new Congress. Southern hostility to any law stopping the importation of slaves, firmly supported by the Constitutional provision that no such law might be passed before 1808, made it difficult to gain a reception for Friends' pleas.[24]

From 1792 on, with slavery taking on new life in the South, Quakers were compelled to direct their energies to what were essentially rear-guard actions. In Maryland and Virginia they called for stiffer laws against kidnaping free Negroes, while the petitions patiently reiterated Quaker beliefs about the iniquity of slavery as an institution and its inconsistency with natural rights and the national welfare. Well into the nineteenth century North Carolina Friends were futilely trying to persuade the legislature of their state to repeal a law forbidding anyone to teach a slave to read and write.[25] For a time, at least, the Quakers' corporate concern for the Negroes had reached a point where no new projects could be undertaken. In the North, after Friends had freed, reimbursed, and educated their slaves, and the governments had begun to abolish slave property and clamp down on the slavers, little remained to be done directly for Negroes except to continue such philanthropic work as that performed by the Association of Friends for the Instruction of Adult Colored Persons. In the South much needed to be done but very little could be.

By contrast, the corporate concern for the welfare of the Indians, which suddenly took a new form in the 1790's, enjoyed a nearly unlimited field for action, though one which was less obviously in need of cultivation for the good of the civil community. Although the new endeavors on behalf of the Indians were based on the long-standing sense of obligation which Friends felt to the Indians whom they had displaced, the missionary work quickly escaped the limits of this original motivation and overthrew several traditional views of how the religious Society should act.

Sporadically, between the days of Fox and the American Revolution, the possibility had occurred to Quakers of helping the Indians by teaching them Christianity and civilized ways of life. When Zebulon Heston visited the Delawares in 1773 with a message from the Meeting for Sufferings at Philadelphia, however, it was the Indians who urged such a project, not the Friends. The Meeting, almost ignoring the request for secular instruction, declared its readiness to send teachers, but only if some should present

298

themselves under a sense of duty; it was not right to preach or teach religion, except as the head of a household, unless stimulated by God within. The Meeting's decision to give little attention to non-religious training probably was due to the discovery in 1760 that Papunahung and his followers could adopt a religion similar to Quakerism without changing their way of life. But no Friends had the inner prompting to evangelize the Indians in 1774. The Christian Delawares sent a statement to the Meeting for Sufferings expressing their satisfaction with Quaker religion, a desire to be as one people with Friends in the future, and an abject plea for temporal and spiritual instruction, since they were "poor & weak," unable to judge for themselves, and apprehensive of what would happen to their children. In spite of the impression the message made on Friends in England and America, nothing was done about it for years. The Revolution forestalled action for a time, but not until the 1790's did events bring an end to waiting.[26]

One important way in which Friends' minds continued to be drawn to the Indians was the old custom of entertaining Indian chiefs who visited Philadelphia. On these occasions the Quakers spoke for peace, sobriety, and Christianity. This practice, also adopted by Friends in Baltimore and New York, revived the concern for the natives after 1789. Indian warfare, which lasted from that year to 1795, though punctuated by lulls and fresh outbreaks, drew the chiefs to the capital at New York and later Philadelphia. Furthermore, the purpose of their visits, the desire to stop the fighting, gave Friends a special cause for parleys.[27]

Quakers began to exhort the Indians, however, to do more than heed the Light Within in order to guarantee peace. Philadelphia Friends advised Cherokee and Creek emissaries, on their way to see President Washington, to pursue a pacific policy which should be reinforced by "tilling the ground, learning useful trades," and finding "proper schoolmasters to teach their children, that they might be brought up to love and obey the great and good Spirit who made them." One crucial economic fact, the reduction of hunting areas by the growth of white settlements, convinced Quakers that the Indians must shift their reliance to agriculture and make it the occupation of the men. The moral and psychological side of the problem deserved equal attention: if peaceful living and conversion to Christianity were to be assured, the Indians would have to give up their spirit of revenge and cultivate "a feeling of love and charity." Farming, Friends believed, would help to bring about this spiritual transformation. Repeatedly, Quakers sought to persuade Indians of the necessity and wisdom of learning a new pattern of living.[28]

The most significant parley between Friends and Indian chiefs at Philadelphia was held early in 1791 when three Senecas — Cornplanter, Big Tree, and Half Town — came to talk with President Washington and the Governor of Pennsylvania. Cornplanter, as his name suggests, had seen the necessity for his people to take up agriculture. In 1791 he did not enjoy the solid backing of his village, but he could say that they wanted teachers and were inclined to trust Friends. He asked that Quakers instruct his son, another Seneca boy, and the son of Joseph Nicholson, their interpreter, as they taught their own children. After receiving approval from the Governor of Pennsylvania and the United States Secretary of War, the Meeting for Sufferings sent word to Cornplanter that they would grant his request, and appointed a committee to find "some examplary prudent Friend in the Country" to train the boys.[29]

Soon Quakers began to take the initiative in approaching the distant natives. Two members of Philadelphia Meeting for Sufferings, Isaac Zane and John Parrish, sent messages to various tribes to explore the possibility of further work to civilize them. Indian deputies on their way to discuss peace with the United States held conferences with Friends at Philadelphia and brought replies to the messages. Interest shown by a group of Senecas led by the Farmer's Brother and a message from Hopackon, a Delaware, encouraged the Meeting to approve the mission which six Quakers felt a religious engagement to undertake. They wanted to visit Indians in their villages on the way to forthcoming parleys at Sandusky to arrange peace.[30]

The six — John Elliott, John Parrish, William Savery, Jacob Lindley, Joseph Moore, and William Hartshorne — after their plan had been approved by Friends and the government, took a message to the Indians, signed by forty-four Quakers. Written in pseudo-Indian fashion, it explained the doctrine of the Inner Light and the virtues of peace, and expressed the desire that the Indians remember the ancient friendship between their ancestors and in the future live peacefully with all their neighbors. The emissaries set off, holding conferences with some Iroquois and religious meetings with a few straggling Quakers and Indians near Niagara on the way. After a voyage to Detroit aboard a British ship, they spent six weeks holding religious meetings and taking "opportunities" to inform bands of Indians heading for the treaty, of Quaker beliefs. When the prospects of holding a treaty dimmed, they sent a message to the chiefs still assembled at Sandusky, and returned home.[31]

The following year David Bacon, John Parrish, William Savery, and James Emlen found themselves "under a concern" to go to a conference to be held at Canandaigua, New York, between United States Commissioners and sachems of the Six Nations. The Iroquois chiefs desired the presence of some Quakers, and the government had no objections. Sent by the Meeting for Sufferings, the four men carried presents and an address to the Indians. They spent about seven weeks at Canandaigua, holding religious meetings for Indians, Quakers, and other whites in the vicinity. Some of the Indians, especially the Oneidas, were found to be Christians, at least in name. Savery reported that they "received the gospel in word only, and not in power," so that it had "but little influence on their conduct"; and they were still "enslaved to all the vices common to the other Indians." He thought it likely that more spiritual missionaries (that is, Friends) would turn the first acquaintance with the Gospel to account, especially since the religious meetings held during the treaty showed promise.[32]

Savery and the other visitors soon concluded that humanity and justice demanded more than just the spreading of Christianity. After talks with Cornplanter, the Farmer's Brother, Red Jacket, Little Beard, and other Seneca braves, the Quaker understood better the importance of teaching the Iroquois nations how to farm. One sachem, "Sagareesa, or the Sword-carrier," who struck Savery as a thoughtful man, "mentioned a desire he had, that some of our young men might come among them as teachers"; Savery supposed he meant as schoolmasters and artisans.[33]

The four missionaries gave their report in the last month of 1794. The interest aroused by the two journeys to the treaties and the establishment of peace in 1795 stimulated Friends attending Philadelphia Yearly Meeting later in the same year to consider their duty to the Indians. They spoke of the "former and present Condition of the Indian Natives," the history of Quakers' relations with them; and, in general, the concern for the Indians was "in a solid manner weightily revived and spread with Life over the Meeting." A committee was appointed to deliberate on what action might be taken. It reported that there were "loud Calls for [Friends'] . . . Benevolence and Charitable exertions to promote . . . the Principles of the Christian Religion" among the natives, as well as to turn the attention of the Indians "to School Learning, Agriculture, and useful Mechanic Employments." The committee recommended that the Yearly Meeting set up a standing committee on aid to the Indians, call on the Quarterly Meetings to raise money for the good work, and apprise other Yearly Meetings. The committee declared that the establishment of peace, the desires of the tribes for instruction, and the favorable disposition of the United States government combined to give an opportunity that should not be missed. A new committee was accordingly named which, after its enlargement in 1796, became the permanent Indian Committee of Philadelphia Yearly Meeting.[34]

The Committee sent circular letters among the Indians of Pennsylvania and New York — accompanied by notes of approval from the United States Secretary of State, to explain Friends' desire to be of service. Only a group of Oneidas in New York showed any eagerness to receive help, however. Appeals from the Committee to local Meetings brought over £5,000 in contributions and several men with a "concern" to teach literacy, agriculture, and the principles of Christianity to the Indians. When the necessary arrangements had been made with government officials, some members of the Committee escorted three missionaries to the Oneida reservation in the summer of 1796. There they found the Brothertown Indians safely under the care of three state-appointed superintendents, two of whom were Quakers; the Stockbridges, whose progress was such that the Friends thought some financial encouragement would be sufficient; and the Oneidas proper, the least civilized of the three elements. So the mission was planted among the Oneidas on unused land, convenient to a sawmill and smithy built by the United States government.[35]

The mission to the Oneidas set a pattern later followed in other places. First, an agreement specified the terms on which the missionaries would conduct their business. They were to have the use of land on which to conduct a model farm, and they would perform certain services for the Indians. The latter were exhorted to be frugal, industrious, and sober, and not to expect to share the missionaries' livestock. The Friends planted fields and built a permanent barn, to show how the work was done and what rewards it could bring. They put the sawmill back into working order and during the first winter held classes at which several Indians learned to read. Occasionally the Quakers visited neighboring villages to distribute farm tools and give stern advice to the men to stop getting drunk and start working the land. But they devoted their ingenuity primarily to popularizing farming among the Oneidas.[36]

The missionaries thought that the old division of labor in which the women worked in the fields would have to be changed and each family encouraged to fence and use its own tract of land. Their success in offering prizes to the Stockbridge men for growing wheat made the missionaries eager to try the system among the Oneidas, but the Committee wanted to make the fruits of labor their own reward. Accordingly, the missionaries experimented with hiring some men as laborers on the model farm, only to find that few except some young ones would work steadily, and they only when they actually lived on the farm. A further discouragement came when attempts to divide the land among the Oneidas met the opposition of the Indians and the law alike; the reservation could not be parceled out without making the Indians' rights to it alienable.[37]

The division of labor was attacked from the women's side, too. The missionaries sent word to Philadelphia that a female colleague

303

would be useful; cleanliness in the Indians' houses and apparel "should go along with many other usefull improvements that might be promoted amongst them." Happily, two qualified Friends, Hannah Jackson and Susanna Gregory, responded to the call. They taught the squaws how to spin, knit, sew, and even read. Susanna's husband, Henry, helped even more. A blacksmith, he could repair the farm implements, and found that Indian men took an interest in his manly trade even if they scorned agriculture as women's work.[38]

By 1799 some of the Indians began to doubt the "single and disinterested views of Friends in the labour" and to suspect the missionaries of wanting to acquire land. To show them their error, the Indian Committee ended the mission before the end of the year, leaving all the implements it had supplied and all the products of the model farm to the Oneidas. The Committee believed that the first mission had succeeded to the extent that when the Indians could no longer depend on the exertions of the young Friends placed among them, they might "be excited to pursue with increasing diligence the example set them." The missionaries concluded their work with additional paeans to the virtues of sobriety and industry, while the Committee promised that it, or its counterpart in New York Yearly Meeting, would give the Indians aid and advice in the future.[39]

The success of the Oneida mission promoted interest in the work among both Friends and Indians. Some communities of Senecas, including Cornplanter's band, living along the Allegheny River on either side of the Pennsylvania-New York boundary, asked for instruction in agriculture. In 1798, the Indian Committee sent two of its members to escort Joel Swayne, Henry Simmons, Jr., and Halliday Jackson, three young Friends who started what proved to be the most extensive of the early Quaker Indian missions. The Committee members acquired a house and land in the middle of the belt of settlement along the river, at a place called Genisenguhta. They made an agreement with the Senecas to give some produce from the model farm to the old and sick, to contribute smith's tools when they could be used, to pay half the price of a sawmill provided the Indians could raise the rest from the annuity given them by the United States, and for a period of four years to award cash prizes to the men for growing grains, hay, and potatoes, and to the women for linen and woolen cloth made from fibers produced on their families' land.[40]

The missionaries began at once to demonstrate how a farm should be established, by planting crops, building a stable, and helping the Indian men clear and fence fields and erect permanent houses. During the first winter the Friends and Senecas built a schoolhouse, but in later years the missionaries instructed the Indian children wherever they could gather them. The Quakers praised all the "marks of industry" they could see in the Indian villages, whether fences, roads, or cucumbers, and recommended further efforts to store winter fodder for the cattle and make roads along the river. They saw in every scrap of progress toward civilized ways "renewed evidence" that the mission was "sanctioned by Divine approbation," and that they "as instruments engaged therein" stood in their "proper allotments." [41]

The missionaries gave little attention to promulgating Christian doctrine; there is no record that they preached it, and their correspondence with the Indian Committee simply ignored the whole subject. They spoke, instead, for those changes in social values necessary to the replacement of hunting with agriculture, changes which would elevate industriousness and pride in individual ownership over the Indians' traditional virtues of generosity and sharing. They accounted it a great triumph when an Indian man, using a sled pulled by a horse, brought in firewood, formerly women's work. They did not want to encourage individualism, however, to a degree that would disrupt the solidarity of the Indian communities; in several ways the missionaries depended on the solidarity for the success of their plans. In the first place, they hoped to use social pressure by those who accepted the agricultural way of life to break down the resistance of the rest; the Friends looked to social pressure especially to help stamp out drunkenness. In the second place, the Indian communities had important legal rights which the members exercised by joint decision and which could be used either to help or obstruct the mission. The communities owned and controlled the use of the land they occupied, and did not have the power to parcel it out into tracts under individual ownership. So if the land was to be assigned for individual use and white men's agriculture introduced, these innovations had to be made with the consent of the communities. Furthermore, the communities decided how to spend subsidies which they received from the United States. So the Quakers had to have the good will of the communities behind the mission to persuade the Indians to stop spending the money on provisions and liquor and to use it instead to buy oxen, plows, and other necessities of the agricultural life. The Committee at first supplied these things as gifts, but knew that the Indian communities could never be self-reliant until they learned to use their own resources prudently.[42]

The Seneca communities' willingness to cooperate with the missionaries became uncertain very early. The half-brother of Cornplanter — Connudiu, or Handsome Lake — had three visions which he believed were divine revelations and which, as he expounded their meaning, subsequently became the basis of a revision of the Seneca religion. The missionaries — especially Halliday Jackson — took keen interest in these events, though they refused to mention them in their official correspondence with Philadelphia; and the Indian Committee, though members of it had been informed of them in private correspondence with the missionaries, would not divulge them to the Yearly Meeting. When the Indians called on Jackson to judge whether the revelations were divine or not, he replied warily and asked for time to meditate. In accord with the Committee's policy of not offending the natives in religious matters, he decided that since the teachings of the new "prophet" called for useful reforms of behavior — specifically, to give up drink and to accept the economic life advocated by the Friends — he should tell them that they "would do well to observe the sayings"; and, as he recorded in his journal, "the answer pleased Cornplanter the Chief." Jackson could not conscientiously be more positive, but he would not rule out the possibility that the revelations were genuine. His decision, tacitly accepted by the Committee later, showed clearly the Quaker policy of starting mission work by teaching a way of life rather than a religion.[43]

The preaching of Handsome Lake created a series of special

problems, for it divided the Indians into antagonistic groups, though it served the mission well by preventing controversy over the white man's religion. The missionaries had to avoid supporting the prophet's accusation of witchcraft against the enemies of the new way of life and called a conference to resolve the quarrel. But even when the furor over the charges had died down the jealousies of those eclipsed by the new leader and the traditional views of a large part of the Senecas interfered seriously with the work of the missionaries. Both the traditionalists and the ardent followers of Connudiu were reluctant to allow the Friends to educate their children.[44]

To find a more satisfactory arrangement of the missionary establishment after the squabbles among the Senecas had subsided, the Quakers in the field recommended at the end of 1802 that the mission be removed to land privately owned by the Committee near the reservation. Set apart from the life of any one village and its inner strife, they hoped to be of greater service. The Indian men, whom the missionaries believed capable of getting along on their own resources, would be compelled to do so if they could not count on the Quakers to share in the life of the village by growing crops, giving tools and labor, and repairing equipment. If a few women Friends could be found "under a concern" to add their strength to the mission they could begin to teach housekeeping, spinning, knitting, and the dairy arts to the squaws. But potentially the greatest advantage in relocating the mission would come from requiring the children to leave home for education. It had been observed that "the unhappy way in which the Indians bring up their Children" made their learning difficult, for the parents generally left them "to act as the rude propen[s]ities of nature" dictated, a poor preparation for being "confined to learning." Away from their families and the advocates of the old tribal ways, they could be trained more successfully in "usefull information tending to eradicate many superstitious notions which prevent civilized ideas from increasing." [45]

The Indian Committee agreed to the relocation in 1803 and sent a delegation to help set up the new center. The Quakers chose a tract then owned by the Holland Land Company at Tunesassa

Creek, between the Seneca villages. There were places for a saw-mill and gristmill, which, if water in the Creek proved sufficient, the Committee agreed to erect; thus the Indian men could be led to clear fields and build houses by having their trees sawed into planks, and encouraged to grow grain by the prospect of having it ground into flour free (which would offer the additional advantage of relieving the women of some of their customary drudgery). When the land had been bought and a family of missionaries added to the force in the field, the Friends looked forward to improved results.[46]

The new arrangements worked well, though training the squaws began slowly over strong traditionalist opposition, and some of the Indian men thought the Quakers ungenerous for stopping loans of tools and refusing to pay the girls who went to learn housekeeping. Cornplanter, who had been in favor of the move from the beginning, regained some prestige, if not his old leadership, while Hand-some Lake and several others became even more cooperative than before. The Quakers began to appeal to the Senecas' consciences to persuade them of "the impropriety of putting away their wifes and marrying others &c," and of the wisdom of staying away from the bottle — appeals to which Handsome Lake added his endorse-ment. The Indian Committee even sent an address explaining the principle of the Inner Light and the two Christian commandments and recommending resort to silent waiting for divine "light, knowl-edge and counsel," which was superior to any that humans could impart, and which would teach the Senecas, as it had taught Friends, "to love all men as brethren" and restrain them "from revenging injuries or returning Evil for Evil." But the missionaries contented themselves with pursuing their own religious customs and allowing the claims of Handsome Lake to stand. The difficul-ties remained, but the chief means of coping with them had been worked out. Gradually more and more Senecas helped with the milling, blacksmith's work, building, spinning, and weaving. The missionaries reported that the idea of individual property and the habits of industry were gaining ground. After a few years of pa-tience and diplomacy and a few tangible results they decided that the best course would be to establish a boarding school to gain a firmer influence over the young.[47]

Tunesassa remained the center of Indian work from Philadelphia for many years, though for a time missionaries went to the village on Cattaraugus Creek as well. As other Yearly Meetings took up the concern for the Indians, western New York became the one field cultivated by Philadelphia. Baltimore and New York soon found territories to work in but North Carolina did not, and New England, though it approved Philadelphia's "solicitude" for the Indians and tried to find some to help in its own territory, discovered little to do after two years of searching. The Meeting for Sufferings helped send a few families to join the Oneidas, but there they came under the jurisdiction of New York Yearly Meeting.[48]

The New Yorkers, sparked by the indefatigable Thomas Eddy, began inspecting the needs of Indians in their state in 1793. Two years later the Yearly Meeting appointed an Indian Committee which canvassed the tribes in the state even more thoroughly. For eleven years members of the Committee and other concerned Friends visited villages, encouraged the inhabitants to sobriety and industry, distributed farm tools, and held religious meetings at which they eagerly looked for points of agreement between the natives' religion and Quakerism. In 1806 New York Yearly Meeting began to raise money for a resident mission. Helped by a gift of £2,250 from the Philadelphia Indian Committee and by contributions from England, New York sent a Friend and his family to live at Brothertown, where one of the sons taught school and all gave practical instruction in the useful arts. In 1809 a Friend and his wife went to live with a village of Oneidas, taking gifts of stock and farm implements from the Committee. During the ten years that followed, additional Quakers extended the work among the Onondagas, and the usual beginnings were made in teaching the smith's trade to some of the men, and spinning, weaving, and sewing to many of the women.[49]

Next to Philadelphia, Baltimore Yearly Meeting carried on the most extensive work with the Indians in the twenty years after 1795. Like New York, it appointed an Indian Committee that year, though the group did little except canvass the situation and send gifts for several years. By arrangement with Philadelphia, Baltimore took for its field the tribes to the northwest of the Ohio River and sent a delegation to look over the territory. The Committee decided that in spite of appeals from various Delaware, Wyandot, and Pottawottami villages, and the interest shown by a Miami chieftain named Little Turtle, there was no hope for missions while illegal traders sold liquor to the Indians.[50]

An appeal to the United States government to ban strong drink from the Ohio area, in which Little Turtle joined the Committee, received an encouraging reply. The Secretary of War arranged to create a trading post at Fort Wayne to keep unscrupulous traders from corrupting the Indians. The Secretary wanted blacksmiths and carpenters to go to the Fort as teachers. Within two years the Indians, deprived of drink, were much more inclined toward farming. After a second request from Little Turtle, two members of the Indian Committee escorted a volunteer named Philip Dennis to Fort Wayne early in 1804, with a team of horses for the spring plowing.[51]

The Quakers called a meeting of Indians — men, women and children — near Fort Wayne to tell them the purpose of the mission and to paint an alluring picture of the benefits to be enjoyed from an agricultural way of life after the white man's pattern. The Friends confessed, diplomatically, that their ancestors had once lived "in the same manner that our red brethren now live . . . they went almost naked" and "procured their living by fishing, and by the bow & arrow in hunting," but had learned better ways from "some who came from towards the Sun rising." Dennis went to work on a farm by the Wabash River, where he raised corn and a large variety of garden vegetables, tended livestock, and taught the Indians who stayed nearby. As originally planned, he returned to his wife and children at the end of the season, leaving all that he had accomplished and the equipment he had used as gifts to the Indians. Before his departure he had begun to discourge the Indian women from working in the fields and had urged them instead to go to Fort Wayne, where the government had sent spinning wheels, to learn to spin and knit. His work drew the attention of other bands of Indians, some of whom relocated nearer his farm. He carried to Baltimore a message of gratitude to Friends from the Indians, and hope that the Committee would send others out to replace him.[52]

At the request of the Committee, the government agent at Fort Wayne sent a man to take Dennis's place, which was fortunate for the project since no Friends with a sense of religious duty appeared in time, and the Committee, in any case, was itself short of funds. The agent informed the Committee that he saw great prospects for the work in the industrious disposition of the Indians, their desire that he spend part of their annuities to get rails for fences, and their energy in clearing lands. With this unexpected encouragement, the Committee redoubled its efforts to collect money (the Philadelphia Indian Committee sent £4,760 8s. 4d.) and found two Friends under a concern for the work. They went to replace Dennis's successor, who had done well, and stayed for several years, until the promising results were vitiated by the re-entry of liquor in 1809, and the work of the mission rendered too difficult to continue by the rise of the Shawnee "Prophet" a year or two later. By that time the work of the Baltimore Committee had branched out, in the fashion set by Philadelphia and New York; gifts of farm and mill equipment were made to several villages in the hope of inspiring interest in future missions.[53]

The Indian missions, Friends kept saying, represented a continuation of the friendship between their ancestors and the Indians. But the missionary help was far from a simple repayment of kindnesses shown the early settlers in Pennsylvania. Actually, the Quakers looked on their obligations to the "aborigines" in such broad terms as to verge on Woolman's concept that the whites, and — after 1776 — the United States, owed a debt for the continent to the Indians collectively. The Indian Committees made payments on this debt only as circumstances made wise or possible. The Quakers, nevertheless, liked to point out elements of similarity between the ideas of the early Friends and their new corporate concern. The missionary movement revived some of the attitudes of late seventeenth-century Quakers who had delighted in the exotic and adventurous side of traveling to powwows and holding religious meetings around flickering campfires. The reports of the Committees transmitted these elements for the vicarious enjoyment of those who stayed at home. The earnestness had come back to Quaker efforts to keep liquor from the natives, too, after relative indifference during the mid-eighteenth century. The emphasis on practical training of the Indians, also, had precedents in the ideas held by Archdale and Budd before 1700. Budd had wanted Indians to go to school with Friends and learn the daily routine of the English settlers. In the 1790's, when the Indian Committees placed Indian children for training in Friends' families, the plan came to fruition on a small scale.[54]

The creation of resident missions, however, marked a departure from older attitudes. The plan contemplated no fusion of Indian and white societies; rather, it was predicated on the belief that merely to forestall their extinction the natives would have to be educated from their own ways to those of the white men. To exchange the tomahawk and scalping knife "for the *plough* and the *hoe*" and replace ranging the forests "in seeming affinity to the wild beasts of the desert" by "cultivation of the earth," was the first step to "many other *temporal* advantages." [55]

The occasional religious visits to the Indians, which had seemed so important earlier, no longer received much stress; such isolated inspired acts in behalf of the natives had little place in the missionary work. Apparently fearing that the rank-and-file Quakers would criticize the de-emphasis on religious teaching, the Baltimore Indian Committee asked rhetorically whether the transformation of economic life might not "*prepare for*, and prove *the means* under the DIVINE BLESSING," through which there would "finally spread . . . that LIGHT and KNOWLEDGE, which so eminently distinguish the true CHRISTIAN." [56] The Committee adopted the cautious approach evident in the whole missionary movement: the teaching of religion could proceed slowly, along the most general Christian lines, appealing only to Indian consciences in what might be called a Quaker vein; the missionaries should neither interfere with existing customs nor train the Indians for religious fellowship with Friends.

The Indian Committee as an institution represented a departure from older Quaker practice, for it was a body of men working systematically and patiently for the "corporate concern." While the Committee expected divine guidance in the conduct of its business, once given duties by the Yearly Meeting, it did not rely on a collective inner prompting to initiate each of its actions; rather, it exercised human ingenuity to find means to its ends. It scrupulously waited for an inner sense of obligation only to bring individual Friends to offer to serve as missionaries; when none presented themselves it could with equanimity hire men to do its work who were not Quakers at all. The concern — both for the Society and its members — was regarded as a case of benevolence, appreciation of the brotherhood of man, as well as fidelity to old promises and "justice," and the outcome of Quaker purity. It needed the continued sense of duty for the work on the part of the Society as a whole, as well as some rational hope of achieving its ends, but not a harvest of converts to justify it.[57]

In obedience to law, the Indian Committees kept clearing their projects with the government. The relations between the work of the Baltimore Committee and that of the United States officials at Fort Wayne showed that Friends were furthering or correcting the policy of the government as well as helping the Indians. The support given to Little Turtle by a memorial to Congress carried the Quaker role of guardian of justice back into an old field. Though they faced less opposition and won more applause in championing the Indians than they did when they fought slavery, the Friends still acted as a minority rightly engaged in the business of the whole nation.

Quakers surely needed no testimony from United States cabinet members to convince them of the value of their religious Society. Yet the endorsement of Secretary of State Timothy Pickering demonstrated that their church earned a good name by its benevolent projects. Pickering declared of the first Indian mission: "The goodness of the design, and the disinterestedness of the motives, must recommend it to the favour and support of all who wish the happiness of their fellow-men." The Quakers prized evidence of the good opinion which Presidents Washington and Jefferson had of their missionary work. The Indian Committee probably felt pleased when Secretary of War Henry Dearborn asked for the services of any available Friends to teach the Choctaws.[58]

The Indian missions, more than any other Quaker activity, demonstrated the purity of the Society of Friends and its ability to mobilize its members for the benefit of the United States. Civic-minded philanthropies engaged only part of the Quaker flock and remained self-serving to the extent that they improved the philanthropists' immediate neighborhood. Friends' care for their ex-slaves had an ulterior purpose — to help enforce the Discipline against slave-owning. War relief during the Revolution had defended the Quakers and the reputation of their religion. But the Indian missions were, as Pickering pointed out, utterly disinterested except as the missionaries would be "capable of deriving pleasure from the happiness of their fellow Men."[59] The Friends could not expect to recruit new members and had no illusions on that score. If they had no desire to bridge by religious fellowship the social gulf that separated them from free Negroes, they certainly could not hope to do so in the case of the Indians. Nevertheless, the Quakers proclaimed that the Inner Light made their preaching useful to anybody with a properly receptive heart, no matter how little doctrine he might hold in common with them. The *modus vivendi* with the religion of Handsome Lake stretched Quaker acceptance of religious pluralism to the utmost, but not to the breaking point.

Among Senecas, as among Presbyterians, Quakers pointed to the general agreement on what constituted virtue and evaluated religious ideas on their ability to elicit good conduct. Since they thought their own beliefs to be the best by this pragmatic standard, Friends had a public obligation to show their virtuous behavior, including disinterested benevolence, and thereby inspire imitation and draw divine favor on their nation. But they demonstrated their qualities most effectively through their religious Society. Indian missions and the fight against slavery were ventures in behalf of "universal righteousness," and so should be made the obligations of the nation as a whole. Quakers would show an example in the face of any wicked hostility. Therefore, in the midst of activities deliberately undertaken for the benefit of the whole nation the Society had a crucial obligation to maintain its solidarity, uniformity, and purity.

The idea that Quakers benefited their nation by precept, example, and corporate purity was not foreign to the seventeenth century, but in that period of their history Friends had expected their efforts to result in mass conversion and the reform of human behavior. As American Quakers developed their community during the second half of the eighteenth century, they put increasing emphasis on the role of their Society as the medium through which they would confer benefits on mankind and converted their ideas about the universality of the Inner Light to forms which suggested that persons in all denominations could find the way to righteous conduct. Friends should be good neighbors in more than the ordinary ways, but they should participate in public life mainly through an ever-purer religious fellowship. The abandonment of large-scale conversion as a goal of their Society allowed social service to become humanitarian — the altruistic expression of Friends' religious convictions. Quakers could honestly justify even the most intensely sectarian operations of their Society as manifestations of benevolence to the civil community, for their church had become a society to do good for all mankind, not solely for its own members.

Humanitarianism among Friends

In the preceding pages, the word "humanitarian" has been reserved for a quality of motivation, a concern for the welfare of mankind. In the narrowest sense, Quakers are not now, and never have been, humanitarian, inasmuch as they have not claimed that virtue consists solely of acts for the benefit of mankind without any reference to a supernatural order. To Quakers, the second commandment, "Thou shalt love thy neighbor as thyself," has never ruled out the first. But neither have Friends always interpreted the second commandment to require philanthropic acts based simply on an intention to aid their fellow men.

Loving one's neighbor, while it can be interpreted as implying a broad program of social service, need not mean more than a consistent day-to-day neighborliness directed toward individuals. In fact, those who thought as Friends did, before 1750, that innate depravity was the chief quality to be reckoned with in natural man, might logically find nothing in the species worthy of affection, and express love of mankind only as a result of divine command. The saving quality of grace which lifted certain individuals from the mass, not the common quality of the species, determined the priority of group solidarity. Beyond the group, love of one's neighbors was a religious duty, something felt by the unusually virtuous, an attribute of those significantly set apart from the ordinary. Such neighborliness partook more of condescension than humanitarianism. When some other attribute set certain people apart from the rest — wealth or hereditary aristocracy, for instance — the obligation of the high to help the low plainly arose not from humanitarianism but a belief in a doctrine of stewardship or *noblesse oblige.* While any help to another may have pleased the giver by demonstrating his superiority or power over the beneficiary, humanitarian motives were kinds of love to neighbors which meant a recognition of likeness among all persons.

Eighteenth-century Quakers never felt "in it together" with the rest of mankind. There was always something to hold Quakers away from a lively sense of equality with others. They kept themselves apart by the special qualities they expressed in their distinctive language and clothing, their conviction that they gave more resolute obedience than others did to the divine will and commands, and by their solicitude for the reputation of Truth, even when they required practical demonstrations of the brotherhood of man. Whatever the rightly concerned Friend did, he expected his acts to afford a gauge for the virtues of his sect.

In the first century of Quakerism there was little evidence of humanitarianism, apart from the desire to convert people or show "the Example of a Meek Courteous, and Loving Deportment" to them.[1] In modern usage, conferring the benefit of one's religion is not defined as humanitarian charity. The distinction may be questionable, but in any case the early Quaker attitude put too much stress on a fellowship of the pure apart from the corrupt to allow comparable devotion to the broader concept of the brotherhood of man. Those of the fellowship in Christ should "not be weary in well-doing," should strive to apply their Savior's command to do unto others as they would have others do unto them, and in general "do justly love Mercy, & exercise brotherly kindness toward all Men the inseparable effect of walking humbly with God."[2] Quakers could and did carry out these duties in the routine of life. It was a departure from existing concepts of duty, however, when men like Woolman and Israel Pemberton postulated the obligation of Friends to perform services for Negroes and Indians in return for their sacrifices of labor and land.

The appearance of motives more specifically humanitarian took place among Friends in the middle of the eighteenth century. Changes in the sentiments and actions of Quakers became pronounced in Philadelphia and the surrounding area about the time when the Great Awakening and the attack on Quaker control of

the provincial government threw the sect on the defensive. Outsiders could challenge the community of Friends in these two ways
— religious and political — because of the failure of Quakerdom to
grow numerically at anything like the rate of the general population around it. Since the Friends remained a leading "people"
among the several classifications of Pennsylvania's inhabitants, their
weakness in numbers left them vulnerable to a challenge by power,
votes, and competitive religiosity.

In the effort to avoid giving up all their importance in society,
Quakers — especially those who could still be rich, but wanted to
be justified in their wealth and to retain their power — turned
more and more to philanthropy in public ways. Some of the first
efforts were the most ambitious — the Pennsylvania Hospital, the
Friendly Association, and the Bettering House — but as the proportion of Friends in the population decreased, the plans grew more
modest. In 1789 the Contributors to the Relief and Employment
of the Poor in the City of Philadelphia ceased to function, and the
Bettering House which they had managed fell under the control
of the public Guardians of the Poor;[3] it no longer accorded with
their diminishing wealth and power as a religious people for Friends
to support such a major institution. As Quakers lost public power
in Pennsylvania, moreover, the decline in the number of high-rank-
ing men in their Society began a levelling process which subsequent
events encouraged.

As the Revolution approached, the challenge from outsiders grew
stronger in Pennsylvania and began to appear throughout the colonies. In this period, projects to do good, though not of the sort that
might be regarded as civic improvement, became matters for the
religious organization of Friends to undertake. The proper limits
to the Society's actions, drawn during the first half of the eighteenth century, were altered step by step until Meetings began to
conduct schools for Negro children and missions for Indians without any intention of making converts.

At the same time that Friends found themselves under attack
and were responding by organizing to do good, they renewed
their fervor to live piously in accordance with their distinctive patterns. The conduct of individual Friends added together would

not be enough to show the virtues of their sect. While insisting on the uniform, salutations, and self-denials which would make them noticeable as individuals, they sought increasingly to make themselves conspicuous in concerted action. They intended to garrison America spiritually, not withdraw to isolated fastnesses. In this strategy, the Meeting assumed the function of guidance on a new scale, became the promoter of humanitarian ideals in petitions and projects, not simply the endorser of neighborly charity as an undefined command. In the main the humanitarianism adopted by Friends was a response to attack by colonial society; the Quakers responded — above all, in Pennsylvania — by withdrawing from governmental office and incorporating their participation in public life into the business of their Society.

In many respects, however, Friends saw these changes in approach as rededication to long-held beliefs. Opponents of slavery did much to gain success for their point of view by relating it to other, better established, moral commitments. John Woolman, though he advocated freedom for the Negroes as an expression of selfless devotion to the welfare of his fellow men, also advocated it for the welfare of his sect, on grounds derived from meditations on the ancient mystical identity of Christ and his church. Quakers should be "a family united in that purity of worship, which comprehends a holy life, & ministers instruction to others," that God might be " 'sanctified in them.' " But they could do so only because of "the love of Christ," who "gave himself for the Church, that he might . . . sanctify and cleanse it." Nevertheless, Woolman admonished his Friends, the "afflictions of Christ are yet unfinished." Those arising by declension from purity within his visible gathered church could be alleviated. But "the sincere in heart who abide in true stillness, and therein are exercised before the Lord for his name's sake, these have a knowledge of Christ in the fellowship of his sufferings." Thus, as Christ's mystical body, Friends in the Revolutionary crisis had the obligation to be "inwardly prepared to suffer adversities" for his sake, and strive to become more worthy to exemplify his role.[4] As the church, Christ would continue to suffer for the errors of the world, such as the slave trade or the wickedness which brought warfare to America in 1755 and 1775.

The church as a body would take on more and more of a corporate life as the mystical exemplification of unity in Christ.

But while taking into account the existence of such other explanations for the developments of the second half of the eighteenth century among Quakers, and putting main emphasis on the historical experience of American Friends, there remains an intellectual movement which requires attention. The attitudes which sprang up in the Society of Friends in this period had a connection with the same or similar ideas outside it. Some influential Quakers pondered the words of leading exponents of humanitarianism.[5]

Ideals of benevolence had been proclaimed on other occasions when Christians turned to philanthropic projects. Anglicans and, to a lesser extent, Dissenters, in England had undertaken a number of charitable projects in the decades just after the Glorious Revolution. Three institutions of the Established Church were noteworthy: The Society for the Propagation of the Gospel in Foreign Parts, the Society for Promoting Christian Knowledge, and the Associates of Doctor Bray. There were lesser activities, too, such as charity schools, societies for the reformation of manners, prison reform movements, and foundling homes.[6] Behind this outburst of benevolence lay several factors: the end of the political conflicts of the seventeenth century, the beginning of the practical divorce of religion from the state, and the disinclination to continue theological bickering when it could be discarded in favor of Christian action.

Cotton Mather and other ministers of the Congregational establishment in New England sponsored similar projects at about the same time; they promoted "Practical Piety" and societies to do good or reform morals alongside the regular church activities, in order to keep their influence after the reduction of government support and in the face of public distrust. The achievement of Cotton Mather also had a profoundly American aspect. The futility of part of the preaching of New England divines had grown as wealth accumulated among the colonists without any corresponding sense of social responsibility. The fixed orders of society having become little more than platitudes, the rich did not accept the moral limitations on their power nor the poor on their appetite to change their condition. Societies to promote pious ends gave strength to bands of ordinary citizens and tacitly revealed that social leadership was open to anyone who would assert it.[7]

Cotton Mather derived some inspiration from works of piety in Holland and from August Hermann Francke's orphanage in Halle, an institution which caught the attention of later leaders in benevolence, including Owen Biddle, the proponent of the Philadelphia Yearly Meeting Boarding School.[8] German Pietism grew in a region where religious strife had been even more protracted and more physically violent than in England. However, Mather thought that the Pietists had demonstrated a proposition which would apply to New England — that in works of practical Christianity all sects could agree and not interfere with one another.

Apart from the flurry of projects for social melioration produced by John Bellers in England and the unrealistic hopes for the Quaker colonies, Friends thus came late to an interest in benevolent organizations. This time sequence confers special importance on the renunciation of political power in Pennsylvania in the middle of the eighteenth century, as well as on Friends' later adoption of ideas regarding benevolence usually traced to the third Earl of Shaftesbury. Lord Shaftesbury, who shared much of his attitude with the Cambridge Platonists before him, examined the gregarious qualities of human beings and suggested that in addition to the various physical senses there was a moral sense which responded with pleasure to acts conducive to society's well-being. The Cambridge Platonists' Reason and Shaftesbury's moral sense, bore strong resemblance to the Quaker Inner Light, though theologian Robert Barclay, in his *Apology for the True Christian Divinity*, took care to distinguish Christ's indwelling spirit from both conscience and the light of reason.[9] Each promised a redeeming feature — a source of correct standards and impulses to virtuous behavior amid the depravity of human nature — on which to rest hope for good decisions, something incorrupt on which to build.

As an inducement to benevolent acts, the moral sense offered something slightly different from the satisfaction of conscience or the peace which came from obedience to the Light Within. Shaftesbury believed that the successful practice of virtue, the disinterested kindness and generosity directed to the public good, would afford the most exquisite pleasure, next to which wine, women, and song would seem trifling — at least to the properly cultivated individual. On a much less abstract and aristocratic level, Cotton Mather preached the same doctrine.[10]

In the mind of the Scottish philosopher, Francis Hutcheson, however, the concept of a moral sense became more elaborate and produced more positively humanitarian moral corollaries. He did not put as much faith as Shaftesbury in the sublime satisfaction to be derived from disinterested acts of charity, but postulated instead a new kind of self-centeredness. If self-love was extensible to embrace a family, and thereby somewhat redeemed, perhaps it could be extended even further with better results. Ultimately, a properly disposed man would draw his nation, then all humanity, into his enlarged concept of self, so that he would act for the good of mankind as avidly as a less virtuous one would act for himself. Selfishness, duly expanded, became a guarantor of the utmost selflessness and at the same time virtually extinct! Hutcheson, went on to argue that a lover of mankind would respond warmly to actions by others directed to the public good, and set up criteria for judging between such actions, giving highest place to those affording the greatest good to the greatest number.[11] For all the earnestness and self-sacrifice of the donor, the widow's mite would not be equal to the Bettering House; nor would John Smith's pennies to beggars have the same value as the Pennsylvania Hospital.

From Shaftesbury's attempt to create a basis for morality independent of anything so repugnant as the threat of hell, philosophers of the eighteenth century spun sets of values that were often distinguished from those of other eras less in connotation than in phraseology. Shaftesbury created some of the vocabulary: "To love the public, to study universal good, and to promote the interest of the whole world, as far as lies within our power, is surely the height of goodness, and makes that temper which we call divine." [12] After him, a spirit of love for all mankind, as well as sentiments and feelings of disinterested benevolence, became standard coins of the philosopher's and moralizer's realm. Nor were they current only among deists and free-thinkers like Shaftesbury and

Holbach: Hutcheson professed to be a Christian; David Hartley, Jonathan Edwards, and his disciple, Samuel Hopkins, undoubtedly could be called by that name — and they were all endorsers of the new ideas.[13]

Some Quakers used both the concept of a moral sense and the ideals of disinterested benevolence and humanitarianism that became popular in the eighteenth century. Woolman, early in life, came to believe that "as the mind was moved by an inward Principle to Love God as an invisible, Incomprehensible Being, by the same principle it was moved to love him in all his manifestations in the Visible world." [14] Later, on his religious visit to Papunahung, he thought of "the difficulties attending the natives," and, as he recorded in his *Journal*: "a weighty and Heavenly care came over my mind, and love filled my heart toward all mankind, in which I felt a Strong Engagement that we [Friends] might be faithful to the Lord while His mercies are yet extended to us, and so attend to pure Universal Righteousness as to give no just cause of offence to the gentiles who do not profess Christianity, Whither the Blacks from Africa, or the Native Inhabitants of this Continent." [15] Woolman probably regarded the sensation of his heart filling with love toward all mankind as a result of his love of God, but in addition to the similarity of the phenomenon to the operation of a moral sense, the fact that the object of his love was the whole of mankind showed kinship with the ideals commonly expressed in the century. Characteristically, his reflection on his experience led Woolman not to super-sensual joy but to self-questioning, in an effort to determine whether he might not improve his conduct. In later years Quaker Meetings began to refer to their love of mankind as "the feelings of Humanity" and to use other expressions which could have implied belief in a moral sense.[16]

An impressive array of the common terms of humanitarian morality appeared in a letter by Israel Pemberton, the younger, as early as 1750. Writing to his brother John, he praised the "spirit of universal benevolence to mankind, and the real pleasure arising from our being conscious of this being the spring of our actions, [which] so farr surpasses any gratification in our comon pursuits & engagements that those may truly be called Happy, who devote their whole time & strength to the discharge of their duties, from this principle." [17]

Not until the time of the American Revolution did this language enter into official minutes, but once accepted, it became commonplace. Meetings began to describe "universal Love to Mankind," "universal good will," or "universal Righteousness" as the mainsprings of their actions.[18] Benevolence, both as a spirit and as something directed to mankind, began to figure prominently.[19] "The disinterested practice of doing good," a less lofty and more specific idea, was also mentioned.[20] Expressions of brotherhood with all men became common, too, in the Revolutionary years, notably in connection with the problems of the Negro and the Indian.[21]

Friends did not pioneer in the development of the phrases and ideas of eighteenth-century humanitarian ethics; they adopted them at the same time that many others did. Nor did the Quakers abandon older ideas, practices, and formulations in embracing the new. Their advocacy of ideas of natural liberty in the Revolutionary period and their application of them to the Negroes similarly followed current intellectual fashion. In both instances, using contemporary ideas helped Quakers to express their virtues in ways which could be appreciated by the general public. "Restoring" freedom to Negroes born into slavery could even be held up to legislatures as a feature of Quakers' conduct superior to that of their neighbors in terms of their neighbors' own convictions. In the same years, feelings of humanity and a spirit of toleration and philanthropy were publicly praised. Notable Friends were lauded at their deaths for such qualities by non-Friends.[22] Meetings knew that their corporate behavior in respect to members' Negroes, their efforts on behalf of all other slaves, or their dedication to disinterested benevolence would come to public attention and would draw the approval of the rightly disposed of their own and foreign nations.[23] Humanitarianism among Friends was sincere; but it was not the totality of the religious outlook of their church. It gave them a bond, which they cherished, to the ideas and political conditions surrounding them.

Humanitarian ideas, while logically acceptable as developments of the distinctive doctrine of the Inner Light, ran into the obstacle of religious fellowship. Devotion to the human race as a unit required an outreach of the imagination which few could accomplish. The church stood as intermediary between individuals and the whole of mankind, and through the years had acquired organizational practices, an inner life, a reality as base-point for social sentiments (that is, charity and the discipline), which continued to stand in the way of practical devotion to universal causes. Quakerism had once been a universal cause itself; the objective — moribund though it might be — of drawing more people into the religious fellowship kept setting a limit to what Meetings might do for outsiders. The value of the religious fellowship, moreover, became its select quality in spite of the inherent equalitarian features of the doctrine of the Inner Light. A tight sect had grown up around a belief that all men can know and obey God's will.

The external forces which beset Quakers in Pennsylvania after 1750 were matched by a crisis within the religious organization itself. Not only were Friends, in "fearfulness of sufferings," reluctant to deny themselves power; they were also finding it harder to agree that they should. The moral reform, with its primary aim the restoration of distinctive, traditional Quaker ways, was to bring solidarity against the seductive errors which political responsibility, social leadership, religious freedom, and wealth had nurtured. In particular, Friends could not agree about the evil of defensive war, the obligations of the citizen to obey a government bent on an evil policy, or the right action for a man to take who could win high office where he could exert a beneficial influence. All these problems were solved, officially, by withdrawal from public office and by mutual encouragement to support the standards set by the stricter consciences in the group. But there was suppressed animosity, and outbursts of action occurred, such as the episode in 1764 when young Quakers armed against the riotous westerners marching on Philadelphia, even before the Revolution brought the little schism by Free Quakers.

Friends achieved a high degree of success in preserving their church in these years because they asserted the solidarity of the fellowship as a supreme value. Doing so, however, posed a dilemma. Disciplinary strictness, which sometimes served as a means of encouraging solidarity, began to appear as a doubtful technique, especially when those who had been excommunicated could acquire church fellowship with Anglicans, or later with Free Quakers, at little social sacrifice. As early as 1758 leading Friends began to believe that membership in their religious Society should be all but permanent, that the mutual love which held the church together should do so irrespective of differing opinions among the members, and that no one should be expected to abide by the Quaker testimonies more completely than his inner conviction required.[24] This position, now held by most Friends, meant an end to disownment except for conduct universally condemned as immoral, and the abandonment of the goal of uniformity in the collective demonstration of the distinguishing Quaker beliefs before the world.

Anthony Benezet confronted but could not resolve the dilemma posed by conflicting desires to preserve the religious community as a social group and yet uphold the sectarian testimonies: he grieved over the expulsion of a Quaker who openly participated in the Revolutionary government in 1777, but he also knew the embarrassment of explaining Quaker pacifism to Patrick Henry, who was sympathetic to the sect and knew some Friends, but no pacifists. In 1774 Benezet reminded him that many Friends had no other claim to Quaker principles "than as they were children or grand-children of those who professed" them.[25] Birthright membership, accepted by American Friends in the mid-eighteenth century, institutionalized the solidarity of the fellowship as a social group, but threatened to subvert its ability to bear witness to its ancient beliefs. The moral reform movement succeeded only in making peripheral changes in "birthrightism," such as requiring that children with but one parent in unity would be under a Meeting's care only when they formally entered into membership and demonstrated their adherence to Quaker "testimonies." The Society of Friends was torn between two views of its basic nature: a social entity with hereditary membership united in love of God and one another, and a group defined by agreement on religious principles and standards of conduct.

Theology offered no reconciliation. The theory of the church supported unity in love before and above particular opinions; agreement on them was expected to follow, but it did not do so invariably. Meditation on this fact suggested forbearance in the face of disagreement. Friends' understanding of the gift of grace and the perfectibility of conduct, however, made it plain that individuals could so disregard the inner monitor as to fall into every kind of error as a result of turning love from God to self. Those with corrupted hearts ought not to be in the visible gathered church. Individual consciences which led their possessors to conformity with the world were bound to be suspect; Christ intended his mystical body to be a model of purity.

The ideal resolution of this deadlock — to hold all Friends together in one orderly and consistent Society without threat of disownment — was not achieved, though dealings in the Quaker way went far to preserve harmony. The creation of halfway disownment in barring erring members from Meetings for discipline, from committee tasks or even contribution to the stock, softened the threat and kept in the fold those members undergoing disciplinary treatment. This technique was useful when Friends were introducing into the discipline new standards of behavior which at the time were not generally required by other Christians — specifically, freeing and compensating slaves, staying out of public office, and giving up liquor. Exaltation of the ideal of purity of the church helped, too. But humanitarianism served the Quakers as a further aid to solidarity.

Humanitarian ideals could support the inner strength of the church provided the benevolent activities which they inspired did not tend to introduce disruptive elements. Consequently, Friends began to use their Meetings to promote projects for the good of outsiders only after they came to believe that practical demonstrations of the love of mankind could be divorced from making new converts for the religious fellowship. The opportunity to effect the separation arrived in the Revolutionary period, at a time when their efforts to strengthen both the purity and social cohesiveness of the religious Society were making progress. Quakers expected the reform of the church to make them, both individually and collectively, better able than ever before to carry out their God-given duty to uphold their sect's "testimonies" in the world. However, during the second half of the eighteenth century they were gradually accepting a new understanding of the usefulness of this duty: to persuade outsiders to act more conscientiously according to the basic moral principles they already professed. Friends, while still believing they had the best knowledge of God's will and how to achieve submission to it, adopted the view that other sects practiced less perfect, not erroneous, religions. Though hidden to various degrees by superstition and formality, the universal Inner Light which gave a uniform morality to all who heeded it and which provided the valid essence of all faiths, enabled people outside as well as inside the Society of Friends to benefit from Quaker preaching; the right-hearted among any religious "people" would recognize a divinely inspired message and could make good use of it within the framework of their particular denomination. For Quakers, the task of bearing witness to divine standards of justice and love thus became a group responsibility which did not entail any major change in the composition of the church.

Benevolent efforts to reform the world also helped the solidarity of the church by reconciling Friends' determination to play a part in public affairs with the duty they accepted to love their neighbors and with the prevailing social philosophy of eighteenth-century America. Particularly as a result of combining theories of natural rights with more traditional morality, Friends were able to set goals of social justice which they were obligated to reach in their personal lives and encourage their fellow citizens to strive for. Quaker opponents of slavery, by postulating a universal right to liberty, found a way to solve the problem of Friends' duty to the Negroes and successfully advanced arguments which persuaded their religious Society first to prohibit slave-owning by its members, then to devise a practical program of aid to former bondsmen, and finally to call on all other people to stamp out the slave trade and free the Negroes by governmental action. Later, zeal to give justice to the Indians in the light of a natural property right inspired a program of missionary activity by the Society and appeals to the government and the public at large to increase honesty in business dealings with the Indians, to stop the liquor traffic, and to teach white men's ways to the natives.

Fortunately for the harmony of the church, however, patriotism and compassion for the oppressed could be harmonized in the support of benevolent projects as well as the long-standing obligation to express love to fellow men and the newly adopted standard of natural justice. Both in the 1750's and in the early nineteeth century, individual Friends looked with suspicion on deism and religious rationalism as well as on the natural rights theories and projects to improve human institutions to which these trends of thought had given support. Though greatly reduced, this suspicion continued during the Revolutionary period. As though mindful of those Friends who were reluctant to endorse natural justice and disinterested benevolence, the Society conceived its efforts to do good for outsiders in the light of more traditional ideals as well. Quakers had long accepted the belief that a nation's collective virtue influenced its temporal welfare; they, like other sects, had a responsibility to improve public morality. In addition to purifying their own conduct, therefore, they called on others to avoid sin and pointed out the need to end slavery and to civilize the Indians as adequate recompense for their lands in order to insure the prosperity and peace of the whole body politic. Even more than devotion to national righteousness, sympathy for the Negroes, Indians, and the poor in their suffering or degradation, encouraged Quakers to undertake social service without fear that it would subtly entangle them with worldliness.

The Society rarely kept these explanations of benevolence distinct, but used them woven together. Combined, they expressed a point of view generally acceptable to Friends in the late eighteenth century, prevented disruptive antagonisms in the Society over specific points, and defined a mutually satisfactory relationship between the church and the civil community. The Society, by accepting social service as a function of the religious fellowship and by endorsing natural justice and disinterested benevolence, kept in step with Revolutionary America and provided activities inside the church by which its members could participate in public life. If the Society had tried to maintain a policy of isolation and aloofness, the aspiration to participate — either intellectually or in organizations to do good — might have driven more members out than left to become Free Quakers or otherwise to find more freedom from their sect's code of conduct.

Although it adopted its own form of humanitarianism and engaged in benevolent activities for outsiders, the Society was willing to undertake only a few projects. It set limits partly because its financial resources were not endless, partly because of lingering opposition to making the fellowship a philanthropic agency, and partly to insure that its efforts would plainly support the sect's distinctive beliefs. Outside of the Meeting individual Friends formed or took part in associations to uplift the poor, improve prisons, reform laws, distribute Bibles, support hospitals, and perform other good works. While fellow Quakers often applauded these efforts, the Society declined to make most of them parts of its business. Most obviously, it never officially backed the Pennsylvania Hospital, the most successful major philanthropic institution predominantly supported by Quakers; the hospital exemplified no special "testimony" of the sect. Acting as a religious organization, Friends in the last quarter of the eighteenth century wished to face the rest of the civil community united as a benevolent society, but they decided to use corporate action to advance Christian principles which they upheld, but believed others did not sufficiently follow, as well as to demonstrate the solidarity and virtue of their Society to an often critical public.

This decision to confine official backing to benevolent projects that would promote distinctively Quaker views resulted in seemingly contradictory policies on the types of assistance which the Society offered to different kinds of outsiders. Since Friends expected other religious or ethnic "peoples" in settled communities of white men to practice mutual aid much as they themselves did, Meetings did not try to assume such responsibilities for outsiders except to provide schooling for children of indigent citizens who were not members of an organized "people." In support of the peace testimony, however, Quakers gave war relief to white men provided they took no part in the warfare, even if they were members of a well-organized religious body. To uphold opposition to slavery, the Society was willing to redress the injustices which it believed had been done to the colored people by advocating manumission, by giving legal protection and rudimentary religious and temporal education to free Negroes, as well as by looking after the welfare of the former slaves of Quakers in an even more comprehensive way. However, it tried to guide the colored folk to participation in the American nation as a distinct people, not as Quakers.

While the Society held that Negroes had a wider claim to its benevolence than whites, it gave to the Indians a claim wider still. It regarded ending Indian wars as so important that in the interest of peace it would offer aid even to braves who had taken part in the fighting. Moreover, for the natives it undertook the most sweeping program of re-education. The size of the task was so great that Friends could not hope to complete it; they could only show other sects and the government what should be done. Although the Quakers hoped to bring the Indians to Christianity eventually, and perhaps to participation in the American civilized community as well, the initial purposes of the missions were less far-reaching: to insure the very physical survival of the Indians, who no longer had a territory sufficient to support their old way of life, and to give a just recompense for lands which the Indians had vacated for white settlements. To carry out these purposes, the Quakers offered to teach agriculture and the full range of daily occupations practiced in American farming communities to any natives willing to learn.

The Society justified every project which it undertook for the benefit of a group of outsiders as meeting a special obligation to the group as well as observing a duty to help all mankind. While Friends acknowledged a variety of bonds to other peoples — from being members of the same civil communities to enjoying lands formerly occupied by the other group — all the additional considerations to some degree diluted a direct expression of brotherhood with mankind and emphasized the existence of the Society as a distinct element in the American nation. This emphasis guarded the Friends against that blending with the world which they were determined to resist and which some of them feared would be the result of extensive philanthropy. The Society made its strongest expressions of humanitarian motives, significantly, in justifying its aid to the Indians, the people separated from Friends by the widest cultural gulf, the least likely to become converts. Although at the time of the founding of the first missions Meetings gave some attention to historical bonds between various tribes and early Quaker settlers, in practice they let their obligation to help the natives rest on the moral debt owed by the American nation and on the duty of men to help each other. Except for the desire to improve national righteousness, the Friends' missions to the Indians in the post-Revolutionary period expressed forthright humanitarian motives. Paradoxically, Friends could acknowledge obligations based on the brotherhood of man most readily to those people in the United States with whom they had least in common. It was not recognition of likeness, but common membership in the species in spite of unlikeness, that inspired Quakers to embrace humanitarian ideals.

Social service — including the Indian missions — and public appeals for better laws or for improvement of individual conduct gave the Quakers a role in American society during the Revolutionary and post-Revolutionary periods. The role satisfied most Friends and was agreeable to such outsiders as paid attention to it, except for defenders of slavery. Owing to events outside the Society of Friends as well as developments within it, the situation changed by the 1820's, leaving Quakers ever since with a divided mind about the wisdom of making benevolent activities a function of the religious fellowship. But for a crucial half-century beginning about 1770, the year when Philadelphia Monthly Meeting founded its school for free Negroes, projects to advance natural justice and express disinterested benevolence to all mankind grew and flourished in American Quakerdom with the blessing of the religious Society. These projects enabled the Quakers to hold their church together and defend themselves as a people from the attacks of outsiders during the French and Indian War and the Revolution.

Before the middle of the eighteenth century, Friends accepted as a fact that they were a people among peoples in colonial America — an organized segment of the population which kept morality and good order in its own ranks, expected no special favor from the government, and thought other elements should do likewise. The Quakers wanted their church to be autonomous, yet tolerated by the British monarchy; as subjects they were willing to observe the laws as fully as their consciences would allow, and desired to exercise political rights equal to those of other colonials. Especially in Pennsylvania they had some hope of influencing public policy in accord with their ideals, but elsewhere they accepted political authority as normally in the hands of outsiders. Although they preserved a traditional belief that their religion would prevail over all other forms of Christianity, in practice they behaved as though they had abandoned this hope. The public hostility and political harassment which they encountered between 1755 and 1783 gave them a choice between withdrawing into an isolated world of their own, giving up their distinguishing "testimonies," or meeting the challenge by making their sect important to the rest of the nation. By following the third of these policies, they responded creatively to the most serious emergency in the history of American Quakerdom. Although they could not hold their previous proportion of the population, they increased their contribution to the American nation. Accepting the demand of Revolutionary patriots that they take a positive part in the new republic, the Quakers chose to act as a lobby for virtue and to some extent as a philanthropic organization. These activities gave a moral purpose to their sect at a time when Friends adopted a theory of religious toleration that acknowledged divine authority for other faiths. In this way the Quakers reconciled themselves with American religious pluralism, which they began to regard as permanent and, to a large degree, morally justifiable.

In the new interpretation of their position as a people among peoples, the Quakers after the Revolution could support the government and contribute to the national welfare in ways which would preserve and express their distinctive views. By benevolent activities they found a way to win a place for themselves in American society without either sacrificing their strict fidelity to their distinctive code of behavior or compromising with worldliness. By declining to seek converts through their philanthropic efforts, they made it possible to avoid any temptation to lower their standards in order to draw in more outsiders. Quaker asceticism and desires to reform human institutions, which had been preserved in colonial Pennsylvania, were reconciled under the aegis of the new American government that expected active participation by the citizens in the political process. Though the Quakers imposed qualifications on the extent and nature of their participation, they became valuable members of the body politic. They purified their own conduct, maintained the solidarity of their church, and by offering examples of philanthropic action for the national welfare in ways which they believed it their special duty to do, showed the way in virtue and public policy to fellow Americans.

SOURCES

NOTES

INDEX

Sources

I. PRIMARY SOURCES

A. Meeting Records

The sources most clearly necessary to any study of Quaker church life before 1800 are the records of the various Meetings. The Men's and Women's Meetings for Discipline and the Meetings of Ministers and Elders were all "Meetings of Record." Books of minutes kept to record their deliberations survive with entries in some cases going back far into the seventeenth century. By the end of the eighteenth century even some of the Preparative or weekly Meetings for Discipline were assembling such records. Minute books were not always kept up to date. The "rough minutes" written by the various clerks occasionally piled up for many years before someone undertook the task of putting them in order, editing, and transcribing them in the ledgers which were to be preserved for posterity. Some bundles of the original notes, or even superseded minutes books, survive. Conceivably, comparison of the various versions of such minutes might yield useful information, but for this study I have consulted only the volumes approved for a final version. The quantities of these tomes extant are highly admirable in the abstract, but stupefying to the historian unless his attention is confined to a small territory or time span. Consequently I make no pretense to having covered the field comprehensively.

Several main repositories contain large collections of Quaker records. Guilford College, North Carolina, has the main accumulation for the region south of Virginia. The two Yearly Meetings held at Baltimore have collections from Meetings in the Chesapeake Bay states. The Department of Records of Philadelphia Yearly Meeting, 302 Arch St., Philadelphia 6, Pa., has a huge accumulation (including all those outside New England which I have consulted in manuscript) from Meetings in Delaware, New Jersey, Pennsylvania, parts of Maryland and Virginia, and even Charleston, S. C. The Friends Historical Library, Swarthmore College, Swarthmore, Pa., has a somewhat smaller collection, though it possesses microfilm copies of many records (chiefly Monthly Meeting minutes and records of births, deaths, and marriages kept by Monthly Meetings) from all parts of the colonial Quaker world. New York records are mostly in a repository in New York City, a description of which was compiled by John Cox, Jr., for the Historical Records Survey, Division of Women's and Professional Projects, Work Projects Administration, under the title: *New York City Church Archives; Religious Society of Friends; Catalogue; Records in Possession of, or Relating to, the two New York Yearly Meetings of the Religious Society of Friends and their Subordinate Meetings* (New York, processed, 1940). New England records are mostly (Newport and Nantucket Monthly Meetings being the notable exceptions) housed in the Yearly Meeting Vault at the Moses Brown School, Providence 6, R. I. A few books of minutes have found their way into historical societies here and there.

The value to the historian of Quaker minute books varies widely from set to set. Meetings for Sufferings (of which I have inspected three volumes covering 1756 to 1802 for Philadelphia, and two covering 1775 to 1842 for New England) proved most consistently valuable. Especially, Philadelphia Meeting for Sufferings with its extensive correspondence provided information about the whole Quaker world. The papers of that Meeting for Sufferings, which include the originals of documents entered in the minutes as well as many others, could well amplify the record.

Yearly Meeting minutes (of which I have consulted three volumes covering 1681 to 1798 for Philadelphia, and two volumes covering 1683 to 1819 for New England) have also been very useful. They dealt not only with inter-Yearly Meeting affairs, but the more general matters of church government, belief, and discipline in their own territories. By the end of the eighteenth century the minutes of the Philadelphia Yearly Meeting were becoming so thoroughly devoted to committee reports, however, that they ceased to be self-explanatory.

Quarterly Meeting Minutes in America, a brief sampling revealed, offer little to the historian. Chester (Pa.) Quarterly Meeting (of which I have read one volume, 1683 to 1767) recorded far less than the Yearly Meeting minutes told of what was going on at its sessions. Sandwich Quarterly Meeting in New England (one volume, c. 1705 to 1779), Rhode Island Quarterly Meeting of Ministers and Elders (one volume, 1701 to 1769) similarly proved of slight value.

Monthly Meetings afforded a great range of usefulness. When evaluating the Quaker community (or, perhaps, communities) even a rather arid set of minutes demonstrated important points. Falls Monthly Meeting in Pennsylvania (three volumes, covering 1683 to 1788) proved typical of rural Monthly Meetings. Into its records went marriages, disciplinary cases, deliberations over certificates, communications from higher Meetings, answers to the queries (when required), and only a few matters relating to other features of the religious fellowship. Concord (Pa.), Evesham (N. J.), Pembroke (Mass.), Dartmouth (Mass.) and New Bedford (Mass.) presented a similar picture of the business of the usual Monthly Meeting. Even Salem Monthly Meeting, which included Salem, Lynn, and Boston, Mass., fell into the same pattern, apparently because the members were just ordinary townsfolk. The only rural Monthly Meeting which came to my attention as operating frequently in more than routine fashion was South Kingstown, R. I., in the Narragansett Planter country, where the Quaker Community in-included men of substance, social pretension, and cultivation in some numbers.

Monthly Meetings held in cities where a sizable group of the leading citizens were Friends regularly proved more interesting for historical purposes. Urban Quakers consistently provided much of the dynamism in the rise of humanitarian concerns and most other changes. Newport Monthly Meeting, nevertheless, provided almost an exception. There the devout were for the most part a different element in the church from the socially and politically prominent. The eighteenth-century records which I read on microfilm at the Rhode Island Historical Society (the originals are at the Newport Historical Society, Newport, R. I.), rarely mentioned familiar names and rarely dealt with the inner ferment of the Quaker world. Still, the range of business of this city Meeting proved wider and confronted the members with more uncertainties than usual in rural Meetings. Burlington (N. J.) Monthly Meeting (five volumes of Men's Minutes covering 1678 to 1788 and two volumes of Women's, 1681 to 1799) showed a much more interesting spectacle, including the striking contrast between the affairs of the two sexes.

But by all tests the Philadelphia Monthly Meeting records are most valuable to the historian of colonial America. In the nine volumes of Men's Minutes which I read (1682 to 1781) there lay a wealth of detail about the affairs of the church from the widows and orphans to the most momentous questions of morality. Though written in a language as stylized as any Quaker minutes, these conveyed a great deal of information about the changing attitudes toward the religious fellowship, the abilities of various members, the objectives of the organization, and the crucial position of Philadelphia in the world of friends. The Women's Minutes (four volumes, 1686 to 1781) similarly stood out in their field. The Philadelphia women, while still in second place to their menfolk, had more to do than other women and far more capacity to do it. Not only did they have funds beyond the reach of their sisters elsewhere, but their records reflect a superior level of education and a greater inclination to write down what went on in their meetings, sometimes including topics of preaching which apparently interrupted the conduct of business but went unrecorded in most Meetings.

Records kept by the Meetings of Ministers and Elders (or Select Meetings), while not often directly useful to the subjects treated in this book, contain more information than has been generally realized. New England Yearly Meeting for Ministers and Elders (of which I have examined one volume, 1707 to 1797) occasionally illuminated events in the Yearly Meeting for business.

Meetings of Ministers and Elders—even more, possibly, than the Meetings for Discipline—failed to provide self-contained records. The clerks set down decisions, but not subjects on which no "sense of the Meeting" appeared; nor did they set down disagreements in the fellowship or the process behind the decisions. As a result, unofficial reports, whenever they turned up, gave keys to the meaning of minutes and opened up new vistas. Such aids appeared so unpredictably as to make it impossible to go searching for them. Fortunately, over a long period of time spent reading official minutes, enough internal evidence comes to light to enable the historian to read between the lines with sufficient success to divine many points at which the minutes may not be taken at face value.

Most Quaker records before 1800 have not been printed. A few epistles were considered important enough to be published for distribution by the Meetings which issued them. The annual general epistles sent by London Yearly Meeting to its subordinate Meetings and the Yearly Meetings in America have been published as *A Collection of the Epistles from the Yearly Meeting of Friends in London, to the Quarterly & Monthly Meetings in Great Britain, Ireland, and Elsewhere, from 1675 to 1820* (New York, 1821). By the end of the eighteenth century the Yearly Meetings were printing their "Disciplines." An outgrowth of collections of important decisions kept and augmented by lower Meetings for the guidance of disciplinary officials, the printed forms usually put the material into a topical arrangement and frequently retained the wording (and even the dates) of the original minutes. In the absence of manuscript records, these books can be very helpful. Large collections of them exist at the Friends Historical Library at Swarthmore, the Haverford College Library, and the Widener Library of Harvard University.

Some special subjects of Meeting action received individual treatment, as in *A Narrative of some of the Proceedings of North Carolina Yearly Meeting on the Subject of Slavery within its Limits* (Greensborough, N. C., 1848), brought out by the local Meeting for Sufferings.

More recently, some valuable documentary histories have been compiled. One that remains useful even though drawn from a limited collection of minute books is Ezra Michener, *A Retrospect of Early Quakerism; Being Extracts from the Records of Philadelphia Yearly Meeting and the Meetings Composing It. To which is Prefixed an Account of their First Establishment* (Philadelphia, 1860). In the twentieth century, Thomas Woody began a series of books which follow roughly the same format, dealing with education, but defining the subject so loosely as to admit data pertaining more directly to other topics. While the Quaker records transcribed in these volumes are not always letter-perfect, they have made clear in a general way the nature and activities of the Quaker churches in places which I have not covered by reading the local minute books, with the exception of New York. Woody himself published *Early Quaker Education in Pennsylvania* ("Columbia University Contributions to Education, Teachers' College Series," No. 105 [New York, 1920]) and *Quaker Education in the Colony and State of New Jersey; a Source Book* (Philadelphia, 1923). Zora Klain continued the series with *Quaker Contributions to Education in North Carolina* (Philadelphia, 1924) and *Educational Activities of New England Quakers; a Source Book* (Philadelphia, 1928). William C. Dunlap produced the book in the series which gives the most comprehensive treatment of Quaker behavior, *Quaker Education in Baltimore and Virginia Yearly Meetings, with an Account of Certain Meetings of the Eastern Shore Affiliated with Philadelphia; Based on the Manuscript Sources* (Philadelphia, 1936). In addition to the minutes contained in these books, the bibliographies give a useful, if now partly obsolete, list of locations of Meeting records.

B. Records of Other Quaker Organizations

In addition to the official documents of Meetings, other Quaker organizations supplied useful material. I have consulted the Papers relating to the Friendly Association (4 volumes) and the minutes and papers of the Indian Committee of Philadelphia Yearly Meeting (up to 1812) kept by the Department of Records, 302 Arch St., Philadelphia. These items are also available on microfilm at the American Philosophical Society Library. The material is described in George S. Snyderman, "A Preliminary Survey of American Indian Manuscripts in Repositories of the Philadelphia Area," in American Philosophical Society *Proceedings*, XCVII (1953), 596–610, and G. S. Snyderman, "The Manuscript Collections of the Philadelphia Yearly Meeting of Friends Pertaining to the American Indian," in Am. Phil. Soc. *Proc.*, CII (1958), 613–20. The Department of Records has the "Minutes of the Committee's appointed by the Three Monthly Meetings of Friends of Philadelphia, to the Oversight and care of the School for Educating Africans' and their descendants," together with a bundle of correspondence actually of the Philadelphia Association of Friends for the Free Instruction of Adult Colored Persons, 1790 to 1798.

Near the end of the eighteenth century Quakers began to inform each other and the general public about activities of such organizations by publishing short historical accounts of them compiled mainly from their minutes, correspondence, and papers of the individuals who took part in them. The Indian affairs received the earliest attention, beginning with *Some Transactions between the Indians and Friends in Pennsylvania, In 1791 & 1792* (London, 1792). As the missionary work began, the series was continued with *A Brief Account of the Proceedings of the Committee, appointed in the year 1795 by the Yearly Meeting of Friends of Pennsylvania, New Jersey, &c. for promoting the Improvement and gradual Civilization of the Indian Natives* (London, 1806; previously printed in Philadelphia); and *A Brief Account of the Proceedings of the Committee, Appointed by the Yearly Meeting of Friends, Held in Baltimore, for Promoting the Improvement and Civilization of the Indian Natives* (London, 1806; previously printed in Baltimore). Subsequently there appeared *A Sketch of the further Proceedings of the Committees Appointed by the Yearly Meetings of Friends of Pennsylvania, &c. and Maryland, for Promoting the Improvement and Gradual Civilization of the Indian Natives in some parts of North America* (London, 1812), after which New York entered the field with *A Summary Account of the Measures pursued by the Yearly Meeting of Friends of New York, for the Welfare and Civilization of the Indians residing on the frontiers of that State. With extracts from two letters relating to the subject* (London, 1813) and *Narrative of Recent Proceedings of the Committee Appointed by the Yearly Meeting of Friends of New-York, in Relation to the Indians in that State* (New York, 1839). Later publications continued to treat the early years, notably in *Some Particulars Relative to the Continuance of the Endeavours, on the part of the Society of Friends in the United States of North America, for the Improvement and Gradual Civilization of the Indian Natives* (London, 1823); the compendious volume by the [London] Meeting for Sufferings, Aborigines' Committee, *Some Account of the Conduct of the Religious Society of Friends towards the Indian Tribes in the Settlement of the Colonies of East and West Jersey and Pennsylvania: with a Brief Narrative of their Labours for the Civilization and Christian Instruction of the Indians, from the time of their settlement in America, to the year 1843* (London, 1844); and *A Brief Sketch of the Efforts of Philadelphia Yearly Meeting of the Religious Society of Friends, to promote the Civilization and Improvement of the Indians; also, of the Present Condition of the Tribes in the State of New York* (Philadelphia, 1866).

Following much the same pattern, Samuel Parrish brought out a documentary history of the Friendly Association, *Some Chapters in the History of the Friendly Association for Regaining and Preserving Peace with the Indians by Pacific Measures* (Philadelphia, 1877), a book which reveals surprisingly little about its subject.

Other Quaker organizations were given official documentary histories during the nineteenth century. Philadelphia Yearly Meeting's record in supporting education was outlined in *A Brief Account of the Concern of the Yearly Meeting of Friends, held in Philadelphia, in Relation to the Guarded Religious Education of their Youth, together with a Statement of some of the Proceedings of the Committee to whom the Subject was Referred* (Philadelphia, 1835). Quaker efforts to provide education for the Free Negroes of Philadelphia were described in *A Brief Sketch of the Schools for Black People, and Their Descendants, Established by the Religious Society of Friends, in 1770* (Philadelphia, 1867) and *History of the Associations of Friends for the Free Instruction of Adult Colored Persons in Philadelphia* (Philadelphia, 1890), published by the respective organizations.

Although not a book about an exclusively Quaker organization, Thomas G. Morton and Frank Woodbury, *The History of the Pennsylvania Hospital, 1751–1895* (Philadelphia, 1895), presents the subject chiefly by means of documents. No published secondary treatment of the institution, in fact, has fully exploited the offerings of this collection.

C. Printed Quaker Writings: Doctrinal and Personal Records

The "Friends' Books" which circulated among American Quakers in the eighteenth century included many titles, some of them dating originally from the days of the First Publishers. As a rule, the full titles and various editions of such works may be found in Joseph Smith's *Descriptive Catalogue of Friends Books*, 2 vols. (London, 1867). Robert Barclay's *An Apology for the True Christian Divinity*, the introduction to which is dated 1675, went through several editions with various additional phrases attached to the main title (for convenience, I have used the edition of Philadelphia, 1908). The standard work on Quaker theology during the eighteenth century, the *Apology* covered its subject in comprehensive and systematic fashion probably mastered by a small minority of those who regarded it as the classical statement of their religious beliefs. Two of Barclay's other works have been of special importance to this study: *The Anarchy of the Ranters, and other Libertines, the Hierarchy of the Romanists, and other pretended Churches, Equally Refused, and Refuted, in a Two-fold Apology for the Church and People of God, Called in Derision Quakers . . .* (to take most of the title page of the edition of London, 1771) and *Uni-*

versal Love Considered, and Established upon its Right Foundation: Being a Serious Inquiry how far Charity may, and ought to, be Extended towards Persons of Different Judgments in Matters of Religion: and Whose Principles, among the Several Sects of Christians, do most Naturally Lead to that due Moderation Required. Written in the Spirit of Love and Meekness, for the Removing of Stumbling Blocks out of the way of the Simple; by a Lover of the Souls of all Men (as the title page reads for the London edition of 1799).

Among the writings of George Fox, probably none was read as often as his primer, *Instructions for Right Spelling, and Plain Directions for Reading and Writing True English. With several other Things, very useful and necessary, both for Young and Old, to read and learn* (of which I have read the Newport, R. I., edition of 1769). The Quaker antidote to "In Adam's fall we sinned all," it worked the fundamentals of Christian doctrine and Friends' distinctive beliefs into lessons for the young. However, *The Journal of George Fox*, 2 vols., ed. Norman Penney (Cambridge, England, 1911), has more specific historical information.

Among other doctrinal and personal writings of the early period of special interest to the study of colonial Quakerdom, William Penn's writings, which I have consulted in *The Select Works of William Penn*, 5 vols. (London, 1782), deserve a special place, but not far ahead of William Edmundson, *A Journal of the Life, Travels, Sufferings and Labour of Love in the Work of the Ministry, of that Worthy Elder and faithful Servant of Jesus Christ, William Edmundson, who departed this Life, the thirty first of the sixth Month 1712* (2nd ed.; London, 1774), which contains not only the record of his travels but numerous epistles of particular importance to the organization of the church and its justification. John Richardson, *An Account of the Life of that Ancient Servant of Jesus Christ, John Richardson* (which I have read in the edition of Philadelphia, 1856), describes the career of a fairly sophisticated Quaker evangelist and his notable encounters with American Indians. Isaac Penington, *The Works of the Long-Mournful and Sorely-Distressed Isaac Penington . . .*, 4 vols. (London, 1784), is highly important to a general understanding of Quakerism, but of little direct bearing on colonial America, as Friends there paid less attention to him than to other early writers. Even more consistently ignored was John Bellers, whose works carried to its best expression an offshoot of late seventeenth-century English Quakerism of interest to colonials only briefly. Following a rather superficial sketch of his life, Bellers' pamphlets are available in A. Ruth Fry, *John Bellers, 1654–1725; Quaker, Economist and Social Reformer. His Writings Reprinted, with a Memoir* (London, 1935).

344

Among the writings of eighteenth-century Quakers of general value in revealing the doctrinal and ecclesiastical views of the time, I have found several especially useful. The Rhode Islander, Job Scott, who acted in this case chiefly as a compiler, produced *A Treatise on Church Discipline, taken, principally, from the Writings of Robert Barclay, William Penn, and Isaac Penington* (Philadelphia, 1824). Moses West, in *A Treatise Concerning Marriage: wherein the Unlawfulness of Mixt Marriages is Laid Open from the Scriptures. Recommended to the Youth of Both Sexes among the People called Quakers* (4th ed.; London, 1780) produced a work widely distributed by Quaker Meetings in efforts to preserve the social solidarity of the fellowship. The edition cited includes advices from London Yearly Meeting of 1777. The English schoolmaster, David Hall, wrote the most explicit recommendations on the related subjects of rearing the youth: *An Epistle of Love and Caution to the Quarterly and Monthly Meetings of Friends in Great-Britain, or elsewhere* (3rd ed.; London, 1750) and *An Epistle to Friends in Great-Britain, or elsewhere, containing Advice and Consolation, particularly address'd to those who are under Tribulation, viz. 1. To the Widows and Fatherless. 2. To the Orphans. 3. To Apprentices. 4. To Men and Maid Servants. 5. To Fathers and Mothers, with their Children. 6. To the Poor, Aged, and Infirm. &c.* (London, 1754). A treatise by another English Friend, Joseph Phipps, illustrated the change in tone of theological speculation perceptible by the end of the eighteenth century: *The Original and Present State of Man, Briefly Considered; wherein is shown the Nature of his Fall, and the Necessity, Means, and Manner of his Restoration, through the Sacrifice of Christ, and the Sensible Operation of that Divine Principle of Grace and Truth, held forth by the People called Quakers . . .* (Philadelphia, 1836). This work gained popularity among Americans by the end of the eighteenth century.

The printed journals of American Quakers, often supplemented by short works on doctrine, church government, or individual conduct, form a voluminous literature. All too often such writings contain little more than chronological records of Meetings attended and stock pious phrases. Among the important exceptions are the products of Thomas Chalkley, John Churchman, Job Scott, John Griffith, and, above all, John Woolman. Chalkley's *A Collection of the Works of Thomas Chalkley . . .* compiled after his death and published at the instigation of Philadelphia Monthly Meeting (Philadelphia, 1749), reported the career and ideas of a colorful Quaker who enlarged his conception of his duty to his fellow men far beyond that of most of his contemporaries. John Churchman, *An Account of the Gospel Labours, and Christian Experiences of a Faithful Minister of Christ, John Church-*

man . . . (Philadelphia, 1779, or London, 1780) offers an account of a pivotal figure in the reformation of Pennsylvania Quakerdom in the mid-eighteenth century, but it has to be supplemented with other sources to yield its full significance. (Citations to this work in the notes to the chapters of this book are to the reprint in William Evans and Thomas Evans, eds., *The Friends' Library*, 14 vols. [Philadelphia, 1837–1859], vol. VI.) Job Scott, *A Journal of the Life, Travels and Gospel Labours of that Faithful Servant and Minister of Christ, Job Scott: with Corrections and Additions* (of which I have used the edition of London, 1815) reveals even less of what it might, though it offers hints about New England Quakerism that are highly valuable. If the "corrections and additions" could be undone, or the manuscript in the Friends Historical Library in Swarthmore used, Scott might be a more valuable source on inner currents of New England Quakerism, but a less accurate index to the prevailing official opinions. John Griffith, *A Journal of the Life, Travels, and Labours in the Work of the Ministry, of John Griffith, Late of Chelmsford in Essex, in Great Britain formerly of Darby, in Pennsylvania* (Philadelphia, 1780) is a more straightforward book, giving illuminating comparisons of Quakers in England and America, as well as the aims of the reformers. John Woolman, *The Journal and Essays of John Woolman, edited from the Original Manuscripts* by Amelia M. Gummere (New York, 1922) is so obviously central to the study of colonial Quakerdom as to need no further endorsement, unless the importance of the essays needs to be underlined.

The Friends' Library edited by William and Thomas Evans, and *Friends' Miscellany* . . . published at Philadelphia by John and Isaac Comly beginning in 1831, offer convenient collections of English and American Quaker writing with emphasis on the journal and short essay genres.

D. Quaker Writings on Special Subjects

Among the specialized writings by Quakers, a few on miscellaneous topics need to be mentioned. Thomas Budd, *Good Order Established in Pennsylvania and New Jersey* (reprinted with Notes and Introduction by Frederick J. Shepard; Cleveland, 1902) is one of the few documents of the social reformist, or utopian, influence in early Pennsylvania. Some others appear in whole or in part in Robert Proud, *The History of Pennsylvania in North America, from the Original Institution and Settlement of that Province, under the first Proprietor and Governor William Penn, in 1681, till after the Year 1742 . . . *, 2 vols. (Philadelphia, 1797–1798), a work full of extracts from documents, Quaker writings of all kinds, and direct personal information.

Anthony Benezet's pamphlets include *The Mighty Destroyer Displayed, In some Account of the Dreadful Havock made by the Mistaken Use as well as Abuse of Distilled Spirituous Liquors* (Philadelphia, 1774), sometimes included in various offerings under the title, *The Potent Enemies of America laid Open: Being Some Account of the baneful effects attending the use of Distilled Spirituous Liquors, and the Slavery of the Negroes;* . . . (1774? and later). This attack on drink was not the first by a Quaker, but it was easily the most important in the eighteenth century, and pioneered in the genre. Also important were Benezet's anti-war pamphlets, *Serious Considerations on several Important Subjects; viz. On War and its Inconsistency with the Gospel* . . . (Philadelphia, 1778) and *The Plainness and Innocent Simplicity of the Christian religion. With Its Salutary Effects, compared to the corrupting Nature and dreadful Effects of* WAR. *With Some Account of the Blessing which attends on a Spirit influenced by divine Love, producing Peace and Good-Will to Men* (Philadelphia, 1783). The latter includes one of the celebrated encomiums on Pennsylvania as proof of the values of pacifism.

Owen Biddle's pamphlet urging the establishment of a Yearly Meeting boarding school, *A Plan for a School On an Establishment Similar to that at Ackworth, in Yorkshire, Great-Britain, varied to suit the Circumstances of the Youth within the Limits of the Yearly-Meeting for Pennsylvania and New-Jersey: Introduced with the Sense of Friends in New-England, on the Subject of Education; and An Account of some Schools in Great-Britain: to which is added Observations and Remarks intended for the Consideration of Friends* (Philadelphia, 1790), is justly famous. Possibly its debt to Moses Brown and the New Englanders needs greater emphasis than it has received. Witness the printed epistle *From the Meeting for Sufferings for New-England, to the several Quarterly and Monthly-Meetings belonging to the Yearly-Meeting* (Providence, 1782?).

The subject of slavery, however, was the one on which Quakers entered the most unusual special pleas during the eighteenth century. Long before Benezet put antislavery propaganda into a highly successful form for distribution among Americans and Europeans in general, other Quakers had developed the main lines of argument. Thomas E. Drake, in *Quakers and Slavery in America* (New Haven, Conn., 1950) gives a comprehensive bibliography of this literature. Happily, since Drake wrote, the Microprint publication of the extant items by the American Antiquarian Society has made the question of the location of the originals of little moment. The antislavery pamphlets by Quakers, American-born or -bred, who did not let their cause fire them to the point of violent controversy with their brethren, have been most important to this study. John Hepburn's *The American Defence of the Christian Golden Rule, Or an Essay to prove the Unlawfulness of Making Slaves of Men* (New York? 1715) is the best early example available. William Burling's statement of a few years later survives only in part, the portion printed in Benjamin Lay, *All Slave-Keepers, That keep the Innocent in Bondage, Apostates Pretending to lay Claim to the Pure & Holy Christian Religion* . . . (Philadelphia, 1737). Elihu Coleman, *Testimony Against that Antichristian Practice of Making Slaves of Men. Wherein it is shewed to be contrary to the Dispensation of the Law and Time of the Gospel, and very opposite both to Grace and Nature* (Boston, 1733) is somewhat less interesting. Woolman's essays (in the volume mentioned above) brought to a climax the creative phase of Quaker antislavery arguments. By comparison, the earliest antislavery papers, such as those by Cadwalader Morgan (printed in T. E. Drake, "Cadwalader Morgan, Antislavery Quaker of the Welsh Tract," *Friends Intelligencer*, XCVIII [1941], 575–76) and Robert Pyle (printed in Henry J. Cadbury, "An Early Quaker Anti-Slavery Statement," *Journal of Negro History*, XXII [1937] 488–93), and the blasts by outraged consciences, such as Ralph Sandiford, *The Mystery of Iniquity, in a brief Examination of the Practice of the Times,* . . . *The Second Edition, with Additions* (Philadelphia, 1730) and Lay's work already mentioned, have less to do with the development of American Quakerism. The impact of Sandiford and Lay on colonial Friends may be evaluated better from Roberts Vaux, *Memoirs of the Lives of Benjamin Lay and Ralph Sandiford; two of the earliest Public Advocates for the Emancipation of the Enslaved Africans* (Philadelphia, 1815), written with the aid of men who had known these unusual characters.

E. Personal Papers

Two collections of correspondence which have been published provided valuable material on the Quaker reformation of the mid-eighteenth century. One, George Crosfield's *Memoirs of the Life and Gospel Labours of Samuel Fothergill, with Selections from his Correspondence* . . . (New York, 1844), I have consulted in the reprint in Evans and Evans (eds.), *The Friends' Library*, vol. IX. The other is George S. Brookes, *Friend Anthony Benezet* (Philadelphia, 1937), which makes available an assortment of Benezet's papers which is much more valuable than the short biography that prefixes it. Brookes's account of Benezet was derived from earlier ones by Roberts Vaux and Wilson Armistead. The volume contains a good bibliography of Benezet's writings, though it probably has not catalogued all the variations to be found under the same title.

348

I have not relied heavily on manuscript papers of individual Quakers. The Pemberton Papers in the Pennsylvania Historical Society have been very helpful as a key to many aspects of colonial Quakerdom; the Moses Brown papers in the Austin Collection (in the Yearly Meeting Vault of the Moses Brown School, Providence, R. I.) have had more restricted value. The bulk of the Moses Brown papers is in the Rhode Island Historical Society, also in Providence. The "Collection of Letters," RS 181, in the Department of Records, Philadelphia Yearly Meeting, 302 Arch St., Philadelphia, consists mostly of letters to or from Henry Drinker or Daniel Drinker; some of the items there have been very revealing.

A sizable volume of personal papers of the early Quaker missionaries to the Indians remains, mostly in manuscript. As in the case of the Indian Committee papers, the personal materials relating to the missions have been investigated and described by George S. Snyderman. John Pierce's "Notes on a visit to several tribes of Indians, 1796" and Halliday Jackson's "Some Account of my residence among the Indians Continued" may be consulted at the Friends Historical Library at Swarthmore. Anthony F. C. Wallace has edited "Halliday Jackson's Journal to the Seneca Indians, 1798–1800," which appears in *Pennsylvania History*, XIX (1952), 117–47, 325–49. This journal provides information on the visions of Handsome Lake and the Quaker's response to them. Appended to Jackson's journal is a parallel account of the visions by Henry Simmons. George Snyderman has edited "Halliday Jackson's Journal of a Visit Paid to the Indians of New York (1806)," in American Philosophical Society *Proceedings*, CI (1957), 570–88. Merle H. Deardorff and G. S. Snyderman have presented the journal of John Philips from the same year as "A Nineteenth-Century Journal of a Visit to the Indians of New York," in Am. Phil. Soc. *Proc.*, C (1956), 594–612.

II. SECONDARY SOURCES

F. The Background of Philanthropy and Humanitarianism

The European background in philanthropic institutions and practices as presented here has been derived mainly from Brian Tierney, *Medieval Poor Law; A Sketch of Canonical Theory and Its Application in England* (Berkeley, Cal., 1959); Wilbur K. Jordan, *Philanthropy in England, 1480–1660; A Study of the Changing Pattern of English Social Aspirations* (New York, 1959); and Lynn Thorndike, "The Historical Background," in Ellsworth Faris *et al.* (eds.), *Intelligent Philanthropy* (Chicago, 1930). The last two chapters of Tierney's book provide a valuable critique of previous estimates of the effectiveness of the medieval church in carrying on various social services. If Jordan's analysis suffers from failure to take into account the great rise of prices during his period, he provides a good account of the institutional forms and purposes of philanthropy as they developed during these years.

Robert H. Bremner, *American Philanthropy* (Chicago, 1960), offers a brief sketch of the colonial period, though with little success in relating philanthropic motives to colonial life, except in the case of the Great Awakening. The relevant portion of Michael Kraus, *The Atlantic Civilization: Eighteenth-Century Origins* (Ithaca, N. Y., 1949) covers the continuing inter-relationship between Americans and Europeans in both philanthropy and philanthropic ideals. Special studies, however, yield greater understanding of the colonial affairs. Perry Miller, *The New England Mind; from Colony to Province* (Cambridge, 1953) explains the rise of societies to do good in New England in a fashion which I have found vastly more effective than any approach directed toward finding the roots of modern institutions. Carl and Jessica Bridenbaugh, in *Rebels and Gentlemen; Philadelphia in the Age of Franklin* (New York, 1942), have put philanthropic achievements in the context of the times with great success.

In the Bridenbaughs' work, as well as Carl Bridenbaugh, *Cities in the Wilderness: the First Century of Urban Life in America, 1625–1742* (New York, 1955) and *Cities in Revolt; Urban Life in America, 1743–1776* (New York, 1938), the records of various religious sects have been compared. Some of the other studies which have helped me evaluate the Quakers by comparison with other denominations have been J. Winfield Fretz, "Mutual Aid Among Mennonites," in *Mennonite Quarterly Review*, XIII (1939), 28–58, 187–209; Edgar Legare Pennington, "The Work of the Bray Associates in Pennsylvania," in *Pennsylvania Magazine of History and Biography*, LVIII (1934), 1–25; Mary F. Goodwin, "Christianizing and Educating the Negro in Colonial Virginia," in *Historical Magazine of the Protestant Episcopal Church*, I (1932), 143–52; Verner W. Crane, *The Southern Frontier, 1670–1732* (reprinted, Ann Arbor, 1956); Leslie F. Church, *Oglethorpe: a Study of Philanthropy in England and Georgia* (London, 1932); the *Festschrift* for Frank J. Klingberg edited by Samuel Clyde McCulloch, *British Humanitarianism* (Philadelphia, 1950); F. J. Klingberg, *Anglican Humanitarianism in Colonial New York* (Philadelphia, 1940); F. J. Klingberg, "The Evolution of the Humanitarian Spirit in Eighteenth-Century England," in *The Pennsylvania Magazine of History and Biography*, LXVI (1942), 260–78; and Samuel Eliot Morison's short biography of John Eliot, chapter x of *Massachusettensis de Conditoribus or the Builders of the Bay Colony* (Boston, 1930).

On the intellectual background of eighteenth-century benevolence and humanitarianism I have been guided by Perry Miller's *The New England Mind; from Colony to Province* and *Jonathan Edwards* (New York, 1949), as well as several studies chiefly of the British currents of thought. Among the latter, James Bonar, *Moral Sense* (New York, 1930); Basil Willey, *The Seventeenth Century Background; Studies in the Thought of the Age in Relation to Poetry and Religion* (reprinted, New York, 1953) and *The Eighteenth Century Background; Studies on the Idea of Nature in the Thought of the Period* (New York, 1950); and Norman Sykes, "The Theology of Divine Benevolence," in *Historical Magazine of the Protestant Episcopal Church*, XVI (1947), 278–91, have been especially important.

G. Quaker History: General

Although short works on Quaker history have not proved very successful in modern times, Friends have enjoyed the possession of a multivolume history of their sect in the "Rowntree Series" which commands respect. William Charles Braithwaite's *The Beginnings of Quakerism* has recently been issued in a second edition with revisions and notes by Henry J. Cadbury (Cambridge, England, 1955). Braithwaite's second volume in the Rowntree Series," *The Second Period of Quakerism* (London, 1919) was very helpful. It has recently been brought out in a new edition (Cambridge, England, 1961) with notes and many textual changes by Cadbury and an introduction by Frederick B. Tolles. Rufus M. Jones, Isaac Sharpless, and Amelia M. Gummere, wrote *The Quakers in the American Colonies* (London, 1911), a volume which does credit to the intuition as well as the diligence of its authors. Among Quaker writers before Frederick B. Tolles, Jones had the firmest historical sense; interested in both the history of ideas and institutions, he produced interpretations of the inter-relationships between the two which are conspicuously inadequate only in some of the many areas where he had little previous work to prepare the way for his. His heavy reliance on Stephen B. Weeks, *Southern Quakers and Slavery; A Study in Institutional History* ("Johns Hopkins Studies in Historical and Political Science," Extra Volume XV; Baltimore, 1896), while it shows what Jones could do with unpromising material, similarly demonstrates the handicap under which he worked. Jones's *The Later Periods of Quakerism*, 2 vols. (London, 1921) forged ahead into eras far less well covered by prior scholarship; that these volumes (which attempt to cover both England and America) have not stood the test of time is hardly to be wondered at. Rather, the many good parts of them are amazing.

Earlier works on Quakerism which remain valuable include William

Sewel's classic *History of the Rise, Increase and Progress of the Christian People Called Quakers* . . . (first published in 1722; I have consulted the edition of New York, 1844), and Samuel M. Janney, *History of the Religious Society of Friends, from its Rise to the Year 1828*, 4 vols. (Philadelphia, 1861).

More recently, several important interpretative articles on Quakerism have appeared. Several of them have been gathered into Frederick B. Tolles, *Quakers and the Atlantic Culture* (New York, 1960). Also stimulating are E. Gordon Alderfer, "Three Faces of the Colonial Quaker Testimony," in *Pennsylvania History*, XVII (1950), 265–80; Howard H. Brinton, "Stages in Spiritual Development as Exemplified in Quaker Journals," in H. H. Brinton (ed.), *Children of Light*; [Essays] *In Honor of Rufus M. Jones* (New York, 1938); and Henry J. Cadbury, "Intercolonial Solidarity of American Quakerism," in *Pennsylvania Magazine of History and Biography*, LX (1936), 362–74.

H. Quaker History: Special Topics and Localities

There is a large literature on William Penn and the founding of Pennsylvania, most of it uncritical (in the scholarly sense), lackluster, or both. Catherine Owens Peare, in *William Penn; A Biography* (Philadelphia, 1957) describes the man's career adequately. William I. Hull, *William Penn; A Topical Biography* (London, 1937) and Edward C. O. Beatty, *William Penn as Social Philosopher* (New York, 1939) treat their subject analytically. Beatty's book suffers from an attempt to make Penn's ideas consistent, with the result that he reduces divergent strains of Penn's views to their least common denominator, thus depriving his subject of much of his vigor. J. H. Powell, "William Penn's Writings: An Anniversary Essay," in *Pennsylvania History*, XI (1944), 233–59, affords in many ways a much more illuminating introduction to Penn's thought. Vincent Buranelli, "William Penn and James II," in American Philosophical Society *Proceedings*, CIV (1960), 35–53, shows what may be done with the story of the great proprietor, and incidentally sheds light on one of the enduring sides of the Quaker attitude toward government. Thomas E. Drake, "William Penn's Experiment in Race Relations," in *Pennsylvania Magazine of History and Biography*, LXVIII (1944), 372–87, is not nearly so successful in its department.

Two recent studies have contributed to the understanding of the Quaker religious fellowship in its early years. Arnold Lloyd, *Quaker Social History, 1669–1738* (London, 1950) treats what Americans would classify as institutional history of the English Quaker church with admirable thoroughness and insight. L. Hugh Doncaster, *Quaker Organization and Business Meetings* (London, 1958) briefly covers the field in its entire time span, though without considering the American practices. In addition, the succinct discussion by Emerson W. Shideler of "The Concept of the Church in Seventeenth-Century Quakerism," in *Bulletin of Friends Historical Association*, XLV (1956) 67–81, and XLVI (1957), 35–39, applies a philosopher's skill to the subject.

A group of special topics of tangential interest to the study of charity and humanitarianism has been covered with some success in Amelia M. Gummere, *The Quaker in the Forum* (Philadelphia, 1910); Isaac Sharpless, *Quakerism and Politics; Essays* (Philadelphia, 1905); and Howard H. Brinton, *Quaker Education in Theory and Practice* ("Pendle Hill Pamplet," No. 9; Wallingford, Pa., 1940). Henry J. Cadbury's discussion of Quaker education in Philadelphia, "Quaker Education — Then and Now," in *Two-and-a-Half Centuries of Quaker Education; The Proceedings of the Anniversary Meeting held under the Auspices of Friends' Council on Education, Tenth Month 20, 1939, in the Meeting-house at Fourth and Arch Streets, Philadelphia* (Philadelphia, n.d.; also in *The Friend* [Philadelphia], CXIII, nos. 9 and 10), pp. 5–18, approaches the subject with great precision.

Quaker interest in philanthropy has been discussed in several works, but with reference either to modern social work or the lesson to be drawn for twentieth-century Quakerism. Auguste Jorns, *The Quakers as Pioneers in Social Work*, translated by T. K. Brown (New York, 1931) was finished in the German original in December 1911. It enthusiastically magnifies all sorts of Quaker activities into the forerunners of modern practices and institutions. This ahistorical approach vitiates the results most strikingly in the passages dealing with events before 1800. Joshua Rowntree, *Social Service: Its Place in the Society of Friends* (London, 1913), and Alice Heald Mendenhall, *Some Social Aspects of the Society of Friends in the 17th and 18th Centuries* (Salem, Ohio, 1914), are focused on the twentieth-century prospects.

Secondary material on Friends and the Indians, until recently, added little to what had been put into the official documentary histories described above. Rayner W. Kelsey, *Friends and the Indians, 1655–1917* (Philadelphia, 1917), written for the Indian Committee of Philadelphia Yearly Meeting, offers a simple description of goodness getting steadily better, with little regard to the circumstances. Although primarily concerned with the Indians involved, the introductions to some journals of Quaker missionaries and inspectors have recently shown how much more can be found in the subject when it is approached with more historical care. The introduction by Merle H. Deardorff and George S. Snyderman to "A Nineteenth-Century Journal of a Visit to the Indians of New York," in American Philosophical Society *Proceedings*, C (1956), 582–94, is especially good; that of Snyderman to "Halliday

Jackson's Journal of a Visit Paid to the Indians of New York (1806)," in Am. Phil. Soc. *Proc.*, CI (1957), 565–70, carries on the story.

On the Quakers' relationship with the Negroes, Thomas E. Drake, *Quakers and Slavery in America* (New Haven, Conn., 1950), is most thorough and scholarly, though the author takes the record as one of virtually inevitable progress, and so plays down the shifts in Quaker attitudes and the problems raised by the close church fellowship of Friends. Henry J. Cadbury, "Negro Membership in the Society of Friends," in *The Journal of Negro History*, XXI (1936), 151–213, treats the subject exhaustively. Alan M. Rees, "English Friends and the Abolition of the British Slave Trade," in *Bulletin of Friends Historical Association*, XLIV (1955), 74–87, gives a valuable sidelight.

The Quakers during the American Revolution have been chronicled by Arthur J. Mekeel, "The Society of Friends (Quakers) and the American Revolution" (MS Ph.D. thesis, Department of History, Harvard University, 1940). Mekeel takes up mainly Quaker opinions about public affairs in these years, their sufferings, the rise of the Free Quakers, and related matters. Isaac Sharpless, *A History of Quaker Government in Pennsylvania:* Vol. II, *The Quakers in the Revolution* (Philadelphia, 1899) has nearly the same emphasis. Henry J. Cadbury, *Quaker Relief during the Siege of Boston* ("Pendle Hill Historical Study Number Four," n.p., n.d.; reprinted from the *Transactions of the Colonial Society of Massachusetts*, XXXIV) covers an important episode, though Mack E. Thompson's introduction (pp. 97–111) in "Moses Brown's 'Account of Journey to Distribute Donations 12th Month 1775,'" in *Rhode Island History*, XV (1956), 97–121, gives a more accurate account in some particulars.

Quakerism in Pennsylvania has been studied on many levels. Isaac Sharpless, *A Quaker Experiment in Government* (Philadelphia, 1898; apparently later thought of as Vol. I. of *A History of Quaker Government in Pennsylvania*) remains valuable in spite of its filiopietism. It contains long extracts from important documents. The whole field of Quaker history, however, has been revolutionized by Frederick B. Tolles, *Meeting House and Counting House; the Quaker Merchants of Colonial Philadelphia, 1682–1763* (Chapel Hill, N. C., 1948). This analysis of the achievements and final tragedy of the men who tried to be Quakers and eighteenth-century colonial aristocrats at the same time constitutes one of those rare triumphs: a successful amalgamation of intellectual, social, and religious history with religious dedication. Interesting sidelights on the subject are provided by Edwin B. Bronner, "The Failure of the 'Holy Experiment' in Pennsylvania, 1684–1697," in *Pennsylvania History*, XXI (1954), 93–108; Bronner, "The Disgrace of John Kinsey, Quaker Politician, 1739–1750," in *Pennsylvania Magazine of History and Biography*, LXXV (1951), 400–15; and the early part of Helen G. Hole, *Westtown Through the Years, 1799–1942* (Westtown, Pa., 1942). Historical accounts of various Meetings have been written, offering normally no more than parochial annals. Among the numerous items of historical information in *The Friend* [Philadelphia], the "Researches into the First Establishment of Philadelphia Yearly Meeting," beginning in Vol. XVIII (1844–1845), 125; and "The Society of Friends in Pennsylvania and New Jersey from 1764 to 1782," started in XIX, 404, but not continued after 1775, are noteworthy. Robert Proud, *The History of Pennsylvania, in North America, from the Original Instituton and Settlement of that Province, under the first Proprietor and Governor William Penn, in 1681, till after the Year 1742 . . .* , 2 vols. (Philadelphia, 1797–1798) treats the subject virtually as Quaker history. The work, like several others of lesser stature, was composed with the aid of documents collected by the Meetings.

Quaker history in other places has not fared as well. S. B. Weeks, *Southern Quakers and Slavery* has already been mentioned. John Cox, Jr., *Quakerism in the City of New York, 1657–1930* (New York, 1930) remains valuable mainly because no further work has been done on the subject. Caroline Hazard, *Narragansett Friends' Meeting* (New York, 1899) has made a beginning to the study of New England Friends in an important place, but the gaps to be filled by detailed studies have been forcefully pointed out by the presence of Frederick B. Tolles's "The New-Light Quakers of Lynn and New Bedford," in *New England Quarterly*, XXXII (1959), 291–319, an article about an episode that clearly belongs in a context which must include the antecedent currents of thought in the region.

1. Biographies of Quakers

The deficiencies of historical accounts have in some measure been remedied by biographical ones. Early Pennsylvania figures have been studied in Frederick B. Tolles, *James Logan and the Culture of Provincial America* (Boston, 1957); Ethyn Williams Kirby, *George Keith (1638–1716)* (New York, 1942); and Roy N. Lokken, *David Lloyd, Colonial Lawmaker* (Seattle, Wash., 1959), a book which is not so informative as could be desired on the religious setting of Lloyd's career. Theodore Thayer, *Israel Pemberton, King of the Quakers* (Philadelphia, 1943), is valuable for the political career of its subject, but woefully deficient on his religious leadership. Isaac Sharpless, *Political Leaders of Provincial Pennsylvania* (New York, 1919) offers some thought-provoking short biographies, but leaves much to be said. The work on Anthony Benezet by Brookes, Vaux, and Armistead has already been described; none of these authors has approached the last word. Two late eighteenth-century Friends have received satisfactory treatment in Frederick B. Tolles, *George Logan of Philadelphia* (New York, 1953), and Francis R. Taylor, *The Life of William Savery of Philadelphia, 1750–1804* (New York, 1925).

Lives of two New Yorkers of the late eighteenth and early nineteenth centuries have gone far to illuminate the condition of Friends there: Samuel L. Knapp, *The Life of Thomas Eddy, comprising an Extensive Correspondence with many of the Most Distinguished Philosophers and Philanthropists of This and Other Countries* (London, 1836; first published in New York, 1834), and Bliss Forbush, *Elias Hicks, Quaker Liberal* (New York, 1956).

The life of the admirable Moses Brown has been recounted with skill and care in Mack E. Thompson, "Moses Brown, Man of Public Responsibility" (MS Ph.D. dissertation, Department of History, Brown University, 1955). Thompson's chapter on Brown's projects for the benefit of Friends and the public generally are especially informative. Moses Brown also figures in James B. Hedges, *The Browns of Providence Plantation, Colonial Years* (Cambridge, 1952).

J. Projects to Do Good Furthered by Friends

Harold E. Gillingham, "Philadelphia's First Fire Defences," in *Pennsylvania Magazine of History and Biography*, LVI (1932), 355–77, supplements the books by the Bridenbaughs. Lawrence H. Gispson, *The Great War for the Empire; The Years of Defeat, 1754–1757* (*The British Empire Before the American Revolution*, Vol. VI; New York, 1956), ch. x, provides the best account of the treatment of the Acadian exiles. W. G. Malin, *Some Account of the Pennsylvania Hospital, its Origins, Objects and Present State* (Philadelphia, 1831), and Francis R. Packard, *Some Account of the Pennsylvania Hospital; from its first Rise to the Beginning of the Year 1938* (Philadelphia, 1938), describe the achievements of this institution.

The cause of the Negro is well surveyed in John Hope Franklin, *From Slavery to Freedom; A History of American Negroes* (New York, 1948). An important part of the subject is dealt with in the classic by William E. B. Du Bois, *The Suppression of the African Slave-Trade to the United States of America, 1638–1870* (Cambridge, 1896). In the literature about free Negroes before 1860, J. H. Franklin, *The Free Negro in North Carolina, 1790–1860* (Chapel Hill, N. C., 1943) is a good example, and gives perspective on the role of Friends in that state.

The upsurge in philanthropic projects after the Revolution is indicated by the range of private efforts described in Robert Proud, "Philadelphia" (MS, Historical Society of Pennsylvania, Philadelphia,

Pa., n.d.), though the work is hardly more than a preliminary sketch.

Quaker interest in educational philanthropy is illustrated in Joseph J. McCadden, *Education in Pennsylvania, 1801–1835, and its Debt to Roberts Vaux* (Philadelphia, 1937); James Mulhern, *A History of Secondary Education in Pennsylvania* (Philadelphia, 1933); and William Oland Bourne, *History of the Public School Society of the City of New York with Portraits of the Presidents of the Society* (New York, 1870).

The subject of penal reform and Quakers' interest in it has been studied largely from the point of view of finding the roots of modern ideas and practices. Albert Post, "Early Efforts to Abolish Capital Punishment in Pennsylvania," in *Pennsylvania Magazine of History and Biography*, LXVIII (1944), 38–53, offers some guidance on this subject. Harry Elmer Barnes, *The Evolution of Penology in Pennsylvania; A Study in American Social History* (Indianapolis, 1927) locates the Friends who played important parts. Negley K. Teeters, *The Cradle of the Penitentiary, The Walnut Street Jail at Philadelphia, 1773–1835* (n.p., 1955); N. K. Teeters, "The Early Days of the Eastern State Penitentiary at Philadelphia," in *Pennsylvania History*, XVI (1949), 261–302; and Robert G. Caldwell, *The Penitentiary Movement in Delaware, 1776 to 1829* (Wilmington, Del., 1946), deal with special branches of the subject. Unfortunately, Quaker interest in penology and several other subjects cannot be properly understood in the absence of careful chronological studies of Friends' ideas about how people can learn and both ideas about and attitudes toward violence. It is well known, for instance, that virtually all eighteenth-century Quakers thought violence was utterly immoral; but the proper lengths to which civil society might go to suppress violence and the morality of Friends serving as police officers remain obscure.

K. Special Topics in Political and Local History

The dramatic events of mid-eighteenth-century Pennsylvania exert undying power to fascinate historians. Robert L. D. Davidson, *War Comes to Quaker Pennsylvania, 1682–1756* (New York, 1957) comes to grief over the question of Quaker pacifism. Gipson's *Great War for the Empire; Years of Defeat* judiciously covers the events, but without special attention to the various Quaker positions. Anthony F. C. Wallace, *King of the Delawares: Teedyuscung, 1700–1763* (Philadelphia, 1949) brilliantly illuminates the Indians' side of the story. Theodore Thayer, *Pennsylvania Politics and the Growth of Democracy, 1740–1776* (Harrisburg, Pa., 1953) puts the provincial politics in a useful, if not always satisfactory, context, supplementing his *Israel Pemberton*. John J. Zimmerman, "Benjamin Franklin and the Quaker Party, 1755–

1756," in *William and Mary Quarterly*, third series, XVII (1960), 291–313, analyzes most ably the issues at the time of the Quaker withdrawal.

Among treatments of part of the public record of Pennsylvania, William C. Heffner, *History of Poor Relief Legislation in Pennsylvania, 1682–1913* (Cleona, Pa., c. 1913), has been particularly useful, though it explains little beyond the legislative events.

The place of Quakers in colonial New Jersey has been made clear in several works, notably Samuel Smith, *The History of the Colony of Nova-Caesaria, or New-Jersey: Containing, an Account of its First Settlement, Progressive Improvements, the Original and Present Constitution, and other Events, to the Year 1721* . . . (Burlington, N. J., 1756); John E. Pomfret, *The Province of West New Jersey, 1609–1702; A History of the Origins of an American Colony* (Princeton, N. J., 1956); Donald L. Kemmerer, *Path to Freedom; the Struggle for Self-Government in Colonial New Jersey, 1703–1776* (Princeton, N.J., 1940); and George DeCou, *Burlington; A Provincial Capital* (Philadelphia, 1945).

Part of the history of Delaware and Friends' part in it have been well described in John A. Munroe, *Federalist Delaware, 1775–1815* (New Brunswick, N. J., 1954). A beginning has been made in the evaluation of the place of Quakers in colonial North Carolina in Hugh T. Lefler and A. R. Newsome, *North Carolina; the History of a Southern State* (Chapel Hill, N. C., 1954). As yet, the role of Quakers in eighteenth-century New England has not been put in proper perspective.

Notes

Explanatory Note on the Documentation

A fuller and more heavily annotated version of the first half of this book may be found in my "Benevolence of American Friends before 1810" (MS Ph.D. thesis, Department of History, Harvard University, 1957) in Widener Library, Cambridge, Massachusetts. The remainder of the thesis has been so thoroughly revised (and I trust improved) that it should be regarded as obsolete.

Citations of minutes of Quaker Meetings here have been simplified by abbreviating Minutes to Min., supplying the geographical name of the Meeting, and indicating its nature by the following code:

MM	Monthly Meeting of men Friends
MW	Monthly Meeting of women Friends
QM	Quarterly Meeting of men Friends
QW	Quarterly Meeting of women Friends
YM	Yearly Meeting of men Friends
YW	Yearly Meeting of women Friends
M for S	Meeting for Sufferings
MM of M and E	Monthly Meeting of Ministers and Elders
QM of M and E	Quarterly Meeting of Ministers and Elders
YM of M and E	Yearly Meeting of Ministers and Elders

The names and locations of Meeting minutes consulted in the original appear in the discussion of sources (pp. 337–340).

The dates (rather than page numbers) which complete the citations of minutes, like all other dates specified in the notes, have been left as they appeared in the documents employed, whether Old Style or New Style, numbered months or named months. For convenience, dates in Quaker sources (which used numbers for months) have been put in the form of day of the month and number of the year in Arabic numerals, separated by the number of the month in Roman numerals. It must be remembered that March 25 was New Year's Day in the Julian Calendar (the Old Style in use in the British Empire before September 2, 1752) and March the First month. So, 25/I/1701 followed 24/I/1700. Following the practice of the colonials, who found this feature of the system confusing, I have given both year numbers for the earlier days in March — for example, 6/I/1712/3.

Chapter I: The Quaker Religious Fellowship in the American Colonies

1. The description of the nature and functioning of the Quaker religious fellowship in this chapter is based on the author's general acquaintance with the subject. Only examples and quotations, as a rule, will be identified in the notes. A longer, more elaborately illustrated, more heavily documented, and on some points less accurate, version of the same description may be consulted in the author's "The Benevolence of American Friends before 1810 . . ." (MS Ph.D. thesis, Department of History, Harvard University, 1957), ch. i. Arnold Lloyd, *Quaker Social History, 1669–1738* (London, 1950), describes the crystallizing of the organization in England.

2. Robert Barclay, *An Apology for the True Christian Divinity, being an Explanation and Vindication of the Principles and Doctrines of the People Called Quakers* (Philadelphia, 1908), 121–23, 262–64. Compare "Antient Testimony of yᵉ People called Quakers revived," in Minutes of Philadelphia and Burlington Yearly Meeting for 1722 (MS, Department of Records, Philadelphia Yearly Meeting, 302 Arch St., Philadelphia 6, Pa.). N.B.: Hereafter, all minutes of Quaker Meetings will be cited by abbreviated references giving the usual name of the Meeting, the type of Meeting it was (MM for Monthly Meeting of Men; MW for Monthly Meeting of Women, and so forth), and the date for the minute (the year only in the case of Yearly Meetings) in number of the day, followed by number of the month (in Roman numerals), followed by number of the year. See "Explanatory Note on the Documentation," above.

3. Virginia Yearly Meeting, *Rules of Discipline of the Yearly Meeting of Friends, held in Virginia* (Richmond, Va., 1826), 2; William Edmundson, "Epistle" to Friends in England and elsewhere, following Minutes of New England YM, 1711; Barclay, *Apology*, 264–65.

4. Barclay, *Apology*, 241, 254–55, 259, 310–11, 320; Edmundson, "Epistle" after Min. New England YM, 1711; Virginia Yearly Meeting, *Rules of Discipline*, 2; Epistle from New England Yearly Meeting of Ministers and Elders, dated 13–16/VI/1755, in Min. Rhode Island QM of M and E, 11/VII/1755; Barclay, *The Anarchy of the Ranters, and other Libertines . . .* (London, 1771), 44–45.

5. Barclay, *Apology*, 332; Barclay, *Anarchy of the Ranters*, 87.

6. Min. New England YM, 1708; Barclay, *Apology*, 261–62; William Edmundson, Epistle "For all Friends . . ." in *Journal* (2nd ed.; London, 1774), 341.

7. William Penn, "Just Measures, in an Epistle of Peace and Love, to Such Professors of Truth as are under any Dissatisfaction about the present Order practised in the Church of Christ" (1692), in *Select Works of William Penn* (3rd ed.; London, 1782), IV, 439, 446.

8. Thomas Woody, *Quaker Education in the Colony and State of New Jersey* (Philadelphia, 1923), 53, 60–63, 75, 79, 95, 102–3, 110, 182, 208, 215.

9. Stephen B. Weeks, *Southern Quakers and Slavery* (Baltimore, 1896), 94.

10. Min. Philadelphia MM, 31/VIII/1701; Min Burlington MM, 2/VII/1759.

11. For example, Min. Burlington MM, 3/III/1760; Min. Philadelphia MM, 25/VIII/1751.

12. Min. Falls MM, 5/V/1756; Min. New England YM, 1755; John Griffith, *A Journal of the Life, Travels, and Labours in the Work of the Ministry, of John Griffith* (Philadelphia, 1780), 394.

13. Frederick B. Tolles, *Meeting House and Counting House* (Chapel Hill, N. C., 1948), 251–52.

14. Epistle to London Yearly Meeting, in Min. Philadelphia YM, 1786; Preface to Chesterfield (N. J.) Monthly Meeting records, in Ezra Michener, *A Retrospect of Early Quakerism; being Extracts from the Records of Philadelphia Yearly Meeting and the Meetings Composing It* (Philadelphia, 1860), 38.

15. Min. Newport MM, 28/IV/1698; Penn, "A Brief Account of the Rise and Progress of the People Called Quakers" (1694), *Select Works*, V, 238; Min. New England YM, 1705.

16. Michener, *Retrospect*, 30–31; Min. New England YM, 1729.

17. Michener, *Retrospect*, 141, 240–42; Min. Half Years Meeting at Treadhaven, 3/VIII/1677, and Min. General Man's Meeting at West River, 18/III/1678, in William C. Dunlap, *Quaker Education in Baltimore and Virginia Yearly Meetings* (Philadelphia, 1936), 347; Min. Philadelphia MM, 9/XII/1684, 24/IX/1699, 28/II/1699, 24/IV/1772.

18. Min. South Kingstown MM, 1/IV/1771; John Cox, Jr., *Quakerism in the City of New York, 1657–1930* (New York, 1930), 111; Min. Philadelphia MW, 31/VIII/1718.

19. Min. Philadelphia YM, 1723, in Michener, *Retrospect*, 158–59.

20. Michener, *Retrospect*, 158–67.

21. The original Meeting for Sufferings, of course, was in London, but it was held to be a unique institution, even an undesirable one in some estimates. After Philadelphia established a similar body, with tighter strings on it, New York Yearly Meeting followed suit in 1758, New England in 1775, Baltimore in 1778, Virginia in 1782. North Carolina did not establish one, but its component Quarterly Meetings did — Eastern Quarter in 1757 and Western Quarter in 1778. (See Rufus M. Jones, Isaac Sharpless, and Amelia M. Gummere, *Quakers in the American Colonies* [London, 1911], 151, 259, 545; Arthur J. Mekeel, "The Society of Friends [Quakers] and the American Revolution" [MS Ph.D. thesis, Department of History, Harvard University, 1940], 7, 297; Dunlap, *Quaker Education*, 542; Min. Philadelphia YM, 1756.)

22. Michener, *Retrospect*, 33–34; Min. Philadelphia MM, 26/XI/1756.

23. Sydney V. James, Jr., "The Benevolence of American Friends before 1810," 49n.–50n.

24. Barclay, *Apology*, 144, 297–99.

25. Griffith, *Journal*, 170; Barclay, *Anarchy of the Ranters*, 36, 39–40, 53–57.

26. Tolles, *Meeting House and Counting House*, 240; Isaac Penington, *Works* . . . (3rd ed.; London, 1784), II, 441, 458–59, 527; Barclay, *Anarchy of the Ranters*, 41.

27. Jones *et al.*, *Quakers in the American Colonies*, 276, 302n.

Chapter II: The Rise and Progress of "Charity"
among the People Called Quakers

1. Brian Tierney, *Medieval Poor Law, a Sketch of Canonical Theory and Its Application in England* (Berkeley and Los Angeles, 1959), chs. iii-v.

2. Tierney, *Medieval Poor Law*, 124–33; Wilbur K. Jordan, *Philanthropy in England, 1480–1660, a Study of the Changing Pattern of English Social Aspirations* (New York, 1959), 54–57.

3. William Penn, "Good Advice to the Church of England . . ." (1687), in *Select Works of William Penn* (3rd ed.; London, 1782), IV, 388; Penn, "One Project for the Good of England: that is, Our Civil Union is our Civil Safety" (1679), *Select Works*, IV, 256, 264–65; Penn, "An Address to Protestants of all Persuasions . . ." (1679), *Select Works*, IV, 170–72.

4. Jordan, *Philanthropy*, 146–47, 207, 229–53, 264, 338, 350.

5. Auguste Jorns, *Quakers as Pioneers in Social Work*, trans. T. K. Brown, Jr. (New York, 1931), 64–65, 67; Arnold Lloyd, *Quaker Social History, 1669–1738* (London, 1950), ch. iii; Robert Barclay, *The Anarchy of the Ranters, and other Libertines . . .* (London, 1771), 29, 36–40.

6. Jorns, *Quakers as Pioneers*, 57, 57n.; Joshua Rowntree, *Social Service; Its Place in the Society of Friends* (London, 1913), 32–46; Lloyd, *Quaker Social History*, 82–83, 91.

7. William Sewel, *The History of the Rise, Increase and Progress of the Christian People Called Quakers* (New York, 1844), *passim*; Penn, "Address to Protestants," *Select Works*, IV, 40–41, 177–79; Penn, "England's Present Interest Considered . . ." (1675), *Select Works*, III, 246, 258–62.

8. Jorns, *Quakers as Pioneers*, 55–56; A. R. Fry, *John Bellers, 1654–1725, Quaker, Economist and Social Reformer* (London, 1935), *passim*, but especially Bellers, Preface "To . . . Quakers," in "Proposals for Raising a College of Industry" (pp. 34–35); Lloyd, *Quaker Social History*, 6, 37, 84; Jordan, *Philanthropy in England*, 212–14.

9. John Bellers, "An Epistle to the Quarterly-Meeting of London and Middlesex," in Fry, *John Bellers*, 149–54.

10. Lloyd, *Quaker Social History*, 40; Fry, *John Bellers*, 7–8; Bellers, "Some Reasons for an European State . . ." (1710), in Fry, *John Bellers*, 99; Jorns, *Quakers as Pioneers*, 80–81; Isabel Grubb, *Quakerism and Industry before 1800* (London, 1930), 138–40; Penn, "England's Present Interest Considered," *Select Works*, III, 258–61; Penn, Epistle "To the Children of Light," *Select Works*, IV, 241.

11. Perry Miller, *The New England Mind; From Colony to Province* (Cambridge, Mass., 1953), 407–18, 464–66; Carl Bridenbaugh, *Cities in the Wilderness* (New York, 1938), 229, 287, 289; Norman Sykes, "The Theology of Divine Benevolence," *Historical Magazine of the Protestant Episcopal Church*, XVI (1947), 281–91; Mary F. Goodwin, "Christianizing and Educating the Negro in Colonial Virginia," *Hist. Mag. Prot. Episc. Church*, I (1932), 143f.

12. John E. Pomfret, *The Province of West New Jersey, 1609–1702* (Princeton, N. J., 1956), 245–53.

13. Ethyn W. Kirby, *George Keith* (*1638–1716*), New York, 1942, 113–14, 127–47; Bridenbaugh, *Cities in the Wilderness*, 263.

14. Lloyd, *Quaker Social History*, 140–43; William C. Braithwaite, *The Second Period of Quakerism* (London, 1919), 180f.

15. Lloyd, *Quaker Social History*, 28, 83–92, 97–105; Advice of London Yearly Meeting, quoted in Braithwaite, *Second Period*, 160; Braithwaite, *Second Period*, 177–78.

16. Rufus M. Jones, I. Sharpless, and A. M. Gummere, *Quakers in the American Colonies* (London, 1911), 63f; S. B. Weeks, *Southern Quakers and Slavery* (Baltimore, 1896), 16f, 50–52, 59–68, 124–25, 351–52; Kenneth L. Carroll, "Talbot County Quakerism in the Colonial Period," *Maryland Historical Magazine*, LIII (1958), 326–27.

17. Lloyd, *Quaker Social History*, 91; Pomfret, *Province of West New Jersey*, 135 Frederick B. Tolles, *Meeting House and Counting House* (Chapel Hill, N. C., 1948), 9–12, 33–38.

18. Min. Philadelphia MM, 31/I/1752; Min. Philadelphia MW, 29/I/1742, 28/VIII/1761; Robert Proud, *History of Pennsylvania in North America*, 2 vols. (Philadelphia, 1797–98), I, 58–61.

19. Penn, "Just Measures," Select Works, IV, 445; Penn, "One Project," *Select Works*, IV, 264–65.

20. Min. Philadelphia YM, 1706, 1721; Penn, "Address to Protestants," *Select Works*, IV, 26; Min. Philadelphia MM, 7/X/1685; William Edmundson, Epistle "Concerning Men and Women's Meetings," *Journal* (2nd ed.; London, 1774), 369–70.

21. Min. Philadelphia YM, 1706, 1719.

22. Proud, *History of Pennsylvania*, I, 74; Penn, "Address to Protestants," *Select Works*, IV, 140, 188; Penn, "Persuasive to Moderation," *Select Works*, IV, 325–26; Edmundson, Epistle "For all Friends," *Journal*, 344–47; Thomas Budd, "A Letter by Thomas Budd, sent to his Friends in Pennsylvania and New-Jersey," from London, 29/VIII/1684, *Good Order Established in Pennsylvania and New Jersey* (Cleveland, 1902), 78–79.

23. Min. Philadelphia MW, 25/II/1763; Min. Philadelphia YM, 1751; Min. Falls MM, 5/XII/1753, 6/VII/1768, 6/I/1773; Min. New England YM, 1708; Min. Salem (Mass.) MM, 13/V/1713, 12/I/1724; Min. South Kingstown MM, 31/I/1774.

24. Min. Falls MM, 6/XII/1786; Moses West, *A Treatise Concerning Marriages* (4th ed.; London, 1780), 20f; Min. Philadelphia MW, 27/IV/1707; Min. Burlington MM, 4/VI/1759; Min. South Kingstown MM, 28/IV/1783; Min. Rhode Island QW, 9/IV/1778; Min. Philadelphia YM, 1721.

25. Lloyd, *Quaker Social History*, 70; Thomas E. Drake, *Quakers and Slavery in America* (New Haven, Conn., 1950), 16–18, 32–33, 77; Min. Philadelphia MM, 24/XI/1769; Min. Philadelphia MW, 31/I/1777; Thomas Woody, *Early Quaker Education in Pennsylvania* ("Columbia University Contributions to Education, Teachers' College Series," No. 105 [New York, 1920]), 99n.

26. Penn, "Just Measures," *Select Works*, IV, 439; Penn, "Brief Examination," *Select Works*, IV, 279; Edmundson, *Journal*, 341–48, 369–70; Proud,

History of Pennsylvania, I, 217–19; Min. Philadelphia MM, 31/VIII/1729, 30/VIII/1771.

27. Min. Philadelphia MM, 29/I/1751.

28. Min. Philadelphia MM, 31/VIII/1729; Epistle to London Yearly Meeting, in Min. Philadelphia YM, 1786.

29. Joseph Phipps, *The Original and Present State of Man, Briefly Considered* (Philadelphia, 1836), 20, 33; Brand Blanshard, "Early Thought on the Inner Light," in H. H. Brinton (ed.), *Byways in Quaker History* (Walingford, Pa., 1944), 169.

30. Min. Philadelphia MM, 29/I/1768, 7/XI/1750, 31/I/1752; Min. Philadelphia MW, 24/VI/1757, 31/I/1766, 25/V/1759; Min. Burlington MM, 7/XI/1750.

31. Min. South Kingstown MM, 1/I/1776; Min Philadelphia MW, 22/II/1751, 23/II/1770, 24/II/1764, 31/X/1766; Min. Philadelphia MM, 25/VIII/1769; Preface to Min. Chesterfield MM (N. J.), in Ezra Michener, *A Retrospect of Early Quakerism* (Philadelphia, 1860), 38; Penn, "Address to Protestants," *Select Works,* IV, 80–81.

32. Phipps, *Original and Present State,* 33.

33. Phipps, *Original and Present State,* 37–38, 53–55; George Fox, MS. Epistles and Advices to Birmingham Friends, 1681, p. 8, as quoted in Lloyd, *Quaker Social History,* 32; Min. Philadelphia MM, 28/I/1757, 24/XI/1769; Edmundson, "An Epistle to Friends in Barbadoes," in *Journal,* 364.

34. For example, Min. Falls MM, 1/IV/1772. See also chap. iv below.

35. Min. Philadelphia YM, 1734; Penn, "To the Children of Light," *Select Works,* IV, 240; John Pemberton, Trawden in Lancaster, England, 27/I/1752, to James Pemberton, Pemberton Papers (MS Historical Society of Pennsylvania), VII, 159; Penn, "No Cross, No Crown," *Select Works,* II, 158; Min. Sadsbury MM 10/XII/1793, Min. Abington MM, 27/I/1749, and Min. New Garden MM 6/III/1773, in Woody, *Early Quaker Education in Pennsylvania,* 144, 107–8, 128.

36. Min. Chester QM, 14/VI/1732; testimony of appreciation of Thomas Chalkley, in Min. Philadelphia MM, 20/II/1749.

37. Min. Falls MM, 6/IV/1683; Min. Philadelphia MM, 26/VI/1715, 28/X/1739.

38. Penn, "No Cross, No Crown," *Select Works,* II, 180; Budd, *Good Order,* 23.

39. Min. Burlington MM, 6/VII/1682; Min. Philadelphia MM, 30/VIII/1696, 27/IX/1696.

40. Min. Philadelphia YM, 1786.

41. Min. Philadelphia MM, 5/X/1759.

42. Tolles, *Meeting House,* 151; Carl and Jessica Bridenbaugh, *Rebels and Gentlemen* (New York, 1942), 229; Proud, *History of Pennsylvania,* I, 58–61.

43. Min. Philadelphia YM, 1726, in Michener, *Retrospect,* 147–48; C. and J. Bridenbaugh, *Rebels and Gentlemen,* 21.

44. Penn, "To the Children of Light," *Select Works,* IV, 241.

45. Min Philadelphia MM, 27/VII/1733, 27/I/1741, 26/IX/1703; "Address" to John Penn, Lt. Gov., Min. Philadelphia M for S, 25/II/1764.

Chapter III: Mutual Aid in the Monthly Meetings

1. Arnold Lloyd, *Quaker Social History, 1669–1738* (London, 1950), 113–14, 116–18; Henry J. Cadbury, "Inter-Colonial Solidarity of American Quakerism," *Pennsylvania Magazine of History and Biography*, LX(1936), 362–67; R. M. Jones, I. Sharpless, and A. M. Gummere, *Quakers in the American Colonies* (London, 1911), 314–15.

2. Lloyd, *Quaker Social History*, 33; Auguste Jorns, *Quakers as Pioneers in Social Work*, trans. T. K. Brown, Jr. (New York, 1931), 87.

3. Lloyd, *Quaker Social History*, 32–42, 111–18; Isabel Grubb, *Quakerism and Industry before 1800* (London, 1930), 63–66, 71–78; Jorns, *Quakers as Pioneers, passim;* W. K. Jordan, *Philanthropy in England,1480–1660* (New York, 1959), 40–46, 240–75.

4. Jones, *et al.*, *Quakers in the American Colonies*, 153–56, 167, 228, 247, 302, 317–21; Kenneth L. Carroll, "Talbot County Quakerism in the Colonial Period," *Maryland Historical Magazine*, LIII (1958), 326, 343–46, 348–50; Min. New England YM, 1743, 1749, 1750; Min. South Kingstown MM, 26/IV/1756, 27/I/1777; Min. Newport MM, 28/X/1708.

5. Carroll, "Talbot County," *Md. Hist. Mag.*, LIII, 331; Min. Philadelphia MM, 9/XI/1682; Min. Burlington MM, 18/VI/1678; Min. Newark MM, ?/III/1686, in W. C. Dunlap, *Quaker Education in Baltimore and Virginia Yearly Meetings* (Philadelphia, 1936), 348.

6. Min. Philadelphia MM, 4/X/1683, 3/XII/1684, 9/XII/1684, 2/IX/1685, 29/VIII/1686, 31/X/1686, 31/III/1689, 30/IV/1689; Min. Philadelphia MW, 28/XI/1686; William C. Heffner, *History of Poor Relief in Pennsylvania, 1682–1913* (Cleona, Pa., c. 1913), 119–20.

7. Min. Burlington MM, 1/XI/1682, 2/V/1705; Min. Philadelphia MM, 4/XI/1682, 26/XI/1699, 25/III/1711, 29/VI/1712, 26/VI/1715, 27/VIII/1773; Min. Philadelphia MW, 28/VII/1694, 25/VI/1699, 27/VIII/1710.

8. See Min. Philadelphia MM, 24/IX/1693, 24/IX/1738, 30/IV/1749, 31/VI/1750, 28/X/1750, 29/VI/1770, 30/VII/1773, 12/X/1778; Min. Philadelphia MW, 26/IX/1714, 31/X/1714; Min. Burlington MM, 4/XI/1765, 7/VI/1779; Min. Falls MM, 4/IX/1771; Min. Newport MW, 27/IX/1716.

9. Min. South Kingstown MM, 30/IV/1746, 27/I/1751, 1/XI/1773; Min. Smithfield MM, 1/I/1779; Min. Salem (Mass.) MM, 13/VII/1744; Min. Sandwich QM, 30/I/1747, 16/IX/1751; Min. New England YM, 1747.

10. Min. Falls MM, 7/XI/1701; T. Woody, *Quaker Education in the Colony and State of New Jersey* (Philadelphia, 1923), 247; Min. Philadelphia MM, 24/II/1702, 30/VII/1715, 25/IV/1725, 29/VII/1732, 27/XII/1771, 24/IV/1772, 26/VI/1772; Min. Burlington MM, 3/I/1774, 7/II/1774; Min. Newport MM, 29/IX/1687, 27/X/1687; Ezra Michener, *Retrospect of Early Quakerism* (Philadelphia, 1860), 215.

11. Min. Philadelphia MM, 31/III/1706, 26/VI/1715, 30/VII/1715, 28/X/1722, 30/XI/1746, 28/II/1766, 24/VI/1768; Min. South Kingstown MM, 1/X/1773, 26/I/1778.

12. Min. Philadelphia MM, 30/II/1742, 28/III/1742, 28/I/1754, 29/I/1773; Min. Falls MM, 4/IX/1771, 5/III/1777; Min. Burlington MM, 2/VI/1777; Dunlap, *Quaker Education*, 116; Min. South Kingstown MM, 26/II/1781;

Min. New England M for S, 12/IV/1783 (including an Epistle from Philadelphia Meeting for Sufferings, dated Philadelphia, 19/XII/1782); Min. New England YM, 1791. Henry J. Cadbury, in "The Passing of Friends' Library," *The Friend* (Phila.), CIII (1929–30), 460, quotes the will of John Pemberton as evidence that the library of Philadelphia Monthly Meeting was primarily for the benefit of "the beloved youth."

13. Min. Newport MM, 26/XI/1741, 31/XI/1748; Min. Philadelphia MM, 30/XI/1701, 27/V/1711, 28/VI/1713, 27/VI/1714, 26/X/1718, 29/IV/1744, 27/VII/1745, 29/IX/1745, 27/X/1745, 25/VI/1749, 29/IV/1750, 25/XI/1750; Min. Philadelphia MW, 24/VII/1714; Min. Burlington MM, 7/X/1696, 3/XI/1703.

14. Min. Philadelphia MM, 29/IX/1702, 25/IX/1705, 30/X/1726, 30/VI/1728, 30/III/1729, 27/XII/1729, 25/XII/1736, 30/VII/1737, 27/XII/1740, 25/IV/1742, 27/XI/1743, 27/IV/1746, 26/X/1746, 28/XI/1755, 30/IV/1762; Heffner, *History of Poor Relief*, 43n.–44n.; Carl Bridenbaugh, *Cities in the Wilderness; the first Century of Urban Life in America, 1625–1742* (New York, 1938), 235–36; David H. Forsythe, "Friends' Almshouse in Philadelphia," *Bulletin of Friends Historical Association*, XVI (1927), 17–20; Min. Philadelphia MW, 31/I/1704, 29/IX/1706.

15. Min. Philadelphia MM, 27/X/1758, 27/II/1744 to 26/III/1773, *passim*; Min. Philadelphia MW, 30/V/1742, 28/XII/1745, 26/II/1760, 26/X/1770.

16. Min. Burlington MW, ?/XI/1694, 5/I/1732/3; Min. Philadelphia MW, 24/II/1775, 21/XII/1691, 30/IX/1694; Min. Philadelphia MM, 29/III/1691, 26/IV/1691, 22/II/1754, 26/VIII/1750.

17. Min. Philadelphia MW, 31/X/1686, 31/VIII/1718, 30/III/1735, 29/X/1721, 26/VII/1707.

18. Min. Burlington MW, 5/I/1732; Min. Burlington MM, 4/XII/1769; Min. Falls MM, 5/I/1757; Min. Philadelphia MM, 25/II/1718; Min. Newport MW, 27/IX/1716, 29/IV/1736; Min. Newport MM, 22/XII/1725, 20/X/1740.

19. Min. Philadelphia MW, 27/VII/1717, 27/III/1761; Min. Philadelphia MM, 29/VI/1701, 31/III/1717; Min. South Kingstown MM, 1/VII/1746, 1/XI/1773; Min. Newport MM, 18/XII/1689, 28/V/1747, 29/I/1748.

20. Min. Philadelphia MM, 26/VI/1709, 28/V/1710, 28/VI/1710, 29/VII/1710, 7/VIII/1710, 25/II/1713, 29/IV/1716; Min. Burlington MM, 2/III/1737, 6/XII/1763.

21. Aid to victims of French and Indians: Min. Philadelphia MM, 23/III/1711, 29/V/1715. Subscriptions: Min. Philadelphia MM, 26/X/1701, 25/VI/1710, 25/II/1735; Min. Burlington MM, 1/X/1690, 2/VI/1697; Min. Falls MM, 5/XII/1695, 4/III/1752. Smaller sums: Min. Philadelphia MM, ?/II/1694, 30/X/1709; Min. Newport MM, 25/V/1727.

22. Dunlap, *Quaker Education*, 310–11, 341, 505; Carroll, "Talbot County," *Md. Hist. Mag.*, LIII, 331; Min. Philadelphia MM, 24/IX/1699, 30/VII/1743, 29/IX/1752, 31/X/1766; Min. Philadelphia MW, 27/VIII/1710; Min. Burlington MM, 5/XII/1749, 5/I/1749/50; Min. Falls MM, 1/VII/1761.

23. Min. Philadelphia MM, 28/VII/1723, 26/XI/1749, 31/VI/1750, 29/V/1752, 27/XI/1757.

24. Min. Philadelphia MM, 28/X/1694, 27/XI/1698, 28/VIII/1709, 31/I/1710, 27/VI/1714, 26/X/1718.

25. Min. Philadelphia MM, 5/V/1686, 13/X/1687, 29/I/1695, 26/I/1703, 25/I/1708; Min. Burlington MM, 7/V/1753; Min. Newport MM, 25/VI/1719, 27/V/1742; Minute of a yearly Meeting on widows and orphans in Maryland, 1732, in Michener, *Retrospect*, 241; Dunlap, *Quaker Education*, 307, 350–51.

26. Min. Philadelphia MM, 27/V/1739, 26/V/1769, 24/IV/1772, 28/I/1774, 28/XI/1777; Min. Chester QM, 14/VI/1732, in T. Woody, *Early Quaker Education in Pennsylvania* ("Columbia University Contributions to Education, Teachers' College Series," No. 105 [New York, 1920]), 153.

27. Min. Philadelphia MM, 27/V/1739, 27/XI/1740, 30/VIII/1745, 27/XI/1748, 29/XII/1752; Min. Abington MM, 27/I/1749, in Woody, *Early Quaker Education*, 107–8. Other bequests for the poor: Min. South Kingstown MM, 27/II/1786, Min. Philadelphia MM, 29/III/1724; Min. Burlington MM, 3/VII/1744; Min. Buckingham MM, 2/IX/1776, in Woody, *Early Quaker Education*, 95. Other bequests for the education of poor Friends' children: Min. Philadelphia MM, 28/V/1732; Min. Burlington MM, 2/I/1786; Woody, *Early Quaker Education*, 74–75, 134–35. Yearly Meeting exhortation: Min. Philadelphia YM, 1754.

28. Min. Philadelphia MM, 28/VI/1724, 25/VII/1724, 30/XI/1753, 29/III/1754, 29/VIII/1755; Jordan, *Philanthropy in England*, 40, 147.

29. Min. Falls MM, 5/VII/1683; Min. Middletown MM, 9/II/1699, in Woody, *Early Quaker Education*, 10; Min. Philadelphia MM, 25/VI/1704, 26/X/1707, 30/VI/1715, 28/X/1739; Min. Burlington MM, 5/VII/1748; Min. Philadelphia YM, 1721; Min. Quarterly Mtg. at Little River, 1715, in Zora Klain, *Quaker Contributions to Education in North Carolina* (Philadelphia, 1924), 299.

30. Min. Burlington MM, 3/VIII/1772, 7/XII/1772; Min. Philadelphia MM, 25/IV/1702, 27/XII/1729, 27/VII/1759; Min. South Kingstown MM, 28/VII/1755, 1/IX/1755.

31. Min. Philadelphia MM, 26/III/1762, 30/II/1731, 25/XI/1750, 27/VI/1766; Min. Falls MM, 2/X/1771.

32. Min. Philadelphia MM, 22/II/1754, 26/VII/1754, 30/VIII/1754, 31/I/1755, 25/VII/1755, 31/X/1755, 26/III/1756, 30/IV/1756, 25/II/1757; Min. Burlington MM, 1/IV/1765, 5/VIII/1765; Min. Philadelphia MW, 29/I/1742.

33. Min. Philadelphia MM, 28/VII/1739, 28/VI/1759, 27/V/1774; Min. Newport MW, 27/VII/1715.

34. Min. Newport MM, 21/XI/1689; Min. Philadelphia MM, 28/XI/1755, 31/VIII/1759, 6/XI/1772; Min. Philadelphia MW, 27/I/1702; Min. Burlington MM, 1/XI/1682, 3/XI/1703; Michener, *Retrospect*, 214.

35. Philadelphia MM, 2/IX/1685 and 25/I/1754 (burden of the poor), 29/VIII/1714 (accepting doubtful poor), 31/VIII/1729, 24/II/1741, 26/VIII/1750, 26/II/1762 (getting them out of the city), 29/I/1745, 4/X/1776

(insisting on other Meetings supporting them). Appearance of similar policies: Min. Newport MM, 30/VI/1748; Min. Burlington MM, 6/II/1764; Min. New England YM, 1778; Min. South Kingstown MM, 28/XI/1785.

36. C. and J. Bridenbaugh, *Rebels and Gentlemen,* 230.

37. Min. Burlington MM, 1/VIII/1757.

Chapter IV: Charity in Education

1. Min. Newport MM, 31/XI/1715.

2. Min. Philadelphia MM, 29/I/1695; *Pennsylvania Colonial Records; Minutes of the Provincial Council* (Philadelphia, 1852), I, 531–32; *A Collection of the Epistles from the Yearly Meeting of Friends in London, to the Quarterly & Monthly Meetings in Great Britain, Ireland, and Elsewhere, from 1675 to 1820* (New York, 1821), 66.

3. Thomas Budd, *Good Order Established in Pennsylvania and New Jersey* (Cleveland, 1902), 44; Thomas Woody, *Early Quaker Education in Pennsylvania* ("Columbia University Contributions to Education, Teachers' College Series," No. 105 [New York, 1920]), 37–38; T. Woody, *Quaker Education in the Colony and State of New Jersey* (Philadelphia, 1923), 235, 235n, 242; Howard H. Brinton, *Quaker Education in Theory and Practice* ("Pendle Hill Pamphlet," No. 9 [Wallingford, Pa., c. 1940]), 96–108.

4. *Collection of the Epistles,* 66.

5. George Fox, *Instructions for Right Spelling, and Plain Directions for Reading and Writing True English* (Newport, R. I., 1769), 11, 44; Charles W. Bush *et al., Friends School in Wilmington* (Wilmington, Del., 1948), 1.

6. *Collection of the Epistles,* 66, 92, 100, 135, 169–71, 196–97, 263–64, and *passim;* Min. Philadelphia YM, 1694, 1721, 1746, 1777, 1786.

7. David Hall, *An Epistle of Love and Caution to the Quarterly and Monthly Meetings of Friends in Great Britain, or Elsewhere* (3rd ed.; London, 1750), 27, 32–34.

8. Hall, *Epistle of Love and Caution,* 15; *Collection of the Epistles,* 197; Min. New England YM, 1708, query no. 4.

9. *Collection of the Epistles,* 92, 100, 119, 169.

10. Min. Philadelphia MM, 24/XI/1769; *Collection of the Epistles,* 92, 100, 135, 197, 213, 226, 263–64; Hall, *Epistle of Love and Caution,* 16, 28–29; Min. Philadelphia YM, 1721.

11. Hall, *Epistle of Love and Caution,* 15, 17, 20, 28–29; *Collection of the Epistles,* 196–97, 213; Joseph Phipps, *Original and Present State of Man, Briefly Considered* (Philadelphia, 1836), 15–16, 111–12.

12. *Collection of the Epistles,* 66.

13. Woody, *Quaker Education in New Jersey,* 2; George DeCou, *Burlington: A Provincial Capital* (Philadelphia, 1945), 176; Robert Proud, *History of Pennsylvania in North America,* 2 vols. (Philadelphia, 1797–98), II, second page sequence, 18, 24; *Pa. Col. Rec.,* I, 91, 93; William Penn, "One Project for the Good of England . . .", *Select Works of William Penn* (3rd ed.; London, 1782), IV, 257–58.

14. Budd, *Good Order,* 43–46.

15. Min. Philadelphia MM, 26/V/1689; Robert Proud, "Philadelphia"

(MS, Historical Society of Pennsylvania, c. 1807), 57; James Mulhern, *A History of Secondary Education in Pennsylvania* (Philadelphia, 1933), 28.

16. Min. Philadelphia MM, 29/III/1691, 31/X/1697, 25/I/1698, 29/II/1698, 28/II/1699; Min. Philadelphia MW, 27/XI/1698.

17. *Pa. Col. Rec.*, I, 531–32; Woody, *Early Quaker Education*, 47–49.

18. Woody, *Early Quaker Education*, 43; Mulhern, *History of Secondary Education*, 28; Min. Philadelphia MM, 28/XII/1700, 28/I/1701, 26/VI/1709, 27/V/1711, 26/I/1714, 29/XI/1719, 25/I/1720, 29/VII/1721, 27/II/1722, 28/III/1725; Min. Philadelphia MW, 29/II/1709.

19. Mulhern, *History of Secondary Education*, 30–35; Proud, *History of Pennsylvania*, I, 344; Min. Philadelphia MM, 31/X/1708, 27/XII/1729, 29/VII/1749, 24/IV/1772.

20. Min. Newport MM, 4/XII/1684, 12/III/1691, 27/II/1703, 25/III/1703, 30/III/1710, 31/VIII/1710, 27/IX/1711, 26/XII/1711, 26/VI/1718.

21. Min. Newport MW, 25/V/1727; Min. Newport MM, 29/XII/1731, 26/I/1734, 24/XII/1735, 29/IV/1736, 25/II/1738, 26/VII/1738, 29/VI/1749, 30/IV/1754.

22. Min. Philadelphia MM, 25/VII/1696, 30/VIII/1696; Min. Abington MM, 29/II/1695, in Woody, *Early Quaker Education*, 105; John E. Pomfret, *The Province of West New Jersey, 1609–1702* (Princeton, N. J., 1956), 231; R. M. Jones, I. Sharpless, and A. M. Gummere, *Quakers in the American Colonies* (London, 1911), 253–54, 505; Min. South Kingstown MM, 29/II/1751.

23. Woody, *Early Quaker Education*, 79–86, 117–18; Min. Philadelphia MM, 25/XI/1733; Min. Newport MM, 14/VII/1703, 31/XI/1709, 29/III/1711, 30/II/1728; Min. New England YM, 1716.

24. Min. Philadelphia MM, 28/VI/1765.

25. *Collection of the Epistles*, 213.

26. Min. Philadelphia YM, 1745, 1746.

27. Min. Philadelphia YM, 1750, 1754; Min. Philadelphia MM, 27/V/1750; Min. Falls MM, 4/X/1751, 5/XII/1753.

28. Min. Burlington MM, 1/V/1751, 5/VI/1751; Woody, *Early Quaker Education*, 23, 131; Woody, *Quaker Education in New Jersey*, 57, 164; Min. Falls MM, 2/VII/1760, 7/VI/1769; Bush, *Friends' School in Wilmington*, 2; W. C. Dunlap, *Quaker Education in Baltimore and Virginia Yearly Meetings* (Philadelphia, 1936), 351–52.

29. Min. Wilmington MM, 13/V/1772, in Dunlap, *Quaker Education*, 352; Woody, *Early Quaker Education*, 149, 181, 217; Min. Philadelphia MM, 25/IV/1760.

30. Woody, *Early Quaker Education*, 79–80, 117–18; Min. Falls MM, 4/IX/1771, 1/IV/1772, 6/V/1772, 2/VIII/1775; Min. Philadelphia MM, 28/VI/1765, 24/XI/1769, 24/IX/1773; Min. Shrewsbury QM, 26/I/1756, in Woody, *Quaker Education in New Jersey*, 38.

31. Min. Philadelphia MM, 29/VII/1774, 26/VII/1776; Min. Falls MM, 7/XII/1774, 3/I/1776.

32. Min. Burlington MM, 4/VIII/1777, 1/XII/1777.

33. Report to Philadelphia Yearly Meeting of 1778, as transcribed at back of third volume of Min. Falls MM.

Chapter V: Charity among Meetings

1. Min. Philadelphia MM, 6/IV/1687; Min. Falls MM, 1/XII/1773; Min. South Kingstown MM, 25/VII/1749; Min. Rhode Island QW, 8/V/1715; Wilbur K. Jordan, *Philanthropy in England, 1480–1660* (New York, 1959), 149–50.

2. Arnold Lloyd, *Quaker Social History, 1669–1738* (London, 1950), 38–40; Min. Philadelphia MM, 24/IV/1692, 24/IX/1692, 25/IV/1697, 26/VI/1698, 30/VII/1698; Kenneth L. Carroll, "Talbot County Quakerism in the Colonial Period," *Maryland Historical Magazine*, LIII (1958), 345–46; Min. Newport MM, 20/VII/1698.

3. Min. Philadelphia MM, 31/X/1725, 25/I/1726; Min. Burlington MM, 6/X/1725; Min. Newport MM, 31/VI/1725; Min. New England YM, 1726; Frederick B. Tolles, *Meeting House and Counting House* (Chapel Hill, N. C., 1948), 70.

4. Min. Concord MM, 5/V/1697; Min. New England YM, 1697; Min. Philadelphia MM, 30/V/1697; Min. Falls MM 4/VI/1697; Min. Philadelphia YM, 1697, 1698; Min. Newport MM, 25/II/1704.

5. Min. Philadelphia MM, 30/VIII/1702, 29/IX/1702, 25/X/1702, 26/I/1703, 27/VIII/1704, 28/II/1772, 27/III/1772, 24/IV/1772; Min. Newport MM, 30/XII/1755; Min. Burlington MM, 1/X/1712.

6. Edwin B. Bronner, "The Center Square Meetinghouse," *Bulletin of Friends Historical Association*, XLIV (1955), 71–72; Min. Philadelphia MM, 27/II/1705, 28/XI/1714, 26/VI/1715, 28/X/1722, 26/XII/1724, 23/III/1741; Min. Burlington MM, 6/VII/1725; Min. South Kingstown MM, 25/IX/1758; Min. Newport MM, 25/I/1746.

7. Min. Newport MM, 30/V/1695, 30/X/1707; Min. New England YM, 1709, 1710; Min. Philadelphia YM, 1710, 1711; Min. Philadelphia MM, 23/XII/1710, 29/VIII/1760, 26/IX/1760; Min. Burlington MM, 7/III/1711, 4/IV/1711; Min. South Kingstown MM, 1/IX/1760.

8. Min. Philadelphia MM, 27/I/1741, 31/V/1741; Min. Philadelphia M for S, 17/IX/1767, 16/VIII/1770.

9. Min. Newport MM, 15/V/1707; Min. New England YM, 1718, 1720, 1723, 1725, 1726, 1734, 1738.

10. Min. Burlington MM, 3/V/1749, 2/III/1767; Min. Philadelphia MM, 30/X/1748, 27/V/1750, 30/IV/1773; Min. Philadelphia M for S, 24/III/1759, 18/IX/1766, 17/XII/1767, 20/II/1783, 30/VII/1790, 17/II/1791.

11. Min. Philadelphia YM, 1727, 1734, 1736, 1750, 1757; Min. Philadelphia M for S, 21/I/1773, 6/XII/1784, 20/I/1785, 18/VIII/1791.

12. Joint Committee of Hopewell Friends, assisted by John W. Wayland, *Hopewell Friends History, 1734–1934, Frederick County, Virginia* (Strasburg, Va., 1936), 124; Min. Philadelphia M for S, 13/VII/1758, 20/VII/1758, 20/V/1762, 17/VI/1762, 21/IX/1786.

13. Min. Chester QM (anachronistically described as Concord QM), 8/V/1758, in W. C. Dunlap, *Quaker Education in Baltimore and Virginia Yearly Meetings* (Philadelphia, 1936), 371; Min. Philadelphia YM, 1756; Min. Philadelphia M for S, 10/VIII/1757, 21/IX/1757.

14. Min. Philadelphia M for S, 10/II/1757.

Chapter VI: Charity to Neighbors Outside the Membership

1. Robert Barclay, *Universal Love Considered, and Established Upon its Right Foundation* . . . (London, 1799), 15; F. B. Tolles, *Meeting House and Counting House* (Chapel Hill, N. C., 1948), 89–93; Min. Burlington MM, 6/VII/1682; Min. Philadelphia MM, 25/V/1701, 31/I/1752, 29/X/1756; Min. Falls MM, 2/XI/1683; Robert Proud, *History of Pennsylvania in North America*, 2 vols. (Philadelphia, 1797–98), I, 55–57; R. Barclay, *The Anarchy of the Ranters, and Other Libertines,* . . . (London, 1771), 29.

2. J. E. Pomfret, *The Province of West New Jersey, 1609–1702* (Princeton, N. J., 1956), 229–30.

3. Barclay, *Universal Love Considered*, 10–11; Min. Philadelphia MM, 26/I/1725.

4. Min. Philadelphia MM, 27/I/1730, 28/VII/1733; William Edmundson, "A Postscript to an Epistle from Leinster Province-Meeting" (1698), in *Journal* (2nd ed.; London, 1774), 359.

5. See Min. Wilmington MM, 13/V/1772, in W. C. Dunlap, *Quaker Education in Baltimore and Virginia Yearly Meetings* (Philadelphia, 1936), 352; Min. Philadelphia MM, 25/IV/1709, 29/V/1715, 27/I/1741; Min. Philadelphia M for S, 25/II/1764.

6. Min. Philadelphia YM, 1685, 1686, 1687; Rayner M. Kelsey, *Friends and the Indians, 1655–1917* (Philadelphia, 1917), 53; Min. Burlington MM, 4/VII/1679; Min. Philadelphia MM, 7/I/1686/7, 3/VII/1687, 31/III/1689; Min. Falls MM, 4/III/1687.

7. London Meeting for Sufferings, Aborigines' Committee, *Some Account of the Conduct of the Religious Society of Friends Towards the Indian Tribes in the Settlement of the Colonies of East and West Jersey and Pennsylvania* (London, 1844), 59–60; Proud, *History of Pennsylvania*, I, 432–33.

8. Min. Philadelphia MM, 6/IV/1687; Proud, *History of Pennsylvania*, 145n.

9. Thomas Chalkley, *A Collection of the Works of Thomas Chalkley* (Philadelphia, 1749), 51n, 308; Proud, *History of Pennsylvania*, I, 195, 212–13; "Samuel Fothergill to His Brother and Sister. Curles, upon James' River, Virginia, Twelfth month 13th, 1754," in William Evans and Thomas Evans (eds.), *The Friends' Library*, IX (Philadelphia, 1845), 146.

10. Kelsey, *Friends and the Indians*, 52; Min. Philadelphia M for S, 10/VIII/1757, 21/IX/1757.

11. Kelsey, *Friends and the Indians*, 52.

12. Min. Philadelphia YM, 1763; Min. Philadelphia MM, 27/IX/1771; Kelsey, *Friends and the Indians*, 52–53.

13. Min. Philadelphia YM, 1719; Kelsey, *Friends and the Indians*, 56–58.

14. London Meeting for Sufferings, *Some Account*, 19–23, 50–54; Kelsey, *Friends and the Indians*, 20–29, 35; Proud, *History of Pennsylvania*, I, 300–301; Pomfret, *Province of West New Jersey*, 220; Dunlap, *Quaker Education*, 367.

15. Proud, *History of Pennsylvania*, I, 301; Thomas Budd, *Good Order Established in Pennsylvania and New Jersey* (Cleveland, 1902), 65, 67;

George Fox, *The Journal of George Fox,* 2 vols., ed. Norman Penney (Cambridge, England, 1911), II, 224.

16. "The Planter's speech," in Proud, *History of Pennsylvania,* I, 227n.

17. Kelsey, *Friends and the Indians,* 29.

18. John Richardson, *An Account of the Life of that Ancient Servant of Jesus Christ, John Richardson* (Philadelphia, 1856), 133–37.

19. Richardson, *Account of the Life,* 134–35. Compare passages in Albert C. Myers (ed.), *Narratives of Early Pennsylvania, West New Jersey and Delaware, 1630–1707* ("Original Narratives of Early American History" [New York, 1912]), 234, 384–85.

20. London Meeting for Sufferings, *Some Account,* 36, 57; George Staughton *et al.* (eds.), *Charter to William Penn, and Laws of the Province of Pennsylvania* . . . (Harrisburg, Pa., 1879), 240–41.

21. Proud, *History of Pennsylvania,* I, 218n, 223n, 229; Min. Philadelphia MM, 29/I/1700; John Archdale in North Carolina to George Fox, 25/I/1686, in Zora Klain, *Quaker Contributions to Education in North Carolina* (Philadelphia, 1924), 322.

22. Chalkley, *Collection of the Works,* 49–51.

23. George S. Brookes, *Friend Anthony Benezet* (Philadelphia, 1937), 115–20; Anthony F. C. Wallace, *King of the Delawares: Teedyuscung, 1700–1763* (Philadelphia, 1949), 176f.

24. Wallace, *King of the Delawares,* 228; A. M. Gummere, "Papunahung, the Indian Chief," *Bulletin of Friends' Historical Society of Philadelphia,* IX (1920), 109–15; A. Benezet, supposed author, "An Account of the Behaviour & Sentiments of a Number of Well-Disposed Indians Mostly of the Minusing Tribe," and "An Account of Papunahung's Second Visit to Friends the 4th of the 8th Month, 1761," in Brookes, *Friend Anthony Benezet,* 481–89. Brookes attributed these writings to Benezet (*Friend Anthony Benezet,* 118, 119n), but the schoolmaster's work was based on reports of the Trustees of the Friendly Association, which he may have helped write, but which in the accounts of meetings of Friends and the Indians follow phrases in Israel Pemberton's letters to his wife, as, for example, Papers Relating to the Friendly Association (MS, Department of Records, Philadelphia Yearly Meeting), IV, 139–51, 159, 163.

25. [Benezet], "Account of the Behaviour," and "Account of Papunahung's Second Visit," in Brookes, *Friend Anthony Benezet,* 484, 488–89; William Penn, "No Cross, No Crown," *Select Works of William Penn* (3rd ed.; London, 1782), II, 25; H. H. Brinton, "Stages in Spiritual Development as Exemplified in Quaker Journals," in H. H. Brinton (ed.), *Children of Light* (New York, 1938), 386–402.

26. [Benezet], "Account of the Behaviour," Brookes, *Friend Anthony Benezet,* 481–82; Brinton, "Stages," *Children of Light,* 397–99.

27. [Benezet], "Account of Papunahung's Second Visit," Brookes, *Friend Anthony Benezet,* 486–87.

28. [Benezet], "Account of Papunahung's Second Visit," Brookes, *Friend Anthony Benezet,* 489.

29. John Woolman, *The Journal and Essays of John Woolman,* ed. A. M. Gummere (New York, 1922), 248–51; George DeCou, *Burlington:*

A Provincial Capital (Philadelphia, 1945), 171–72; Min. Burlington MM, 7/II/1763.

30. Woolman, *Journal and Essays*, 259–61.

31. Woolman, *Journal and Essays*, 254–55.

32. Min. Philadelphia YM, 1762.

33. Kelsey, *Friends and the Indians*, 33–34; London Meeting for Sufferings, *Some Account*, 94.

34. Epistle of Philadelphia Meeting for Sufferings to the Delawares and other Indians, 8/VII/1773, as quoted in London Meeting for Sufferings, *Some Account*, 95–96.

Chapter VII: Charity and the Negro Slave

1. Thomas E. Drake, *Quakers and Slavery in America* (New Haven, Conn., 1950), 5–11; George Fox, *Instructions for Right Spelling, and Plain Directions for Reading and Writing True English* (Newport, 1769), 39.

2. John Hepburn, *The American Defence of the Christian Golden Rule, or an Essay to Prove the Unlawfulness of Making Slaves of Men* (New York? 1715), [iii].

3. Drake, *Quakers and Slavery*, 5–7; George Fox, *The Journal of George Fox*, 2 vols., ed. Norman Penney (Cambridge, England, 1911), II, 191, 195, 200, 201, 255.

4. William Edmundson, *A Journal of the Life, Travels, Sufferings and Labour of Love in the Work of the Ministry, of . . . William Edmundson* (2nd ed.; London, 1774), 81, 85–86.

5. Edmundson, *Journal*, 86; William Penn, "A Brief Examination and State of Liberty Spiritual" (1681), *Select Works of William Penn* (3rd ed.; London, 1782), IV, 279; Edmundson, Epistle to Friends of Virginia and Maryland (1675), as quoted in William C. Dunlap, *Quaker Education in Baltimore and Virginia Yearly Meetings* (Philadelphia, 1936), 434; letter by Edmundson, dated Newport, 19/VII/1676, in Drake, *Quakers and Slavery*, 9–10.

6. Edmundson, Epistle to Friends in Virginia and Maryland, in Dunlap, *Quaker Education*, 434; letter by Edmundson, Newport, 19/VII/1676, in Drake, *Quakers and Slavery*, 9–10.

7. Drake, *Quakers and Slavery*, 8–9.

8. Min. Philadelphia YM, 1688.

9. Min. Philadelphia YM, 1688.

10. Min. Philadelphia YM, 1688.

11. Min. Philadelphia YM, 1688

12. Drake, *Quakers and Slavery*, 14–15, 20.

13. Drake, *Quakers and Slavery*, 15.

14. Drake, *Quakers and Slavery*, 19–20; T. E. Drake, "Cadwalader Morgan, Antislavery Quaker of the Welsh Tract," *Friends Intelligencer*, XCVIII (1941), 575–76 (including the whole text by Morgan).

15. Drake, *Quakers and Slavery*, 11, 17, 75–77; Robert Pyle, "A Copy of Robert Pile's Paper About Negoes," following Henry J. Cadbury, "An Early Quaker Anti-Slavery Statement," *Journal of Negro History*, XXII (1937), 492–93.

16. Hepburn, *American Defence*, 30; Min. Philadelphia MM, 28/VIII/ 1698, 30/VII/1756; Zora Klain, *Quaker Contributions to Education in North Carolina* (Philadelphia, 1924), 55–57; Henry J. Cadbury, "Negro Membership in the Society of Friends," *Journal of Negro History*, XXI (1936), 152.

17. Drake, *Quakers and Slavery*, 19; Min. Philadelphia YM, 1696.

18. Min. Philadelphia MM, 29/I/1700; Min. Philadelphia YM, 1696.

19. Min. Philadelphia MM, 26/III/1756, 25/XI/1757; Dunlap, *Quaker Education*, 440; Klain, *Quaker Contributions*, 310–11.

20. Min. Philadelphia YM, 1715, 1719; Dunlap, *Quaker Education*, 439, 451; Drake, *Quakers and Slavery*, 16–18.

21. Pyle, "A Copy of Robert Pile's Paper," *Jour. Neg. Hist.*, XXII, 492–93.

22. Penn, "An Address to Protestants," *Select Works*, IV, 212–15.

23. Min. Philadelphia MM, 30/VII/1698; Drake, *Quakers and Slavery*, 21–22; H. J. Cadbury, "Another Early Quaker Anti-Slavery Document," *Jour. Neg. Hist.*, XXVII (1942), 211–12.

24. Drake, *Quakers and Slavery*, 22; John H. Franklin, *From Slavery to Freedom; a History of American Negroes* (New York, 1948), 95–96.

25. Min. Philadelphia YM, 1712.

26. Drake, *Quakers and Slavery*, 50, 73, 81–83; John Cox, Jr., *Quakerism in the City of New York, 1657–1930* (New York, 1930), 57; Franklin, *From Slavery to Freedom*, 62–64.

27. Drake, *Quakers and Slavery*, 30, 62, 64; Cox, *Quakerism in the City of New York*, 57.

28. Drake, *Quakers and Slavery*, 34; Penn, "A Brief Examination and State of Liberty Spiritual," *Select Works*, IV, 286.

29. Robert Barclay, *Universal Love Considered, and Established upon its Right Foundation* (London, 1799), 31–32, 32n.

30. Maurice Ashley, *England in the Seventeenth Century* (London, 1952), 207–12; Pierre Muret, *Le Prépondérance Anglaise (1715–1763)* (3rd ed.; Paris, 1949), 32–33; Louis B. Wright, *The Atlantic Frontier* (New York, 1951), 241.

31. Min. Philadelphia YM, 1714; Drake, *Quakers and Slavery*, 25–26.

32. Hepburn, *American Defence*, [iii–iv], 15; Drake, *Quakers and Slavery*, 34–36.

33. Drake, *Quakers and Slavery*, 28; Min. Philadelphia YM, 1711, 1715, 1716.

34. Min. Philadelphia YM, 1711, 1715, 1716; Drake, *Quakers and Slavery*, 28–29, 40.

35. William Burling, "Address to the Elders of the Church . . .", in Benjamin Lay, *All Slave-Keepers That Keep the Innocent in Bondage, Apostates* (Philadelphia, 1737), 7–8.

36. Cox, *Quakerism in the City of New York*, 55–57.

37. Min. Newport MM, 27/IX/1716; Drake, *Quakers and Slavery*, 30.

38. Min. New England YM of M and E, 15/IV/1717, 17/IV/1717; Min. New England YM, 1717, 1718.

39. Drake, *Quakers and Slavery,* 32; Min. Philadelphia MM, 28/VIII/1720.
40. Penn, *Select Works,* IV, 283–85, 444; Robert Barclay, *The Anarchy of the Ranters, and other Libertines* (London, 1771), 55, 88–89.
41. Roberts Vaux, *Memoirs of the Lives of Benjamin Lay and Ralph Sandiford* (Philadelphia, 1815), 63–65; Revised Discipline in Min. Philadelphia YM, 1719; Drake, *Quakers and Slavery,* 39–41.
42. [Ralph Sandiford,] *The Mystery of Iniquity, in a Brief Examination of the Practice of the Times, By the Foregoing and the Present Dispensation . . .* ([Philadelphia,] 1730), 25–26, 87; Drake, *Quakers and Slavery,* 40–41.
43. Min. Philadelphia YM, 1729, 1730.
44. Drake, *Quakers and Slavery,* 41–43; Lay, *All Slave-Keepers,* 18–21.
45. Drake, *Quakers and Slavery,* 45–46; Lay, *All Slave-Keepers,* 21, 29–30, 151; Vaux, *Memoirs,* 25–29, 34–35.
46. Franklin, *From Slavery to Freedom,* 65–66, 77, 95, 105.

Chapter VIII: The Victory of Abolitionist Principles among Friends

1. Min. Virginia Yearly Meeting, 1722, 1758, in W. C. Dunlap, *Quaker Education in Baltimore and Virginia Yearly Meetings* (Philadelphia, 1936), 451; Thomas E. Drake, *Quakers and Slavery in America* (New Haven, Conn., 1950), 41, 50, 62–66; John Cox, Jr., *Quakerism in the City of New York, 1657–1930* (New York, 1930), 56.
2. *A Narrative of Some of the Proceedings of North Carolina Yearly Meeting on the Subject of Slavery Within its Limits* (Greensborough, N. C., 1848), 6–7.
3. Drake, *Quakers and Slavery,* 42, 60–62, 64–66, 71; Dunlap, *Quaker Education,* 442, 451, 453; Min. Philadelphia YM, 1758.
4. Elihu Coleman, *Testimony Against that Antichristian Practice of Making Slaves of Men* ([Boston,] 1733); John Hepburn, *The American Defence of the Christian Golden Rule, or an Essay to Prove the Unlawfulness of Making Slaves of Men* ([New York?] 1715), 29–34.
5. Benjamin Lay, *All Slave-Keepers That Keep the Innocent in Bondage, Apostates . . .* (Philadelphia, 1737), 53–54.
6. Lay, *All Slave-Keepers,* 54–55.
7. John Woolman, *The Journal and Essays of John Woolman,* ed. Amelia M. Gummere (New York, 1922), 188–90, 195–96, 215–17, 234–38.
8. Woolman, *Journal and Essays,* 180, 191–92, 339–42, 346.
9. Woolman, *Journal and Essays,* 181; Min. Philadelphia YM, 1753, 1754 (including an "Epistle of Caution and Advice," drafted by Woolman [see Drake, *Quakers and Slavery,* 56n. for ascription]).
10. [Philadelphia Yearly Meeting of Friends,] *An Epistle of Caution and Advice, Concerning the Buying and Keeping of Slaves* (Philadelphia, 1754), 3.
11. [Phila. Yearly Mtg. of Friends,] *Epistle of Caution and Advice,* 3.
12. Woolman, "Some Considerations," *Journal and Essays,* 344–46.
13. John Churchman, *et al.,* "An Account of the Gospel Labours and

Christian Experiences, of . . . John Churchman," in William Evans and Thomas Evans (eds.), *The Friends' Library*, VI (Philadelphia, 1842), 236–37.

14. C. and J. Bridenbaugh, *Rebels and Gentlemen; Philadelphia in the Age of Franklin* (New York, 1942), 254; John H. Franklin, *From Slavery to Freedom; a History of American Negroes* (New York, 1948), 107–8.

15. Drake, *Quakers and Slavery*, 50.

16. Theodore Thayer, *Israel Pemberton, King of the Quakers* (Philadelphia, 1943), 33, 198–99; Woolman, *Journal and Essays*, 190–95, 199–200, 237.

17. Min. Philadelphia YM, 1755, 1758; examples of dealings with slaveholders in Min. Philadelphia MM 25/II/1757, 26/VIII/1757.

18. Min. Burlington MM, 2/III/1761; Min. Falls MM, 5/XII/1759; Dunlap, *Quaker Education*, 439, 451, 463 (including paper from Wilmington Monthly Mtg. quoted here), 464; Zora Klain, *Quaker Contributions to Education in North Carolina* (Philadelphia, 1924), 310; Drake, *Quakers and Slavery*, 65–66.

Chapter IX: Government, Benevolence, and the Quaker Revival

1. Frederick B. Tolles, *James Logan and the Culture of Provincial America* (Boston, 1957), 13, 28, 35, 155–56; Theodore Thayer, *Israel Pemberton, King of the Quakers* (Philadelphia, 1943), 45.

2. Isaac Penington, "A Brief Account of what the People called Quakers desire, In Reference to the Civil Government," *The Works of the Long-Mournful and Sorely-Distressed Isaac Penington* (3rd ed.; London, 1784), II, 191.

3. William W. Comfort, *William Penn, 1644–1718; A Tercentenary Estimate* (Philadelphia, 1944), 8; William Penn, *Select Works of William Penn* (3rd ed.; London, 1782), IV, 243–46, 430; F. B. Tolles, *Meeting House and Counting House; the Quaker Merchants of Colonial Philadelphia, 1682–1763* (Chapel Hill, N. C., 1948), 16–17.

4. Robert Proud, *History of Pennsylvania in North America*, 2 vols. (Philadelphia, 1797–98), I, 198, 207n, 479, and II, 224n; Penn, Preface to "Frame of Government" of Pennsylvania (1682), in *Pennsylvania Colonial Records; Minutes of the Provincial Council*, I (Philadelphia, 1852), 29–31; Penn, *Select Works*, II, 216, and IV, 40.

5. Penn, *Select Works*, II, 216, and IV, 178–79; Proud, *History of Pennsylvania*, I, 197.

6. Penn, *Select Works*, IV, 247–52.

7. Penn, *Select Works*, IV, 256–65, 347, 354.

8. Proud, *History of Pennsylvania*, I, 6–7, 427–28, and II, 153n, 158; Penn, *Select Works*, IV, 353.

9. Penn, *Select Works*, IV, 15–16, 40–41, 177–82, 237–42; Min. Philadelphia M for S, 4/I/1770.

10. *Pa. Col. Rec.*, I, 29–31; Penn, *Select Works*, IV, 179, 325–26.

11. Penn, *Select Works*, IV, 215; Penington, *Works*, II, 192.

12. Declaration dated at Boston, 14/IX/1711, presented to Gov. Joseph Dudley, in Min. Salem (Mass.) MM, on p. 45 of Vol. I; Min. New England YM, 1731.

13. Charles M. Andrews, *The Colonial Period of American History*, 4 vols. (New Haven, Conn., 1934–38), III, 154, 167, 223–35, 272; Hugh T. Lefler and A. R. Newsome, *North Carolina* (Chapel Hill, N. C., 1954), 53–58, 125–26; Donald L. Kemmerer, *Path to Freedom; the Struggle for Self-Government in Colonial New Jersey, 1703–1776* (Princeton, N. J., 1940), *passim*; Rufus M. Jones, I. Sharpless, and A. M. Gummere, *The Quakers in the American Colonies* (London, 1911), 191–207.

14. Memorial "To the Mayor, Aldermen and Commonalty of the City of Philadelphia," Min. Philadelphia MM, 28/VII/1733; Address of Lt. Gov. Keith and the General Assembly of Pennsylvania to George I, May, 1718, in Proud, *History of Pennsylvania*, II, 101–2; Tolles, *Meeting House*, 34–38; John E. Pomfret, *The Province of West New Jersey, 1609–1702* (Princeton, N. J., 1956), 93–97, 128–30.

15. Pomfret, *Province of West New Jersey*, 93–97, 128, 184–85; *Pa. Col. Rec.*, I, 32–47, 52, 455–56, and II, 56–58.

16. William Penn, "Letter . . . to the Committee of the Free Society of Traders, 1683," in A. C. Myers (ed.), *Narratives of Early Pennsylvania, West New Jersey and Delaware, 1630–1707* ("Original Narratives of Early American History" [New York, 1912]), 239; Justin Winsor (ed.), *Narrative and Critical History of America*, 8 vols. (Boston, 1884–89), III, 487–88; Robert Barclay, *The Anarchy of the Ranters, and Other Libertines* (London, 1771), 40f; Thomas Budd, *Good Order Established in Pennsylvania and New Jersey* (Cleveland, 1902), 50; Pomfret, *Province of West New Jersey*, 97, 184–85; Proud, *History of Pennsylvania*, II, 288–89; *Pa. Col. Rec.* I, 38, 582.

17. Harold E. Gillingham, "Philadelphia's First Fire Defences," *Pennsylvania Magazine of History and Biography*, LVI (1932), 357; William C. Heffner, *History of Poor Relief Legislation in Pennsylvania, 1682–1913* (Cleona, Pa., c. 1913), 24, 27–33, 44–47; Proud, *History of Pennsylvania*, I, 157n; Thomas Woody, *Quaker Education in the Colony and State of New Jersey* (Philadelphia, 1923), 262; Arnold Lloyd, *Quaker Social History, 1669–1738* (London, 1950), 36; *Pa. Col. Rec.*, II, 544.

18. *Pa. Col. Rec.*, I, 91, 93, 531–33, and II, 216, 553; Proud, *History of Pennsylvania*, I, 334–45, 345n; Min. Philadelphia MM, 28/I/1701; Thomas Woody, *Early Quaker Education in Pennsylvania* ("Columbia University Contributions to Education, Teachers' College Series," No. 105 [New York, 1920]), 43–44; James Mulhern, *A History of Secondary Education in Pennsylvania* (Philadelphia, 1933), 30; George DeCou, *Burlington: A Provincial Capital* (Philadelphia, 1945), 176; Woody, *Quaker Education in New Jersey*, 1–2.

19. Heffner, *History of Poor Relief*, 25–27, 34–38, 43n–44n, 45–47, 60, 119–20; *Pa Col. Rec.*, II, 9–10, 232; Carl Bridenbaugh, *Cities in the Wilderness: the first Century of Urban Life in America, 1625–1742* (New York, 1938), 8, 83, 237.

20. Heffner, *History of Poor Relief*, 24, 44–45, 52–54; Min. Philadelphia YM, 1712, 1714; Min. Philadelphia MM, 30/VII/1698.

21. Pomfret, *Province of West New Jersey*, 93–97, 128–30, 135; Proud, *History of Pennsylvania*, I, 139, 196–97.

22. Pomfret, *Province of West New Jersey*, 183, 219; Min. Philadelphia MM, 12/VII/1685; Isaac Sharpless, *A Quaker Experiment in Government* (Philadelphia, 1898), 71–72, 74; Winsor (ed.) *Narrative and Critical History*, III, 490–91; Tolles, Meeting House, 231; "The Planter's speech . . ." (1684), known only from extracts in Proud, *History of Pennsylvania*, I, 226n–227n.

23. Budd, *Good Order*, 23, 41–42, 77–79; *Pa. Col. Rec.*, I, 93, 236; Pomfret, *Province of West New Jersey*, 92, 135; Proud, *History of Pennsylvania*, I, 142n.

24. John Woolman, *The Journal and Essays of John Woolman*, ed. A. M. Gummere (New York, 1922), 153, 157, 247–48, 399, 461–66; Roberts Vaux, *Memoirs of the Lives of Benjamin Lay and Ralph Sandiford* (Philadelphia, 1815), *passim;* Thomas E. Drake, *Quakers and Slavery in America* (New Haven, Conn., 1950), 19n; George S. Brookes, *Friend Anthony Benezet* (Philadelphia, 1937), 196; "Memoirs of Joshua Evans," in John and Isaac Comly (eds.), *Friends' Miscellany*, I (Philadelphia, 1831), 242–44.

25. Pomfret, *Province of West New Jersey*, 99, 125–26, 129, 134; Rayner M. Kelsey, *Friends and the Indians, 1655–1917* (Philadelphia, 1917), 44–45, 48, 54–55; *Pa. Col. Rec.*, I, 28; Proud, *History of Pennsylvania*, I, 145n, 266n–227n, 428–33, and II, 148–49; Sharpless, *Quaker Experiment*, 158–72; London Meeting for Sufferings, Aborigines' Committee, *Some Account of the Conduct of the Religious Society of Friends toward the Indian Tribes* (London, 1844), 26–27; Budd, *Good Order*, 72–73.

26. London Meeting for Sufferings, *Some Account*, 56–60, 79–85; Kelsey, *Friends and the Indians*, 65; F. B. Tolles, *James Logan and the Culture of Provincial America* (Boston, 1957), 100–103, 112, 167–85.

27. Kemmerer, *Path to Freedom*, 50–52; Sharpless, *Quaker Experiment*, 74.

28. Sharpless, *Quaker Experiment*, 186–87, 202–21, 227–42.

29. Tolles, *Meeting House*, 20–21, 231–32.

30. Heffner, *History of Poor Relief*, 44, 49–50, 55–59, 61–64, 73–77, 123–24; J. T. Mitchell and Henry Flanders (compilers), *Statutes at Large of Pennsylvania from 1682 to 1801*, IV (n.p., 1897), 59–64; C. and J. Bridenbaugh, *Rebels and Gentlemen; Philadelphia in the Age of Franklin* (New York, 1942), 232.

31. George Crosfield, "Memoirs of the Life and Gospel Labours of Samuel Fothergill, with Selections from his Correspondence," in William Evans and Thomas Evans (eds.), *The Friends' Library*, IX (Philadelphia, 1845), 189; John Hepburn, *The American Defence of the Christian Golden Rule* ([New York?] 1715), 15.

32. Thayer, *Israel Pemberton*, 32–33, 49–50, 56; John Churchman, *et al.*, "An Account of the Gospel Labours and Christian Experiences, of that Faithful Minister of Christ, John Churchman, late of Nottingham, in Pennsylvania," in William Evans and Thomas Evans (eds.), *The Friends' Library*, VI (Philadelphia, 1842), 236, 251, 254.

33. W. H., Jr., "The Life and Travels of John Pemberton, a Minister of the Gospel of Christ," in W. Evans and T. Evans (eds.), *Friends' Library*, VI, 282–84; Thayer, *Israel Pemberton*, 17, 136–37, 202; Isaac Sharpless, *Po-*

litical Leaders of Provincial Pennsylvania (New York, 1919), 214, 218, 221.

34. *Friends' Library*, IX, 166; Theodore Thayer, *Pennsylvania Politics and the Growth of Democracy, 1740–1776* (Harrisburg, Pa., 1953), 56.

35. *Friends' Library*, IX, 148; Jones *et al.*, *Quakers in the American Colonies*, 128, 410.

36. *Friends' Library*, IX, 151, 153–56, 159–65; George Churchman, East Nottingham, Pa., 3/IV/1807, to [Henry Drinker?], Collection of Letters, RS 181 (MS, Department of Records, Philadelphia Yearly Meeting, 302 Arch St., Philadelphia 6, Pa.), 191; Min. New England YM of M and E, 1755.

37. *Friends' Library*, IX, 146, 189–90.

38. *Friends' Library*, IX, 190.

39. *Friends' Library*, IX, 155, 159–63; Min. New England YM, 1743, 1755, 1759, 1760; Min. South Kingstown MM, 28/VII/1755, 1/IX/1755; Min. New England YM of M and E, 1755; John Griffith, *A Journal of the Life, Travels, and Labours in the Work of the Ministry, of John Griffith* (Philadelphia, 1780), 397–98.

40. *Friends' Library*, IX, 189–90; George Churchman, East Nottingham, Pa., to [Henry Drinker?], Collection of Letters, RS 181, 191. The moral reform movement spread to English Friends by 1760. (Griffith, *Journal*, 293–324; John Hunt, London, 14/VI/1760, to Israel Pemberton, in Papers of the Friendly Association, III, 479.)

41. *Friends' Library*, IX, 165.

42. *Friends' Library*, IX, 167–68.

43. *Friends' Library*, IX, 165, 174; Thayer, *Israel Pemberton*, 98.

44. Woolman, *Journal*, 177n.

45. [John Woolman,] Epistle "To Friends on the continent of America," sent by Philadelphia Yearly Meeting of Ministers and Elders which sat 29/III/1755–1/IV/1755, as printed in Woolman, *Journal*, 177–79.

46. Woolman, *Journal*, 492–93; Epistle from Philadelphia Quarterly Meeting to London Meeting for Sufferings, 5/V/1755, in Sharpless, *Quaker Experiment*, 237–41.

47. Thayer, *Pennsylvania Politics*, 42–47; *Friends' Library*, IX, 170, 173; Woolman, *Journal*, 208–10.

48. Thayer, *Pennsylvania Politics*, 55–56; Thayer, *Israel Pemberton*, 113–19.

49. Tolles, *Meeting House*, 26–28; Sharpless, *Quaker Experiment*, 263–72; Min. Chester QM, 13/VIII/1759.

Chapter X: Coping with the Crisis of 1755

1. Anthony Benezet, Philadelphia, 13/XII/1757, to John Smith, in George S. Brookes, *Friend Anthony Benezet* (Philadelphia, 1937), 224–25; John Woolman, *The Journal and Essays of John Woolman*, ed. A. M. Gummere (New York, 1922), 207.

2. Min. Philadelphia YM, 1755.

3. Min. Philadelphia YM, 1756.

4. Min. Philadelphia YM, 1756, 1757.

5. Min. Philadelphia M for S, 10/II/1757, 10/VIII/1757, 21/IX/1757, 13/VII/1758, 20/VII/1758.

6. Min. Philadelphia M for S, 29/IX/1760.

7. Min Philadelphia M for S, 24/III/1759, 22/V/1759, 25/II/1764.

8. Min. Chester QM, 11/VIII/1755, 10/XI/1755, 9/V/1757, 8/VIII/1757, 8/V/1758, 12/II/1759.

9. Min. Philadelphia MM, 27/XI/1761; Min. Falls MM, 3/V/1758; Min. Burlington MM, 3/IV/1775; Min. Philadelphia MW, 29/VII/1774; Min. Chester QM, 9/II/1756, 10/V/1756, 14/II/1757, 11/VIII/1760.

10. Min. Falls MM, 6/I/1762, 1/XII/1762.

11. Min. Falls MM, 1/XII/1762.

12. Min. Philadelphia MM, 28/VIII/1761, 30/X/1761, 16/I/1762, 25/III/1763.

13. Anthony Benezet, Philadelphia, 1/VIII/1760, to John Smith, in Brookes, *Friend Anothony Benezet,* 241; Min. Philadelphia YM, 1759; *A Collection of the Epistles from the Yearly Meeting of Friends in London, to the Quarterly and Monthly Meetings in Great Gritain, Ireland, and Elsewhere, from 1675 to 1820* (New York, 1821), 252–53.

14. Woolman, Journal, 214–15.

15. Woolman, *Journal,* 214–15.

16. Papers of the Friendly Association, I, 531; Min. Philadelphia M for S, 17/XII/1756.

17. Min. Philadelphia M for S, 17/XII/1756, 10/VIII/1757, 15/XII/1757; Theodore Thayer, *Israel Pemberton, King of the Quakers* (Philadelphia, 1943), 133.

18. Papers of the Friendly Association, I, 103; Thayer, *Israel Pemberton,* 98–101; Anothony F. C. Wallace, *King of the Delawares: Teedyuscung, 1700–1763* (Philadelphia, 1949), 93.

19. Thayer, *Israel Pemberton,* 106–7, 110.

20. Wallace, *King of the Delawares,* 109–10.

21. Papers of the Friendly Association, I, 167; Thayer, *Israel Pemberton,* 124–25.

22. Thayer, *Israel Pemberton,* 125–28.

23. Wallace, *King of the Delaware,* 25–29, 133–35, 147.

24. Wallace, *King of the Delawares,* 30, 58–59.

25. Wallace, *King of the Delawares,* 134–35.

26. Thayer, *Israel Pemberton,* 125; Papers of the Friendly Association, I, 247, 285.

27. Thayer, *Israel Pemberton,* 135–59.

28. Thayer, *Israel Pemberton,* 140–47; Wallace, *King of the Delawares,* 158–59; Papers of the Friendly Association, I, 531.

29. Wallace, *King of the Delawares,* 174–82; Thayer, *Israel Pemberton,* 148–49.

30. Wallace, *King of the Delawares,* 185–89; Papers of the Friendly Association, I, 527, and II, 55.

31. Thayer, *Israel Pemberton,* 159; Theodore Thayer, "The Friendly Association," *Pennsylvania Magazine of History and Biography,* LXVII (1943), 371.

32. Thayer, *Israel Pemberton*, 154–55.

33. Wallace, *King of the Delawares*, 193, 204–207.

34. Papers of the Friendly Association, II, 395, 399, 469, and III, 39; Thayer, *Israel Pemberton*, 158–59, 171–74.

35. Papers of the Friendly Association, II, 399, 403, and III, 103; Thayer, *Israel Pemberton*, 174–76.

36. Papers of the Friendly Association, III, 339, 395, 415, and IV, 189; Thayer, *Israel Pemberton*, 191.

37. Min. Philadelphia M for S, 25/II/1764.

38. Papers of the Friendly Association, II, 127; Thayer, *Israel Pemberton*, 152–53, 185; Wallace, *King of the Delawares*, 241, 249.

39. Thayer, *Israel Pemberton*, 185–187.

Chapter XI: Private Societies To Do Good

1. Min. Philadelphia MM, 20/II/1749.

2. Benjamin Bagnall, Boston, 1/IX/1755, to Israel Pemberton, Pemberton Papers (MS, Historical Society of Pennsylvania, Philadelphia, Pa.), Vol. X, No. 163; Theodore Thayer, *Israel Pemberton, King of the Quakers* (Philadelphia, 1943), 39, 196; William Penn, *Select Works of William Penn* (3rd ed.; London, 1782), IV, 99; Perry Miller, *The New England Mind; from Colony to Province* (Cambridge, 1953), 409.

3. John Smith, MS Diary, Vol. III (Feb. 20, 1747), as quoted in F. B. Tolles, *Meeting House and Counting House; the Quaker Merchants of Colonial Philadelphia, 1682–1763* (Chapel Hill, N. C., 1948), 71; Penn, *Select Works*, II, 180; Robert Proud; *History of Pennsylvania in North America*, 2 vols. (Philadelphia, 1797–98), II, 158.

4. Min. Philadelphia MM, 27/VIII/1704, 29/VI/1712; Thomas Woody, *Early Quaker Education in Pennsylvania* ("Columbia University Contributions to Education, Teachers' College Series," No. 105 [New York, 1920]), 148–49.

5. Miller, *New England Mind; from Colony to Province*, 409, 413; Maurice Ashley, *England in the Seventeenth Century* (London, 1952), 123–24, 157–58, 239–41.

6. Isaac Sharpless, *A Quaker Experiment in Government* (Philadelphia, 1898), 68, 107–8.

7. Sharpless, *Quaker Experiment*, 74; Carl and Jessica Bridenbaugh, *Rebels and Gentlemen* (New York, 1942), 11, 22–26, 243.

8. Tolles, *Meeting House*, 151, 155–56, 220–22; Harold E. Gillingham, "Philadelphia's First Fire Defences," *Pennsylvania Magazine of History and Biography*, LVI (1932), 368–70; Sharpless, *Quaker Experiment*, 74; George DeCou, *Burlington; A Provincial Capital* (Philadelphia, 1945), 172–73.

9. Gillingham, "Philadelphia's First Fire Defences," *Pa. Mag. of History and Biog.*, LVI, 358–74; C. and J. Bridenbaugh, *Rebels and Gentlemen*, 24–25.

10. Tolles, *Meeting House*, 220–22.

11. Tolles, *Meeting House*, 156.

12. DeCou, *Burlington*, 171.

13. Papers of the Friendly Association, I, 427, 505–506, and II, 75,

195; Donald L. Kemmerer, *Path to Freedom; the Struggle for Self-Government in Colonial New Jersey, 1703–1776* (Princeton, N. J., 1940), 259, 265; DeCou, *Burlington*, 171–72.

14. George S. Brookes, *Friend Anthony Benezet* (Philadelphia, 1937), 63–66, 74–75; Lawrence H. Gipson, *The Great War for the Empire; the Years of Defeat, 1754–1757* ("The British Empire Before the American Revolution," Vol. VI [New York, 1946]), 310–12; Wilson Armistead, *Anthony Benezet from the Original Memoir* [by Roberts Vaux] *Revised, with Additions* (London, 1859), 101; William C. Heffner, *History of Poor Relief Legislation in Pennsylvania, 1682–1913* (Cleona, Pa., c. 1913), 78.

15. Brookes, *Friend Anthony Benezet*, 64–68, 75; Armistead, *Anthony Benezet*, 101n, 102; Gipson, *Great War for the Empire; Years of Defeat*, 312.

16. Brookes, *Friend Anthony Benezet*, 66–75; Gipson, *Great War for the Empire; Years of Defeat*, 313–19.

17. Brookes, *Friend Anthony Benezet*, 68–73, 239–40.

18. Anthony Benezet, Philadelphia, 25/XII/1755, to Joseph Spangenberg, in Brookes, *Friend Anthony Benezet*, 212–14.

19. Brookes, *Friend Anthony Benezet*, 212–14.

20. Brookes, *Friend Anthony Benezet*, 214–19.

21. Tolles *Meeting House*, 227–29; Benjamin Franklin, "Autobiography," *The Writings of Benjamin Franklin*, ed. Albert H. Smyth, Vol. I (New York, 1905), 377; Thomas E. Morton, assisted by Frank Woodbury, *The History of the Pennsylvania Hospital, 1751–1895* (Philadelphia, 1895), 10–13.

22. "An Act to encourage the establishing of an Hospital . . ." in Morton and Woodbury, *History of the Pennsylvania Hospital*, 10; C. and J. Bridenbaugh, *Rebels and Gentlemen*, 244–47, 271–75.

23. Tolles, *Meeting House*, 229, 229n; Morton and Woodbury, *History of the Pennsylvania Hospital*, 14.

24. John Smith, Philadelphia, 6/V/1751, to John Pemberton, Pemberton Papers, VII, 80; Morton and Woodbury, *History of the Pennsylvania Hospital*, 35, 345, 347, 357–59, 378, 384, 387; Tolles, *Meeting House*, 229; C. and J. Bridenbaugh, *Rebels and Gentlemen*, 273; Gillingham, "Philadelphia's First Fire Defences," *Pa. Mag. of Hist. and Biog.*, LVI, 373–74.

25. Morton and Woodbury, *History of the Pennsylvania Hospital*, 9, 13–15, 49, 377, 385.

26. Morton and Woodbury, *History of the Pennsylvania Hospital*, 14–15, 18–20.

27. Morton and Woodbury, *History of the Pennsylvania Hospital*, 21–23, 27–28, 33; Edwin Bronner, "The Disgrace of John Kinsey, Quaker Politician, 1739–1750," *Pa. Mag. of Hist. and Biog.*, LXXV (1951), 403–14.

28. Morton and Woodbury, *History of the Pennsylvania Hospital*, 42–46, 248, 265–67.

29. Morton and Woodbury, *History of the Pennsylvania Hospital*, 43–44, 47–48.

30. Morton and Woodbury, *History of the Pennsylvania Hospital*, 49–69, 248–63, 276–85, 376, 401.

31. Heffner, *History of Poor Relief*, 77–78, 81–86.

32. C. and J. Bridenbaugh, *Rebels and Gentlemen*, 233–35, 292–93.

33. C. and J. Bridenbaugh, *Rebels and Gentlemen*, 235–36, 250–53, 259; Harry E. Barnes, *The Evolution of Penology in Pennsylvania* (Indianapolis, 1927), 80.

34. See, for example, Benjamin Franklin, Philadelphia, April 13, 1738, to Josiah Franklin, in *Writings*, ed. Smyth, II (New York, 1905), 215; or the project for a United Party for Virtue, "The Autobiography," in *Writings*, ed. Smyth, I, 340–41.

35. J. Arrowsmith, March 26, 1698, "Papers Relating to the American Church, Pennsylvania," 7, quoted in Sharpless, *Quaker Experiment*, 38n.

36. Morton and Woodbury, *History of the Pennsylvania Hospital*, 33–34; Luke 10:34.

37. C. and J. Bridenbaugh, *Rebels and Gentlemen*, 253.

Chapter XII: Justice to the Negro

1. John Woolman, "The Journal of John Woolman," in *The Journal and Essays of John Woolman*, ed. A. M. Gummere (New York, 1922), 219–20.

2. Min. Philadelphia MM, 12/III/1761, 10/XII/1761, 8/IV/1762, 31/XII/1762, 25/III/1763, 2/V/1763; Woolman, *Journal and Essays*, 193–94, 342–46, 355; Min. Burlington MM, 5/XI/1764.

3. Min. Philadelphia MM, 25/XII/1761, 26/III/1762, 30/IV/1762, 10/VI/1762, 25/XI/1763.

4. Min. Burlington MM, 2/III/1761, 1/VI/1761; Min. Philadelphia MM, 28/II/1759, 28/III/1760, 25/IV/1760, 12/VI/1760, 13/VIII/1761, 28/X/1763, 31/V/1765.

5. Min. Philadelphia MM, 27/IV/1759, 29/II/1760, 25/IV/1760, 12/VI/1760, 13/VIII/1761, 27/VIII/1762; Min. Burlington MM, 5/II/1770.

6. R. M. Jones, I. Sharpless and A. M. Gummere, *The Quakers in the American Colonies* (London, 1911), 159–63, 255–56; Min. South Kingstown MM, 28/XI/1757.

7. Min. South Kingstown MM, 1/XII/1760, 1/XI/1762, 27/I/1766, 30/XII/1771, 31/XII/1771, 2/VI/1772, 29/VI/1772, 28/VI/1773.

8. Woolman, *Journal*, 237; Min. New England YM, 1760; Jones *et al.*, *Quakers in the American Colonies*, 163, 256–57.

9. Min. Philadelphia M for S, 18/XII/1760; Min Philadelphia YM, 1760, 1762; William C. Dunlap, *Quaker Education in Baltimore and Virginia Yearly Meetings* (Philadelphia, 1936), 454–56; Thomas E. Drake, *Quakers and Slavery in America* (New Haven, Conn., 1950), 79–86.

10. Min. Philadelphia MM, 25/IV/1760; Anthony Benezet; "Caution and Warning to Great Britain and her Colonies on the Calamitous State of the Enslaved Negroes in the British Dominions" (1766), in A. Benezet and John Wesley, *Views of American Slavery, taken a Century Ago* (Philadelphia, 1858), 29; Woolman, *Journal*, 190, 216, 380; Min. Philadelphia YM, 1765; Min. New York YM, 1768, in Jones *et al.*, *Quakers in the American Colonies*, 257.

11. See, for example, Min. Philadelphia MM, 22/IX/1775, 29/XI/1776; Min. Fairfax MM (Va.), 25/IV/1767, in Dunlap, *Quaker Education*, 464;

Min. Burlington MM, 7/XII/1767; Min. Philadelphia YM, 1773, 1775; Min. New York YM, 1775, in Bliss Forbush, *Elias Hicks, Quaker Liberal* (New York, 1956), 31.

12. See, William Penn, *Select Works of William Penn* (3rd ed.; London, 1782), IV, 279; Robert Barclay, *Universal Love Considered, and Established upon its Right Foundation* (London, 1799), 34; Joseph Phipps, *The Original and Present State of Man, Briefly Considered* (Philadelphia, 1836), 15–16.

13. Woolman, *Journal*, 216.

14. Min. Philadelphia YM, 1767, 1769, 1770, 1774; Min. Falls MM, 6/IV/1768, 6/XII/1769, 4/II/1771, 6/I/1773.

15. Min. Philadelphia MM, 12/VIII/1762, 26/XI/1762, 29/VII/1763, 28/X/1768, 25/XI/1768, 31/III/1769; Min. Falls MM, 3/V/1773, 4/VIII/1773.

16. Min. Virginia YM, 1772, in Dunlap, *Quaker Education*, 456; [North Carolina Yearly Meeting, Meeting for Sufferings,] *A Narrative of Some of the Proceedings of North Carolina Yearly Meeting on the Subject of Slavery within Its Limits* (Greensborough, N. C., 1848), 6–7; Min. Philadelphia MM, 29/IV/1757, 24/VI/1757, 27/VII/1759, 12/VIII/1762, 30/III/1770.

17. Min. Falls MM, 4/VIII/1773; Min. Philadelphia MM, 25/II/1774, 25/III/1774, 29/IV/1774.

18. Min. Philadelphia YM, 1774.

19. Min. Falls MM, 3/I/1776; Min. Philadelphia YM, 1775, 1776; Min. Philadelphia MW, 29/XI/1776.

20. Min. Philadelphia YM, 1779; Thomas Woody, *Quaker Education in the Colony and State of New Jersey* (Philadelphia, 1923), 277–82.

21. Min. New England YM, 1763, 1769, 1770, 1771, 1772.

22. Min. New England YM, 1773, 1774, 1778; Min. Salem MM, 9/III/1775, 14/III/1776, 12/II/1778; Drake, *Quakers and Slavery*, 79.

23. Forbush, *Elias Hicks*, 31–32; Jones *et al.*, *Quakers in the American Colonies*, 258; Drake, *Quakers and Slavery*, 80.

24. Drake, *Quakers and Slavery*, 81–83; Dunlap, *Quaker Education*, 440, 442–43, 479 (Min. Black Water MM, 15/VIII/1789), 456–47 (Min. Virginia YM, 1779), 457–58.

25. Zora Klain, *Quaker Contributions to Education in North Carolina* (Philadelphia, 1924), 311–12; Drake, *Quakers and Slavery*, 83–84; [North Carolina Yearly Meeting, Meeting for Sufferings,] *Narrative of Some of the Proceedings*, 11–23.

26. Min. Philadelphia YM, 1778; Dunlap, *Quaker Education*, 457.

27. Min. Philadelphia YM, 1774, 1775, 1777, 1779; Dunlap, *Quaker Education*, 440–41, 450–57; Klain, *Quaker Contributions*, 55–56.

28. Drake, *Quakers and Slavery*, 76–78, 80; Min. Burlington MM, 4/VIII/1783.

29. Min. Falls MM, 4/II/1767; Min. Philadelphia MM, 25/XI/1757, 30/XI/1759, 25/I/1760; Drake, *Quakers and Slavery*, 76, 81–84; Stephen B. Weeks, *Southern Quakers and Slavery* (Baltimore, 1896), 208–14; Min. Chesterfield MM, 3/VIII/1775, in Woody, *Quaker Education in New Jersey*, 276.

30. Min. Philadelphia MM, 26/III/1756, 25/XI/1757; Klain, *Quaker Contributions*, 310; Dunlap, *Quaker Education*, 440.

31. Dunlap, *Quaker Education*, 473–74; Min. Philadelphia YM, 1778, 1779, 1787, 1791; Woody, *Quaker Education in New Jersey*, 126, 278–83; Min. Burlington MM, 7/VIII/1780. On deficiency in spiritual training, see, for example, Min. Falls MM, 6/IX/1780; Min. Philadelphia YM, 1781, 1783.

32. Min. Chesterfield MM, 5/VIII/1779, in Woody, *Quaker Education in New Jersey*, 276.

33. Woody, *Early Quaker Education in Pennsylvania*, 246–47.

34. See, for example, Min. Warrington and Fairfax MM, 16/IX/1776, in Dunlap, *Quaker Education*, 470; Min. Philadelphia YM, 1781, 1783 (summary of answers to seventh query).

35. Epistle to London Meeting for Sufferings, in Min. Philadelphia M for S, 21/I/1780; "Minutes of the Committee's [sic] appointed by the Three Monthly Meetings of Friends of Philadelphia, to the Oversight and care of the School for Educating Africans' and their descendants" (MS, Department of Records, Philadelphia Yearly Meeting, 302 Arch St., Philadelphia, Pa.), Vol. I (1770–1811), pp. 38–39, 64. Hereafter, these minutes will be cited as Min. Philadelphia MM Africans School, with a page reference.

36. Min. Philadelphia MM, 26/I/1770, 30/III/1770; Min. Philadelphia MM Africans School, 33; *A Brief Sketch of the Schools for Black People and their Descendants, Established by the Religious Society of Friends, in 1770, Published by Direction of the Committee having Charge of the Schools* (Philadelphia, 1867), 4.

37. Min. Philadelphia MM Africans School, 8–60.

38. Min. Philadelphia MM Africans School, 30–68.

39. Min. Philadelphia MM Africans School, 68–76, 112–13.

40. Woody, *Early Quaker Education*, 247–59; Woody, *Quaker Education in New Jersey*, 278–81; Dunlap, *Quaker Education*, 353, 471–76.

41. Woody, *Quaker Education in New Jersey*, 281–82; Min. Burlington MM, 5/VIII/1782.

42. Epistles to London Yearly Meeting, in Min. Philadelphia YM, 1772, 1773; William Tuke, York, England, 26/X/1772, to Reuben Haines, in Woolman, *Journal*, 317; Min. Philadelphia M for S, 1774–1780, *passim*.

43. Min. Wilmington MM, 12/X/1783, in Dunlap, *Quaker Education*, 353.

Chapter XIII: American Quakers and Social Service during the Revolution

1. Rufus M. Jones, I. Sharpless, and A. M. Gummere, *Quakers in the American Colonies* (London, 1911), 560; Epistle from London Meeting for Sufferings, dated London, 22/VIII/1766, in Min. Philadelphia M for S, 20/XI/1766.

2. Epistles to London Meeting for Sufferings, in Min. Philadelphia M for S, 4/VIII/1769, 21/VII/1774; Min. Philadelphia MM, 4/VIII/1769, 25/V/1770, 4/X/1770, 30/VIII/1771, 26/VII/1776.

3. Arthur J. Mekeel, "The Society of Friend (Quakers) and the American Revolution" (MS Ph.D. thesis, Department of History, Harvard University, 1940), 345–55.

4. "Representation" to the President, Executive Council and Assembly

of Pennsylvania, in Min. Philadelphia M for S, 22/XI/1781; Robert Proud, *History of Pennsylvania in North America* (Philadelphia, 1797–98), I, 479, and II, 227–30; Min. Burlington MM, 3/X/1774; Min. Philadelphia MM, 26/VIII/1774, 27/I/1775, 24/II/1775.

5. Min. Philadelphia M for S, 5/XI/1774 (Epistle to London Meeting for Sufferings), 20/I/1776; Min. Philadelphia YM, 1776; Proud, *History of Pennsylvania*, I, 292–93; Bliss Forbush, *Elias Hicks, Quaker Liberal* (New York, 1956), 32–35.

6. Isaac Penington, "A Brief Account of what the People called Quakers desire, In Reference to the Civil Government," *The Works of the Long-Mournful and Sorely-Distressed Isaac Penington* (3rd ed.; London, 1784), II, 192.

7. Proud, *History of Pennsylvania*, I, 427–28, and II, 23; Min. Philadelphia YM, 1776.

8. Report of Meeting for Sufferings to Quarterly Meetings, in Min. Philadelphia MM, 31/VII/1778.

9. Epistle to London Yearly Meeting, in Min. Philadelphia YM, 1777; Isaac Sharpless, *A History of Quaker Government in Pennsylvania*: Vol. II, *The Quakers in the Revolution* (Philadelphia, 1899), 152–68.

10. Forbush, *Elias Hicks*, 37, 44, 48; Min. New England YM, 1777, 1778, 1779; Min. Philadelphia YM, 1777.

11. Sharpless, *Quakers in the American Revolution*, 172–206; Min. Philadelphia M for S, 4/XI/1779, 20 and 21/I/1780, 18/V/1780, 18/I/1782.

12. Min. New England M for S, 13/XI/1780; Min. South Kingstown MM, 27/I/1777; Forbush, *Elias Hicks*, 45; Min. New England YM, 1780, 1781.

13. Min. Philadelphia M for S, 20 and 21/I/1780.

14. "Representation" to President, Executive Council and Assembly of Pennsylvania, in Min. Philadelphia M for S, 22/XI/1781; Proud, *History of Pennsylvania*, I, 50.

15. Min. New England YM, 1743, 1744, 1754, 1755.

16. Min. New England YM, 1760, 1761, 1762, 1763, 1767; Min. Salem MM, 13/X/1757, 1758 and 1759 *passim*.

17. Min. South Kingstown MM, 31/I/1763; Min. New England YM, 1774, 1778.

18. Min. New England YM, 1772, 1773, 1774, 1775.

19. Min. Salem MM, 9/IV/1778; Min. New England YM, 1787, 1788.

20. Min. New England M for S, 10/IX/1776, 1/XI/1784; Min. New England YM, 1782.

21. Min. New England YM, 1774, 1775, 1776; Min. New England M for S, 10/VII/1776.

22. Forbush, *Elias Hicks*, 29, 51, 52.

23. Min. Philadelphia YM, 1756; Jones *et al.*, *Quakers in the American Colonies*, 151, 259; Mekeel, "The Society of Friends and the American Revolution," 7, 286, 297; Min. New England M for S, 10/VII/1776, 14/V/1781.

24. Min. Philadelphia M for S, 16/V/1771, 20/VI/1771, 24/XI/1774; Min. Burlington MM, 2/VI/1777; Min. Philadelphia MM, 29/I/1773, 29/XI/1776; Min. New England M for S, 12/IV/1783.

25. Min. Salem MM, 9/VII/1772; Min. Philadelphia MM, 28/II/1772; Min. Philadelphia YM, 1727, 1728, 1734, 1736, 1750, 1757, 1776; Min. Philadelphia M for S, 21/I/1773, 6/XII/1784; Proud, *History of Pennsylvania,* I, 3–5; Samuel Smith, *History of the Colony of Nova-Caesaria, or New Jersey* . . . (Burlington, N. J., 1765).

26. Min. Philadelphia MW, 29/VII/1757, 29/VII/1774, 31/I/1777; Proud, *History of Pennsylvania,* I, 76–81; Min. Philadelphia MM, 31/VII/1767, 24/XI/1769; Min. Burlington MW, 6/XII/1779; Min. Burlington MM, 1/XII/1777; [Anthony Benezet,] *The Mighty Destroyer Displayed, In Some Account of the Dreadful Havock Made by the Mistaken Use as Well as Abuse of Distilled Spirituous Liquors* (Philadelphia, 1774), 18.

27. Min. New England YM, 1779, 1780, 1788; Min. New England Meeting for Sufferings, 11/XI/1782, 1/XI/1784; Zora Klain, *Educational Activities of New England Quakers* (Philadelphia, 1928), 13–15, 36–37.

28. Forbush, *Elias Hicks,* 54–55; William C. Dunlap, *Quaker Education in Baltimore and Virginia Yearly Meetings* (Philadelphia, 1936), 105–6, 171–72, 300–304, 508.

29. Min. Philadelphia YM, 1778, 1779; Min. Burlington MM, 1/XII/1783, 6/XII/1784; Min. Burlington QM, 30/VIII/1779, in Thomas Woody, *Quaker Education in the Colony and State of New Jersey* (Philadelphia, 1923), 26.

30. Min. Burlington MM, 6/VIII/1781, 2/VIII/1784; Min. Falls MM, 5/II/1777, 3/IX/1783; Min. Philadelphia MM, 31/VII/1778; Woody, *Quaker Education in New Jersey,* 60–62, 78, 95 facs., 120, 139 facs., 183; T. Woody, *Early Quaker Education in Pennsylvania* ("Columbia University Contributions to Education, Teachers' College Series," No. 105 [New York, 1920]), 99, 99n, 149–50, 171; Dunlap, *Quaker Education,* 98–100, 255, 309–14, 352–53.

31. Min. Philadelphia MM, 25/V/1759, 10/XII/1761, 16/I/1762, 26/III/1762, 31/XII/1762, 25/III/1763.

32. Min. Philadelphia MM, 28/II/1777, 25/IV/1777; Min. Philadelphia YM, 1777; Min. Falls MM, 4/XII/1776; [Benezet] *Mighty Destroyer,* 11n, 26; Min. New England YM, 1784.

33. Min. New England YM 1784; Min. Philadelphia YM, 1777, 1788.

34. [Benezet,] *Mighty Destroyer,* 5–9, 14–15, 20, 20n, 28, 36, 38–39, 43–47.

35. [Benezet,] *Mighty Destroyer,* 12, 21; Min. Philadelphia YM, 1777; Epistle from New England Meeting for Sufferings, in Min. Philadelphia M for S, 21/X/1784.

36. Thomas E. Drake, *Quakers and Slavery in America* (New Haven, Conn., 1950), 85–91, 97; Dunlap, *Quaker Education,* 441–42; Min. Philadelphia M for S, 21/VII/1774, 21/XI/1776, 25/IX/1779, 20 and 21/I/1780, 15/VIII/1782, 15/IV/1784.

37. Robert Proud, "Philadelphia" (MS, Historical Society of Pennsylvania, Philadelphia, Pa.), 43–45; Drake, *Quakers and Slavery,* 90, 90n, 94, 98n; Theodore Thayer, *Israel Pemberton, King of the Quakers* (Philadelphia, 1943), 200.

38. Epistle to London Meeting for Sufferings, in Min. Philadelphia M for S, 5/XI/1774; Min. Salem MM, 9/III/1775; Henry J. Cadbury, *Quaker Re-*

lief During the Siege of Boston ("Pendle Hill Historical Study," No. 4 [n.d., n.p.], reprinted from Colonial Society of Massachusetts, *Transactions,* XXXIV), 3–5, 8.

39. Min. New England M for S, 12/IX/1775; Min. Philadelphia M for S, 6/VII/1775, 2/XI/1775, 6/XI/1775, 9/XI/1775, 9/V/1776; Cadbury, *Quaker Relief,* 13; Mack E. Thompson, "Moses Brown's 'Account of Journey to Distribute Donations 12th Month 1775,'" *Rhode Island History,* XV (1956), 103–7.

40. Min. New England M for S, 13/I/1776, 13/II/1776, 11/III/1776, 12/III/1776, 15/VI/1776; Min. Philadelphia M for S, 25/IX/1776; Cadbury, *Quaker Relief,* 20–21. Figures on numbers of recipients differed by New England and Philadelphia reckoning.

41. Mekeel, "The Society of Friends and the American Revolution," 145–48, 318–26, 334–35; Min. New England M for S, 11/VIII/1777, 10/IV/1778, 6/I/1779, 8/II/1779.

42. Min. Philadelphia MM, 27/XII/1776, 25/VII/1777, 26/XII/1777; Min. Philadelphia M for S, 21/VIII/1777.

43. Min. Philadelphia MM, 31/X/1777; Min. Falls MM, 7/I/1778; Min. Philadelphia M for S, 20/XI/1777, 11/XII/1777.

44. Min. Philadelphia M for S, 17/XII/1778, 18/II/1779; Min. Philadelphia MM, 26/VI/1778.

45. Mekeel, "The Society of Friends and the American Revolution," 332, 344; Min. Philadelphia M for S, 19/X/1778, 20 and 21/I/1780, 19/VII/1781, 15/XI/1781, 19/II/1784.

46. Min. Philadelphia M for S, 18/II/1779, 20 and 21/I/1780, 15/XI/1781, 15/VIII/1782, 9/II/1784; Mekeel, "The Society of Friends and the American Revolution," 328, 332–40.

47. Min. Philadelphia M for S, 16/VI/1785, 21/VI/1787, 3/VII/1787, 19/VII/1787, 16/VIII/1787, 17/I/1788, 26/IX/1789; Mekeel, "The Society of Friends and the American Revolution," 341–44.

48. Min. Philadelphia MM Africans School, 104.

49. Min. Philadelphia MM, 16/I/1762, 26/III/1779; Epistle to the Quarterly and Monthly Meetings, in Min. Philadelphia YM, 1776.

50. Min. Philadelphia M for S, 4/XI/1779, 25/II/1764, 21/IX/1786, 7/IX/1778, 18/V/1780.

Chapter XIV: The Society of Friends in Post-Revolutionary America

1. Min. New England YM of M and E, 1788; Min. New England YM, 1789; Min New England M for S, 11/II/1782, 13/V/1782, 8/IX/1788.

2. Min. Falls MM, 4/I/1786; Min. Philadelphia YM, 1795; *Gwynedd Monthly Meeting of the Religious Society of Friends, 1699–1949* (n.p., n.d.), 17; William C. Dunlap, *Quaker Education in Baltimore and Virginia Yearly Meetings* (Philadelphia, 1936), 457, 458, 485; Zora Klain, *Quaker Contributions to Education in North Carolina* (Philadelphia, 1924), 160.

3. Stephen B. Weeks, *Southern Quakers and Slavery* (Baltimore, 1896), 131; George Churchman, East Nottingham, Pa., 3/IV/1807, to [Henry Drinker?], Collection of Letters RS 181 (MS, Dept. of Records, Philadelphia Yearly Meeting, Philadelphia, Pa.), number 191.

4. Min. Falls MM, 4/I/1786; Min. New England YM, 1787.

5. Min. New England YM, 1787; Min. New England YM of M and E, 1788, 1792.

6. Bliss Forbush, *Elias Hicks, Quaker Liberal* (New York, 1956), 53, 89–90; Min. Philadelphia YM, 1784, 1788, 1794, 1795; Weeks, *Southern Quakers*, 128–29.

7. Min. New England YM, 1784, 1787, 1788, 1794.

8. Frederick B. Tolles, *Quakers and the Atlantic Culture* (New York, 1960), 89–90; Forbush, *Elias Hicks*, 52–53; George Churchman, East Nottingham, Pa., 3/IV/1807, to [Henry Drinker?], Collection of Letters, RS 181, number 191.

9. Thomas Woody, *Quaker Education in the Colony and State of New Jersey* (Philadelphia, 1923), 20; Min. Philadelphia YM, 1787, 1789; Forbush, *Elias Hicks*, 90–92; Zora Klain, *Educational Activities of New England Quakers* (Philadelphia, 1928), 37–51, 116–24, 129–32.

10. Min. Falls MM, 4/VIII/1784; Min. Burlington MM, 2/VIII/1784, 4/XII/1786, 3/XII/1787; Min. Philadelphia YM, 1784, 1785, 1789, 1792, 1798; Woody, *Quaker Education in New Jersey*, 53, 79, 249; T. Woody, *Early Quaker Education in Pennsylvania* ("Columbia University Contributions to Education, Teacher's College Series," No. 105 [New York, 1920]), 76, 111–12, 139–40.

11. Dunlap, *Quaker Education*, 28–39, 62–63, 107, 171–72, 177–85, 207–8, 300–304, 508; Klain, *Quaker Contributions*, 56, 58, 112, 181–82, 243–45; Epistle to London Meeting for Sufferings, in Min. Philadelphia M for S, 16/VI/1785.

12. Klain, *Educational Activities*, 51, 119, 124, 145; Dunlap, *Quaker Education*, 255–64, 353–57; Woody, *Quaker Education in New Jersey*, 60–62, 102–3, 113, 167–69, 183, 202; Woody, *Early Quaker Education*, 72, 126–28, 170; Min. Philadelphia YM, 1787.

13. Min. Philadelphia YM, 1789; Forbush, *Elias Hicks*, 92.

14. Min. New England YM, 1780, 1788, 1797, 1800; Min. New England M for S, 11/XI/1782, 8/VI/1785, 13/III/1787, minutes for 1815, *passim*.

15. [Owen Biddle,] *A Plan for a School on an Establishment Similar to That at Ackworth, in Yorkshire, Great-Britain, Varied to Suit the Circumstances of the Youth Within the Limits of the Yearly-Meeting for Pennsylvania and New-Jersey* (Philadelphia, 1790).

16. Woody, *Early Quaker Education*, 60, 60n, 73–74; Min. Philadelphia YM, 1792, 1794, 1796, 1798; Woody, *Quaker Education in New Jersey*, 47, 126, 176; Dunlap, *Quaker Education*, 357.

17. Rufus M. Jones, *The Later Periods of Quakerism* (London, 1921), II, 682; Woody, *Quaker Education in New Jersey*, 47; R. M. Jones, I. Sharpless, and A. M. Gummere, *The Quakers in the American Colonies* (London, 1911), 262.

18. Dunlap, *Quaker Education*, 289–97.

19. *Historical Sketch of the Friends Academy, prepared for the Centennial Year* (New Bedford, Mass., 1876), 3–20, 30–35; Frederick B. Tolles, "The New-Light Quakers of Lynn and New Bedford," *New England Quarterly*, XXXII (1959), 304–18.

20. Klain, *Educational Activities*, 57, 71, 73, 75; Dunlap, *Quaker Education*, 324.

21. Klain, *Quaker Contributions*, 69–71, 109–10, 112–17.

22. Henry J. Cadbury, "Negro Membership in the Society of Friends," *Journal of Negro History*, XXI (1936), 170–77, 185; John H. Franklin, *Free Negro in North Carolina* (Chapel Hill, N. C., 1943), 175.

23. Hunt's diary, as quoted in Cadbury, "Negro Membership," *Jour. Neg. Hist.*, XXI, 175; Min. Chesterfield MM, 5/VIII/1779, in Woody, *Quaker Education in New Jersey*, 276.

24. Min. New England M for S, 12/IV/1783 (Epistle from Philadelphia Meeting for Sufferings, dated Philadelphia, 19/XII/1782), 8/IX/1788.

25. Min. Philadelphia M for S, 21/X/1790, 16/XII/1790, 17/II/1791; Ezra Michener, *A Retrospect of Early Quakerism* (Philadelphia, 1860), 123.

26. Min. Philadelphia YM, 1786; Min. New England YM, 1789.

27. Francis R. Taylor, *Life of William Savery of Philadelphia, 1750–1804* (New York, 1925), 417, 450–51; Robert Proud, *History of Pennsylvania, in North America*, 2 vols. (Philadelphia, 1797–98), II, 338–39, 356–59; Robert Barclay, *Universal Love Considered, and Established upon its Right Foundation* (London, 1799), 23; Joseph Phipps, *The Original and Present State of Man, Briefly Considered* (Philadelphia, 1836), 73–74.

28. Min. Philadelphia YM, 1783, 1787, 1789; Min. Philadelphia M for S, 20/XI/1783; Min. New England YM, 1787.

29. Thomas E. Drake, *Quakers and Slavery in America* (New Haven, Conn., 1950), 103–10; Min. Philadelphia YM, 1789 (Epistle to London Yearly Meeting), 1790 (Epistle to London Yearly Meeting); Min. Philadelphia M for S, 20/X/1786 (Message to Congress), 21/II/1793 ("Address" to the Pennsylvania legislature); Min. New England M for S, 10/XII/1787 (Memorial "To the General Assembly of the State of Rhode Island"), 25/II/1788 (Epistle to New York Meeting for Sufferings), 8/XII/1788; Min. New England YM, 1793 (Memorial "To the President Senate & House of Representatives of United States").

30. Min. Philadelphia YM, 1789; Min. Philadelphia M for S, 18/XI/1790 (Epistle to New England Meeting for Sufferings).

31. Min. Philadelphia YM, 1784 (Epistle to London Yearly Meeting), 1791 (Epistle to London Yearly Meeting), 1797 ("Memorial & Address" to Congress); Min. Philadelphia M for S, 20/XII/1793, 16/X/1788 ("Memorial & Address" to the General Assembly of Delaware); Min. New England YM, 1793 (Memorial "To the President Senate & House of Representatives of United States"); rhetorical question by Rep. Jackson (Ga.) quoted in Drake, *Quakers and Slavery*, 103.

32. Proud, *History of Pennsylvania*, II, 236; Min. Philadelphia YM, 1789, 1796; Min. Philadelphia M for S, 18/I/1782 ("Address & Memorial" to the Pennsylvania Assembly).

Chapter XV: The First Flowering of Humanitarian Concerns

1. Robert Proud, *History of Pennsylvania, in North America*, 2 vols. (Philadelphia, 1797–98), I, 61.

2. George DeCou, *Burlington: A Provincial Capital* (Philadelphia, 1945), 175–76; Thomas Woody, *Quaker Education in the Colony and State of New Jersey* (Philadelphia, 1923), 246–47.

3. Robert Proud, "Philadelphia" (MS, Historical Society of Pennsylvania, Philadelphia, Pa.), 81–82; Bliss Forbush, *Elias Hicks, Quaker Liberal* (New York, 1956), 129; William C. Dunlap, *Quaker Education in Baltimore and Virginia Yearly Meetings* (Philadelphia, 1936), 487; Zora Klain, *Educational Activities of New England Quakers* (Philadelphia, 1928), 55–57.

4. William O. Bourne, *History of the Public School Society of the City of New York* (New York, 1870), 2–12; Samuel L. Knapp, *The Life of Thomas Eddy* (London, 1836), 128–29.

5. [Providence, R. I.,] *U. S. Chronicle*, April 28, 1785; *Historical Sketch of the Friends Academy, prepared for the Centennial Year* (New Bedford, Mass., 1876), 4; Samuel Mickle, "Diary," in Frank H. Stewart (ed.), *Notes on Old Gloucester County, New Jersey* (n.p., 1934–37), I, 159, 163, 164, and II, 112, 114, 117, 161, 162; Woody, *Quaker Education in New Jersey*, 137n; DeCou, *Burlington*, 174–75; Knapp, *Life of Thomas Eddy*, 123–24.

6. Knapp, *Life of Thomas Eddy*, 73–75.

7. Knapp, *Life of Thomas Eddy*, 28–29, 40–42, 44–47, 50–52, 57, 114; Harry Elmer Barnes, *The Evolution of Penology in Pennsylvania; A Study in American Social History* (Indianapolis, 1927), 19–20; Negley K. Teeters, *The Cradle of the Penitentiary, the Walnut Street Jail at Philadelphia, 1773–1835* (n.p., 1955), 11–12, 19–20; Michael Kraus, *The Atlantic Civilization: Eighteenth-Century Origins* (Ithaca, N. Y., 1949), 132–34.

8. Teeters, *Cradle of the Penitentiary*, 29–62; Barnes, *Evolution of Penology*, 74–118; N. K. Teeters, "The Early Days of the Eastern State Penitentiary at Philadelphia," *Pennsylvania History*, XVI (1949), 261–62.

9. Robert G. Caldwell, *The Penitentiary Movement in Delaware, 1776 to 1829* (Wilmington, Del., 1946), 143–49; Knapp, *Life of Thomas Eddy*, 42–58.

10. Thomas E. Drake, *Quakers and Slavery in America* (New Haven, Conn., 1950), 94, 101, 104, 118–20; DeCou, *Burlington*, 177–78; Mickle, "Diary," in Stewart (ed.), *Notes on Old Gloucester County*, II, 118; James B. Hedges, *The Browns of Providence Plantations: Colonial Years* (Cambridge, 1952), 17; Proud, "Philadelphia," 43–46, 65.

11. *History of the Associations of Friends for the Free Instruction of Adult Colored Persons in Philadelphia* (Philadelphia, 1890), 3–7; Burlington School Society for the Free Instruction of the Blacks, Burlington, 1/III/1794, to Philadelphia Association for the Instruction of Adult Colored Persons (MS, Dept. of Records, Philadelphia Yearly Meeting, Philadelphia, Pa.).

12. *History of the Association of Friends for the Free Instruction of Adult Colored Persons in Philadelphia*, 3–7, 10–13.

13. Correspondence of the Philadelphia Association for the Instruction of Adult Colored Persons (MS, Dept. of Records, Philadelphia Yearly Meeting, Philadelphia, Pa.), items dated Baltimore, 24/V/1792; Baltimore, 15/

IX/1792; Burlington, 20/XI/1790; Burlington, 3/III/1792; Burlington, 2/II/1793; Philadelphia (to Burlington), 11/I/1794; Burlington, 1/III/1794; Burlington, 10/XII/1797.

14. Kraus, *Atlantic Civilization,* 152; Correspondence of the Philadelphia Association for the Instruction of Adult Colored Persons, items dated Philadelphia (to Obadiah Brown, Providence), 11/I/1794; Newport, 25/IV/1791; Newport, 16/IV/1794; Burlington, 2/II/1793.

15. Dunlap, *Quaker Education,* 173–77, 458–59; Zora Klain, *Quaker Contributions to Education in North Carolina* (Philadelphia, 1924), 199, 237, 314–15; John H. Franklin, *The Free Negro in North Carolina, 1790–1860* (Chapel Hill, N. C., 1943), 25–26, 166–68.

16. Min. Philadelphia YM, 1788, 1792; Thomas Woody, *Early Quaker Education in Pennsylvania* ("Columbia University Contributions to Education, Teachers' College Series," No. 105 [New York, 1920]), 252–54; Dunlap, *Quaker Education,* 479–82.

17. Henry J. Cadbury, "Negro Membership in the Society of Friends," *Journal of Negro History,* XXI (1936), 153–55.

18. Klain, *Quaker Contributions,* 55–57, 112, 199, 237, 312–15; Franklin, *Free Negro in North Carolina,* 68, 165–66.

19. Dunlap, *Quaker Education,* 63, 443–45, 450–51, 457–61 (including quotation from Min. Virginia YM, 1817), 485–88.

20. Min. Philadelphia MM Africans School, 68–208; Forbush, *Elias Hicks,* 129; Woody, *Early Quaker Education,* 243–44, 256; Dunlap, *Quaker Education,* 480–83.

21. Min. Philadelphia M for S, 20/XI/1783, 15/IV/1784, 18/XI/1784, 6/XII/1784, 17/II/1785, 20/X/1786, 21/XII/1786; Min. Philadelphia YM, 1783; Drake, *Quakers and Slavery,* 92–95.

22. Min. Philadelphia M for S, 15/VIII/1782, 18/XI/1784, 17/XII/1785, 27/XII/1785, 21/XII/1786, 21/VII/1791, 18/VIII/1791; John A. Munroe, *Federalist Delaware, 1775–1815* (New Brunswick, N. J., 1954), 157–59; Dunlap, *Quaker Education,* 477–78; Drake, *Quakers and Slavery,* 95–98.

23. Min. Philadelphia M for S, 17/I/1788, 17/IV/1788, 15/V/1788, 22/V/1788, 17/VII/1788, 16/X/1788, 18/XII/1788,15/I/1789, 19/II/1789; Epistle to London Yearly Meeting, in Min. Philadelphia YM, 1788; Drake, *Quakers and Slavery,* 97–98; Munroe, *Federalist Delaware,* 158–59; Min. New England YM, 1787; Min. New England M for S, 10/XII/1787, 25/II/1788, 9/IX/1788, 8/XII/1788.

24. Min. Philadelphia YM, 1787, 1789; Drake, *Quakers and Slavery,* 101–6.

25. Min. Philadelphia M for S, 19/X/1792; Dunlap, *Quaker Education,* 436–37, 445–47, 459–60, 483–84; Klain, *Quaker Contributions,* 315–16.

26. Min. Philadelphia M for S, 8/VII/1773 (Epistle to the western Indians), 25/IX/1773 (message dated Kekailammapaikung, 28/VII/1773), 5/XI/1774.

27. Epistle to London Meeting for Sufferings, in Min. Philadelphia M for S, 15/III/1792; London Meeting for Sufferings, Aborigines' Committee, *Some Account of the Conduct of the Religious Society of Friends towards the Indian Tribes in the Settlement of the Colonies of East and West Jersey*

and Pennsylvania (London, 1844), 106–7; Epistle to London Yearly Meeting, Min. Philadelphia YM, 1794.

28. Min. Philadelphia M for S, 16/II/1792; London Meeting for Sufferings, *Some Account*, 100, 119–20; Dunlap, *Quaker Education*, 376.

29. Min. Philadelphia M for S, 18/II/1791, 21/IV/1791, 19/V/1791, 16/VI/1791, 20/X/1791; London Meeting for Sufferings, *Some Account*, 99.

30. Min. Philadelphia M for S, 21/II/1793, 28/II/1793, 21/III/1793; Rayner W. Kelsey, *Friends and the Indians, 1655–1917* (Philadelphia, 1917), 111.

31. John Parrish, Jacob Lindley, William Savery, John Elliott and William Hartshorne, Philadelphia, 2/XII/1793, to Philadelphia Meeting for Sufferings, in Papers of the Indian Committee of Philadelphia Yearly Meeting (MS, Dept. of Records, Philadelphia Yearly Meeting, Philadelphia, Pa.), Box I.

32. London Meeting for Sufferings, *Some Account*, 107–10 (extracts from Savery's Journal).

33. London Meeting for Sufferings, *Some Account*, 110–13 (extracts from Savery's Journal and "Abstract of the Report of the Committee appointed to attend an Indian Treaty in the Year 1794"); Epistle to London Yearly Meeting, in Min. Philadelphia YM, 1794.

34. Min. Philadelphia YM, 1795, 1796.

35. Minutes of the Committee appointed to attend to the Indian Concern in the recess of the general Committee, in Papers of the Indian Committee of Philadelphia Yearly Meeting (MS, Dept. of Records, Philadelphia Yearly Meeting, Philadelphia, Pa.), Box I, minutes for 5/I/1796, 8/III/1796, 22/IV/1796; Minutes and Papers of the Indian Committee of Philadelphia Yearly Meeting (MS, Dept. of Records, Philadelphia Yearly Meeting), 29/III/1796, 20/V/1796, 26/IX/1796; John Peirce *et al.*, Stockbridge, N. Y., 1/VII/1796, to Indian Committee, Papers of Indian Committee, Box I.

36. "Minutes of Conclusive Conferences, and Agreements, between the Friends settling on the Oneida Reservation, and the Indians there, proposed on the 25th. and agreed to on the 30th. of the Sixth Month 1796," Papers of the Indian Committee, Box I; Minutes and Papers of the Indian Committee, 17/III/1797, 16/VI/1797; Jonathan Thomas *et al.*, Oneida, N. Y., 3/IV/1797, to Indian Committee, Papers, Box I.

37. Jacob Taylor *et al.*, Oneida, N. Y., 13/XII/1796, to Indian Committee, Papers, Box I; John Drinker and Joseph Sansom, Philadelphia, 18/I/1797, to Oneida missionaries, Papers, Box I; Jacob Taylor *et al.*, Oneida, 8/XI/1798, to Indian Committee, Papers, Box I; Jonathan Thomas, Oneida, 4/XI/1797, to Indian Committee, Papers, Box I.

38. Henry Drinker *et al.*, Philadelphia, 12/V/1798, to Oneida Nation, Papers Box I; Jacob Taylor *et al.*, Oneida, 9/IV/1799, to Indian Committee, Papers, Box I; [draft of] Henry Drinker, Philadelphia, 23/X/1799, to Thomas Eddy, Papers, Box I.

39. [Draft of] Indian Committee, Philadelphia, 21/X/1799, to Jacob Taylor *et al.*, Papers, Box I; [draft of] Henry Drinker, Philadelphia, 23/X/1799, to Thomas Eddy, Papers, Box I; Jacob Taylor *et al.*, Oneida, 25/XII/1799,

to Indian Committee, Papers, Box I; Address "To the Chiefs of the Oneida Nation," in Minutes and Papers of the Indian Committee, 19/II/1801.

40. Joseph Shauquethqueat *et al.*, Stockbridge, N. Y., 9/IX/1797, to Indian Committee and Friends generally, Papers, Box I; Minutes and Papers of the Indian Committee, 17/III/1797; Joshua Sharpless and John Peirce, Conuscotago, N. Y., 31/V/1798, to Thomas Wistar, Papers, Box I; Address of Joshua Sharpless *et al.*, Allegheny River, Pa. (?), 22/V/1798, to Cornplanter *et al.*, Papers, Box I.

41. Henry Simmons, Jr., *et al.*, Genesinguhtau, N. Y., 29/VII/1798, to Indian Committee, Papers, Box I; Henry Simmons, Jr., and Joel Swayne, Genesingohta, 16/XI/1798, to Indian Committee, Papers, Box I; H. Simmons, Jr., *et al.*, Genesinguhta, 22/VIII/1799, to Indian Committee, Papers, Box I; "Copy of Speech delivered to Cornplanter & several other Chiefs of the Seneca Nation . . . by Joshua Sharpless" *et al.*, Genesinguhta, 14/IX/1799, Papers, Box I; J. Swayne and Halliday Jackson, Genesinguhta, 10/XI/1799, to Indian Committee, Papers, Box I; [copy of] missionaries, Genesinguhta, 3/IX/1800, to Indian Committee, Papers, Box I; [copy of] missionaries, Genesinguhta, 20/XI/1800, to Indian Committee, Papers, Box I; [copy of] a missionary, Canusatega (Cornplanter's town), Pa., 28/II/1801, to a member of Indian Committee, Papers, Box I.

42. [Copy of] a missionary, Canusatega, Pa., 28/II/1801, to a member of Indian Committee, Papers, Box I; [copy of] missionaries, Genesinguhta, 3/IX/1800, to Indian Committee, Papers, Box I.

43. Anthony F. C. Wallace (ed.), "Halliday Jackson's Journal to the Seneca Indians, 1798–1800," *Pennsylvania History*, XIX (1952), 117–47, 325–49 (especially 332–33).

44. White Seneca *et al.*, Cataraugus, N. Y., Apr. 11, 1801, to David Mead and other Friends, Indian Committee Papers, Box I; [draft of] Henry Drinker *et al.*, Philadelphia, ?/V(?)/1801, to Muncy, Cataraugus and Cornplanter Indians, Papers, Box I; Jonathan Thomas *et al.*, Ginasingohta, 28/VI/1801, to Indian Committee, Papers, Box I; J. Swayne *et al.*, Ginasingohta, 3/VIII/1801, to Indian Committee, Papers, Box I.

45. [Copy of] a missionary, Canusatega, 28/II/1801, to a member of the Indian Committee, Papers, Box I; Jacob Taylor and Joel Swayne, Ginasingohta, 11/XII/1802, to Indian Committee, Papers, Box I.

46. Minutes and Papers of the Indian Committee, 18/VIII/1803, 15/XII/1803, 15/III/1804, 7/XII/1804, 17/XII/1804, 19/IX/1805; Joel Swayne *et al.*, Tunesassah, N. Y., 7/XI/1804, to Indian Committee, Papers, Box II; David Bacon *et al.*, Philadelphia, 7/I/1805, to Jacob Taylor *et al.*, Papers, Box II.

47. John Elliott, Philadelphia, 23/II/1800, to Joel Swayne and Halliday Jackson, Papers, Box I; Jonathan Thomas *et al.*, Ginasingohta, 20/VI/1803 to Indian Committee (?), Papers, Box II; Speeches of Conudiu (Handsome Lake) and Cornplanter, 30/VIII/1803, to Jacob Taylor and Joel Swayne, Papers, Box II; David Bacon *et al.*, Philadelphia, 7/I/1805, to Jacob Taylor *et al.*, Papers Box II; Jonathan Thomas *et al.*, Tunesassah, 26/VI/1805, to Indian Committee, Papers, Box II; Jacob Taylor, Tunesassah, 2/XI/1805, to Thomas Stewardson, Papers, Box II; "Some Account of a visit paid to the

Indians in the 9 mo. 1806, by John Philips, Halliday Jackson, and Isaac Bonsall," pp. 15–17, 23–28, Papers, Box II; Minutes and Papers of the Indian Committee, 14/VIII/1806, 13/IV/1809; Joel Swayne *et al.*, Tunesassah, 21/III/1810, to Indian Committee, Papers, Box II; J. Thomas *et al.*, Tunesassah(?), 12/II/1811, to Indian Committee, Papers, Box II.

48. Minutes and Papers of the Indian Committee, 21/VII/1797; Min. New England YM, 1796, 1797, 1798; Min. New England M for S, 9/VI/1798, 9/X/1799, 7/I/1800.

49. London Meeting for Sufferings, *Some Account*, 106–7, 128, 155–64; Kelsey, *Friends and the Indians*, 114–17.

50. Goldsmith Chandler and Caleb Kirk, Pipe Creek, Md., 23/V/1796, to Thomas Wistar, Papers, Box I; Minutes of the Committee appointed to attend to the Indian Concern in the recess of the general Committee, 17/VI/1796, Papers, Box I; John Brown, Baltimore, 2/XII/1798, to Thomas Fisher and Thomas Stewardson, Papers, Box I; John Brown, Baltimore, 9/III/1799, to Thomas Wistar, Papers, Box I.

51. *A Brief Account of the Proceedings of the Committee, appointed by the Yearly Meeting of Friends, held in Baltimore, for promoting the Improvement and Civilization of the Indian Natives* (London, 1806),16–23; Dunlap, *Quaker Education*, 377–83.

52. Extracts from Minutes of Baltimore Yearly Meeting Indian Committee, describing council near Ft. Wayne, 11/IV/1804, Papers of Philadelphia Indian Committee, Box II; *Brief Account of the Committee Appointed by the Yearly Meeting in Baltimore*, 23–40; Dunlap, *Quaker Education*, 383–85.

53. *Brief Account of the Committee Apointed by the Yearly Meeting in Baltimore*, 40–47; London Meeting for Sufferings, *Some Account*, 128, 225–26; Kelsey, *Friends and the Indians*, 136–37.

54. See, for example, Minutes and Papers of the Indian Committee, 21/X/1796, 18/XI/1796, 7/X/1797, 16/XII/1797, 14/IV/1803.

55. *Brief Account of the Committee Appointed by the Yearly Meeting in Baltimore*, 45.

56. *Brief Account of the Committee Appointed by the Yearly Meeting in Baltimore*, 45.

57. Minutes and Papers of the Indian Committee, 21/IV/1797, 17/VIII/1809; Benjamin Coope *et al.*, Clear Creek, N. Y., 18/XII/1809, to Indian Committee, Papers, Box II; "Advertisement," preceding *Brief Account of the Committee Appointed by the Yearly Meeting in Baltimore*, vi.

58. Timothy Pickering, Philadelphia, Feb. 15, 1796, to Israel Chapin, in Minutes of the Committee appointed to attend to the Indian Concern in the recess of the general Committee, 8/III/1796, Papers, Box I; Minutes and Papers of the Indian Committee, 26/IX/1796; Henry Dearborn, Washington, D. C., Jan. 7, 1802, to Henry Drinker *et al.*, Papers, Box I; Henry Dearborn, Washington, D. C., May 18, 1802, to Henry Drinker, Papers, Box I.

59. Timothy Pickering, Philadelphia, Feb. 15, 1796, to Jasper Parrish, in Minutes of the Committee apointed to attend to the Indian Concern in the recess of the general Committee, 8/III/1796,

Chapter XVI: Humanitarianism among Friends

1. Testimony on Thomas Chalkley, deceased, in Min. Philadelphia MM, 20/II/1749.

2. Sophia Hume, Manchester, England, 25/V/1749, to Mary Pemberton, Pemberton Papers (MS, Historical Society of Pennsylvania, Philadelphia, Pa.), Vol. V, No. 132; Min Black Water MM, 15/VIII/1789, in William C. Dunlap, *Quaker Education in Baltimore and Virginia Yearly Meetings* (Philadelphia, 1936), 479; Epistle to Standing Committee of North Carolina Yearly Meeting, in Min. Philadelphia M for S, 17/III/1791.

3. William C. Heffner, *History of Poor Relief Legislation in Pennsylvania, 1682–1913* (Cleona, Pa., c. 1913), 105–6.

4. John Woolman, "Epistle to the Quarterly and Monthly Meetings of Friends," *The Journal and Essays of John Woolman*, ed. Amelia M. Gummere (New York, 1922), 479, 484, 487.

5. Frederick B. Tolles, *Meeting House and Counting House* (Chapel Hill, N. C., 1948), 176–77; Anthony Benezet and John Wesley, *Views of American Slavery, taken a Century Ago* (Philadelphia, 1858), 41–45.

6. Verner W. Crane, *The Southern Frontier, 1670–1732* (Ann Arbor, Mich., reprinted, 1956), 303–5, 310.

7. Perry Miller, *The New England Mind: from Colony to Province* (Cambridge, 1953), 408–16.

8. [Owen Biddle,] *A Plan for a School on an Establishment Similar to that at Ackworth . . . varied to suit the Circumstances of the Youth within the Limits of the Yearly-Meeting for Pennsylvania and New-Jersey* (Philadelphia, 1790), 33n.

9. Basil Willey, *The Seventeenth Century Background* (New York, 1953), 78–80, 140–43; B. Willey, *The Eighteenth Century Background* (New York, 1950), 58–59.

10. James Bonar, *Moral Sense* (New York, 1930), 37; Miller, *New England Mind: from Colony to Province*, 413; Robert Barclay, *An Apology for the True Christian Divinity* (Philadelphia, 1908), 142–48.

11. Bonar, *Moral Sense*, 75–77.

12. Anthony Ashley Cooper, third Earl of Shaftesbury, "A Letter Concerning Enthusiasm," in *Characteristics of Men, Manners, Opinions, Times, etc.*, ed. John M. Robertson (London, 1900), I, 27.

13. Willey, *Eighteenth Century Background*, 150, 159; Perry Miller, *Jonathan Edwards* ("American Men of Letters Series" [n.p., 1949]), 285–87; George Sherburn, "The Restoration and Eighteenth Century," in A. C. Baugh (ed.), *A Literary History of England* (New York, 1948), 826, 969.

14. Woolman, *Journal*, 156.

15. Woolman, *Journal*, 255.

16. See, for example, "Address" to the Pennsylvania Assembly, in Min. Philadelphia M for S, 17/I/1788; *A Brief Account of the Proceedings of the Committee, appointed by the Yearly Meeting of Friends, held in Baltimore, for promoting the Improvement and Civilization of the Indian Natives* (London, 1806), 44; Epistle to London Yearly Meeting, in Min. Philadelphia YM, 1784.

17. Israel Pemberton, the younger, Philadelphia, 3/XII/1750, to John Pemberton, Pemberton Papers, VI, 166.

18. Min. Philadelphia YM, 1776 (Epistle to Quarterly and Monthly Meetings), 1789 (Address to the President of the United States); Epistle to New England Meeting for Sufferings, in Min. Philadelphia M for S, 18/XI/1790.

19. See, for example, Min. Philadelphia YM, 1776 (Report of the committee on the political situation), 1795 (Report of temporary committee on Indians); William Morgan, Baltimore, 15/IX/1792, to "the Society for promoting the Education of the Blacks at Philadelphia" (MS, Dept, of Records, Philadelphia Yearly Meeting, Philadelphia, Pa.).

20. See Epistle to New England Meeting for Sufferings, in Min. Philadelphia M for S, 7/IX/1778.

21. See Min. Burlington MM, 3/III/1783; Dunlap, *Quaker Education*, 446 (Min. Baltimore M for S, 4/XI/1809), 479 (Min. Black Water MM, 15/VIII/1789); "Burlington School-Society," Burlington, N. J., 2/II/1793, to "Philadelphia school Society for the instruction of the Blacks;" and Benjamin Hadwen, Newport, R. I., 16/IV/1794, to the Philadelphia Association for the Free Instruction of Adult Colored Persons (MS, Dept. of Records, Philadelphia Yearly Meeting, Philadelphia, Pa.).

22. [Providence, R. I.,] *U. S. Chronicle*, Jan. 29, May 20, July 29, 1784, July 21, 1785, and March 16, May 11, 1786 (including notices of the deaths of Anthony Benezet and ex-Friend Stephen Hopkins); François Jean, Marquis de Chastellux, *Travels in North-America, in the Years 1780, 1781, and 1782*, 2 vols., trans. anon. (London, 1787), I, 278.

23. Min. Philadelphia YM, 1783, 1784 (Epistle to London Yearly Meeting), 1790 (Epistle to London Yearly Meeting); Min. Philadelphia M for S, 7/IX/1778 (Epistle to New England Meeting for Sufferings), 20/X/1786 (Message to Congress).

24. George S. Brookes, *Friend Anthony Benezet* (Philadelphia, 1937), 141–42.

25. Anthony Benezet, Philadelphia, 23/X/1774, to Samuel Allinson, in Brookes, *Friend Anthony Benezet*, 322.

Index

Abolition societies, 291–92
Academy of Philadelphia, 199
Acadian "Neutrals," 201–3
Affirmation privilege, 30, 45, 118
Aimwell school (Philadelphia), 288
Alcoholic beverages, 88, 182, 255–57, 271
Allen, William, 206, 207
American Philosophical Society, 199
Archdale, John, 149, 312
Associates of Doctor Bray, 320
Association for the Instruction of Adult Colored Persons (Philadelphia), 291–93
Association Library (Philadelphia), 199, 200

Bäcon, David, 301
Baltimore Yearly Meeting: and education, 254, 273, 277; and laws permitting slave trade, 297; and Negro education, 294; and Negro slavery, 129, 221, 228, 230; appointment of Indian Committee, 309–10
Barbados, 79, 104–7, 115
Barclay, David, 236
Barclay, Robert, 3, 18, 174, 249, 321
Basset, John, 229
Bellers, John, 26–28, 287, 321
Benevolence, 1, 166, 176–77, 285, 320–24
Benezet, Anthony, 18, 74, 97, 131, 136, 154, 159, 171, 173, 202–5, 214, 222, 235–37, 253–57, 265, 326
Bernard, Francis, 201
Bettering House (Philadelphia), see Contributors to the Relief and Employment of the Poor in the City of Philadelphia
Biddle, Owen, 275–76, 321
Big Tree, 300
Birthright membership, 55, 70–71, 175
Board of Island Managers (New Jersey), 65
Bond, Dr. Thomas, 206
Boston, Massachusetts: meetinghouse in, 79; war relief in, 258–60
Bristol, England, Quakers in, 261

Brothertown Indians, 302–3, 309
Brown, Moses, 18, 253, 259–60, 277, 289
Brown, Obadiah, 293
Budd, Thomas, 61, 66, 94, 153, 165, 312
Burling, William, 121, 123, 131
Burlington Monthly Meeting (New Jersey): and free Negroes, 237–38; and poor Friends, 46–47, 55
Burlington Library Company (New Jersey), 199
Burlington School Society for the Free Instruction of the Blacks (New Jersey), 291–93
Burroughs, Edward, 246

Cambridge Platonists, 321
Carter, William, 54
Cattawissa Monthly Meeting (Pennsylvania), 273
Certificates, 8, 13-14, 55, 58, 249
Chalkley, Thomas, 49, 89, 95, 194
Charity (Quaker), 2, 10, chap. ii, 76, 81–82, 84–87, 95, 113
Charleston, South Carolina, 42, 79
Cherokee Indians, 299
Chester Monthly Meeting (Pennsylvania), 280
Chester Quarterly Meeting (Pennsylvania): and slavery, 120–21, 124–25
Chesterfield Monthly Meeting (New Jersey), 48, 279
Choctaw Indians, 314
Church: in Quaker theology, 3–5, 10, 16, 33, 35, 117, 123–24; relation between Quaker and other, 4, 24, 26–28, 42, 152–53, 281, 314–15
Church history, Quaker views on, 4, 20, 174–75
Churchman, George, 272
Churchman, John, 136, 157–59, 162, 215
Clarke, Joseph, 294
Clerk (officer of Quaker Meetings), 10–11
Coleman, Elihu, 131
Connecticut, Quakers in, 45–46, 219
Connudiu, see Handsome Lake

399

INDEX